DIRECTIVE 19

THE MEMOIRS OF SS STURMBANNFÜHRER ROLF OTTO SCHILLER

ROLF SCHILLER.
TRANSCRIBED BY PAUL K. HARKER

Outskirts Press, Inc.
Denver, Colorado

Directive 19
The Memoirs of SS Sturmbannführer Rolf Otto Schiller
All Rights Reserved
Copyright © 2006 Rolf Otto Schiller
Transcribed by Paul K. Harker

Outskirts Press
http://www.outskirtspress.com

ISBN-10: 1-59800-392-5
ISBN-13: 978-1-59800-392-5

ACKNOWLEDGEMENT

Sincere thanks to my parents, Ken and Elaine, and my brother James for their understanding, encouragement and assistance in seeing this to fruition.

Additional thanks to Susan LaBorde for her editing and format advice, and to Ed Easley and Richard Hart for research assistance.

CONTENTS

While the events in this book are well documented and archived, the author's descriptions and accounts remain subjective. Some names have been changed with respect for personal privacy requests. As some of the author's personal claims can not be verified through research, the reader is invited to form his or her opinions and conclusions.

FOREWORD
SS MAJOR ROLF O. SCHILLER

There are several reasons why I have chosen to tell my story, the first of which is a litigious matter. The Holocaust has been qualified, taught and told from the distinct aspect of the Jewish people. There is no cogent validation for the actions committed by Germans at that time. However, the political climate of the modern world has been reshaped by past genocide and conversely, it remains virtually passive to its present occurrences. It is a great mistake to attempt to understand the methodology of genocide from the perspective of the survivors of the persecuted race. Such people tend to speak about it from the perception of dominated victims and in such; illogical presumptions of the reasons are perpetuated. The aggrieved race will often state reasons that are outside the sphere of the intended political objectives. During the government of the Reich, Jews were not persecuted because they were Jews. What we Germans did was not instigated from one-dimensional hatred. Stating that the motive for the Holocaust was German hatred toward the Jews is naïve. There were numerous German political, social, economic and collectivist reasons for what happened. The Jews were considered enemies of the Reich for many reasons including their illegal seizure and control of German banking, industry, trade, commerce and assets. At the end of the First World War the German veteran and common citizens found themselves dispossessed, unwaged, starving and in ruin as a result of the illegal Jewish seizure of political, social and economic power. Had the Russians or Catholics illegally seized control of Germany, the ambition of the Reich would have been to annihilate the Russians or Catholics. For Germans this was a matter of political objective and social, economic and collectivist preservation.

I served the Third Reich as an Officer of the SS Totenkopfverbände. The war ended for me when I was captured by the American Army in the Ruhr Valley in 1945. At that time I wore the rank of Major. I fought and was decorated in many battles. Before those battles, I ordered, planned and participated in the executions of over 6,000 civilians, mostly Jews, in Poland, France, The Netherlands, the Ukraine and Russia. From 1939 until 1944 I witnessed the methodical executions of approximately 150,000 Jews and European civilians and I drafted legal documents of these actions for analysis by my Superior Officers in Berlin. The documents I drafted were evidentiary conclusions based upon the cost effectiveness and the overall efficiency of the systematic liquidations. Based upon the information my comrades and I provided, our Superior Officers would eventually manufacture the blueprint for what became universally known as the Final Solution to the Jewish Question. I was one of 130 Legal Affairs Officers drafting such reports and throughout our assignments; each of us had comprehensive knowledge of what we were doing. I knew that at any moment I could have deliberately compromised my findings on such reports and that doing so would have tied up the bureaucracy. Though compromising the facts would have delayed matters, it would not have prevented the Final Solution. However, compromising the facts may have saved a few hundred thousand lives. I knew this. I chose not to do it.

By regulation and in agreement with the laws that authorized punishment for War Criminals of the Third Reich, I should have been hanged. The majority of my comrades had been earlier convicted based on the clamor of world opinion. I was tried in Poland after the Nürnberg Trials and when the Americans and British were reluctant to issue death sentences as they held it made them analogous to the men they were convicting. The Polish were satisfied to condemn us to unmitigated terms of confinement. By not putting me to the gallows, the Prosecution imposed upon me the worst sentence possible. They allowed me to live each day from that one until now with the memories of what I have done.

The Prosecution sentenced me to 30 years. I represented myself at trial and though the Prosecution presented a most persuasive case against me, its indictment was greatly flawed. I never once denied the charges against me. However, I disputed the dubious legal basis and precedents with which they were presented. The indictment existed as an ex post facto statement for the sake of imposing Allied Occupational Law upon former Officers of the Reich. I decided not to dispute the evidence, but argued the manner in which it was used against me. In discrediting portions of the indictment I was able to establish a defense that directly pertained to the reliable evidence and arguments introduced against me. On many occasions the Prosecution established that my unit had conducted operations in a specific area. Due to not having established the Commanding Officer present during the action, the tribunal presumed that suitable to my rank, I was accountable. Such arguments were without merit but there existed a biased practice on behalf of the Prosecution to advance such theories at trial.

I had chosen to represent myself as I had authored Reich policy and understood its laws. It seemed logical to refuse civilian counsel as the non military legal representative possessed no formal comprehension of the laws I had studied as a Reich Legal Affairs Officer. All defendants were granted complete authorization to speak as long as required in answer to any and all charges presented against us. I used the opportunity to educate the Prosecution on the conception, development, authoring, arbitration and processing of Reich law. I was able to satisfy the Prosecution that the Reich maintained a sound legal basis for the formation of its laws and legal codes. However, my argument was obstructed by the rejoinder that all Reich laws were products of an illegal regime which in turn, was a result of the ex post facto indictment.

I have no respect for the Reich Officers who denied the charges against them while claiming they were only following orders. The trials were not a series of legal proceedings against common soldiers. We were being tried because we had committed grievous crimes against the population of Europe. We were the men that conceived and gave the orders.

Another reason for conveying my accounts is that I watched many comrades go to their deaths under the Allied slogan that "Such crimes must never happen again". One needs to look no further than the newspaper to see such events in Croatia, Serbia, Rwanda, Uganda, Ethiopia, Iraq, Albania and ironically, between Palestine and Israel. One needs to look into the Killing Fields of Pol Pot in Cambodia or at the landfills of Nicaragua, Honduras and El Salvador where in the 1980s, Death Squads similar to the Einsatzgruppen murdered politicians, tax collectors, teachers, priests and other members of the intelligentsia.

Ethnic cleansing, religious cleansing, it all equals genocide. The Bible is filled with accounts of genocide. During the Middle Ages the Catholic Church raised banners bearing the Holy Cross and disguised genocide as The Crusades. The solitary principle of the European forays into the Middle East was intended to annihilate the Muslims or, as the Church favored to call them, the infidels. The British destroyed numerous African and Asian collectives, the Spanish destroyed the Incans, Mayans and Aztecs and today we are but 59 years removed from the end of the European Holocaust. When the Holocaust officially began in 1939, the United States was but 62 years removed from its final act of genocide upon the native Tribes of the Dakotas. Genocide took place before the European Holocaust and it continues to happen despite the many German Officers hanged by Tribunals to "make certain it never occurred again".

I dispute the current popular misconception that men such as me qualify as psychopaths and sadists. This is another attempt to assist an overprotected world in the acceptance and understanding of such horrible and unspeakable acts. Philosophers have stated that good and bad are like comparisons and have no basis but opinion. I can not defend the German annihilation of the Jewish people nor can I excuse it. However, I can speak of the character and moral standing of the men I served with. If one believes the current popular misconception that men such as me qualify as psychopaths and sadists, one must investigate the legal basis under which we were made to stand trial. To correlate the misconception to comparable current standards, one may argue that we were not mentally competent to stand trial and therefore, wrongfully processed and convicted. To accept the popular misconception, one must conversely evaluate this theory.

No man aspires to do the things we did. We were ordinary men made to cope with extraordinary situations. In order for genocide to happen, even under a fascist dictatorship, the government must have the support of its people. Any elder German that denies knowledge of the Holocaust is a liar. Such an atrocious occurrence can only come about when political and social agendas are aligned. I was at the forefront of planning, organizing and carrying out the deportations to the concentration camps. I submitted recommendations to my Superior Officers in Berlin on the most cost effective and efficient methods to utilize in the camps to ensure the maximum number of executions on a daily basis. I participated in the killings of civilians and Jews conducted by Einsatzgruppen Units in the Ukraine and continued to offer proposals on means to expedite the process. I have killed with ruthless disregard for humanity. I ordered young German soldiers to kill with the same ruthless disregard for humanity. I personally authorized favorable reports on the use of Zyklon B as a gassing chemical and personally pulled the trigger of a machine gun to shoot civilians on the snowy steppes of the Ukraine. I hanged Polish, French and Dutch civilians during summary and reprisal executions. I am a criminal.

I have chosen to tell my story for many reasons but above all, in the hope that my words will explain how such heinous madness can be taken from an idea to a reality and how we all have the ability to slip from our comfortable lives and spiral into an abyss to which we are irrevocably committed. The ability to kill is encoded in the genetics of every human being and, the wisdom and ability to control it are fragile guardians.

"If I am wicked, woe to me. If I am righteous, I still shall not lift up my head, being filled with disgrace, and conscious of my affliction."

Job 10:15

CHAPTER ONE
LIGHTING THE FLAMES

I decided whether you lived or died. That was my job as a Reich arbitrator and Legal Affairs Officer of the SS Totenkopfverbände. In the early years I would travel to the various concentration camps to hear death sentence appeals from inmates. "I did not do it", and, "I am innocent", became tedious rejoinders. It was the responsibility of each inmate to utilize resources to prove their innocence. In those days I was objective; perhaps even helpful in some ways. Once the mass incarcerations of Jews and political enemies began, the issue of overcrowding created infection control problems in the camps. Outbreaks of typhus and dysentery threatened not only the SS garrisons in the facilities, but the local populace surrounding them. Because of these epidemics the Ministry of Health and Hygiene was constantly applying pressure on my office to reduce the number of inmates in each facility. That is when my objectivity and helpfulness ceased to exist. I had a job to do. If you had been sentenced to death, whether you lived or died did not so much depend on the presentation of your appeal. It depended on my mood.

My enlistment in the SS was not the result of a fanatical interest in political philosophy, ideology, or the advancement of society. I viewed it as suitable employment for a man of employment age. The SS existed as an exclusive faction and membership was mostly granted by means of sponsorship. A friend of my Father had convinced him it was a glorious path of the New Order and so my Father encouraged me to accept the endorsement. I officially joined the Nazi Party in 1937 and was sent to the SS Training Depot at the Dachau facility. I was immediately placed in the Totenkopfverbände Regiment under the command and direction of Major General Theodor Eicke.

As recruits we were drilled in Eicke's firm conviction of inflexible harshness toward enemies of the Reich. We were to become guards and administrators inside the Detainment Facilities that housed such criminals and we were to exude no compassion. Eicke's motto was: "Tolerance and mercy are weaknesses." By advancing this theory among us, we became instruments that enforced controlled obedience of the prisoners through unrestricted cruelty. That is what our commander demanded. That is what we gave him.

Our training often included standing witness as sentences of corporal punishment were carried out on the inmates. We were ordered to jeer at the prisoner and encourage the SS man performing the whipping. At first it was very difficult to endure these events. You see a man being beaten, hear him scream with each blow of the whip or cane, and it is problematical to circumvent personal ethics and morals to stoically accept it. The Hauptscharführer in charge of our training brigade jovially said that witnessing a beating or an execution was like learning to eat raw clams on the shell. "The first few are difficult," he said, "but the rest become easier."

Eventually we each had to use the whip or cane on an inmate. The Hauptscharführer would ask for volunteers and, if you did not shout out a willingness to do this, a punishment of a revoked pass, extra guard duty, or confinement awaited you.

I was selected to administer the punishment in a cold, driving rain. The prisoner had been sentenced for possessing contraband or some other trivial reason, and was lying facedown on a wooden plank with his arms and legs bound to posts. He was a Jew of perhaps 40 or 50 years, and his eyes asked me why I was going to beat him. The whole of my training brigade was shouting insults at him and encouraging me. I took a wooden rod and struck him sharply across his back.

"Ein!" shouted the Jew. He was obligated to count out each of 25 strokes in a loud voice. I struck him again. *"Zwei!"*

"No, no, no," said the Hauptscharführer. "You are striking him like a girl!" He took the cane from me and struck the prisoner with all his strength. The man wailed and shouted, *"Drei!"*

"Drei?" My instructor leaned over and looked at him. "That was not the third stroke," he said. "I am teaching him how to do this." He handed the cane to me and said, "Now start again."

I struck the man and as ordered, he again shouted, *"Ein!"*

"Halt!" shouted the instructor. "Put your strength and body into each blow. Do not be reserved when striking him! Now, start again."

It was cold, raining, and the Hauptscharführer and I just delivered four extra blows to the man. To get it over with quickly, I mustered all my physical strength to administer the strokes. The screaming of the Jew and the awareness that I was dispensing his pain enraged me. I beat him harshly while hoping he would not lose count of the blows. If he did, he would be punished by having it start over again. I was relieved to hear him shout, *"Zwanzig fünf!"* Handing the cane to a veteran from the Punishment Block, I took my place among the training brigade with shouts of congratulations and fellow recruits touching me with awe as if I was some kind of luminary.

We were also trained as soldiers. Each day was a regimen of physical exercise, marching, learning how to salute, memorizing ranks, performing military customs and courtesies, mastering the K98 rifle, and long runs with a full backpack. We also practiced tactical offensive and defensive maneuvers. At the end of each day we were put into classrooms to learn Reich Administrative duties late into the night.

Following my graduation, I was assigned to the Staff at KZ Sachsenhausen as an arbitrator. My duties included the monitoring of prisoner affairs, the administration of the SS garrison, and serving as a liaison to the Central Office of Concentration Camp Inspectors in Oranienburg and the SS Main Office in Berlin. Because of the additional duties this position required, I was promoted to the rank of Untersturmführer.

"Prisoner Affairs" was a very plain term applied to a most complex set of duties. Each inmate arriving at Sachsenhausen was required to stand before me. I would evaluate his personal information, review the legality of his conviction and sentence, and then officially remand him to custody and assign him to a barracks and job function. All prisoners were required to work in at least one of the industries established inside the camp or one of its subcamps.

Corporal punishment, and Directive 19; the official administrative designation for a death sentence, were also my responsibilities. In cases where prisoners violated the rules of Sachsenhausen, a hearing was conducted to determine the outcome. SS guards and officers were not the only personnel permitted to levy legal charters against an inmate. Accusations could be presented by civilian foremen, owners, operators, and shareholders of industrial plants associated with the camp through labor contracts. If a prisoner was not delivering an expected product quota, or not giving a satisfactory employment performance, legal charters could be filed. Civilians outside the camp who encountered Sachsenhausen inmates during the course of work details were also at liberty to submit allegations. As an arbitrator I listened to both sides and made my ruling in the matters. The majority of my decisions resulted in some form of corporal punishment being dispensed as it had been made clear by Eicke that I was to never take the word of an enemy of the Reich. There were very few cases that I ruled in favor of the accused, and these were mainly instances where the charges had been obviously invented.

Directive 19 was requested in the most severe cases. Striking a guard, inciting a riot, thefts, and attempting to escape, were inflexible mandates for death sentences. In such cases I would draft the warrant, dispatch it to the Central Office in Oranienburg, and carry it out when it was approved and returned.

Nothing could have prepared me for what I witnessed at this concentration camp. I had read and heard various accounts of the Detainment Facilities, the conditions within them, and the general administrations which governed them. The facilities housed a variety of criminals who were considered dangers to the political and social structures of Germany. A colored triangle was sewn onto the breast of the prison garb to designate the crime each individual inmate had been convicted of. Red was worn by Communists, Bolshevists and all other political enemies. Purple was given to Jehovah's Witnesses; green to regular criminals, and pink to homosexuals. Black triangles were reserved for gypsies, vagrants, lesbians and prostitutes. Jews wore two yellow triangles, one of which was placed upright and the other inverted to create the six pointed Star of David.

The Party loyalists believed most fervently that professional criminals and asocials who were not subject to incarceration under the prevailing laws needed to be confined for the interests and security of Germany. Therefore, no precise validation existed for sentencing a criminal to any one of the Detainment Facilities. Construction had begun on Sachsenhausen in 1936 and, it had been moderately operational by the end of 1937. Additional construction had been ordered to build two subcamps at Wittenberg and one in Oranienburg.

It is a rampant misconception to believe that at this time Jews and criminals were capriciously rounded up and imprisoned by the SS. There existed a very elaborate judicial procedure to place a criminal inside a Detainment Facility. Clerical errors and violations of this strict protocol could result in the overturning of the conviction and warrant the release of the criminal. If such happened, the delinquent officer was made to stand inquiry before the German High Court to explain himself. It was a formality that no excuse for errant behavior was accepted in these matters and any officer guilty of such was demoted, transferred, or sentenced to six months inside a military prison.

I had been ordered to author many Reich Warrants of Arrest. I would use a printed form and type in the crime, details, causes and information, and affix my signature as a representative of the Totenkopfverbände. The document would then be forwarded to the German High Court for consideration, and if approved, it would be stamped and signed by a judge to make it official. The Reich Warrant of Arrest would then be returned to me in order to be referred to the appropriate Police Agency to execute its terms.

The Reich held the position that Jews had been provided with a reasonable amount of time to emigrate from Germany. In the case where a Jew failed to comply with these orders, he was classified as a threat to interior German interests. This was more of a political matter than a common crime, so I would forward the signed warrant to the Gestapo who would visit the Jew either at his home or place of employment to execute the warrant. Once taken into custody, the Jew would be transported to the local municipal police station or Gestapo Office if the latter was closer. The Jew would then be permitted to read the Reich Warrant of Arrest and this would be followed by a formal verbal declaration of the legal charters against him. The declaration was made by the senior ranking Police or Gestapo Officer at the location.

Once this had been done, the Jew was made to answer a series of personal questions regarding health, education, family, employment, and whom to notify in the matter of death or illness. He was then examined by a German physician and placed in a temporary holding cell until being transported to the local municipal or state court at the first availability for a hearing. Again the declaration of arrest was repeated by a judge and the accused was permitted to speak in his defense. In some cases financial penalties were levied as punishment and the Jew was awarded an additional 30 or 60 days to emigrate. In matters where an emigration extension had been awarded but not adhered to, the Jew was pronounced guilty of violating a Reich order. A Writ of Incarceration was drafted according to the length of time the convicted was obligated to serve as penalty. Once the writ was made formal by the signature of a judge, the Jew was remanded to custody in a Detainment Facility.

In cases where warrants had been drafted and approved for common offenders, the KRIPO would arrest the accused and these people would be subjected to criminal trials. If found guilty, appropriate penalties would be levied in the form of financial payments, incarceration in a municipal jail, or in the most severe cases, confinement in one of the Detainment Facilities.

The SD was responsible for executing warrants against enemies of the state, whether political, social or religious.

Homosexuals, lesbians, vagrants, and prostitutes were considered civil criminals. The Order Police was responsible for the execution of warrants against these lawbreakers. Each arrested person received a formal process of law regarding their individual cases. Confinement to a Detainment Facility was only possible in instances where a judge authorized it. The German High Court was constantly under pressure from the Ministry of Health and Hygiene to seek alternative placement for the criminals it convicted as overcrowding in the Detainment Facilities led to outbreaks of typhoid and dysentery.

Once a convicted criminal arrived at a Detainment Facility he was granted an additional arbitration of his case. As the presiding officer at Sachsenhausen, I reviewed all court documentation and the case history of the particular criminal in question. I could not overturn the conviction, but I possessed the authority to remand the criminal to an alternate facility provided it was appropriate for the terms of the conviction. This is to say that a prostitute sentenced to one year at Sachsenhausen could be transferred to the Oranienburg municipal jail to serve the sentence. Conversely, a murderer sentenced to Sachsenhausen could be transferred to a more secure environment such as Buchenwald. There existed a desire within each Facility Commander to oversee the least amount of prisoners as possible. The details and stress of supervising a large facility with thousands of prisoners attracted attention from the Reich Ministry of Economics in the form of auditors, inspectors from the Ministry of Health and Hygiene and, an interminable chain of clerical accounting.

The Kommandant of Sachsenhausen, Rudolf Höss, was a difficult man of moody disposition. He had been ordered by Eicke to give me a complete tour of the facility and we began in the Appellplatz which had been turned to mud during a previous rain. I witnessed the evening muster call of the prisoners and watched the kapos as they read from lists and shouted out the names. Those who did not answer loud or quickly enough received a few sharp blows from a truncheon. When roll was completed, the SS Block Sergeant conducted a conversation with the Chief Kapo. After several minutes the kapo shouted out five names at which five prisoners gathered at the center of the assembly. I could not hear what the Chief Kapo said to them, but each laid facedown in the mud of the Appellplatz. The SS Sergeant immediately pulled his pistol from its holster and leaned over to shoot each prone inmate in the back of the head. The five shootings occurred in less than ten seconds and when finished, the Sergeant removed the magazine from his pistol and presented it to an SS Lieutenant so that the remaining bullets could be inventoried. I learned that during the carrying out of a formal execution, orders from the Central Office in Oranienburg specifically stated that prisoners sentenced to death were to receive the "coups de gras" to the back of the head in the form of a pistol shot. To ensure the executions were carried out, and to ensure it was carried out effectively without error, the magazines of the weapons used were required to be inspected by a Senior Officer present at the action. The Senior Officer was to inventory the unfired bullets under the scrutiny of a witness, and record the number of remaining rounds on his After Action Report which he submitted to the Central Office to verify that all scheduled prisoners were executed and that no further shots were fired than the number required. This proved that no additional executions took place and that there had been no errors in the administration of the "coup de gras".

I asked Höss what the prisoners had done to be shot in such a manner. Höss answered that it did not matter. He stated they were enemies of the Reich and such was the only cause required for execution.

When the assembly of prisoners was dismissed, I stood there for quite some time staring at those lifeless bodies in gray and blue striped pajamas. I had no emotion for them. Nothing about their deaths created any emotion. They were simply summoned from the ranks and they laid down without objection. I did not know them. They did not cry out for mercy. I felt no connection to them or their predicament whatsoever. They obeyed, laid down, and were shot to death. None of the witnessing SS troops or prisoners reacted. Everyone simply permitted it to happen without intervention. Perhaps I felt no emotion because of the collective stoic acceptance. It was all very orderly and precise. "First time?" asked Höss. "You will become accustomed to it."

We continued through the Appellplatz and came to a gallows from which the corpses of five or six inmates hung. Höss explained that the hanged persons had been caught with food rations in the barracks. Birds had picked at the bodies and the odor of death was overwhelming. Höss explained it was the policy of the facility to leave the bodies hanging for twenty four hours as a visual deterrent to the other prisoners.

He showed no emotion when he told me these things. Whereas the execution in the Appellplatz did not affect me, the sight of the hanging bodies deeply disturbed me. I fought the nausea to appear strong in the eyes of Höss. For a reason I cannot explain, it was important to me at that time that he held a favorable opinion of me.

I noticed the behavior of the inmates as we traversed the different compounds. When we approached, they would stop whatever they were doing, remove their caps, and stand at attention with their eyes toward the ground until we passed. At one instance Höss remarked, "Is this not grand? They obey and fear us because we tell them to."

On two different occasions I witnessed the violent beatings of prisoners at the hands of the guards. One inmate was on his knees next to a pushcart. Two guards continued to beat him with stones clutched in their hands. They repeatedly ordered the prisoner to stand and each time he obeyed, they knocked him down again and shouted the same orders. Another was an elderly man curled into a fetal position. He attempted, without success, to defend himself from the violent kicking of three guards. Höss said nothing, nor did he do anything to put cease to this ill treatment. He simply stood there until our eyes met. When I looked at him he assumed I had seen enough and was ready to continue with the tour. At one point I asked if such things happened every day. He probably sensed my feelings and responded that it was best to remain detached. Höss echoed that I should never allow sympathy or mercy for enemies of the Reich.

There was a curious duality about Sachsenhausen. While it existed as a place where cruelty was acceptable and expected, it also existed as a place unlike a prison. The barracks were overcrowded but provided the required air space each prisoner was entitled to. I noticed the roofs of the barracks had been papered and tarred which certainly intensified heat from the sun during the summer months. Conversely, there was but a single wood burning stove in each that was not efficient to adequately heat the structures during the winter. Upon inspection of the barracks I could hear the rats and mice scurrying beneath the bunks and under the floorboards. I also heard a steady crackling noise which Höss explained. It was lice and fleas jumping onto the wooden planks of the beds.

Major General Eicke joined us for dinner in the quarters of the Kommandant. When he asked for my impressions of the facility, I knew it would be wise to choose my words carefully. I stated that in my opinion, it could bear some modifications. I wanted so much to say something about the treatment of the prisoners, but it was obvious from the tone of the conversation that this was not even a topic to approach. I spoke of the tarred and papered roofs and replacing them with thatch or wood. I suggested forging slopes into the sides of the walkways and roads to prevent water pools and mosquito infestations. They were trivial suggestions and each flowed easily. The General asked for an answer. I gave him one. That was all.

Over the next few months the protocol for sentencing and the principles for arbitration hearings were called into question. With such a volume of cases, situations had arisen that required rulings from higher sources. I was constantly in communication with the Legal Affairs Officers and arbitrators assigned to the other camps. We asked each other for advice in difficult situations, such as a Directive 19 issued for a well known person in custody. There were also relatives of Reich political allies incarcerated in the camps and we feared corporal punishment or a Directive 19 might hinder diplomatic relations. SS Judges at the Central Office in Oranienburg and at the Main Office in Berlin reviewed most of these questions. This brought about a meeting of all camp Legal Affairs Officers and arbitrators in Berlin. The purpose was to discuss the drafting of new legislation to govern the administration of justice and police matters inside the camps.

CHAPTER TWO
FANNING THE FLAMES

The meetings I attended were always held in Conference Room B on the third floor of RSHA Headquarters. The entrance was a set of ornate double doors equal to a meter and a half wide. Upon entry, the room extended a full 3 meters to the left and right, and it was approximately 4 meters across. A gilded conference table had been placed in the center and the far right corner of the room contained a lectern from which the presiding official conducted the meetings. Portraits of Hitler, Party flags, and national eagles adorned the room, and a small table containing silver coffee and tea pots rested against the far wall. The time of day never mattered as this table always contained a collection of pastries that smelled and tasted as if they had been baked only moments before our arrival in Conference Room B.

The participants at these meetings fashioned a most curious and eclectic lot. It seemed I was always surrounded by bemedalled gentlemen in their military uniforms. The army wore gray, the navy and airforce wore blue, and the SS wore either black or gray. It was about four or five weeks of attending these meetings before I realized the elder veterans were subordinate in rank to their younger counterparts in the emerging Reich. I found this a most intriguing observation as the elder gentlemen had elevated their careers on the hardships of long service and combat during the Great War. Yet, I was sharing the room with newly appointed Reich Colonels and Generals in their early twenties and thirties. The elders spoke with experience and dictated the course of the meetings with political, social and economic observations. They offered their findings based on the years preceding the Great War; evaluated the change in current collective standards, and offered hypothetical reasons for the negative influences that dominated the present German social order. Despite the soundness of their conclusions and reasons, the younger Reich officers consistently held that all destructive conditions in the German communal structure were the results of Jewish, Communist and Bolshevist influence. Many times the elders argued that reform was required to oversee financial security in matters of commercial, industrial and trade practices, and they argued a case of intemperate spending by Reich officials for the rebuilding of the military in defiance of the terms of the Versailles Treaty. They made many good points and sound arguments. The younger Reich officers maintained that these conditions would not exist if not for the damage caused by the presence of Jews, Communists and Bolshevists in the German state.

The elders would depart from the meetings with exasperated expressions and raised eyebrows that clearly indicated they believed it had been a waste of time. The gatherings were nothing more than formalities. The Reich had previously drafted its agenda and the assemblies served the purpose of presenting the façade that the elder statesmen agreed with the new policies.

Was it possible to object to the arguments presented by the young Reich officers? Of course it was, though such was far from prudent. I was present when two objections were raised by elder veterans at these meetings. During one, a Surface Fleet Commander of the Navy banged a fist on the table and shouted that the current state of affairs was the direct result of the weaknesses of former politicians. The elder did not disparage against Hitler or the Reich, but he made his speech with passion. He claimed in a forward manner that it was unsophisticated to blame the social collapse upon Jews, Communists and Bolshevists. The young officers listened to him in silence and then continued the meeting. A few days after the assembly it was reported that the Surface Fleet Commander had suffered a fatal heart attack in his home.

The second matter was an elder veteran of the army who claimed the same argument, but with much less passion. He too was found dead days later though it was reported he took his own life with a pistol. One did not have to look far outside of Conference Room B to find the true causes of death for these men. Everyone knew it and nobody said a word about it.

A collection of civilians consisting of aristocrats, industrialists, bankers and contractors also attended these assemblies. While the meetings existed under the headings of Urban Zoning or Civil Industry, the underlying premise always surfaced in relation to the Jews, Communists and Bolshevists. Each gathering began with an announcement of the agenda articles, but the discussion of each topic transferred into an open argument of ways and means to harass the enemies of the Reich into a forced evacuation of the German state.

I must note that the discussion of eradicating these enemies never officially surfaced at the meetings I attended at RSHA Headquarters in 1938. I was not aware of these plans then. However, it was an educated conclusion that if such measures as deportation, forced evacuation, and harassment were being discussed at the low level assemblies I attended, more radical actions were being considered at higher level meetings.

Most of the aristocrats that attended the meetings were not Germans, but were members of foreign ruling families. I attended several assemblies with relatives of the Austrian Schuschnigg, Renner, Petznek and Eigruber families. French aristocrats from the Houses of Orleans, Guise, and Bourbon had also been present, as well as members of the Italian Vercellana and Bergolo families. RSHA officials did not entertain the fervent loyalists from these Houses and families, but instead had courted the disinherited outcasts from each. In exchange for immunity and honorary titles within the Reich, these aristocrats openly provided classified information about their respective governments as well as current situational reports on industry, armaments, trade and commerce.

It was in these particular meetings that we discussed the treatment of camp inmates who had blood ties to influential families or direct relations to owners of commercial and industrial enterprises engaged to the Reich by legal contracts. I took great interest in these conversations and freely volunteered my thoughts and opinions. I was the only officer present with practical experience as I was overseeing an incarcerated man at Sachsenhausen who had kinship ties to Optique Iena. This company had been secured under contract to provide eyeglasses to all Wehrmacht and SS personnel and I had received numerous appeals from its owners to release the associated inmate or grant him privileged concessions in the Detainment Facility. Within weeks after denying the requests, Optique Iena reported negative figures for its production quota and made a bold statement to the Ministry of Economics that these figures were due to the absence of its manufacturing foreman. The company formally stated that it was unable to meet product demands due to a lack of qualified supervision on the plant floor. The Ministry of Economics upheld the contract and cited a production quota by covenant. Optique Iena countered by quoting a clause in the contract that permitted the company access to qualified personnel to meet the agreed upon needs. The Reich and Optique Iena enlisted lawyers to resolve the matter through civil litigation. In the meantime, the company produced the number of units required to meet the covenant, but eighty per cent of the product failed quality control standards.

This was clearly a ruse on behalf of Optique Iena to coerce the Reich into releasing the relative of its owners. The Reich had no interest in appeasing the owners of Optique Iena and entered civil litigation for the sole purpose of establishing the legal premise to rescind the contract. Putting the matter before a court meant that governmental and public interest was at the root of the issue. However, all judges were Party loyalists and this made it virtually impossible for private industry and citizens to receive a ruling in their favor.

Each of these matters was explored through precise debate. The Reich had incarcerated many famous personalities including Nobel Prize winners, scientists, researchers, political activists, mathematicians, actors, and radio hosts. In relation to the social infrastructure of Germany, nobody presented an objection to the absence of local criminals. However, the arrests of people who had foreign and public recognition, such as the Nobel Prize winners, actors, and radio hosts, drew outside attention to German internal matters. The welfare of these inmates often became the interest of the Red Cross and other international agencies. The Reich was extremely concerned with what these organizations knew and reported about the conditions, administrations, and treatment of the prisoners inside the camps.

This had been a particular problem since 1936 when a representative of the Helvetic Red Cross called upon a Nobel Prize winner imprisoned in our Esterwegen facility. A report was published that stated the inmate had been starved and mistreated, and this strained diplomatic relations with several important foreign departments. As a measure of good faith, the Reich transferred the prisoner to a public hospital where he stayed until his death in 1938. This event led to the establishment of several Transitional Facilities throughout Germany. These places became large, general holding camps for newly arrested civilians. The numbers of prisoners kept in these places never met or exceeded the occupational capacity of the barracks, and this was intentionally done to present an illusion to inspecting foreign agencies such as the Red Cross. These facilities were well maintained, landscaped, and supplied with excess food stores. Work was optional for each prisoner, but those who chose to work received wages. Mistreatment of the inmates was forbidden, and all these details convinced outside inspectors that the Reich had gone to great lengths to operate its prison system with the dignity and welfare of the inmates in mind.

These inmates were sentenced to the camps on a regular basis, and replaced by recently arrested people. The presence of new prisoners in the Transitional Facilities convinced outside inspectors that the Reich had rehabilitated its criminals and returned them to society as loyalists and productive citizens.

Maintaining this illusion was an extreme financial burden. Legislation was therefore proposed and passed allowing the seizure of assets from all arrested persons. These items were appraised by Reich officials and then sold to the German public to generate revenue for the maintenance of the Transitional Facilities. It also became a Reich policy to present monthly incarceration invoices to the families of those detained in our prisons. The families who did not or could not pay were held liable, and their personal assets became duly marked for seizure in order to pay the debts.

The Transitional Facilities served a very important function for the prison administration system. It satisfied foreign agencies that Germany maintained a benign and tolerable incarceration complex for its citizen-offenders, and it demonstrated we were willing to adhere to international humanitarian demands by correcting conditions observed at Esterwegen and Füllen. Some of these prisons were upgraded to Transitional Facilities while others were "closed" on only an administrative and social information level. As far as the German public and international agencies knew, the intolerable prisons ceased to exist. On an administrative level, they existed on paper. In truth they continued to operate under the strictest degrees of confidentiality.

Meetings were held to address many problems that were emerging throughout the whole of the Reich. Another assembly took place under the heading of Foreign Art and Culture. It directly focused on the presence of outside art, monuments, paintings, literary works, statues and treasures displayed in German museums and places of public gathering. It was declared at this meeting that all German, Prussian, Hessian and Nordic pieces had been approved to remain, but all other items bearing foreign, and especially Jewish influence, were to be removed, destroyed, bricked over or stored in secure areas not accessible by German citizens. Since our forces occupied Austria in agreement with the terms of the May 1938 Anschluss, all pieces residing in Austrian museums and places of public gathering were subject to the same terms. All items crafted of gold, silver, pewter and any other metal deemed to have value, such as copper and bronze, were to be transported to Metalworks facilities inside the Greater Reich for the purpose of being melted down and applied to the manufacture of items necessary for the rebuilding of the German military. All paintings, literary works and sculptures of foreign influence residing in Austria and not of German origin were to be destroyed. The order for the destruction of foreign culture in Germany was most distressing to me. Countless were the days when as a young boy I would lose myself for hours in the museums admiring such wonderful art.

It was difficult at that time to understand the purpose and consequences of these orders. The idea of Germanization had rooted well in the interior of the state, and though it seemed natural to impress this philosophy upon the Austrians, it disturbed me to confront the destruction of such masterpieces. However, there also existed within me a conflict at that time that such icons, books and works were enemy influences designed to distract Germans from the ambitions of the Reich. Whereas I appreciated the intrinsic beauty of such items, I somewhat abhorred them as creations inserted into my personal domain by enemies determined to destroy me. The fear of foreign and Jewish influence, fuelled by daily reminders from the Ministry of Propaganda, generated my neutral acceptance of these demands.

Each meeting ended with an announcement of which Staff officers were to attend the next assembly. The elder veterans were the first to be dismissed and I eventually found myself to be a member of a very private and powerful gathering. I had never hesitated to speak my thoughts and made each of my statements in favor of the Reich. Personally, I recognized the Jewish problem as a threat to German interests though I did not agree with all the radical ideas being proposed at that time. I was a strong advocate for forced emigration and the incarceration of those Jews that refused to comply. My training under Eicke's philosophies was alive in everything I said. Tolerance and mercy were weaknesses. At those meetings I preached to my fellow officers that leniency and negotiations with Jews and political enemies would do nothing but encourage rebellious behaviors.

Our discussions led to the drafting of new legislation. We were amending the Nürnberg Laws and forging new legal codes to be applied against our enemies. Our proposals were crossing the desks of General Best, Reinhard Heydrich, and Reichsführer-SS Heinrich Himmler. These works were finalized by German High Judges and placed before Hitler in the Chancellery where they became formal law. Though none of us were aware of it, we had created the rumblings for an avalanche of disaster.

On Monday, 14 November 1938, I returned to my duties at Sachsenhausen and attended the promotion ceremony of a fellow officer in the square of the SS Administrative buildings. Weeks earlier the pogrom called The Night of Broken Glass had commenced. Thousands of Jews and criminals had been arrested, processed, and sentenced to the Detainment Facilities at Sachsenhausen and Dachau. Trucks filled with prisoners had come through the gates during the promotion ceremony. Members of the Transport Staff unloaded the human freight with the assistance of violent dogs. Though we did not see this from where the ceremony took place, the barking of the dogs, shouting of the Transport Staff, and wailing of the prisoners was heard from inside at the Appellplatz.

Eicke stated he would not often be present at Sachsenhausen as the recent actions required his supervision at Buchenwald, Dachau, Nordhausen, and their subcamps. He informed me that I was to question Kommandant Höss for any requirements I had. My orders and duties were prepared and stacked on the desk, and I officially began work at the camp.

One of the sealed packets of orders contained the stamp and wax seal of RSHA Headquarters. The documents stated that I was required to operate as a liaison between the Totenkopfverbände and RSHA Headquarters. Because of my Executive Police Authority, the RSHA assigned me to operate as Chief of the Sachsenhausen Administrative Police. This required me to monitor and report on the activities of Eicke and Höss in relation to the orders they received from their superiors. SS General Reinhard Heydrich wished to know about every step Eicke and Höss took inside Sachsenhausen and I was ordered to report this to him with strict confidentiality.

I received all incoming orders addressed to Höss and Eicke regarding activities at the camp and it was my responsibility to ensure that all directives were carried out accordingly. I was bound to report any discrepancies to RSHA Headquarters and this put me in a most unique position. Most of my time was spent compiling reports on the details of legal matters at Sachsenhausen as Headquarters was most interested in keeping aware of the costs of operation, contractors, supplies, inventory, and the efficiency of the facility.

For the first few months I managed to contain my activities to the SS Administrative area without having to visit the inside of the facility. During April 1939, I was summoned to a meeting with Höss and Eicke. The Major General announced that Sachsenhausen would be receiving a shipment of 500 Jews from Salzburg, Austria. The Detainment Facility had already exceeded its maximum number of inmates, and overcrowding was an issue attracting adverse attention from the Ministry of Health and Hygiene. Eicke demanded that I find a legal cause to refuse the shipment while Höss arranged the details of diverting the train to another location. My precedent existed in that overcrowding was an infection control problem. I felt certain the Ministry of Health and Hygiene would approve my request to refuse the shipment.

As anticipated, the precedent met agreement in Berlin, but diverting the train to another location became a problem. Dachau, Buchenwald, Nordhausen, Esterwegen, Flössenberg and Mauthausen were overpopulated with inmates, and Ravensbrücke was attempting to control an epidemic. The Kommandants at all potential destinations refused to accept our diverted shipment with sound legal reasons of their own.

On or about 10 April, I again met with Eicke and Höss in hopes of finding an alternate solution. Though we had received official authority to divert the train, there was nowhere to reroute it to. Despite that the Ministry of Health and Hygiene agreed that Sachsenhausen could not receive the shipment due to overcrowding, Höss was bound by law to accept it if another suitable location could not be found to divert it to. It was a circular bureaucratic dilemma which no one could clarify. This raised the question: Would Höss and Eicke be subjected to disciplinary measures for receiving the shipment and consciously increasing the risks for the spread of disease and infection within the Detainment Facility?

By legal standards, Sachsenhausen was overcrowded at that time. However, the Ministry of Health and Hygiene permitted a margin for such cases. While an excess population increased the risk of epidemics, it was controlled by having SS physicians conduct weekly visual examinations of the prisoners. This was considered to be a depletion of valuable resources and such matters were constantly under discussion by superiors at RSHA Headquarters. The visual examinations were conducted in the Appellplatz where approximately 10 or 20 SS physicians sat at tables. The inmates were ordered to undress and form lines before each doctor and step up to each table where an SS physician would look for obvious signs of illness. The unfit inmates were directed to an assembly area and loaded aboard trucks to be taken out of the Detainment Facility. The prisoners never came back, and I learned in July 1939 that the unfit inmates were taken to a sanatorium in Wittenberg where each was given a lethal phenol injection to the heart.

Facility Kommandants all over Germany were preparing to receive shipments of Jews from Austria that they could not accept due to overcrowding. I was constantly speaking to the Legal Affairs Officers at other camps in attempts to resolve the matter. We tried to talk each other into accepting lesser numbers of Jews from our intended shipments, but nobody was in the position to do this. A visual medical examination of the prisoners was scheduled for the middle of that week and Eicke asked me to urge the Chief Physician to raise the standards for physical fitness. The Major General hoped this would result in a higher quota of prisoners removed from the camp.

The Chief Physician said he would instruct his medical staff to be more observant in the examinations, but he could not alter the standards for medical protocol. At the end of the visual inspections, approximately 200 inmates had been listed as unfit and were loaded aboard trucks to be taken away. The arrival of the shipment from Austria was two or three days away, and this meant that at the currently exceeded occupancy of Sachsenhausen, we needed to remove an additional 300 inmates.

Höss and I worked late into the night reviewing the files of potentially transferable prisoners. Shortly after midnight we dispatched a courier carrying approximately 300 files to Headquarters in Berlin. It was our hope that Department IV would review and approve the transfers of the lesser criminals we had selected. We had mainly chosen vagrants, prostitutes and petty thieves with the hope that Headquarters would grant transfers from Sachsenhausen to municipal prisons, thus making the space available for the incoming shipment from Austria.

By the end of the following day we had received word from Department IV. We were not the only Detainment Facility Administration requesting inmate transfers. To grant an impartial decision, Department IV agreed to transfer 50 lesser criminals from each facility to municipal jails. This left us with an excess of 250 prisoners and less than 24 hours to find a place for them before the Austrian shipment arrived. We exhausted all options. Before noon on or about 13 April, Höss entered my office and ordered me to appeal to Headquarters for permission to enact Directive 19 for a total of 500 prisoners.

Eicke had given Höss the orders with the reasoning we needed to make room to accommodate the incoming shipment. Höss said it was rumored Headquarters approved the use of Directive 19 at Dachau, Flössenberg, Mauthausen and Buchenwald due to the present circumstances. I argued with Höss that our facility would exceed maximum capacity by a total of only 250, and he answered that Eicke was aware of this, but the Major General specifically requested Directive 19 for 500 prisoners. Höss relayed Eicke's desire that I was to formally make the request.

I never thought Headquarters would approve a telephoned request for 500 death warrants. This kind of demand required accompanying paperwork and formal documentation. I reached an officer in Department IV, and once I identified myself and the facility from which I was contacting him, apologized for the inappropriate manner in which I had to request Directive 19 for 500 prisoners. To my astonishment I received verbal approval and was told it would become official in the form of an authorization number once Headquarters confirmed the request with Höss. Less than one hour later the process was official. Höss came to me and said I was to arrange the executions of 500 prisoners with strict consideration for the legal constraints of the action. He declared I was to choose the 500 prisoners and that I could do this during the muster call at the Appellplatz, or I could select them based upon any other legal means. Höss announced he expected my roster by 2000 hours.

There I sat in my tiny office with the gruesome burden of selecting 500 people to be executed. It did not seem to happen in any form of reality. How was I to choose? My first thought was to execute the 500 prisoners arriving from Austria the moment they stepped off the transports. Not knowing what to do, I telephoned Untersturmführer Fritz Stammler, a fellow officer who had attended the meetings with me in Berlin

Stammler did not know what to do and said he did not envy me for having to make this decision. He warned me to use caution in making the determination to execute the new arrivals. What, he asked, would I do if they were only women and children? Stammler stated that if the decision was his, he would probably choose the elderly at Sachsenhausen. He informed me that superior officers at RSHA Headquarters were monitoring my management of the situation.

I methodically entered the names of the eldest prisoners on my roster until early in the evening. I had charted 500 names of prisoners who were between the ages of 55 and 80 years. I processed the documentation necessary for the enactment of a Directive 19 Order, and presented the packet to Höss at 2000 hours.

I used a telephone and typewriter to authorize the slaughter of 500 people. Selecting names from a list had not been as impersonal as I hoped it would be. I was cognizant that each represented a living person. I did not sign off on that order. Rudolph Höss did. Though the entire process of the Directive 19 followed Reich protocol, it took place without having to affix my signature to a single document that admitted my complicity in the arranging, planning and carrying out of the orders.

On the morning the train arrived from Austria, affairs seemed to be normal throughout the facility. I had heard nothing about the carrying out of the scheduled Directive 19, nor did I inquire about it. Shortly before noon, Höss entered my office and informed me that the 500 condemned prisoners had finished digging a trench near the northwest section of the security wall. He said the executions were going to begin in approximately an hour and that Major General Eicke demanded my presence at the site to ensure the action was carried out legally and within the protocol of Reich codes. I did not know what the standards were. It required a quick and intensive reading of the Directive 19 articles in the Reich legal books at hand. The articles stated that the presiding Officer or Kommandant was to select shooting or hanging as the method for execution. If shooting was chosen, all ammunition magazines would need to be stored, sorted and inventoried for accounting purposes, and this information was to be entered on the After Action Reports. Höss had selected shooting and assigned the task to an SS Sergeant. It was required that all executed prisoners be formally pronounced dead by an attending physician and this information had to be conveyed in writing to a Legal Affairs Officer also present at the action.

I was driven through the prison to the area designated for the carrying out of the Directive 19 where I met the facility doctor, Captain Lutz. A pit had been dug that was approximately 9 meters long by 2 ½ meters wide and 4 ½ meters deep. A machine gun had been mounted on a tripod approximately 3 ½ meters from the edge of the hole, and it was there that the Sergeant shouted vulgarly at his juniors. Now and then he would walk to where 20 elderly prisoners were standing and shout vicious obscenities, point his pistol at them, and strike them with a piece of wood he carried in his other hand. The prisoners were the people I had chosen.

Doctor Lutz carried a satchel that contained a stack of small cards. Each was printed with the words *"Bescheinigung des Todes"* and contained spaces and lines for the name of the prisoner, the custody number, and the time of death. Lutz began filling out the dates on each. 14 April 1939.

It was necessary to traverse over the crest of a small hill to reach the area designated for the executions. Prisoners would be led to the pit in groups of 20. The remainder was kept under guard and out of view from where the shootings were to take place. I assumed it would be quite obvious for those out of view to know their fate from the sound of the gunfire. Truthfully, I did not know what to expect or how I would react when the Directive 19 officially commenced. At approximately noon, the Sergeant shouted, "It is time for the circus! Fetch the animals!"

The elderly men and women were ordered to disrobe and were then kicked, beaten and pushed to the edge of the pit. The Sergeant looked at a Corporal who had taken position behind the machine gun and shouted, "Shoot them, damn it!" The Corporal tried, but a defect had occurred in loading the weapon. Several SS guards opened the loading latch and reset the belt of ammunition while the prisoners looked at each other. Again the order was given to shoot and again the machine gun failed to operate. The prisoners began to weep and plead. The Sergeant opened the loading latch and realigned the ammunition belt and called his juniors to observe how it was properly done. He explained that the belt needed to rest between the guiding rails and then called the lot a "Group of stupid Bavarians". On the third order the machine gun fired and the 20 prisoners were torn apart. At such a close range, arms and legs were instantly severed by the bullets and innards were scattered across the pit and on the ground.

Confusion followed this horror. Captain Lutz had been so engaged in writing the dates on the Death Certificates that he did not record the names of the twenty executed prisoners. He shouted this to the gun crew at which the Sergeant insubordinately replied, "You can go down in the pit and ask them for their names Sir, but I do not think you will receive any answers!"

I told Lutz that all the information was on a roster in my office and that if he was careful to obtain the subsequent names, we could check his results against my list to figure the names of the first twenty.

A Schütze shouted that some of the prisoners were moving in the pit. A group of SS troops ran to the edge and began firing their rifles without orders. The Sergeant began yelling for them to stop. He screamed, "You dumb bastards know the damned procedure! I need to know which of you fired and how many rounds! Then I need your magazines! What in hell is wrong with you people? You fools know better! This is not the first time we have done this!" The Sergeant wrote down the names of the soldiers who fired into the trench and accounted for the number of rounds discharged. He then assigned three soldiers to deliver the coup de gras to any prisoner still moving after the round of machine gun fire.

Lutz or I should have chastised the Sergeant for his abominable behavior, but neither of us did so. I can say the reason I did not discipline him was because he operated with complete authority over the firing squad. That was something I wished to have no part of. Therefore, I allowed him to conduct the action in his own manner.

The next group of twenty was led over the hill and was forced to disrobe. As they walked to the edge of the pit, each paused to give his or her name and custody number to Doctor Lutz. There was great emotion among them when they saw the severed limbs and innards and, when they saw their dead comrades at the bottom of the pit, they began to weep, sing and pray. They were instantly shot and the action was followed by the coup de gras where necessary.

As the shootings continued, the behavior of the SS guards worsened. A Corporal picked up the severed arm of a prisoner and used it to slap inmates on their way to the edge of the pit. It took everything in me to maintain the demeanor of an officer. Lutz looked on with no emotion, but the Doctor had witnessed such actions many times before. The men of the firing squad had obviously participated in previous actions as they went about their duties with a jovial manner. I was speechless when the shootings halted due to the arrival of a horse drawn soup wagon. The executions were suspended for half an hour so the men could eat. During that time an enlisted man brought me an empty ammunition crate and turned it on its side and told me to use it as a seat. I sat there watching the SS eat potato soup in the middle of a sea of blood. Lutz brought me a cup of coffee and I spilled most of it because my hands were trembling. The doctor produced a vial of pills from his tunic and gave me one. He said it would calm my nerves and stated he took two before coming to these actions. I never questioned what it was. I took the pill and soon my nerves were calm and the nausea had subsided. I sat there for the remainder of the executions and then collected the Sergeant's written records and loaded all the magazines and machine gun belts into the car. The SS poured cans of petrol in the pit and set the corpses aflame.

Lutz and I were able to ascertain the names and custody numbers of the first twenty prisoners that were executed. I stared at the walls in my office for quite some time after the doctor left. When I looked at the magazines and empty machine gun belts, I began shaking and weeping without control. I felt the urgency to regain my senses, for if Höss or Eicke entered my office and found me weeping at my desk, I would be ridiculed and punished. I bit into the back of my fist to cause enough pain to diminish my emotions. When I drew blood from my hand it took me from the grief and forced me to tend to the wound. While washing it in the basin, Höss entered my office long enough to say, "Have your After Action Report on my desk first thing in the morning."

I formally stated as a witness, that the Directive 19 had been conducted in accord with the codes of Reich legal protocol. I affixed my signature and obtained the signature of Doctor Lutz. I presented it to Höss in the morning as ordered.

The Kommandant signed my report and its three copies. I dispatched the original to Headquarters, gave one copy to Höss, another copy to Eicke, and dispatched the third copy to SS General Heydrich's office.

During the following days I was assigned the task of investigating a problem with the military postal mail. Many parcels posted from the facility were not reaching their destinations, and those that did arrive were badly damaged or delivered open and with portions of the contents missing. This did nothing to remove my thoughts from the execution of the prisoners.

Doctor Lutz came to my office on a frequent basis. He always inquired of my health and well being as if suspecting that the horrible experience of the Directive 19 had somehow affected my mental state. It had, and he was the only person I felt comfortable in confiding this. He said he understood and was always ready with a kind word or amusing story to take my thoughts from things.

Lutz finished medical studies in 1933 and had built a small, but successful private practice in Hamburg until the Nürnberg Laws decreed that Jews could no longer enlist the professional services of Germans. He said most of his patients had been Jews, and the new laws deeply affected his practice. He received an invitation to join the

SS in 1936 due to a shortage of medical personnel. His enlistment carried the automatic rank of Hauptsturmführer and he believed it was the most favorable means to continue his profession. We became close friends over the months that followed.

During May, the Gestapo arrived at Sachsenhausen and interviewed me at great length in regard to the After Action Report I had submitted concerning the April Directive 19. Accompanying the Gestapo were two SS officers who were gravely concerned about the adverse remarks I had written about the conduct of the SS Sergeant who had been in command of the gun crew. I had not intended to cause personal trouble for the Sergeant, but I had sought to make Headquarters aware of the unprofessional manner in which the Directive 19 was carried out. The Gestapo was not concerned with the fact that no dignity had been extended toward the prisoners. Their concern existed in that I had entered the adverse remarks on my report in the form of a complaint, but had not listed any means of formal discipline against the Sergeant. The Gestapo reminded me that as an officer with Executive Police Authority, I should have arrested him. The accompanying SS officers stated it was my duty as an attending officer, or the duty of Hauptsturmführer Lutz, to have intervened in the action to correct the errant behavior and to have proceeded in an appropriate manner at that time so as to avoid entering inconclusive remarks in the report. Because a copy was sent to Heydrich's office, the General was greatly displeased to learn of such unruliness and demanded the Sergeant be demoted and transferred to another facility. In addition, adverse conduct reports were to be written by the SS officers and placed into Lutz's and my personnel records. The Gestapo and SS officers then personally escorted the Sergeant to their vehicle and took him from the facility.

Höss was unforgiving over this incident. He called me into his office and shouted at me for half and hour. He stated that the Sergeant was the product of excellent training; that he had earned the respect of the prisoners, and his reputation alone kept Sachsenhausen free of treachery from the prisoners. Höss mocked my appointment to Junior Lieutenant and accused me of being a failure as an officer. He further claimed that it would be his ambition to have me removed from the Sachsenhausen facility.

Major General Eicke was not pleased with the situation, but was very civil and professional. He was disappointed that I entered adverse remarks on my report about an enlisted man under his command. He said I should have discussed the Sergeant's behavior with him or Höss before dispatching the reports, and then admitted he knew I was reporting to Heydrich about his actions. Eicke stated my career at Sachsenhausen was all but over as there was no anticipated resolve with Kommandant Höss. This seemed a good thing as I wanted nothing more than to be away from such a horrible place.

My final day at Sachsenhausen was 27 June 1939. Major General Eicke summoned me to his office that morning and told me I was being assigned to a Waffen SS Regiment. He announced quite clearly that this was by no means a punitive measure, but had been ordered at a higher level. Eicke had been asked to select an officer under his command with Executive Police Authority who had demonstrated aggressive measures. The General said that my loyalty to the SS and devotion to duty had been noticed in that I did not hesitate to claim unprofessional military behavior in Eicke's Regiment. He informed me that most Junior Officers would never have taken the risk of defying or embarrassing him and that he was ultimately praised for my report because it demonstrated the men under his command represented the integrity expected by Reichsführer-SS Heinrich Himmler.

Eicke told me I was to be assigned to Waffen SS Regiment Deutschland, VII Panzer Division Kempf under the command of SS Brigadeführer Paul Hausser. He informed me of a confidential matter in which German Intelligence had revealed a Polish plot to move against the Reich by inciting riots within the interior of Germany. He explained that if such happened, it would be considered an act of war and the Reich would be forced to move against Poland. Eicke said that in this event, I would serve as a front line liaison to RSHA Headquarters and serve the Totenkopfverbände as a Forward SS Police Chief in the Occupied Zone. He explained it would be necessary for the Totenkopfverbände to subjugate the population and oversee the application of Reich military and civil law. This was the reason for my assignment to the Waffen-SS Regiment. Eicke said if the Reich went to war against Poland, I would serve him by establishing Detainment Facilities in the Occupied Zones.

On the following day I reported to Brigadeführer Paul Hausser at Regimental Headquarters at Dresden. He received me with great respect and remarked that he was pleased and honored to have a representative of the RSHA as a member of his staff. My arrival created an obvious state of tension among the men as I wore the SS Police uniform which was different from all other members of the unit. My insignia clearly identified me not only as a representative of the RSHA, but as an officer of the SS Police which now included a personal membership in Gestapo affairs. Hausser instructed me not to visit the quartermaster to draw new patches and insignia. He ordered me to keep and wear what I arrived with as he believed my presence and appearance would help maintain discipline in the Regiment. At the next general formation he introduced me as "General Heydrich's representative".

Following this introduction it was astounding to witness the manner in which officers and enlisted men reacted to my presence. At that time, I represented the RSHA which made me an agent of the Reich Central Security Office, the Gestapo, the Military Police, Criminal Police, Order Police and the SS Security Police. I had been given absolute jurisdiction to enforce all aspects of Reich law and had complete authorization to place military and civilian personnel under investigation or arrest.

When I entered a barracks the men would immediately come to attention and some would stutter in great fear when they spoke to me. All responded in the formal language of the Reich believing that I wanted to hear nothing but their loyalty and devotion to Hitler and the SS. All offered me unconditional assistance and knew I possessed the power and means to alter their lives. They had conceived the notion that I was harsh and cruel, and that I would not tolerate the slightest form of insolence or lack of discipline. The rumor circulated that I exposed an insubordinate member of Eicke's Regiment and the men believed I had been assigned to the Waffen SS Regiment to weed out any soldier not in compliance with Reich expectations.

I enjoyed this respect as a young Lieutenant. I permitted their fear of me to fan the flames of my own arrogance, and I easily developed into what they thought I was. During July and August I found fault with the men of Waffen SS Regiment Deutschland. I punished them for laziness, improper salutes, and uniform violations. I issued fines and imposed 72 hours confinement for insubordination. The men came to fear me, avoid me, and ultimately hate me. I enjoyed the power my position afforded me, and it was here that I first abused it.

CHAPTER THREE
THE STORM IN THE EAST

During the final weeks of August the Regiment moved east to the city of Gorlitz where an old school campus had been modified as a barracks. I regularly received directives from Headquarters requiring my attendance at meetings in the nearby town of Cottbus. Senior RSHA and Gestapo officers presented me with documentation at these assemblies that outlined proposals for Reich Occupational Law. We discussed the information, suggested alternative measures, and offered addendums and amendments to the proposals. By that time we believed Poland posed an inevitable threat to Reich security because public and military broadcasts no longer concealed Polish plans to seize our radio towers and border installations. It was clearly stated that if Polish attacks manifested, German forces would be ordered to cross the border.

On the afternoon of 31 August, 1939, Waffen SS Regiment Deutschland, VII Panzer Division Kempf, received orders to organize and proceed east to the Neisse River near the Polish border. The mobilization was an event unlike anything I had ever experienced. Men ran about gathering backpacks and equipment, others hurriedly wrote letters to loved ones, and some inspected vehicles and supplies. Piercing whistles continued to blow and the stench of exhaust burned my nose and throat as the panzers, kampfwagons, halftracks and transport trucks turned over their engines. Soldiers greased the sliding bolts on their rifles, stuffed grenades into their belts and stored ammunition. After another series of piercing whistles, the men boarded the vehicles.

As an officer of the SS Police, I was not certain of my

responsibilities during the mobilization. I did not know where I was supposed to be or what I was supposed to do. I had been given no direct orders, and as I was separate from the Waffen SS, there was no one for me to directly command. I tried to appear casual as I searched for my Commanding Officer. I eventually located Hausser at the head of the tank column, but he did not permit me the opportunity to ask questions. Instead, he pointed toward a row of Kubelwagens and told me to get in one of them for transport. Other officers were carrying rifles and combat equipment and I felt quite awkward being armed only with my briefcase and a pistol. An enlisted driver opened the back door for me to enter and then he took a seat behind the wheel. With great excitement he asked, "Where are we going, Sir?" I was very calm as I answered.

"Poland."

Two Waffen SS officers joined me in the car and we sat there for twenty or thirty minutes before the remainder of the column had organized into an Advance Formation. With the shrill sound of those damned whistles and the shouting of men, the panzers opened their throttles and the column began moving forward.

We came to the Neisse River in less than an hour and the column turned northward onto the Frankfurt an der Oder road. The river was on our right side. Its far eastern bank was Polish territory. At some places we watched Polish civilians washing garments and filling buckets in the river. Polish children swam and splashed in the water, and pointed and waved when they saw us. The elder Poles watched us with great caution as the political climate between our countries had been greatly strained over the past several months.

The column halted southeast of Cottbus where a stone bridge spanned approximately 15 meters over the Neisse River. On its other side was a Polish border gate, a guardhouse with a flag, and approximately 50 Polish soldiers armed with rifles and light artillery. They had taken precautions against an impending invasion. Beyond the border gate was an open expanse of land that disappeared at the top of a rolling hill in the distance.

The column turned off its engines and we sat there for a long time in the heat. The Poles on the opposite side continued to watch us. Several hours later, Waffen SS Infantry and a Wehrmacht Mechanized Regiment came southward on the road from Frankfurt an der Oder and met us at the bridge. Observers constantly kept field glasses trained on the Polish territory. By the time our kitchen wagons arrived, the Poles had reinforced with perhaps 300 additional soldiers.

A Polish Officer bearing a flag of truce came halfway across the bridge with an enlisted man. A Waffen SS Colonel met him at the midpoint and they spoke through the translation of the enlisted Polish soldier. The opposing officers eventually shook hands and returned to their respective sides. I never knew what was said on the bridge, but from the gestures of the Waffen SS officer, he seemed to indicate to the Poles that we posed no threat. The entire meeting seemed quite suspect.

None of our superiors told us what awaited on the following day. It was obvious that a major action was in store as high ranking officers kept to themselves and continued to come and go from the tent serving as Hausser's Command Post. By evening, the uncertainty of our purpose, and the fact that the Poles were still reinforcing across the river began to manifest in many ugly ways. Fistfights erupted over card games and a soldier playing an accordion was berated for the tunes he chose. In this restlessness, a Sergeant informed me that Hausser required my immediate presence in the Command Post.

"You look nervous", was the first thing Hausser said to me. I thought such a statement never needed be made. It was obvious I was nervous. We all were nervous. Hausser looked nervous but I would be a damned fool to tell him that. He turned the pages of several documents and announced the Gestapo had intercepted a credible Polish message revealing the time and date of a planned attack on a German border installation. I knew my Commander was lying. I understood the workings of the Reich Departments and, as the representative of RSHA Headquarters in the field, I knew that if such a credible message had been intercepted, I would have been the first informed. It would have been my duty to relay the information to Brigadeführer Hausser. The fact that he informed me revealed the alleged Polish plans to be suspect, and that the impending German action was of military motive rather than in defense of a security matter. He told me that Polish militants planned to seize a German radio tower and broadcast anti German propaganda in an effort to incite Jews, Communists and Bolshevists to rebel against the Reich. When he told me this I was certain that if such a thing happened, it would be a well staged maneuver orchestrated by the Reich. Poland had a weak military as a result of the Great War and stood in no beneficial position to draw Germany into a war.

The Brigadeführer said if we were forced to cross the Polish border, I would serve in the capacity of the SS Chief of Police and Security in an Occupied Zone. He gave me a roster that contained the names of officers and enlisted men among us at the moment. 26 of them had previous experience as Civil Servants before joining the military and had served as members of Civil Fire Brigades and as local police, postmen, and administrators for mayors. I was to conscript these men as members of my Occupational Police Force and assign them duties based upon rank. Hausser pointed to a map and I first heard the name of our objective. Porajów.

The town contained a population of approximately 6,500 of which perhaps 1200 men, women and children were Jews. Hausser presented me with orders stating that in the event German Forces occupied this town, I was to account for each of the Jews. In addition, I was given a roster of approximately 400 names of known Bolshevist and Communist sympathizers residing there. On dismissal from the Command Post, I enlisted the assistance of a Sergeant to collect the 26 former Civil Servants and took them to an area away from the others to introduce myself and explain our purpose.

The men were confused and I could not yet explain matters to them. They asked many questions which I could not answer. All of them were eager to assist me because my reputation as Heydrich's representative had quickly circulated. One of the men asked, "Sir, are the Poles going to attack us?" I answered him in the silence of my mind. "Most assuredly," I thought. "And what great fortune for us that our entire army happens to lie on their borders tonight!"

I do not believe anyone slept that night. I continued to stress the importance of adhering to Reich Occupational Law and making certain all 26 men under my command understood this. After midnight, approximately a dozen panzers employed the manual crank mechanisms to silently turn their turrets toward the Polish border. We heard the foreign voices across the river and though I did not know what they were saying, German Intelligence Officers were writing down every word with great eagerness and then running into Hausser's Command Post.

Before dawn the SS Infantry Regiment began taking places along the riverbank. The Polish would occasionally sweep a spotlight across our troops and we would do the same to them. I believe that all men on both sides knew it was a matter of hours before we engaged in combat, though both armies acted in a manner that pretended we did not know this was about to happen.

At approximately 0500 hours on 1 September, the skies turned a mild red with the dawn of a beautiful day. The sun had just appeared when German radios were turned on. Our men gathered around them with great excitement. I heard a portion of the broadcast and learned that Polish militants had seized a German radio tower on the border. The sounds of shooting could be heard behind a voice with a heavy Polish accent. The broadcaster condemned the Reich and called for the citizens of Germany to take arms and fight against our government. Orders circulated through the chain of command to prepare for combat.

The broadcast had gone silent for a matter of moments before our planes soared over the trees into Poland. By God what a spectacular sight that was! Formations of Stuka dive bombers roared overhead at low level permitting us to see the pilots, read the tail numbers, and view the great black crosses underneath the wings! We could smell the exhaust and fuel from the wash of the propellers. As rapidly as they flew overhead, we watched them become dots on the horizon over the Polish frontier.

An internal radio order was issued to the tank commanders and a dozen panzers opened fire on the Polish positions across the river. I was sitting in the back of the Kubelwagen when this occurred and did not have the foresight to exit the vehicle and take cover. When Polish bullets struck the transport truck parked near my Kubelwagen, I needed to find something safe to hide behind. The bullets striking the truck sounded like someone pounding on metal with a carpentry hammer.

As I rolled out of the car a tremendous explosion forced me from my senses and I instinctively peered over the back of the tank I was cowering behind. I was not the only man huddled there. I was in the company of officers and enlisted men alike. The Polish had mined the stone bridge with dynamite but made the mistake of setting the charges on the sides of the bridge. Our engineers noticed the charges on the previous day, but could not attempt to disarm them without revealing German intentions. The detonation of the bridge was completely ineffective. Dynamite combusts outwardly. As a result, the bridge across the Neisse had absorbed half the power of the explosives and remained intact.

An enlisted man was crouched behind the tank with a rifle slung over each shoulder, a sidearm in his holster, grenades in his belt, and an MP38 machine pistol clutched in his hands. When he saw that I was armed with a pistol and briefcase, he offered a rifle to me. I refused it and demanded the MP38. I had given an average performance with the Mauser rifle during my training and I preferred the security of the MP38 machine pistol. It increased my chances for survival to point and spray with the weapon rather than being forced to fumble with a five round clip and the sliding bolt of a rifle. The enlisted man was reluctant to give me the MP38. In my opinion, this was the first advantage of having rank. I appeared as a fool for not knowing how to lock the charging handle but the enlisted man showed me with great patience and respect, and gave me additional ammunition.

I heard continuous shooting, the bursts of tank fire and orders being shouted. During the initial attack I kept myself out of harm's way by crouching behind the tank. As frightened as I was during that battle, I could have completely hid myself behind a box of matches.

After ten or fifteen minutes the shooting stopped and a roar of rejoicing voices erupted from our troops. The tank I was hiding behind turned over its engine and the sudden noise nearly frightened me out of my skin. I was trembling, but I was not the only one. The SS Infantry returned from their positions along the riverbank with ashen faces and expressions of terror. We took approximately 50 casualties during the battle, but not a single German soldier had been killed. The armored vehicles crossed the bridge, followed by an orderly column of men. On the other side I took a moment to survey the carnage we had visited upon the Polish army. Some enemy soldiers had been mutilated so badly by our bullets that one could scarcely identify them as former human beings. Others lied in a peaceful state as if they were sleeping. The border guardhouse was gone. Aside from a hole in the ground and flames, one would never know it existed if he had not first seen it. The Polish artillery was smoldering and bent. Our planes now flew overhead in both directions as they came and went from their bombing raids on the Polish interior.

I suppose my experiences at Sachsenhausen tempered my feelings toward the dead Polish soldiers. I felt nothing for them, nor did the sight of their twisted open bodies affect me. They were the enemy and we had vanquished them. In my thoughts I truly knew that the alleged Polish attack on a German radio tower had been the product of RSHA planning. It appealed to no logic for Poland to draw us into a war. At that moment, there on Polish territory, I had a troubling sense that we as Germans had committed our first grievous act as a country. The elder officers seemed angry, and their facial expressions seemed to reflect my thoughts. Most of our troops were shaking hands and congratulating each other on victory. They believed the Polish first attacked us and that the slaughter at the bridge was justified. I remember thinking that perhaps the officials at RSHA Headquarters manufactured the invasion as a preemptive measure to counter an impending Polish attack. Perhaps we struck first? One had to take comfort in thinking our superiors in Berlin knew what they were doing, and that the invasion of Poland served the interests of Reich security.

Waffen SS Regiment Deutschland, VII Panzer Division Kempf, advanced as the left flank of the Wehrmacht Mechanized Regiment. We moved forward at a steady pace toward the rolling hills in the distance all the while being over flown by Stukas heading into and out of Poland.

On 12 October 1939, Brigadeführer Liszka formally pronounced me SS Chief of Police and Security for the Occupied Polish Zone of Porajów. The position held a great amount of responsibility. As the SS Chief of Police and Security, I became the ultimate authority over all matters of misconduct committed by civilians and military personnel. I had been granted liberty to author original legal codes necessary for the effective protection of Reich forces and for the general overseeing of the city. This was not uncommon. All SS Chiefs of Police and Security in the Occupied Zones were given this privilege as it was deemed we knew what measures needed to be enforced to guarantee safety, efficiency and pacification of the subjugated civilians. As a result, activities that I may have deemed legal in Porajów could very well be considered illegal in Debno or Kostrzyn. The code of Occupational Law was left to the discretion of the acting SS Chief of Police and Security in each individual town or city. It was the responsibility of each German soldier to first familiarize himself with local Occupational Law when traveling from town to town. Excuses and ignorance were never valid reasons for breaching the law.

Porajów had not been the site of many partisan attacks at that time. As a small town virtually cut off from industrial civilization, it remained unimportant as a strategic location but, vital for its railroad. The rails running east of Porajów connected to six switching stations east at Kalisz. These stations provided rail access south to Czestochowa, Tarnow, Bielsko-Biala and most importantly, Karków. The station at Kalisz provided vital supply shipments to reach distribution centers north at Konin, Wloclawek, Torun, Plock and Ciechanow. The most important aspect of the rails at Porajów was the provision of a direct line from Dresden in Germany, to the switching stations at Kalisz in Poland. East of those six stations were areas in need of German troop reinforcements, especially at Lodz, Lublin, Lomza, Skierniewice, Radom and of course, Warsaw.

Though other small border towns contained rails, this one was near the major German industrial center at Dresden. As a result, German trains were a constant on my lines at Porajów. It was not long before Polish partisans disputed my control over the rails.

30 October was the first shooting execution of a Pole in my town. An SS Schütze submitted a report detailing the refusal of a Pole to surrender a knife. I did not particularly care, and the report was not necessary. In my opinion, the Pole earned his fate for carrying contraband in my area of operations.

My primary responsibility was the safety and security of Reich forces in the Occupied Zone. Being entrusted with the protection of my fellow countrymen was a task I performed most seriously. I have no remorse for hanging or shooting any person that threatened the safety, security, welfare and lives of my fellow patriots. Such executions do not weigh whatsoever on my conscience. I had been given the duty to guarantee safe passage for all Reich forces and through my devotion and efficiency, and according to Reich records, Porajów was indeed one of the most secure Occupied Zones during my administration. I did not tolerate the slightest threat to Reich forces whether it was shots fired at SS troops, or a stone thrown at a tank column. The people knew this and I was very clear and efficient at circulating this information among them. By November 1939, civilians suspected of attacking or harassing Reich forces adopted a policy of suicide when they learned I issued warrants for their arrest. I had earned a reputation among the local population as being brutal and merciless.

I promptly learned that containment and restrictions were the most efficient means of controlling the subjugated population. I no longer recall the minor laws I enforced, but I will list the general rules I imposed:

- Polish civilians are not permitted on the streets before 0800 hours.
- Polish civilians are to adhere to the 2000 hours curfew. Any Pole arrested after curfew is subject to Directive 19.
- Polish businesses may operate between the 1000 hours and 1600 hours.
- Polish businesses and civilians must refrain from all social and business contact with Jews, Communists and Bolshevists.
- Polish civilians are ordered to surrender all radios, weapons, ammunition and medicines to the SS or Order Police.
- Polish civilians sympathetic to Jewish interests - specifically Christians married to Jews and children of mixed lineage - are forbidden from using sidewalks, public facilities and public transportation.
- Polish civilians are ordered to provide the names and addresses of all Jews, Communists and Bolshevists known to them. Failure to do so will result in Directive 19.
- Polish civilians, unless first addressed by Reich forces, are not permitted to initiate conversation with Reich forces in the Polish language unless such conversation is proven to provide safety and security for Reich forces. Failure to comply will result in Directive 19. Polish civilians are permitted to first address Reich forces in the German language.
- Polish civilians must immediately surrender upon order by Reich forces, all property, money, portable wealth, vehicles and any other items so requested by Reich forces. Failure to

comply will result in Directive 19.

- Polish civilians must immediately produce Identity Documents upon order by Reich forces. Failure to comply will result in immediate seizure and arrest.
- All Polish criminals and Jews exempt from confinement must wear a 7.5 by 7.5 centimeter green square on the left breast for identification.

My orders demanded the pacification of the subjugated population, and as a means to form harmony with the Poles, I submitted a proposal to Headquarters requesting the formation of a Polish City Council in Porajów. My goal was to keep the council as a puppet system to serve as liaison between the Polish civilians and the Occupying German forces; primarily the SS. Berlin forwarded my request to Major General Eicke who approved the idea, but strongly cautioned that I keep rigid control over the council.

The former Polish mayor of Porajów was receptive to the idea and he submitted several rosters containing the names of those Polish citizens he wished to represent the council. Background investigations had stricken a few from his proposal, but after several arbitration meetings we settled on an acceptable cabinet. The administration housed itself in the former police station which had undergone serious damage as the result of several direct artillery strikes during the invasion.

I ultimately dictated the law in Porajów. The former mayor, Bartlomiej Nieuzyla, understood and acknowledged my control. His two primary administrators consisted of the former Municipal Chief, Henryk Cholewa, and the former Police Chief, Piotr Wietrzychowski. The remaining eight members of the cabinet were former school teachers, tax officials, and civil servants. It was my idea to appoint eleven members to the council so that all matters requiring a vote would never be deadlocked. I told them that when an item required votes, the position of being "undecided" would result in a formal dismissal from the administration.

My personal staff met with Nieuzyla's council every Thursday and I attended the meetings provided my schedule allowed the time. It was in those meetings and through updates from my staff, that I developed an intense dislike for the Poles. I had been most generous in modifying some of the Occupational Laws that directly affected the Polish citizens of Porajów, but instead of being grateful for my benevolence, Nieuzyla and his council saw it as a means to request more concessions. The Poles were very greedy with their demands and inundated my office with inquiries and proposals. When I told Nieuzyla that the conduct of his council bordered on sabotage, he defended his position by reminding me that I conceived and initiated the Polish administration in an effort to pacify relations between German forces and the subjugated people. Nieuzyla would often ask, what is the purpose of having this council if we cannot advocate our needs?

I grew very suspicious of them and on many occasions threatened to dissolve the council. Usually my impatience with them would produce favorable results, and the Poles would tend to minor internal problems for a period of time. Eventually they would again become bold enough to submit unreasonable demands.

Ultimately the council became an entity that processed all the complaints of the populace. The citizens took it upon themselves to line up at the doors with grievances about stolen rabbits, lack of clothing, ration shortages, vandalism, petty thefts, and assaults and, some even dared to protest their treatment by Occupying German forces. Nieuzyla and his council became so overwhelmed at processing the local complaints that it became impossible to meet with my staff more than once a month. The meetings then focused on what the SS Police was willing to do to solve local complaints. My staff and I assured Nieuzyla we would investigate and remedy such matters, but we never did. This encouraged dissention and infighting between the Poles and their council, and ultimately left my Police Units free to address matters of security.

CHAPTER FOUR
AUTHORITY AND JUSTICE

A series of brazen partisan attacks began during the first week of December and conjured a wave of rebellion within a faction of the townspeople. The first incident occurred when saboteurs blew apart a section of the railroad tracks approximately 2 kilometers east of Porajów. The second took place 24 hours later and involved the ambush of our supply trucks west of the town.

Headquarters put intense pressure on me and my staff to bring the guilty parties to justice. We arrested local Polish labor leaders and former town officials who we believed would have pertinent information regarding these attacks. Nieuzyla and his council verbally objected to my policy of house to house searches and arrests and seizures. I warned Nieuzyla that if he had information, or knew someone who did, it would be in his best interest to comply. He said he might be able to gather names and intelligence within 48 hours. I saw this as a potential deception wherein he could set the guilty free and provide innocent parties willing to accept the blame. The Poles would do this. They would offer up the innocent so the organized resistance could continue. I gave Nieuzyla 12 hours and cordoned off Porajów.

Early the next morning an incendiary device was thrown at a Blitz Opel truck from the upper window of an apartment on Brzozowa Street in the western quarter of the town. Following a thorough investigation, credible witnesses from the Wehrmacht and Order Police identified the window from which it had been thrown. I ordered Junior Lieutenant Mahler to assemble a unit of enlisted SS Police, and I accompanied them to the apartment on Brzozowa Street to conduct the arrest of its occupants.

We made entry during the afternoon meal. A woman moved around the dining table with obvious anxiety and she seemed to expect our visit. At her sides were three children of whom two were boys in their teens, and a young girl that appeared to be ten to twelve years of age. Six of the enlisted SS investigated the apartment by throwing the contents of drawers, closets, cabinets, and armoires to the floor. They gathered photographs and documents for review and began tearing open the floorboards and walls.

The woman spoke imperfect German, but it was enough to render a conversation. I asked her who had thrown the incendiary bomb from the window. She claimed not to know and insisted she nor had her children committed the act. Referencing a wedding portrait, I inquired of the whereabouts of her husband. She answered he was a soldier in the Polish army and had been reported captured by German forces at Zlotow. She also stated that she did not share her apartment with other tenants. I demanded to know who else owned a key to her apartment, and she responded that no one had one. Mahler inspected the door and reported that it showed no signs of stress or unnatural entry. She declared that on the day and at the time of the attack, she and her children had been at the market in town. She confirmed locking the door though she had not been in the habit of doing such before German forces occupied the town. She admitted locking it to prevent Germans from entering in her absence.

An enlisted SS soldier suggested that the building custodian would more than likely hold a key to all the apartments for the sake of making necessary repairs. I ordered him brought before me.

When the search of her apartment was complete, my units announced they had not located any items of contraband. The young girl began weeping at the sight of her destroyed home and Mahler ordered the mother to quiet her.

The building custodian was forced into the apartment by two enlisted units and one smacked him in the back of the head, knocking his hat off. The SS soldier ordered the man to stand at attention. He apparently did not speak German and I was required to rely on the woman for translation. I ordered her to ask him if he had access to all the apartments and he responded by showing me the iron ring containing many keys. Ordered to produce the specific key for that door, he found it without delay. The enlisted soldier tore the ring from his hands, locked the door and verified that the designated key opened it. I demanded to know who else owned such a key. The man stated that perhaps the owner of the building held spare keys, but that he lived in a distant town far to the northeast. I inquired if he had thrown the incendiary device from the window and he denied committing the act.

I explained to him and the family that a problem existed. The door contained no traceable evidence of having been forced open, and there were but two people holding keys to its lock. How would someone else have known the door was unlocked? Did someone enter the apartment with an incendiary device for the purpose of attacking German forces? I explained that if this was the case, the unknown person who entered must have been very bold. Bold enough to take the risk of doing such a thing without knowing the loyalty of the apartment owner. Unless, of course, the loyalty of the apartment owner or custodian rested in Polish favor. I stated that anyone intent on committing such an attack would either had to have known the owner of the apartment was sympathetic to Polish partisan activity or risk being turned over to the SS by the occupant. Or, the person who entered knew the occupant was not home at that time and that the door was unlocked. This created grounds for conspiracy. I asked the woman and the building custodian, what was I to do?

The custodian began to prattle in Polish and the woman translated his theory that painters or electricians might have thrown the device. That was very clever but what, I asked, was his duty if others were performing the work he was supposed to do? He continued talking after my explicit order for silence. Mahler raised his pistol and discharged a round through the head of the custodian. I remember the shell casing bouncing once from the table before landing in a bowl of broth. The man was dead before his body touched the floor.

The woman screamed and the children began crying. The shorter, and I presume the younger of the two boys, slightly raised his hand and stepped forward. He patted himself on the chest and said, "Tak, ten ja zrobił", - "Yes, I did this." I ordered him to be placed under immediate arrest at which my SS units seized him. Mahler proceeded to shoot the woman and the two remaining children. As we exited the building we heard the slamming and locking of doors from those who had been listening.

At my office I processed the paperwork to hang the boy as a partisan. Mahler reminded me that in accord with Occupational Law, a summary Directive 19 was required, and because it was a partisan attack on Reich forces, 10 civilians were to be executed along with the guilty boy. Considering the four people Mahler shot in the apartment, six more prisoners were arbitrarily selected from the records of those being held in the local prison. Mahler selected three men and three women.

When this action had been reported to the Polish council, they demanded an immediate meeting with me. I humored them in my office though I had no genuine concern for their complaints and protests. I explained the boy had admitted to throwing the device from the window and Bartlomiej Nieuzyla argued that we had no right to shoot the family and building custodian. I coldly told the insolent Pole that as the SS Chief of Police and Security, I had the legal right to commit any action I deemed appropriate and that anyone challenging my authority would be led to the gallows under the charter of subversion. Nieuzyla inquired why we had shot the family and custodian, and I was not at the least inclined to explain my actions or the policy of my government to a Pole. I reminded him that as I permitted his council to exist, so could I disband it. Nieuzyla asked about those selected for the summary Directive 19 and I allowed him to view the list. At once Nieuzyla began to advocate for the sparing of the women. He provided reasons which I am sure he thought were logical, but I had no concern for his words. I looked at Mahler and he recognized my urgency to end the meeting. Mahler stated that he had no concern for the gender provided that six Poles were hanged in retaliation for the attack. He removed the women from the list and arbitrarily selected three male names. The Poles were not satisfied. Nieuzyla begged for a specific man on the list to be spared. I told him that either the list would remain as it was or that I would strike three names and replace them with the three Polish men before me. That was sufficient in putting an end to his pleading.

I had arrived at the town square an hour prior to the scheduled Directive 19 for a formal inspection of the gallows. Headquarters had dispatched SS Obersturmführer Elberich Gersten and Waffen SS Oberscharführer Arnulf Schumann as observers to the action. To our astonishment, Oberscharführer Schumann wore a summer uniform on that freezing morning. He stood at a height of approximately 185 centimeters and appeared to be comprised of nothing but muscles. His face was badly scarred and two fingers were missing from his left hand. He later told me he sustained his injuries in 1917 during the Great War when he had served as an artillery loader. He openly blamed Jewish sabotage for his wounds by claiming a defective primer had caused an artillery shell to detonate before he could close the breech of the cannon. He enlightened me about a legal action brought against the Jewish owned munitions firm after the war in which the company was accused of knowingly manufacturing and distributing defective artillery shells. The action had been dismissed and Schumann had since concentrated on visiting his personal disdain and retribution upon the Jews.

Prior to being introduced to him, I observed the observer. I approximated his age to be 40 to 45 years and his very presence commanded authority. He shouted obscenities and orders at the Wehrmacht soldiers that lingered about the square, and he impressed me as a natural leader with abrasiveness only earned in combat.

The Obersturmführer had pointed to me while he spoke to the Oberscharführer, and I stood firm when Schumann walked across the square to greet me. He took the position of attention and raised a clipped salute. I returned it and he reported his name and rank with appropriate military courtesy.

Schumann explained the reason for his visit had been the conception of a plan for the Waffen SS to assist the Police in matters of enforcing security. His superiors in Berlin had thought it necessary to incorporate specialty members of the Waffen SS to oversee the actions of the Order Police. As this Police detachment belonged to the general army, Berlin sponsored an idea to make it subordinate to the Waffen SS, who in turn would be subordinate to the SS Chiefs of Police and Security. This would be a benefit in removing an enormous amount of supervisory detail from my office by placing it upon the Waffen SS. Schumann had been dispatched to Porajów in response to the partisan attacks taking place. He presented orders that obligated me to allow him direct supervision of the Order Police during the campaign of hunting the criminals.

At the designated time the local populace was marched into the

town square under the rifles of the Wehrmacht. While awaiting the
arrival of the prisoners scheduled for the Directive 19, Schumann said
that partisans were attacking because they did not respect and
acknowledge my authority. I argued that my rights as SS Chief of
Police and Security were exercised to the absolute limits of Reich Law
and that I could not find a logical explanation as to why, when I held
the power to execute Poles and Jews, the people would continue to
demonstrate aggression against us. He declared that I concentrated too
much on the applications of formal law and that perhaps I failed to
recognize less orthodox methods not referenced in the general codes as
being acceptable. He said that as I exercised absolute discretion of the
law in Porajów, I could benefit by considering his suggestion of
unconventional techniques to gain complete control of the populace.
As a means to demonstrate, he formally requested my permission to
oversee the carrying out of the Directive 19. Always eager to distance
myself from such a responsibility, I authorized his supervision.

While the six condemned prisoners and the boy waited under
guard, Schumann ascended the empty gallows and kicked the wooden
benches from beneath the empty ropes. This action quieted the crowd
as everyone acknowledged the benches had been placed there for the
reason of creating a drop upon their removal. This action broke the
necks of the condemned and provided a quick death. Without them,
the prisoners would need to be hoisted from the platform of the
gallows and would slowly strangle to death.

Schumann ordered my SS units to escort the condemned to the
gallows where their hands were bound behind their backs prior to
being put in a line on the platform. He stepped down and opened the
hood cover of a Blitz Opel, removed its massive lug wrench, and
returned to the gallows with it. The ropes were placed around the
necks of each prisoner, but Schumann stopped my enlisted SS soldier
when he came to the boy. With one hand he violently lifted the boy by
his coat and slammed him facedown onto the platform. Schumann
smashed the head of the boy with one ferocious blow of the lug
wrench and the assembled crowd shrieked in horror as the weak of
constitution lost consciousness.

Schumann approached the first condemned prisoner who stood on
the platform with hands bound, and a rope around his neck. He raised
the lug wrench and struck the man below the knees to break both tibia

bones. When the prisoner collapsed, Schumann ordered my SS soldiers to hoist the condemned man off the platform by pulling the rope over the crossbeam of the gallows. When raised to a height of approximately one meter over the platform, Schumann instructed my soldiers to release the rope. The prisoner fell to the wooden planks with the weight of his body crushing down on his shattered legs. Schumann continued to hoist and release the prisoner in such a manner until the legs resembled raw pork with bones protruding through the red and purple flesh.

I did not form the thought to put a halt to this cruelty. The assembled Poles looked upon Schumann as a barbarian, but more importantly, they looked upon me as the barbarian with the authority to permit it. Schumann executed each of the six condemned prisoners in this manner. Though he had been informed of the four shootings inside the apartment, the population was mostly unaware. It had disseminated among the civilians as a rumor, and Schumann threatened the crowd of Poles that four of them would be condemned to the fate they had just witnessed if the names and location of the partisans responsible for attacking the railroad and supply convoy were not revealed. What followed was astounding. The Poles began to prostrate themselves while pleading for mercy and shouting the names of those accountable. The names were consistent, and it was promptly revealed that a young man and his wife, Cyryl and Katarzyna Oleszak, were guilty of organizing the attacks. Schumann ordered my SS units to escort two women and two men from the assembly to the base of the gallows. He paced the platform alone for a very long time before speaking to the silent crowd.

"I will ask this only once. Where are the partisans hiding?"

A voice immediately answered, "The ore mine".

Schumann had literally beaten Porajów into submission. From that day until the end of my duty as SS Chief of Police and Security of the town, I was forced to deal with only four subsequent acts of partisan subversion.

The four people called to the base of the gallows by the Waffen SS Oberscharführer were released. In my office we studied the census records of Porajów to learn of Cyryl and Katarzyna Oleszak. Cyryl had worked as a leather smith and Katarzyna had been a music instructor. The pair was not the characteristic sort to have become partisans.

I made the decision to arrest their former neighbors, comrade workers, and employers for questioning. With the assistance of the Polish council, we determined the location of the ore mine in the forest. The neighbors, comrade workers, and employers did not attempt to confuse me with lies after the executions they had witnessed at the hands of Schumann. All of them revealed similar information about the Oleszaks. According to statements, the couple fled Porajów at the very onset of our invasion. A few people interviewed said it was rumored that two former pupils of Katarzyna were providing medicines, food, and essential items to the couple, but each insisted they did not know the names of the students. I also learned that Cyryl was known to have an unstable disposition and temper, and that his unruliness had caused him to be arrested twice in the past by the Porajów Civil Police. In my professional opinion, this classified him as a threat to the security of Reich forces and I issued the order to use lethal force if necessary.

Days later I accompanied my SS units into the forest under the guided assistance of a Pole familiar with the location of the ore mine. Schumann had extended his stay for the apprehension of the partisans, and there in the dense frozen woodlands he still wore the summer uniform. We reached the mine and noticed signs of habitation in the form of depressions in the snow at its entrance.

I ordered the soldiers to take cover in a half circle formation at a distance of six meters from the entrance and to establish clear lines of fire. As we were in a horseshoe formation I did not want my soldiers injured by our own crossfire. My first tactic was to heave sulfur and smoke grenades into the mine. The weapons detonated and we could scarcely tolerate the stench of the sulfur in the open air. After six or seven minutes the partisans stumbled out of the mine like drunkards with blistered eyes and hindered sight. They obeyed our commands to lie on the ground and my soldiers encircled the five men and two women. We identified Cyryl and Katarzyna Oleszak; pronounced the remaining people guilty as partisans, and in accord with Occupational Law, declared them subject to Directive 19. I ordered my SS units to shoot them and then posted guards on the mine until it could be safely entered for a search. The Oleszak couple was marched back to Porajów where I declared them guilty as partisans, ordered a Directive 19, and hanged them from a tree alongside the road leading to the rail station. On the following day a stock of weapons, ammunition, medicine, food, petrol, and supplies was located inside the mine.

Weeks later Oberscharführer Arnulf Schumann was permanently transferred to my command. During operations prior to the one we conducted at the ore mine, there had been much confusion regarding the role, responsibilities and deployment of the SD and Order Police. While arresting the Oleszaks, Schumann had seized control of the Order Police with expert authority and discipline, and it was the first time I was not required to concern myself with their actions. His transfer came with a recommendation for promotion to Junior Lieutenant.

I refused to sponsor the endorsement for his promotion. Schumann and Mahler promptly developed a mutual appreciation for each other through their shared indifference toward the suffering of Poles and Jews. Despite my senior rank, I believed that promoting Schumann would somehow strengthen the bond he had with Mahler and that it would inflate their combined power. I viewed the matter as a personal threat and since I was genuinely apprehensive to deliver that amount of authority into Schumann's hands, I denied his promotion.

I can not claim that I am dismissed from sharing the same opinion at that time. Within three months after we invaded Poland I found myself to have no patience for Poles and Jews. There was a flicker of common human compassion in me that forged the effort to minimally appease those peoples, and to grant them dignity. However, that flicker eventually faded to where I felt nothing at all for the people we subjugated.

I refer to this in my own words as the Evolution of German Superiority. I was never cognizant of the various stages of the evolution while it was happening. The Reich manifested as a cell. It formed from splinter groups of the Free Corps and various political groups that were considered dangerous, radical, and in some cases, illegal. In my personal analysis, Hitler's coming to power was the spawn of the evolution. It would have been very possible for the Free Police agencies and the non-attached members of the Free Corps to rise up and crush Hitler at the outset. When Hitler came to power, nobody believed he would be any different than any other politician who had bankrupted Germany in the past. His words against the Jews,

Communists, and Bolshevists were regarded as heated wind by some, and to others it was a refreshing inspiration to think we could take Germany back from those peoples.

I consider the second stage of the evolution to be the rebuilding of the German military in open defiance of the legal terms of the Versailles Treaty. The world had limited Germany in terms of armaments and mechanized infantry. Hitler rebuilt the military under the very nose of the world while it idly watched. History has recorded that there never existed a single formal objection from any nation in response to rebuilding our military.

The third stage existed in the authoring of the Nürnberg Laws. Those bills became active legislation that openly legalized the discrimination of Jews, Communists, and Bolshevists. Our politicians asked the nations of the world to take German Jews. The nations of the world refused. Ocean liners departed our port at Hamburg laden with Jewish refugees, and country after country refused them entry. In 1935, the U-Boats were given orders to sink Ocean liners returning to Germany with Jews. Two were sunk outside the 12-Kilometer Sound before England initiated an investigation that halted this policy. I do not accuse the nations of the world of complicity in the German design to annihilate the Jews, but it must be firmly acknowledged that the world was aware and did nothing.

Despite our efforts to confuse the Red Cross, the world knew about Auschwitz, Chelmno and Treblinka, and it knew precisely what was happening in those Detainment Facilities. Roosevelt knew. Stalin and Churchill knew. It was only at the end of the war when the Allies were close to seizing our Detainment Facilities that they developed a contingency to address them. And when the war was over they shouted, "What horror!" and pretended they had just learned of it.

This was a great factor in the Evolution of German Superiority in that we were implementing such policies with the knowledge of the world. That we were not challenged only served to encourage what we believed to be our inherent rights as Germans.

Of course the Ministry of Propaganda played a critical role in the fourth stage of the evolution. Government doctrine was in every aspect of daily life. Placards, billboards, songs, radio addresses and public speakers declared National Socialism as the reason for our prosperity and well being. The swastika and likenesses of Hitler were on shop fronts, motor cars, trolleys, trains, buses, and existed in remote forms such as being embroidered on napkins and stamped onto coins. There was a social code that transcended chivalry and that was exclusive to Germans of pure lineage. This code, and the Nürnberg Laws, gave us legal rights to malign and mistreat our social and political enemies.

The evolution halted there for most German civilians. The people had been given legal rights and what they chose to do with them and how they decided to act and live their lives was primarily their own choice. As soldiers, our evolution advanced to a fifth stage where we were trained and indoctrinated as servants to the Reich. When we graduated from our military academies we all had a cultivated intolerance for anyone not of pure German lineage. What we chose to do with that was partially our own doing. We were bound to advance the ambitions of our government.

This must not be confused or interpreted that I only followed orders. I conceived and gave the orders. I never questioned the ethics or morality of orders I was given. There existed reliance in our Commanders that all orders were valid and necessary. A true soldier does not question the orders he is given. He carries them out.

The Reich certainly did not encourage free thinking among its troops. However, I was in a very ambiguous position as SS Chief of Police and Security at Porajów. At that time I was genuinely a mere cog in the system and there existed no consistency in my day to day activities. Each problem was unique and very seldom could each be solved by referring to the manuals of Reich Occupational Law or codes of protocol. It was astonishing that in cases where the law was not clear; my personal ruling was accepted without a challenge from any level or Department of the Reich. I had absolute power and authority over the population.

Mahler and Schumann possessed an open indifference to the executions of Jews and civilians. They often spoke of such duty in a casual manner and neither voiced objections to doing it. Whereas my selection of prisoners at Sachsenhausen had been a difficult task, I rationalized it as a bureaucratic assignment. It was lawful and in accord with Reich policy to shoot those people. But, I admit to being deeply disturbed by the entire process. It did not enter my mind at that time that I or any soldier of the Reich would be held criminally liable for these actions. I did not know the plans of the Reich, or that a world war would ensue. I truly believed that my government had no military plans of conquest beyond Poland. The capitulation of France created rumors that England would withdraw its Declaration of War against Germany. But, as early as January 1940, a town in eastern Poland called Oswiecim had been selected as the site for a massive Detainment Facility. In the German language that town was called Auschwitz. My adversary from Sachsenhausen, Rudolf Höss, would become its Kommandant.

By March 1940, I had established a most efficient Police force in Porajów. Schumann commanded the SD and Order Police units while I directed the activities of the SS, Gestapo and KRIPO.

The SD existed as an arm of the Reich Intelligence Service and it was the duty of the SD at Porajów to monitor Polish civilians suspected to be enemies. This force was comprised of 24 men who concentrated their efforts on circumventing partisan activity.

The Order Police was a unit of 62 men that had originally served as Wehrmacht Field Police. These men were ordered under my supervision by the RSHA, and they acted as order keepers in the town by performing civil police duties.

By my own appointment, I was the personal Commander of the Porajów Gestapo. This department consisted of five agents subordinate to my rank. The function of the Gestapo was to identify all enemies of the Reich and because of the importance for state security, this department monitored not only civilians, but all members of the Occupying German military as well. My Gestapo unit was nothing like the popular misconceptions believed about this agency. My five juniors were common SS soldiers elevated to a different police service. They wore the gray uniform and were often far from discreet in their investigations. The Gestapo had means and abilities that differed from the protocol of standard Occupational Law, but these methods were never clearly defined. In truth, it was enough of a deterrent for the military forces and civilian population to simply know a Gestapo Office existed in the town.

Gestapo investigations were different from standard police inquiries and subject to many different forms of approval by the RSHA that we simply did not know how to properly conduct such an investigation. To inquire for clarity would demonstrate the weakness of our lack of knowledge. It was easier to mention a Gestapo matter at our weekly meetings and if it required investigation, we would formally defer it to our department of the SS Police. The formality was necessary for the paperwork. I believe that if Josef Stalin had walked through Porajów, he would have been gone before my Gestapo Office could have devised the proper method to arrest him.

The KRIPO served as the Criminal Police and processed all matters of judicial arbitration. 40 men were responsible for the administrative workings of civilian criminal trials as well as military trials and court martial proceedings.

CHAPTER FIVE
EXPERIMENT MGW-3

Near the end of March 1940, I received directives to travel to the Nordhausen facility in Germany. I appointed Mahler as the interim Police Commander and departed as ordered.

Major General Eicke greeted me upon arrival and explained that I had been summoned to provide legal evaluation for the carbon monoxide poisoning of Jews. He introduced me to Walter Rauff who claimed the invention of a truck capable of pumping its exhaust into an airtight chamber located behind the driving compartment. Rauff had won the approval of RSHA Officials to begin experimenting with the vehicle, and I had been asked by superior officers in Berlin to author reports on the tests.

Rauff showed me the vehicle inside a large garage. The exterior appeared as any normal freight truck until one crouched to see the rubber piping that extended from the exhaust manifold. The piping ran the length of the chassis and disappeared inside the rear freight compartment. The inside was very unnatural. Sealing rubber had been molded into every joint where the compartment had been welded together, and there was a metal grated floor. Beneath the grate was a flat piece of sheet metal that had also been sealed with rubber at the joints. It was between the sheet metal and the grate that the exhaust piping was housed. The ceiling of the compartment contained another grate with a centrally mounted electric fan. Above the fan was the roof of the compartment. Rauff explained that when the truck was mobile, the fan was turned on by the driver to circulate the carbon monoxide exhaust being piped in from beneath the floor. When the van reached its destination, the roof of the compartment which was also sealed with rubber, was opened by a manual release by the driver in order to ventilate the compartment so the next group of Jews would enter the vehicle without suspicion.

After explaining the workings of the vehicle, he stated that in his estimation, it would require 15 minutes to asphyxiate a capacity freight load of 30 Jews. The plan had been approved to have the truck travel to a destination 15 minutes away from the Nordhausen facility. The location had been prepared by the SS, and Jews from the Nordhausen facility had dug a mass burial pit and were waiting to unload the bodies when the truck arrived. After the final transport of the day, the Jews working at the location would be shot in the pit. With the smile of an eager child, Doctor Rauff asked, "Shall we try it?"

Eicke dismissed himself from the tests saying he was required at a meeting in Ellrich. Rauff directed a unit of SS to initiate the process and moments later 30 Jews were marched from the south gate of Nordhausen and waited while the SS maneuvered the truck out of the garage. The soldiers assured the Jews they were being taken to cut lumber in the forest and said they should be happy to be out of the facility and in the fresh air.

The SS opened the freight compartment and the Jews climbed inside without the least hesitation or suspicion. Once the door was latched and locked, Rauff and I got into a Staff Mercedes and followed. I began my report in the back of the car and noted that the loading procedure had been without incident. I also made notations on the vehicle and its specifications as explained by Doctor Rauff and as witnessed by myself. Whatever I was writing at the time was interrupted by the most unworldly screams of panic from inside the truck ahead of us. I heard the sounds of fists pounding on the inside of the freight compartment door and I recall looking at Rauff who was intensely staring at his pocket watch. The screaming and pounding inside the truck endured for ten or more minutes.

When we reached the destination, the driver unlocked the roof and the stench of exhaust permeated the Mercedes. The SS opened the freight compartment door and fifteen or more of the occupants stumbled out of the truck as if they were drunk. They fell to the ground, stood, staggered, and fell again. Rauff gave me a very concerned glance and muttered a curse. The SS began shooting the survivors on the road between the truck and the Staff Mercedes. On final inspection, only 6 Jews had perished inside the truck.

Rauff inquired if I intended to notate the 6 deaths in my report and when I confirmed it, he pleaded with me to destroy my records so that he could configure the variables for a second experiment. He urged me to disregard the first test. I told him that I would file my report as ordered by Major General Eicke and in accord with my orders from RSHA Headquarters, and that if he suggested I consider any further impropriety, I would have him arrested.

Five or six subsequent tests produced similar results. Rauff experimented with increasing the time of transport by fifteen minutes, but this was not effective in accomplishing the goal. The SS was required to shoot a minimum of five to ten prisoners after a 30 minute transport and I put a halt to the experiments at Nordhausen. Rauff continued to search for answers while claiming the tests should have been successful. He requested the opportunity to assess the rubber piping for cracks and leaks, and asked for a resumption of tests the following day. In thoroughness, I assigned an SS mechanic to examine the rubber piping and when no leaks were found, Rauff asked for additional time to investigate the sealing rubber around the joints and freight door. If I did not permit him leisure to inspect the vehicle for flaws, my reports would hold no merit in Berlin. I authorized Rauff and the SS mechanic to make the necessary inspections. At the end of the day I was informed that the vehicle was mechanically sound. I put an official halt to the experiments and filed my reports.

I was certain my superiors would deny future requests for experiments of this kind. My reports outlined the cost for the liters of petrol and the expense of munitions. I also included an itemization of time, number of soldiers required, additional resources expended, and a copy of the report given to me by the SS mechanic verifying the vehicle was sound. My concluding statement on the report was to the effect that, after observation, the use of mobile carbon monoxide trucks as a means of disposing of Jews was found to be inefficient and a squandering of Reich finances.

CHAPTER SIX
RESTRUCTURING THE PLAN

During my journey through Germany on the route back to Porajów, I noticed many combat vehicles and troops being deployed to the south and west of the Fatherland. While changing trains in Erfurt, the soldiers were speaking quite openly about invading France. I had heard nothing of such a plan, nor would the military have had any reason to inform me, but the news was a surprise.

It seems I had not returned to Poland more than a week when I learned our forces had invaded Denmark and Norway. The information regarding both invasions had also been kept as a well guarded secret. At first I believed our attacks to be the product of pure madness. I wondered how a German population of approximately 70,000,000 people could sustain wars in Poland, Denmark, and Norway and, possibly in France. It was logical to assume we would be internationally reproved and penalized with sanctions and embargos. If international commodities were denied to us, it stood to reason we would have to maintain the zones we had conquered. It was the only means to gain the resources that foreign countries would be certain to deprive us of. To our fortune and at the sparing of German and Danish life, Denmark capitulated within 24 hours after its occupation by Reich forces. Norway had resisted.

New orders had been given by RSHA superiors to all German Commanders in Poland. The directives stated that all Jews were to be resettled into concentrated ghettos in each major city. Those Police Commanders in towns not capable of fostering ghettos were to arrange rail transports of Jews to the nearest ghettos. These specified areas of resettlement were to be walled in to make them separate from the occupied areas.

Porajów was to erect a 6 block by 12 block walled hold to accommodate 10,300 Jews being transported to my city from Germany, Austria and Moravia. Officials of the RAD and engineers from the Todt Labor Service appeared to inspect the area and build a wall at the precise height of 3.6 meters with an additional 0.61 meters of barbed wire planted into the cement along its top. The wall was completed near the end of April at approximately the same time the ghetto at Lodz was sealed. Within days of the completed work I received officials from the Ministry of Health and Hygiene, Ministry of Economics, and SS Standartenführer Leopold Eisenberg from the RSHA Department of Resettlement. The delegation arrived to inspect the ghetto and the arrival of the Jews. Their reports were to be forwarded to Himmler, Heydrich and Eicke.

Eisenberg instructed me on the methods to be employed during the arrival of the transports. The trains would come in from the west at Dresden, unload the human freight on the ramps at Porajów, and then proceed northeast to Sieniawka to reload with munitions, supplies and dry goods to be transported to the Polish interior.

The Jews arriving at Porajów were to be marched into the town square to be registered, and then taken to the open market where SS physicians would conduct visual physical examinations. Those considered fit for work would be taken inside the ghetto. Those considered unfit would be taken into the forest to be shot.

Members from the Ministry of Economics and from the Armaments Board had invited private industrialists to Porajów. Owners from the Metall Union, Siemens, Krupp, and Daimler Benz companies were being lavishly entertained by Ministry officials as they inspected the few industrial plants in town to evaluate them for operational status. All of this overwhelmed me.

"I will need more soldiers to guard the ghetto," I said. Porajów had existed as a small town with very few security problems. Suddenly it was being considered as an industrial site.

Eisenberg explained that the advantage of its location provided timely shipments of manufacturing materials and finished products to and from Germany. He said the labor forces for the newly established corporations were to be provided from the shipments of Jews arriving from Germany, Austria, and Moravia, and that I was required to learn the workings of the forced labor policies enacted by the Reich. Each German company establishing itself in Porajów was entitled to Jewish laborers who were to earn no wages. Instead, each company would pay a minimal fee to the Ministry of Economics for each Jew it employed. As the SS Chief of Police and Security, and as the ranking SS Administrator for the town, I was to monitor the operations of these businesses, review their weekly production reports, oversee the labor units on the plant floors, and resolve all problems between Jewish laborers and German owners and personnel.

Eisenberg took me to the rail station and we examined maps of the town to devise an unencumbered plan to ensure an efficient arrival and disembarkation process of the transports.

He was proficient at establishing unloading points and explaining what needed to be done. He ordered the engineers to construct sawhorses to be used as roadblocks and cordons that would provide a direct lane from the unloading area to the town square. More engineers placed wooden ramps at intervals along the rails. He was so busy, direct, and constantly issuing orders that I did not have the opportunity to inquire about the effects of what was to come. I simply watched and learned by committing as much to memory as I could.

Late in the day I asked him how Porajów was to accommodate and sustain 10,300 additional people. "That will not be necessary," he replied. "After the selections, Porajów will probably receive 8,000 people." I knew what this meant. 2,300 people were to be shot in the southern forest.

"Who will process the people not selected?" I inquired. "Who will complete the paperwork for the Directive 19 requests?"

Eisenberg smiled and shook his head. "You will not need the documentation," he responded. "Actions like this one are quite different."

That night I dined with Eisenberg, the officials from the Ministries of Economics and Health and Hygiene, and the private industrialists. The meal was so formal and the guests so important, that I was more concerned about placing my napkin properly and using the correct utensils. A Colonel from RSHA Headquarters began by saying, "The Governor General of Poland is very concerned about industrial output in his territories. Porajów has been chosen to host industry because of its proximity to Germany and its natural security."

I was the only one present who did not understand what "natural security" intoned, but I later learned that the location of Porajów provided its safety. As it was close to the German border, its industry could be promptly defended by military means if the city was attacked. I was grateful to be in Western Poland because it was far enough away from the Russian lines to the east. A Non-Aggression Pact had been secured between the Reich and the Soviet Union, but officers spoke of this document being nothing more than a temporary restraining order being honored by both countries. A common phrase among us was, "Zum *Osten in vierzig fünf*", or, "To the East in '45." We all knew diplomatic relations were strained between the Reich and the Soviet Union, and we were aware that Russia was occupied with the Japanese invasions on its far eastern borders. We logically assumed a war would come between the Reich and Russia, but we believed it would not occur until 1945.

With the capitulations of Belgium, the Netherlands, Norway, Denmark, and France; and with the Anschluss of Austria and the annexation of Czechoslovakia, Porajów was to become an industrial center nestled in the center of many buffers. If the Russian war came before 1945, key Polish cities such as Warsaw, Czestochowa, Gdansk, Poznan, and Kraków would be attacked long before Porajów was considered as a target.

"How would you describe the local Jewish labor force here, Schiller?" I was greatly unnerved by the ranks, ages and prominence of the men I was dining with. It was difficult to answer without a cracking voice and the fear I would make a fool of myself.

"Half unskilled, Sir. One quarter skilled, and one quarter technical."

"Doctor Frank believes Jews can be trained," said the RSHA officer. "Do you concur with this, Schiller?"

Who was I to argue with the Governor General of Poland? "Yes, Sir. I believe they can be trained. They have demonstrated this by being put to work at repairing the city structures and roads."

The industrial representative from Daimler Benz sat there in a fine silk suit. He reeked of money and power. He stared at the wine in his glass and said, "Setting scaffolding and laying cobblestones is different from manufacturing piston engines and ball bearings."

"I am certain they can be trained, Sir."

"You better be certain," he replied. "I do not have the time or liking to explain production failures and shortcomings to the Ministry of Economics."

"I prefer Polish foremen in my factory," said the representative from Krupp. "I do not trust Jews to have a committed effort to German production."

"How many Jews are in this city?" asked the RSHA Officer.

"Approximately 1,200," I answered. "Perhaps 800 are of employment age." There was a slight pause around the table.

"What is the age of employment for Porajów Jews?" inquired the man from the Ministry of Economics.

"Fourteen years to sixty years," I answered.

The man looked at me as if I had no place among them and asked, "By what authority do you decide the employment age of Jews? Doctor Frank has ordered all Jews in Poland between the ages of eight years and seventy years to work."

"Perhaps 1,000 are eligible for employment," I responded.

"Perhaps?" He was mocking me. "You do not know the numbers? You have come to this meeting unprepared?"

Eisenberg put a halt to my embarrassment. "I am certain the Junior Lieutenant was not told this information would be required at this gathering."

"Nonetheless!" argued the man from the Ministry of Economics. "Am I to assume we have appointed Chiefs of Police and Security who do not know facts about the populations they are governing?"

"So," said the Daimler Benz representative while calculating numbers on a pad, "We have 400 unskilled, 200 skilled, and 200 technical. Give or take another 200, and assuming the lot of these to be children, I will project they can make modest contributions to the work effort." He looked at the RSHA and Ministry officials. "How many of the new arrivals will be useful?"

Eisenberg opened a folder. "Approximately 4,800."

"And the remaining 5,500?" he inquired.

"Wives, offspring, and the elderly," answered Eisenberg. "The essential workers will be selected after registration. The healthy, including the wives, offspring, and elderly, will be put into the ghetto."

"How will labor shifts work?" asked the man from Metall Union.

"Am I responsible to transport them from the ghetto to my plant? What about security? Will I be responsible if a worker tries to escape or if one sabotages production?"

The official from the Ministry of Economics assuaged his concerns by warranting each corporation with immunity. "Transportation and all aspects of security will be the responsibilities of the SS and the police."

"What will be done if a worker escapes or is arrested for security violations?" asked the agent from Siemens. "How will I be compensated?"

The man from the Ministry of Economics replied, "You may file Form 61/d for damages. If our investigation validates your claim, you will receive financial reimbursement or a replacement worker. If production is disturbed, you will receive consideration for the consequences of the loss and will be given a reasonable extension to resume quota."

"What if there is a security problem or rebellion inside the plant?" asked the man from Metall Union. "I do not want the guards shooting up my production facility."

"Dogs," proposed the agent from Krupp. "We have had great success with shepherds and wolfhounds at Dachau, Flössenberg, and Ravensbrücke. The mere sight of them is an effective deterrent."

"Dogs?" countered the agent from Daimler Benz. He appealed to the man from the Ministry of Health and Hygiene. "How sanitary can it be to have dogs on the production floor?"

His answer was that it had been approved. This did not please me because at that time I had no affinity for dogs.

"I am not confident in a Jewish labor force," said the Daimler Benz agent. "I do not believe those people can be trusted to make a commitment to German production efforts. Look what we learned during the last war."

"You can use Poles," answered the man from the Ministry of Economics, "But it will be more expensive and you will not find an adequate number of skilled workers here."

"Then I shall import Austrians or Czechs," he stated.

"That is not an option," said the agent from the Ministry of Health and Hygiene. "The new arrivals will stress Porajów to the limits of its sanitation capabilities. You will choose from the local Polish population or the Jews."

The Daimler Benz agent was not pleased. "Günther," he asked with a surprising tone of familiarity, "Why should I bring industry here to Porajów when it seems it is being marked for failure?"

The man from the Ministry of Economics answered him succinctly. "Cheap labor."

"I do not know about this," he replied. After some thought he said, "I will bring industry here provided the Ministry of Economics permits me to send all products manufactured at Porajów to undergo quality control tests at my plants in Snèzka or Králové."

The man from the Ministry of Economics laughed. "Czechoslovakia, Walther?" He paused but there was no change of mood. "Very well! You can conduct quality control tests in France for all I care. Do we have a resolve?"

All four business agents agreed and contracts were distributed and signed. I affixed my signature to each, vowing against my better judgment, to oversee the safety and security of production.

On the following morning I was awakened by the sounds of truck engines, barking, and shouting. A driving rain was splattering against the windows as I dressed, and I heard Eisenberg's voice in the office connected to my private quarters.

I joined him and saw Mahler, Schumann, and a few enlisted men taking coffee and reading morning reports. There was a very subdued and almost unnatural mood about the men that morning. As I poured myself a cup of ersatz, Eisenberg quietly said, "The first transport pulled out of Hradec a few hours ago. It should be here by 0730 hours."

Mahler and Schumann looked at me as if I should have said something. I nodded, sat down, and stared into my coffee as if expecting to find comfort or an answer there.

"Morning duty rosters," said an enlisted man while placing papers before me. I paged through them but did not read them. Mahler eventually asked Eisenberg the question that was on our minds.

"What are we to do today, Sir?"

Eisenberg looked up from a stack of documents. "I want you and Mister Schumann to oversee the escorts to the registration station in the town square. Tell your units that they are only authorized to shoot people who threaten security or try to escape. If the people refuse to comply, you may beat them into submission. I want to keep the shootings to a minimum. Let us try to do this as cleanly as possible."

He looked at me. "Lieutenant, you will assist me with the unloading on the rails and with the selection process in the market. You will be told what to do."

At 0600 hours I called a general assembly of my troops and Eisenberg addressed them with instructions. The Jews were to be unloaded, escorted to the town square, and registered by name, gender, age, work experience, and country of origin. They would then be taken to the market to undress and undergo a visual physical examination by SS physicians. Those considered fit would be given a housing assignment inside the ghetto. Those considered unfit would be taken into the forest south of Porajów and shot.

Those deemed fit would retrieve their luggage at the entrance to the ghetto and sort through it under the supervision of the SS. All watches, money, jewelry, and portable valuables were to be surrendered to the police. Each person would be permitted to carry 6.8 kilograms worth of personal belongings into the ghetto. Items exceeding the allowed weight were forfeited as Reich property.

At 0730 hours Eisenberg and I walked to the arrival point. The Waffen SS had taken positions on both sides of the rails to prevent the new arrivals from escaping and they appeared formidable in their wet rain smocks. Machine guns and rifles were slung over their shoulders or hanging at waist level, and the rain beaded on their helmets. Other soldiers paced up and down the rails with ferocious shepherds and wolfhounds on short chains. A field telephone clattered inside a guardhouse and moments later the sentry leaned out and shouted, "Train!"

The circular front of the locomotive came closer with its eagle and swastika set above its running lamp. Two Party flags extended from each side and flapped above the clouds of steam from the wheels and below the black smoke pouring from its stack. The shrill and hollow whistle blew three times to announce its arrival and it braked with a loud, high pitched grinding noise and hard bursts of steam.

I was surprised to see one passenger wagon behind the coal tender that carried SS soldiers. The remainders were cattle and freight wagons. The soldiers pulled back the locking handles on the wagons and slid the doors open to reveal a collection of well dressed, but very confused people. They stepped onto the unloading ramps and began complaining about the journey and requesting directions to latrines. Most of them thought they were in Austria or Germany, and many others were approaching our officers and senior enlisted men to claim that errors had been made and that they should not be here.

The Waffen SS herded the people into a crowd and forced them into the cordoned lane to be marched to the town square. The soldiers pulled or pushed those who moved slow, fired rifles in the air, and struck those who did not comply. Eisenberg walked toward the end of the train and I followed him. We could see a crowd had gathered, and when we arrived, the Waffen SS was struggling with a corpulent Jewish man who was sitting on the ground and refusing to move. The soldiers struck him with rifle stocks and pulled at him, but he refused to cooperate. Eisenberg shouted above the rain and noise, "What is the problem with this man? Why has he not joined the others?"

A Corporal replied, "Sir, he is refusing to move until we tell him where he is." The other people had moved away and were being led off.

"You are in Poland," shouted Eisenberg. "Now get moving!"

"Poland?" asked the man. "This is not my home. My home is in Paderborn. I am a German!"

"You are a Jew!" shouted the Corporal.

"I am a German!" he responded.

Eisenberg had no patience for this spectacle. He turned to the Corporal and said, "Put the damned dogs on him!"

The Corporal smiled wryly and nodded as if he enjoyed receiving the orders. I stepped back as he called the handlers and the dogs were released. The corpulent Jew fought for his life and shouted, "I am a German! I am a German!" while having his flesh torn from his body by the hounds.

As we walked toward the locomotive we were approached by a woman wearing a fine fur coat and traveling hat. "Gentlemen," she said, "I object to this treatment!" Before another word could be spoken, an SS guard struck her in the kidney with the stock of his rifle. The woman involuntarily urinated, fell to the muddy ground and began vomiting blood. "I apologize, Sirs," stated the guard. "These people will not speak out of turn like that again!"

We heard gunfire and shrieking near the locomotive and ran to the location. A young man was lying in the mud next to a silver candlestick with his legs crossed and his arms stretched out. An SS guard looked nervous but explained, "He tried to strike me with the candlestick." More shots were fired from within the town. Then more on the other side of the train.

"Damn it," muttered Eisenberg. "Go see what happened over there!"

I crossed the tracks over the coupling irons of two cars and saw guards going through the pockets of three or four dead people. A soldier pointed at them and explained, "They tried to escape. They ran toward the forest. We shouted at them to stop, but they did not heed the orders."

Eisenberg was shouting my name and I peered between two freight wagons. "What happened over there?"

"Some people tried to escape. They have been shot."

"Get over here! They are rioting at the registration station!"

I joined him and we were driven to the town square in a Kubelwagen. Upon arriving we saw that the SS was dangerously close to losing control of the people. The Jews were arguing with our guards, refusing to surrender their luggage, and objecting to being separated from their loved ones. Eisenberg called Schumann to the car. While waiting for him he began cursing. "Such chaos before the eyes of my superiors! This will be the end of me!" Schumann arrived and Eisenberg lowered the window. "Get this situation under control at once."

Schumann stared at him for a moment. I suppose he was waiting for orders or suggestions.

"Shoot the troublemakers!" shouted Eisenberg.

Schumann did not even blink. He opened his holster, removed and cocked his Walther PPK and walked toward a man who was very animated in an argument with an SS guard. Schumann grabbed the man's shoulder, spun him around and fired a round through his face. A woman fell to her knees over the man's body and began wailing in sorrow and cursing at us. Schumann lowered his pistol and shot her as well. He looked at the people until finding someone else he recognized as having argued. He walked toward the man with his pistol extended and fired two rounds into his chest.

The SS guards reacted to Schumann's behavior by assuming a general order had been given to shoot. They raised their weapons and began firing into the crowd. Eisenberg covered his face and released a heavy sigh followed by curses.

Schumann gave the order to halt the shooting, and then walked to a radio truck. He took the transmitter and broadcasted his voice over the amplified speakers. "You will proceed to the registration tables in an orderly manner or you will be shot. The choice belongs to you."

Silence came over the crowd and they behaved in a calm and civil manner. I watched them and thought, "So this is the enemy." They were the people who refused to pick up arms to defend Austria and Germany in the last war. Germans and Austrians from all walks of life had left families, homes, businesses and jobs to fight in the trenches. The Jews claimed exemption from fighting by citing themselves as a displaced people without formal citizenship. It is true that some Jews enlisted to fight during the Great War, but their numbers were a minimal contribution to the effort.

While our comrades were being gassed in the trenches and machine gunned on the fields, Austrian and German Jews used foreign money to purchase our national businesses. Banking, industry, commerce and trade were seized by Jews while we were away defending our political interests. Our citizen-soldiers found themselves disadvantaged by military pay, and though our governments granted the soldiers extensions to pay debts and loans, the Jewish owners who seized our banking erased these policies. German homes went into foreclosure and were sold by Jews to fellow Jews. The jobs we had vacated were filled by Jews. Our furniture and livestock were auctioned off and sold to Jews. Our veterans returned from heartbreaking defeat to a life of squalor. The Jews furthered their illegal usury by financing the shattered government to gain more influence and power at our expense.

The world did not react to the illegal seizure of German and Austrian control by the Jews. We were viewed and regarded as defeated nations who committed the grievous errors that brought the world into war. However, when we regained political advantages and began taking our personal property back from those who stole it from us in the first place, National Socialists were declared an evil lot by world opinion. The *"Eigenschaft Rückkehr Vereinbarung"* was passed in 1935. This "Property Return Declaration" gave all Jews amnesty to return homes, automobiles, livestock, furniture, and finances to the Germans and Austrians it had been stolen from. Some Jews complied, but most did not. A few years following this act, the Reich permitted the seizure of all German property owned by Jews.

Yes, that was the enemy before me at Porajów. I was angered by the audacity of the corpulent Jew that sat in the rain by the freight wagons shouting, "I am a German!" There was no doubt in my mind that 25 years ago he stood before the German Enlistment Board stuffing pastries into his fat face while shouting "I am a Jew! I am exempt!"

A motorcycle rider pulled alongside the Kubelwagen and announced the next scheduled transport was due in 30 minutes.

Eisenberg looked at his pocket watch. "This is going to go on late into the night," he sighed. "We must expedite the process before Pohl gets word of this."

Oswald Pohl served as the Chief of the Main Office for Racial and Settlement Affairs. He insisted that all deportations and transports ran efficiently on schedule. Pohl did not accept excuses and was harsh to those who disappointed him.

"Take us to the Selection Station," ordered Eisenberg. The driver maneuvered the Kubelwagen out of the square and took us to the market.

The people stood naked in quiet obedience. There came an overwhelming feeling of vulnerability among the masses when huddled together without clothes. We watched as the SS physicians separated the fit to the right, and the unfit to the left. I expected the unhealthy to be a collection of the elderly, but there were young people, women, and children in the group. Some wore artificial limbs, others coughed, and a few were not well enough to stand. This crowd became larger as the selections continued.

Unpleasant incidents arose when the SS attempted to separate an unfit loved one or child from the healthy. The anguished screams of women and the frightened crying of abandoned children and infants stained my soul. The SS beat the knuckles of mothers to release grips on their children. The women dropped to their knees with folded hands bobbing back and forth at us to plead for mercy. Now and then a child would waddle toward its mother, fall to the cobblestones and cry out in pain, loneliness and confusion. A duality was present in the SS. Some soldiers picked up these children tenderly and took them to one side or the other to be cared for by Jewish strangers. Other SS soldiers shouted at the children, picked them up and heaved them aside.

Eisenberg gulped from a flask and extended it toward me without looking in my direction. I took a drink and asked, "This is our duty assignment today? Here?" He stepped out of the car and told me to go back and supervise the arrival of the transports throughout the day.

Dispatchers came and went with new orders every hour. Instead of taking their luggage with them to the town square where it was loaded aboard trucks and driven to the ghetto entrance, the new arrivals were to deposit their bags along the rails. It was loaded on the trucks after the trains departed and then taken to the ghetto gates. What difference did any of this make? It rained all morning and afternoon, and instead of following orders about the placement of baggage, I was concerned with dragging away the dead Jewish bodies before the next train pulled in.

Each transport brought the same problems. People argued about being brought here; the SS must have made a mistake; my pets were left in Austria; I have fields to plant in the spring; I need a latrine; I must change my baby; Sir, can I speak with you? There were more shooting instances than I could count and I took a drink from anyone who offered me a flask. Mahler came to me late in the afternoon with orders to report to Eisenberg at the Selection Station.

I could hear the chattering of an MG34 machine gun to the south when I reported to Eisenberg. It did not require an explanation as the crowd of unfit Jews was greatly reduced. "There are four more transports due to arrive," he said. "We should be done here by 2200 hours. Jörg Neudorf wants you at the ghetto gates." He must have recognized my blank stare. "He's the representative from the Ministry of Health and Hygiene."

The weather started clearing when I arrived at the gates. The Jews, who came to Porajów well dressed and energetic, walked into the ghetto as an exhausted and disheveled lot. Neudorf approached me the moment I stepped from the car.

"I have splendid news," he announced. "At this time, 7,800 Jews have been brought to Porajów, and 1,150 have been declared unfit. I can mark one fourth of those yet to arrive as unfit and seal off the ghetto with approximately 8,550 residents. This will leave you 1,450 persons short of occupational capacity, and this will keep you well within sanitation policies." He was smiling as if he had just won a Nobel Prize.

"Begging your pardon. Mister Neudorf, but how can you mark off one fourth of those yet to arrive?"

"Lieutenant, I will seal the gates when 8,550 Jews have passed through them. The rest will be marked as unfit."

"But what if they are fit essential workers, Sir?"

"I am trying to perform a favor for you, Lieutenant. I do not expect you wish the Ministry of Health and Hygiene here on a weekly basis because this ghetto is overcrowded. That would bring very adverse attention upon you, young man."

"Very well," I said. "Mark one fourth as unfit."

"You will have to authorize it," he stated while pushing documents and a fountain pen at me. I looked at the papers to see nothing but approximately 600 blank lines. The names would be filled in later. I signed it.

One month later, due to a follow up inspection by the Ministries of Economics and Health and Hygiene, I was ordered to double the number of guards inside the ghetto to 80 men. Requisitioning forces for such a task proved easier than I imagined. The SS promptly dispatched 40 additional Order Police soldiers and I learned all of them had been placed on various disciplinary probations for infractions such as falling asleep on guard duty or being drunk. It became a popular and effective threat to the soldiers of all divisions of the military that violations of regulations would be punishable by reassignment to the Order Police.

Conditions inside the Porajów ghetto had become repulsive. The Jews had converted the streets into a bazaar where they traded and sold the few possessions they had. All of them appropriately vacated from the sidewalks as we traversed the area and each bowed respectfully as expected. Some were dressed in finery, others in rags, and some walked about without any clothing as if they did not know or care that they were naked.

The Officials from the Ministry of Economics were busy gathering information on the availability of labor in the ghetto. They kept most of their discussions to themselves and selected buildings they thought had potential to serve as barracks for a workforce. The officials from the Ministry of Health and Hygiene unsurprisingly recorded every violation they noticed.

Lieutenant Colonel Eisenberg walked with me and informed me of the necessity of the Judenrat inside the ghetto. This was to be a delegation of Jewish officials assigned to arbitrate matters inside the ghetto in accordance with Reich Law. The Judenrat was also designed as a place where the ghetto occupants could lodge complaints. Eisenberg stated that all complaints would be registered, logged and handed over to the German senior ranking Order Policeman and a copy would be presented to me. I was to record the names of those Jews that frequently lodged serious objections about matters related to the Reich. This included any Jewish complaint about treatment or the management of resources inside the ghetto such as food distribution, electrical service, and water supply. Those Jews that registered frequent objections were to have their names forwarded to my SS, SD or Gestapo departments for investigation and if necessary, their arrests.

During our tour of the ghetto a Jewish boy of about 10 years of age ran to us and asked in our tongue, "Do you have a cigarette for me?" Certainly the boy was old enough to comprehend the regulations of the ghetto and knew better than to approach us and speak without a prompt. I was frustrated by thinking I would have to appease the Lieutenant Colonel by administering a form of discipline upon the boy. One of the two Order Policeman escorting us raised the stock of his rifle to strike the boy, but Eisenberg intervened. He leaned over and asked the boy, "And what would you do with a cigarette?"

The boy promptly responded he would trade it for an egg. Eisenberg then asked where he would obtain an egg inside the ghetto. The Jewish boy told us the occupants had taken to raising chickens and pigeons in the buildings as a form of food production. Eisenberg denied the request and encouraged the boy to adhere to proper protocol in the future. As we continued our walk, the Lieutenant Colonel said something such as, "So they trade cigarettes for eggs. What else is available for trade here?" The tone of his voice implied that he suspected arms and munitions might have been available. He then stated his wish to observe a full search of the ghetto.

I detested those sorts of measures when they were ordered by officers who did not have to coexist with the Jews and Poles as I did. There had been no partisan activity in or around Porajów since Schumann conducted the brutal public executions of the six Poles. There had been a mutual understanding gained between Germans and Poles, and Germans and Jews. Searching the ghetto for the amusement of Eisenberg would earn us more anger and resentment from the Jews. I said out loud, "May heaven stop us from finding a weapon or radio." Such contraband would necessitate a Directive 19. It was dangerous to conduct the search itself. Even if we found nothing we would stir the detestation of the Jews by ravaging their squalid dwellings. There was wisdom in keeping the peace. This is not to say that I neglected the possibility the Jews were stockpiling arms or planning an uprising. However, this is to say that certain conditions and signs precede such events. I promised the Lieutenant Colonel that I would organize and initiate a full search of the ghetto before dawn on the following day. I chose the time of 0400 hours for two reasons. First, we would encounter a more favorable opportunity to surprise the Jews. Second, I wanted to inconvenience the Lieutenant Colonel by forcing him to rise before dawn.

My orders for ghetto searches were consistent. To confuse and confound the population, it was necessary to move into the heart of the ghetto with great speed, a tremendous show of force, and to do both as loudly as possible. Marching into the square in an orderly fashion afforded the occupants the time to process what was happening. Roaring in with halftracks while blowing whistles and shouting created a disorganized panic. In those situations criminals are prone to mistakes and irrational behavior. I always told my men to look busy and directed. Even if they did not know where they were going, I ordered them to move with a sense of purpose. Appearing in control of all aspects at all times created a mood of submission and fear.

The Porajów ghetto was spanned in length by five streets between 6 blocks and the width spanned eleven streets between 12 blocks. Two blocks in the center of the ghetto had been razed to form a general assembly area. The trucks, Kubelwagens and halftracks drove through the streets with amplified speakers broadcasting the message in Polish, Yiddish and German, for all Jews to evacuate their dwellings and assemble in the center square. Those refusing to comply would be shot.

For the search of the ghetto, I had issued specific orders that my soldiers were only to shoot if their lives or the life of a comrade was at risk. I explicitly issued orders to use physical force upon any Jew refusing to comply and this directly conflicted with the message being broadcast from our vehicles. The difference rested in that the SS did not want to shoot. The Jews, however, did not know this.

Eisenberg had joined me at a makeshift Command Post at the entrance to the ghetto. By noon the north side had been searched and the only contraband located had been a Polish cavalry sword. My troops had thrown Jewish belongings out the windows and off balconies into the streets below where the SD and Order Police sorted through the items. When it was over, the Jews would have to sort through the scattered mess to reclaim their possessions.

Late in the evening my soldiers concluded the search. Sixteen and a half hours later I presented Eisenberg with the cavalry sword as it was the sole item of contraband we had located. Out of obligation to duty I inquired, "Shall I organize the Directive 19?" The Lieutenant Colonel waved off the action.

As we organized in formation to depart the ghetto I could clearly hear the wailing of the Jews as they sorted through the chaos we created. One week later, two of my Order Police units on patrol in the ghetto had blocks of concrete dropped on them from a fifth floor window. Both were killed when their necks broke under the weight. Their weapons and ammunition were stolen but had been returned by the Judenrat before I carried out the Directive 19 on 20 ghetto occupants. I firmly believe the cause of the attack on German forces was revenge for having torn apart the ghetto.

During one of the meetings with the Polish council, Bartlomiej Nieuzyla informed me that Poles in Porajów were entering into illegal agreements with those Jews permitted to leave the ghetto on work passes. At that time only a small number of Jews and Poles were in collaboration, and Nieuzyla told me because of his fear that the problem would escalate if not addressed.

The illegal agreements mainly consisted of bartering for contraband items, and false work papers and identity documents were being manufactured somewhere in Porajów and being sold to ghetto residents. Nieuzyla realized the guilty would need to be punished and preferred it to happen before more people became involved in the schemes. He introduced me to the Pole who brought the matter to the attention of the council.

It was intriguing that such illegal business took place under our occupation, especially when the population knew the risks it carried. The Pole confessed that he had become involved in trading cigarettes, medicines and alcohol to Jews in the ghetto, and he had come forward because of a change in heart about being caught. He did not want his family harmed, nor did he wish to be punished. The man believed his honesty would bring him leniency.

He explained how the scheme worked. Jews who left the ghetto on work passes would be marched through the streets to various employment details. The workers would deposit personal items that escaped confiscation, such as jewelry, money, silver photograph frames, and gold brocade, under bales of hay, under porches, and in a collection of other clever hiding places. After curfew, Poles would risk death by investigating the hiding locations to learn what items had been left behind. Everything was then taken to a meeting place where the Poles would determine the black market value and replace the items with things that were needed inside the ghetto. These goods were shuttled back to the hiding places under the cover of darkness and the Jews retrieved them the following day.

It was more of an honor system among them than an equal exchange for value. I learned that the Jews kept a cryptic written inventory of who donated what items. One could trade a copper ring for a packet of cigarettes. A silver photograph frame might bring two eggs, two turnips, and a bottle of wine. The items received from the Poles were divided accordingly inside the ghetto.

The man before me attested he knew of no firearms being traded, but I had to assume such transactions were taking place. He provided me with a list of known deposit locations and I posted guards. That night we arrested approximately 15 Poles and, while watching the same locations on the following day, apprehended 10 Jews.

I met with Mahler and Schumann to devise an appropriate punishment and disrupted their conversation regarding the new appointments of superior officers to the prison administration system.

Major General Theodor Eicke had been given his own regiment of Waffen SS, and Richard Glücks succeeded him as Inspector of Concentration Camps.

Porajów was not considered a camp, but the establishment of a ghetto in its municipality and the organization of industry in the zone provided complex problems for the administration of law. Punishing 10 Jews was no longer a simple matter of civil, criminal, or Reich Occupational Law.

The offenders were essential workers used for the construction and renovation of the buildings intended for industry. These Jews thus became a concern for SS Chief Gerhard Maurer in Berlin, because as the head of Office D II, he was responsible for all affairs regarding prisoner employment, training, and profits. If I was to impose corporal punishment on these people, I risked the possibility of crippling an essential worker which would in turn reduce the number required for the work detail. This would equal a loss on the administrative training budget since another worker would require instruction to replace him, and finally result in a temporary loss of profits until the new worker could receive appropriate job lessons.

This matter also gained the attention of Höss who was now head of Office D I, and the overseer of Prisoner Affairs. He became locked in a power struggle with Maurer over what was considered an appropriate punishment for the smuggling and trade offenses committed at Porajów. As if not complicated enough, Max Burger also became involved in the matter as his Office, D IV, was responsible for laws, taxes and contracts. Burger wanted to maintain amicable relations with the private industrialists and wished to appease them by not hindering the construction and renovations.

Schumann stated his opinion that I should hang one Pole and one Jew, and administer 20 lashes to the remainder. I agreed with his idea, but there was no sound precedent or provision of Reich Occupational Law permitting me to proceed with these measures. I had complete authority to exercise my discretion under Eicke's administration, but these liberties began dissolving in the new system Glücks was creating. Berlin expected me to maintain control over the subjugated population of Porajów and did not tolerate lawlessness in Occupied Zones, but placed intolerable restrictions on how I was to enforce Reich authority.

This simple matter blossomed into a very complex debate at higher administrative levels. The most important interest remained the amicable relations between the Reich and private industrialists. Several of the businessmen were present in Porajów while the issue was being arbitrated in Berlin, and the representatives from Daimler Benz and Metall Union told me they had no concern with its outcome. They believed that Jews who dabbled in smuggling and illegal trade equaled untrustworthy workers and this subversion and criminal activity was not welcome in their respective plants. They admitted surprise that the matter was going through such scrutiny in Berlin and confessed its result would have no bearing on business relations with the Reich. One of them merely asked me, "Why have you not hanged them all?" The detainment of the 10 offending Jews had set the process of training replacement workers into motion and this cancelled the purpose of the debate in Berlin.

The matter was brought to the attention of Hans Frank who referred it to one of his most trusted assistants, Brigadeführer Odilo Globocnik. Days later I received a visit from Globocnik's deputy, Untersturmführer Amon Göth.

Lieutenant Göth exited a Staff Mercedes to reveal his 198 centimeter height. He was a very crude and insensitive man regarding Jewish affairs; however, he was an extremely intelligent, articulate, and shrewd officer concerning Reich matters. After frowning at the buildings and appearance of Porajów, he introduced himself by shaking my hand and asking, "Who in hell did you offend to be put in command of this commode?"

We sat across from each other in my office and I began to tell him about the smuggling and black market traders I had captured. He knew more than me about the situation and the developments in Berlin. "People in Berlin enjoy the sounds of their own voices," he said. "We had it good when Eicke was in command. But, Glücks? Glücks requires a meeting for everything. He does not have the intestinal fortitude to make a decision on his own. No, not Glücks. He needs support from all offices and departments before gaining the courage to approach the Reichsführer-SS to propose an idea."

His statements were bold and I asked, "What am I to do? I have been placed under administrative restrictions. How am I expected to enforce the law when such trivial decisions are being placed before committee?"

Göth laughed. "You do not understand how any of this works, do you, Schiller?" He stared at me with an expectant smile.

"How what works?" I did not know what he was specifically referring to.

"This!" he said while lifting both hands with palms upward. "All of this. You, me, the Reich, Germany." He laughed again. "Oh, Schiller. This is not about the government or the Fatherland. This is about you and me. Those men in Berlin are for the most part nothing more than uniforms stuffed with straw and hot air. Very few of them have the stomach to make a decision, and fewer have anything of importance to say. You and me. That is what it is about. Us. Out here in the field we are forced to make decisions while the bureaucracy is stalling."

I looked at him for quite some time because I did not understand what he was saying. "Are you suggesting I make a decision regarding the punishment of the smugglers without waiting for the ruling from Berlin?"

"You see that?" asked Göth, "You sound like Glücks." He sat there as if expecting me to figure out his meaning. When this did not happen he leaned forward in his chair. "The Reich hopes to appease the private industrialists with a decision about the smugglers, yes? The industrialists are here in this commode!" He wore a wide smile and motioned back and forth with his finger while saying, "Go to them and ask them what they want done about the smugglers. Then do it."

"What if the industrialists want them executed?"

"What if they do? I will help you string them up. The point is, Pohl and Globocnik want industry in Polish towns and cities. Make the industrialists happy and word will spread. Industry in this commode means revenue. Revenue means taxes. Taxes mean that Pohl and Globocnik can enforce a certain amount of, how shall I say this?" He nodded while thinking and said, "A certain amount of funds to be placed in your budget for operating costs."

"What operating costs?" I inquired. When he shook his head from side to side I realized he was insinuating financial impropriety.

"It is not a misappropriation of Reich money if that is what you are thinking."

That was precisely what I was thinking.

"These industrialists expect certain things," he explained. "Things that are not specified in civil law. They take care of you when you take care of them." He saw that I was not convinced. "I suggest this. Let us talk to the industrialists and learn what they wish to have done about the smugglers. If they want them executed, we will do that for them. If Berlin is not happy about this, I will take responsibility for it. I can personally assure you that General Heydrich will be impressed by your initiative."

I agreed thinking that if the meeting with the industrialists did not go well; I would have the option of declining to commit to a decision. The representatives voted in favor of executing the 10 Jews. Only one regarded the meeting as a complete waste of time, declared his lack of interest in the outcome, and departed. Göth was pleased with the 3:1 resolve. "Let us now inform the Polish Council," he said.

Nieuzyla was greatly distressed by our decision. He soundly argued that we were not within our rights to enact a Directive 19 on ten people accused of smuggling. Göth smiled and asked me, "Who is this jester?" Then he looked at Nieuzyla and coldly stated, "The SS possesses the authority to decide what is done here. Argue with me again and I will personally hang you."

While getting in the Staff Mercedes outside Nieuzyla's office I said, "He will inform a higher authority." I was nervous that we were making legal decisions beyond our rights.

"I am telling you," Göth replied, "Frank and Globocnik want industry in Polish towns and cities. Make the industrialists happy and you will forge beneficial alliances."

"This is western Poland," I reminded him. "This area is the now comprised of the Free states of Danzig. Globocnik and Frank do not have legal authority."

"Do not concern yourself with who makes what decisions," answered Göth. "Hans Frank commands the Government General for the Occupied Polish Territories. Concern yourself with him and what he wants." He ordered the driver to take us to the city jail for the purpose of interviewing the Polish and Jewish smugglers.

Our subordinates snapped to attention as we entered the facility and we were escorted through a locked door into a corridor with cells on each side. Göth paced up and down several times before stopping before one of the compartments. The man on the other side of the bars removed his hat and stood at attention.

"You are a smuggler?" asked Göth. "You are one of those who smuggled items outside the ghetto, hid them and returned the next day to retrieve illegally traded goods?"

The man denied the accusations. "No, Sir. I am not a smuggler."

Göth looked at me. "Is this one of the Jews arrested by your subordinates for smuggling?"

I nodded.

Göth shrugged to open a needless debate with the prisoner. "Lieutenant Schiller said you were arrested for smuggling, yet you told me you are not a smuggler. Are you lying to me?"

"No, Sir," said the man.

"Then you are implying that Lieutenant Schiller is lying. Is that it?"

Again he replied, "No, Sir."

"There is no logic in your answers," said Göth. "One of your statements must be false but you insist they are both true. Since both can not be true, I therefore pronounce you a liar."

"But, Sir," said the prisoner. He tried to explain his predicament, but Göth quieted him by raising a hand.

He stared at the prisoner before saying, "The truth will grant you leniency."

At this, the man admitted his participation in smuggling items outside the ghetto, hiding them, and retrieving the goods left by the Poles on the following day. He explained to the best of his knowledge how the operation worked and gave the names of other people involved. When finished, he asked Lieutenant Göth to confirm the promise of leniency.

"I am an officer of my word," he replied. "Leniency will be granted as promised. You will be shot instead of hanged."

The man began trembling and stammering. "Calm yourself, and trust me" said Göth. "A prompt death from a bullet is much more lenient than being hanged."

Untersturmführer Göth wasted no time in carrying out the executions. He instructed the Order Police to remove nine prisoners from the cells and escort them to the town square where Göth hanged them before an audience of pigeons and blackbirds.

By God, what had we done? I was yet concerned that we had not officially applied for Directive 19 orders to conduct the executions.

Göth was not in the least manner worried. He turned to me while a couple of the condemned kicked and twisted on the ropes. "What about this business of people manufacturing illegal work cards and identity documents?"

I recently learned about this matter and certainly had not spoken of it to anyone other than Mahler and Schumann. Either one of them had shared confidential information with someone who circulated it, or my subordinates knew about the activity and were talking about it before it had been reported to me.

"You have twenty five Poles in the holding cells," said Göth. "I say we bring them here and show them the hanged Jews. I think the sight of them swinging will be enough impetus to get the Poles talking about the printing press."

We returned to the municipal police station where Göth gathered more SS and Order Police units. He led the way into the corridor of cells where only the Jew who confessed remained. Göth pulled his pistol, placed it between the bars on the door and squeezed off three or four rounds. The man inside the cell tried to run in a panic to avoid the bullets but there was nowhere for him to go. After the shooting, his body laid slumped in a corner on top of a puddle of blood. The percussion from the pistol inside the enclosed concrete hallway had muted our hearing. Göth looked at me while laughing. "Was that not louder than you thought it would be? Are your ears ringing too?"

The Order Police unlocked the door at the far end of the corridor and we descended a staircase to the lower level of the holding area. The 25 arrested Poles were confined there and each was very nervous from hearing the pistol shots on the floor above. The cells were opened and the SS and Order Police cuffed the prisoners before escorting them to the town square.

Göth ascended the stairs to the gallows and walked up and down in front of the hanged Jews. He looked at the Poles and said, "This could be you on the ends of these ropes. Take a look." He stared up at one of the hanging bodies and then gazed at the Poles. "Is this what you want?" Göth paused without taking his eyes from them. "Think about that."

He walked back and forth for some time and I saw the fear forming in the eyes and on the faces of the Poles. Lieutenant Göth turned to them and said, "Some of you fancy yourselves as printers."

His tone became sarcastic and condescending as he continued. "I believe this is an apprenticed job in Poland which, and correct me if I am wrong, would make it guild worthy." No one would have corrected the Lieutenant if he had been wrong. He was insulting the Poles as he spoke to them.

"As you all know, or at least should know, the Reich disbanded all guilds in Poland. This means you are engaging in illegal enterprise. This carries severe penalties. Think about this too." He paced again to allow the Poles more time to absorb the festering fear. He pointed to the bodies once more and stated, "This could be you." Göth shrugged in a most casual manner and asked, "Who wishes to tell me where I can find the printing press?"

No one responded and his disposition immediately changed. "Sergeant! Hang five of those bastards!"

As the SS and Order Police set hands upon five Polish prisoners, a woman among them began shrieking out for mercy. "It is in the attic above the restaurant on Marszalek Street!"

Göth raised a hand to halt the Order Police from bringing the five prisoners onto the gallows. "Marszalek Street?" he asked with suspicion. He nodded slowly and said, "Very well. We shall see." The Lieutenant ordered the enlisted SS to dispatch a detachment of soldiers to search the location. Perhaps 20 or 30 minutes later a motorcycle roared into the town square and an SS Corporal conferred with Lieutenant Göth. From his appearance of satisfaction I presumed the printing press had been found.

The Lieutenant made the announcement that the press had indeed been located and the Poles shared a collective sigh of reprieve. Göth looked at them from atop the gallows and said, "Your cooperation in this matter has been most appreciated."

As he descended the stairs and walked toward the Staff Mercedes the Sergeant of the Order Police asked, "Sir, shall we take the prisoners back to the holding cells?"

"No," replied Göth. "Hang them all."

That evening I dined with Göth, Mahler and Schumann. The three of them were quite pleased with the 35 executions carried out that day and were discussing the fates of the restaurant owner, his wife, and the seven people arrested in connection with the printing press. I was the

SS Chief of Police and Security at Porajów and I allowed my authority to be undermined by Göth and his will. I should have formally applied for the Directive 19 warrants, but the Lieutenant's altered logic, and his promise that General Heydrich would be impressed had fogged my judgment. I was angry at myself for allowing my command to be usurped, and I was angry with Göth for taking advantage of my inexperience. Before finishing our meals, I ordered Mahler and Schumann to leave us.

Göth sensed what I was going to say and this made me realize he had acted like this on other occasions with different people. "Something is troubling you?" he inquired.

"We had no authority to do that today," I said. "The Central Office at Oranienburg is going to receive copies of the arrest records. They are going to want to know why my prisoner census is short by thirty five persons at the end of this month. One or two they might understand. But thirty five people, Amon?"

"Did not the industrialists say they wished the executions?" He continued eating with a lack of emotion that reminded me of Höss. "Frank and Globocnik will take care of this. You will see."

"Glücks and Höss will have me sent to prison for this," I added.

Amon shook his head from side to side. "Glücks is a conventional bureaucrat," he said. "Do you honestly believe he knows what is happening out here in the field? Sure, he might hear of this and ask you questions about it, but Glücks only sees what he wants to see. Globocnik and Frank are always saying that Glücks will not acknowledge that things out here in the Occupied Zones are different. He dwells on the thought that everything Eicke implemented for the Detainment Facilities is also practical for the administration of ghettos and cities. It is not. You know this. You have been at the camps. I do not have to tell you that a city or ghetto can not be governed by the same legal codes practiced in the camps. You did well today, Schiller. You did the right thing. The industrialists are happy and everyone will make money."

I could not displace myself from the thought that I would be relieved of command and sent to a military prison. I had become an officer in the elite SS and this provided doorways to become part of a newly emerging aristocracy. A professional and honest career would equal the means to provide for my parents and siblings. It would result in a security for the rest of my life that was usually reserved for the landed gentry. I was a simple young man from Füssen given formal SS training in Reich law. I had promptly elevated myself to the rank of Junior Lieutenant, impressed and gained the favor of my superiors, and was granted command of a subjugated population in Poland. My path to the new aristocracy of successful SS officers was open and unobstructed before me, and now I could see the road ending because I used personal discretion instead of Reich protocol.

Göth departed the following morning and was gone for two or three days at which I received an official summons to appear before my superior officers at RSHA Headquarters. My attendance was demanded by Glücks and I was not surprised to see the orders had been signed by Rudolf Höss and Max Burger. I was under enormous stress at thinking this was the end. I believed I was going to prison.

I arrived at RSHA Headquarters on the designated day and did not have to wait one moment after announcing myself. I was shown to a lavish conference room on the second floor and was introduced to the General Inspector of Concentration Camps, Richard Glücks. He did not say much to me, but gestured to a chair and I sat down while he paged through several documents. Moments later we were joined by Höss who gave me a very disdainful look and sat down in silence without returning my offer of a handshake. Max Burger was the last fellow to enter the room and he formally greeted me.

Glücks and Höss busied themselves with paperwork while Burger walked to a coffee cart and poured a cup. He added cream and sugar and after stirring the cup he gestured toward the coffee urn. I was too nervous and afraid that my trembling hands would spill a cup on Glücks. I silently declined and sat there for a very long time.

The doors banged open and a Hauptsturmführer called us to attention. All of us stood in a clipped and rigid manner as SS General Reinhard Heydrich entered the room and took a seat at the head of the table. I was relieved when the General told us to sit because my heart was thumping in my chest like a drum and my knees were shaking. He took a few documents from his leather satchel and spread them out on the table. Without looking at any of us, he said, "Good morning, gentlemen."

I did not respond because I did not think the General was particularly speaking to me. His icy gaze found me and with the tone of a school master repeating a lesson he again said, "Good morning."

There was no mistaking that he was addressing me. "Good morning, General."

Heydrich folded his hands and said, "Schiller, tell me something about yourself that I do not already know." His black uniform had been steamed and pressed to perfection and his features were mesmerizing. So mesmerizing that I did not answer his question promptly.

When I did not answer, the General told me what he knew about me, which was everything. He knew when and where I was born, where I attended school, he quoted my grade averages, the names of my relatives, the military career of my Father, and the two menial jobs and the names of the employers I had before enlisting in the SS. Heydrich was known for his amazing capacity to memorize every detail about each man serving beneath him. He did not expect an answer. His goal was to inform me that he knew all he needed to know.

He then asked, "Do you care for the music of Wagner?"

I replied that I did, and he told me to name my favorite piece. I responded, "The Valkyrie", and he rapidly asked why I chose this composition as my favorite. I was greatly confused and intimidated by the odd line of questioning but managed to answer I found the piece of music exciting to the senses. He agreed it was and without hesitation said, "Thirty-five executions at Porajów. Tell me about this."

The thought did not enter my mind to blame Göth or make excuses for a decision I was ultimately responsible for. "Sir, I made the decision. It was a courtesy extended to the industrial representatives. I had to demonstrate that errant behavior on behalf of the workers will not be tolerated in the Occupied Zone I am in command of."

Höss promptly interjected, "You breached the law, Lieutenant. The Central Office in Oranienburg did not receive a written or verbal request for Directive 19 warrants."

"I operated within my discretion," I replied. Then I realized I might have made a grievous mistake with those words, but my emotions got out of control because I was speaking directly to Höss.

"Discretion," repeated Burger. "I admire that."

I did not expect his support as Burger chaired Office D IV and arbitrated all matters of law in the ghettos, camps and Occupied Zones.

"I do not admire it," said Glücks. "If we allow our SS Chiefs of Police and Security to operate with personal discretion we will have miniature fiefdoms springing up all over Poland. What gives you the right to ignore Occupational Law and enforce penalties as you see fit? Your responsibility is to oversee the safety and security of Reich forces, manage the civilian population, and exercise authority over the Jewish residents of the ghetto. What is so difficult about this?"

Höss made a few remarks about how I did not properly manage the situation at Porajów and Burger maintained a very neutral position. Höss did not bother me as the history of our personal conflicts provided his animosity. Glücks did not seem at all concerned whether there had been a breach of law, but was worried the matter would bring ramifications upon him from his superiors. Göth was correct that Glücks was the emblematic bureaucrat.

I explained the situation to General Heydrich and articulated the reasons for my decision. It was necessary to demonstrate authority and control and to reinforce the philosophy that no tolerance or mercy would be extended toward those committing crimes against the Reich.

To my surprise, Glücks did not make a conflicting statement to my quote of Eicke's training philosophy. Since succeeding Eicke as Inspector of Concentration Camps, Glücks impressed a more kind and gentle attitude upon the new Totenkopfverbände units. There was a peculiar aura about him in that he seemed to encourage and support a reformation of policy in the camps and Occupied Zones, yet he believed that all policies already in place could not be amended or reversed.

General Heydrich calmly said, "The reason for this meeting is not to decide whether you violated Reich protocol, Schiller. You used a very aggressive approach and your initiative was brought to my attention by Frank and Globocnik."

This was obviously the result of Junior Lieutenant Amon Göth. I was satisfied and relieved to know I was not at the meeting to decide if I was to be sent before a military tribunal.

"Pohl is making plans to bring agricultural industry to Porajów," said General Heydrich. "What are the problems in the city?"

"There is no consistency in the administrative operations," I replied. "Berlin is constantly issuing new directives for governing the population. There is too much time being wasted in filing the required documents with the Central Office in Oranienburg and the SS Main Economics Department in Berlin. Many situations call for immediate action so that other circumstances do not cause delays."

"Who are you to question decisions made in Berlin?" asked Höss.

The General interrupted. "I meant, what are the local problems in Porajów, but you have opened a new discussion here. Please continue."

I explained that the directives and protocol from Berlin had limited bearing on the tangible aspects of SS Police and Security business in Occupied Zones. While these measures may have been effective in the Detainment Facilities, an occupied town or city was not a confined area of operations. The ghetto at Porajów served as a kind of prison, but the residents were permitted free passage inside it, had their own administrative and judicial committees, and its Judenrat freely conferred with the Polish Civilian Council in the town. This created a floodgate through which poured a liberal amount of details regarding SS business. The residents inside the ghetto were well informed of what was happening outside its walls, and the contact with Polish civilians created a perilous atmosphere for rebellion and criminal activity. Whereas in the camps such information was virtually unobtainable, there was no reasonable method to safeguard police and military details among an open urban population. When Polish civilians and Jews violated the laws, immediate action was required to rectify the problem.

As with the smugglers, I believed immediate action was necessary. Holding the prisoners while filing the requests for 35 Directive 19 warrants and waiting for the Central Office at Oranienburg to receive, process, approve and return the orders, would have allowed more time for other smugglers to increase their criminal activity. Once they knew we had penetrated and discovered their circle of illegal operations, time lost by the SS Police would have been time gained for the criminals. In this period they could have easily foregone simple barter for eggs and cigarettes, and initiated the acquisition of firearms and explosives. I asked the gentlemen if in their opinion, Jews and Polish civilians with guns and explosives would create a stable environment for private industry. Burger and General Heydrich nodded their understanding.

"Now, locally," asked the General, "What are the problems at Porajów?"

"The Jews," I answered. "The Polish population is quite manageable but is easily influenced by criminal activity committed by the Jews."

"What do you suggest we do with the Jews?" he inquired.

"I am not certain of the answer to that question, General. However, I do not understand why they are being deported from Austria, Moravia, and Germany to Poland, when the Reich has plans for lebensraum there."

"You see?" Burger asked the General. "That is what I have been saying to Eichmann. Why are we making room for Germans in Austria and Moravia by deporting the Jews to Poland? Poland is also intended to become living space for Germans. Why shuttle the Jews to Poland when we will be forced to endure additional expenses to resettle them again?"

"The Jews are necessary labor," said Höss. "The Reich will have to make concessions for where they are put."

General Heydrich said, "The Reichsführer-SS is considering the construction of certain industrial prison complexes. These will be larger camps with the purpose of industrial and commercial production. For now we must use the ghettos as Jewish population centers until additional Detainment Facilities can be constructed in the interior of Poland. Once these facilities are completed we will liquidate the ghetto populations by deporting them to the camps."

The General read one of the documents he had set on the table. "Schiller," he said, "Höss has reported on the inmate population at Sachsenhausen. As you have experience at this facility, how would you describe the differences between the Jews at this prison, and the Jews in the Porajów ghetto?"

"I consider the Jews at Sachsenhausen to be a successfully confined and controlled prison population," I responded. "At Sachsenhausen or any other facility of its kind, we direct every aspect of their lives. The Jews live in barracks we provide, they follow rules we enforce, they eat the food we give them, and they do what they are told. Constant monitoring from towers, roving guard patrols, kapos, and barracks searches erase the mere thought of reverting to criminal Jewish behavior. We can not do this in the ghettos. In the ghettos, the Jews are confined but they are not controlled."

"So there is a prevalent objection to German authority?" asked Burger.

"I would not call it a prevalent objection to German authority," I replied. "I would say it is a prevalent adherence to Jewish customs and behaviors. I do not believe a Jew inside Sachsenhausen would risk lighting a menorah or performing a Jewish prayer ritual. However, we can not stop them from doing this inside the ghettos."

Höss asked, "You are saying you can not effectively police the ghettos? This sounds like a matter of incompetence."

No one paid any heed to his obvious attempt to insult me. I ignored him and stated, "It is impossible to monitor every Jewish activity inside the ghetto. They do not live in barracks, they live in apartment buildings. There is a degree of organized Jewish resistance, but in my opinion, this is to be expected when you concentrate criminals in an area with very little supervision. This immoral disease spreads when the Jews infect the local Polish population with notions of wrongdoing. It must be stemmed. It must be cured."

"I have heard enough," said General Heydrich. "Glücks, Burger, and Höss, you are excused from this meeting." The men gathered their belongings and left, but not before Höss made sure I received his contemptuous gaze.

There was tremendous anxiety inside me while sitting alone with General Heydrich. He continued to read several documents for a very long time before putting them away and staring at me.

"You were influenced by Göth at Porajów, were you not?" he asked.

"No, Sir. It was my decision."

His expression turned to a hatred for me. "I have no patience for lies."

"Göth suggested the action," I admitted.

He squinted at me. "And you went along with it. Why?"

"To appease the industrialists, Sir."

"Without formal application for Directive 19 from the Central Office in Oranienburg?"

"Yes, Sir."

"What did you feel when the Jews and Poles were hanged?"

"Feel, Sir? I felt nothing. They were criminals. They deserved it."

"How did you feel when Göth suggested this?"

"I am not certain, Sir."

"Did you feel confused? Did you feel torn between administering a sort of justice you knew was righteous yet could be denied by the officers at the Central Office in Oranienburg? Did you feel that you saw the crimes they committed and that you knew they were guilty, but the Central Office might rule against the Directive 19? Did you hang them because you were entirely convinced of their guilt and wanted no one to overrule your absolute certainty? Do you believe the hanging of those 35 criminals was a matter of inflexible justice?"

"Yes, Sir!"

"Glücks and Höss do not care for you," he said. "Personally, I am not convinced of your loyalty either. However, Pohl, Frank and Globocnik believe you have potential. My personal deputy requires a field liaison and I believe your initiative and observations may qualify you for this position. However, I prefer that all my field officers have combat experience."

"I served during the invasion of Poland, Sir."

"Yes," he replied quite disparagingly. "And what combat awards did you earn?" He knew I had won no medals and that the only reason I wore the Polish Occupation Ribbon was because I had simply been present while others did the fighting.

"I am going to send you to the Western Front," he said. "The Reich is planning an assault on the Low Countries, including Belgium and the Netherlands." He signed a few documents and slid them across the table to me. "Our objective is Paris," he declared. "Therefore, I am assigning you to the 7th Motorcycle Police Battalion. You will invade France with the SS and Wehrmacht. Once France capitulates, and if you are still alive, we will discuss your transfer to my deputy's department."

"Thank you, General," was all I could think to say. A transfer to RSHA Headquarters was a step into the elite circle of the SS. "May I inquire what duties will be required if I am honored with the selection to your deputy's department."

"My God, Schiller," he said with disgust. "There is a difference between gratitude and groveling." He mocked my words by repeating, "Honored with the selection." After putting his documents away he stood and said, "Come. It is better to show you than explain."

It was a privilege to walk next to him in the halls as everyone we passed saw me in the presence of General Heydrich. We eventually entered a large room through a door with an opaque window. On the glass was painted: *Büro für jüdischen Auswanderung.* This ordinary office hosted many clerks and administrators who sat at desks and spoke on the telephones or busied themselves at typewriters. The General took me to the far side of the room and opened a wooden door with an engraved plaque reading: *SS-Hauptsturmführer Adolf Eichmann, Direktor der jüdischen Auswanderung.* General Heydrich briefly introduced me to Captain Eichmann, and then left us there to discuss matters.

"This is the Office for Jewish Emigrations," said Eichmann. "What we do here is quite simple. My office reviews the census records for each populated area in the Reich and its territories. We issue the orders and arrange the transports for forced Jewish emigration."

I was very confused at how I could possibly serve a beneficial role in Captain Eichmann's office.

"You have just come from the occupied Polish territories, correct?" Eichmann was very soft spoken and amicable. It did not seem as if there was a separation in ranks between us. He spoke to me in a most pleasant and cordial tone.

"Yes," I responded. "Porajów."

Eichmann searched through a filing cabinet and read from a set of documents. "Yes, Porajów. Several weeks ago my office sent you a cargo of 10,300 Jews from Lower Germany, Austria, and Moravia. You admitted 8,550 to the ghetto." He handed me the documents with a smile. "You witnessed this arrival. What was it like? Was it efficient?"

His reports were accurate and I handed them back saying, "No. It was very chaotic."

Eichmann seemed very concerned about this. "That is why I asked General Heydrich for a field liaison. I need someone out there to oversee the transports and inform me where the problems exist. My office has received word that the volume of these transports is expected to increase fivefold by the end of next year."

A Lieutenant entered his office and informed Captain Eichmann of a meeting. "You will have to excuse me," he said, "But I will look forward to talking with you again." He gathered his briefcase and some papers before saying, "France, is it?"

"Yes, Captain. I am being dispatched to France."

He placed a hand on my shoulder in the doorway of his office. "Be careful there," he advised. "I will put in a good word for you with General Heydrich."

I telephoned my office at Porajów and placed Mahler in temporary command while I was performing my assignment in France. A train took me from Berlin to Aachen and I found the city to be a hive of military activity. I reported to XXV Panzer Regiment, VII Armored Division under the command of General Erwin Rommel.

CHAPTER SEVEN
THE STORM IN THE WEST

Rommel made no distinctions between SS or Wehrmacht. In his eyes, all troops were equal as soldiers or officers. He understood the necessity for a police presence in his Division, but made it quite clear to me that I would uphold the duties of an officer-soldier before those of the police.

On 10 May 1940, XXV Panzer Regiment, VII Armored Division crossed the border and made an unopposed run to the Belgian town of Butgenbach. We met light resistance on the southwest road to Francorchamps but the Belgian Army did not counter with effective tactics. Most of the enemy soldiers cast their weapons to the ground and immediately surrendered while others huddled in the ditches and fields alongside the road to avoid detection.

During the invasion, my duty was unique and dangerous. I directed the armored vehicles and infantry across the border. The last German element to cross was the 7th Motorcycle Corps and it was the responsibility of Scharführer Bastian Lesser, to wait until all units had passed. I would then seat myself in the gondola of Lesser's motorcycle and we would race to the head of the armored column. I would employ a wireless radio to announce my arrival at which Rommel or one of his officers would identify a tank by its number. Lesser would then pull alongside the designated tank and while moving, a crewman would climb out of its hatch and lean over to hand me the latest handwritten intelligence reports concerning terrain, potential enemy emplacements, civilians, towns, and resources. All forward tank crews would gather this information based upon observation and communication with Luftwaffe reconnaissance pilots and forward SD and Order Police units.

Lesser would then reverse our direction to connect with the Wehrmacht, Order Police and SD in the center of 7th Motorcycle Corps. We halted long enough to relay the intelligence information and issue commands for secondary detachments of the SD, Order Police and Wehrmacht to race ahead and relieve their comrades at the front. Those returning from the front would fall into a rotation in the center of the Advance Formation. One order was clear above all others. Keep the column moving!

The Belgians had fortified at Francorchamps but the shells from our tanks had the town in flames within an hour. When Belgian artillery shells landed amidst our tanks, the Panzers would throw open their throttles and fan out so that no two tanks were within six meters of each other. This was deemed a safe and suitable range to avoid having a tank damaged or disabled from a direct hit to one on either side of it. Most of the time enemy shells were ineffective against us. The heavy Panzers were well armored and could withstand numerous hits. However, the light Panzerjager 101 tanks were easy prey in our spearhead column. Because of their light armor and superior speed, Rommel had chosen to use them as armored reconnaissance vehicles and as quick-strike shock weapons. The problem with the Panzerjager was that its only topside protection was a raised gun shield that was open at the top and rear. There was no enclosed turret. If an enemy shell landed inside the Panzerjager by skill or with the help of God, its ammunition stores erupted into an explosion that obliterated the tank and anything in a 5 meter radius of it. The Belgians employed suicide cavalry officers that would ride into our tank column in ranks of fifty or a hundred. Most were effectively machine gunned before they penetrated the column, but those who made it through specifically searched out the Panzerjagers. If they were successful in reaching the vehicle they would throw a grenade or satchel charge into the back of the tank. The fuses were always shortened to make certain our crews could not retrieve the explosives to throw them out. The report of an exploding Panzerjager was so distinct and louder than any incoming or outgoing report. When we heard this far behind the front lines someone would always remark, "There goes another Panzerjager!"

By evening the Belgian army had evacuated Francorchamps and the armored column turned southwest. The strategy was to bypass

Bastogne to the north by means of woodland roads in the Marche-En-Famenne valley. Rommel would then swing the column sharply to the southeast and meet up with the IX Wehrmacht Infantry to provide rear tank support for the capture of Arlon near the border of Luxembourg. On 21 May we established radio communication with the IX Wehrmacht. The Infantry was poised on the east side of Arlon when Rommel's VII Panzer Division moved in behind the city from the west. The pincer move worked like a vice and the Belgian army at Arlon surrendered within 4 hours.

Rommel took us into France on the evening of 26 May and thus we began the parallel drive south of the Maginot defenses. The towns ahead of us glowed from the flames caused by Luftwaffe bombs, and French soldiers came out on the roads with their hands in the air. In sixteen days we had captured approximately 30,000 Belgian and French Prisoners of War. I had turned the prisoners from Francorchamps over to the Wehrmacht for transport to a holding facility at Essen in Germany. In France I had to turn the prisoners over to the Wehrmacht to be escorted to a sports arena in Arlon. It was the only suitable location to use as a temporary holding facility.

At this time my duty became the most dangerous. French snipers enjoyed the sport of shooting at me while Lesser raced to the head of the tank column. After gathering the information on one such mission we turned to head back to the SD and Order Police. As Lesser spun the motorcycle around, a bullet tore a hole through the fuel tank and soaked me with petrol. We had enough fuel to accelerate and when out of danger Lesser asked if I had been hit. I replied I was in perfect health. Lesser said, "Do not light a cigarette!"

In the time it took to reach the Maginot defenses we had changed motorcycles four times. The first had its fuel tank ruptured, and the second had its gondola separated after we bounced deeply in and out of a shell crater we had not seen in the darkness. Once again I escaped without injury, but there I was, spinning like a top in the gondola. Lesser found me in the darkness and laughed like a Bavarian madman when I staggered from the dizziness. The next motorcycle had its rear tire torn from the connectors after hitting another crater. The fourth took two sniper rounds through the engine, but the fifth would carry us into Paris.

Rommel was most successful in his attacks on the Maginot

defenses. He simply staggered the armored column and launched shell after shell into the fortifications. The French had designed the emplacements with all guns and artillery pointing toward Germany. The weapons were only capable of pivoting in a 180 degree radius to attack forces in front of them. The French were powerless as it was impossible for them to turn their massive guns to the rear. Emplacement after emplacement fell and after clearing them, the Wehrmacht and SS elements on reserve in Germany were given orders to cross the border through the gaps. Rommel next turned to the southwest with his focus on taking the city of Reims.

He was irate at having to halt his column for resupply 26 kilometers east of Reims. The Wehrmacht fuel and ammunition supply trucks had become bottlenecked on the narrow logging roads of the Ardennes, and there on the frontlines of France we were dangerously low on necessary provisions. Rommel could not attack Reims at our current level of stores and we were given orders to dig in to await resupply.

Lesser and I dug a trench and placed the canvas of our tent above it. We brewed coffee and ate sausage while the Mechanized and Armored units made light repairs to their vehicles. Now and again the reassuring sight of the Luftwaffe appeared overhead. They had marked our position on the ground and knew precisely where we were in the event we needed them for support.

That night was my first true experience of combat. Shortly after midnight a French Infantry unit broke through our southern flank and rushed our encampment. Lesser and I had been at the rear, approximately 60 meters away from the nearest tank. The shooting and shouting awoke me and Lesser was pushing an MP38 machine pistol into my hands. I pulled the charging handle as taught by the soldier on the Polish border, and I crouched in the hole to peer out beneath the lip of our canvas tent. I could see outgoing and incoming muzzle flashes and I heard German and French words being shouted. A group of German soldiers fired a burst before running toward the safety and cover of the tanks to the west. Moments later I heard French voices growing louder as they approached. I looked back at Lesser to see he had abandoned our hole and left me there alone. I distinguished two silhouettes in the darkness and when I heard them speaking French, I pulled the trigger of the MP38. At that moment I did not know if I had hit them. I instinctively leapt out of the hole with the agility of a rabbit and ran toward the safety of the tanks as if Lucifer himself was chasing me.

It was determined that the French made the mistake of thinking our tanks and halftracks had halted due to a complete lack of fuel. They believed our vehicles to be stationary targets but learned the truth when the engines turned over, floodlights lit the landscape, and our halftracks cut down the French Infantry with machine guns. I recall the French discarding their weapons and rucksacks for the sake of being able to run faster. It served them no good. As the French retreated away from our floodlights they fell to the ground in scores under the storm of bullets.

Following the engagement, the Field Commanders were angry and demanded full accountability from those who let the French penetrate our perimeter. I found Lesser near an artillery gun and angrily asked why he had abandoned me. He replied with words I could not argue with. He said, "Sir! You are the officer! I waited for you to give the order to fall back to the tanks! When you gave no orders to stand or fall back I took it upon myself to exercise initiative!" He was correct. In that situation I had been responsible for his safety. As he said, I had issued no orders. I had been too frightened under fire to coherently think of commands.

Returning to our tent, I walked several paces to the south and came across the bodies of two dead French soldiers. Both of them were riddled with machine gun bullets. I had done that. I shot them. Lesser stood at my side and discerned from my silence that I was responsible for their deaths. He inquired, "Did you shoot them Sir?" I replied that I did. Lesser was obviously uncertain of what I was feeling and he had no information about the events I witnessed at Sachsenhausen or at Porajów. He next asked, "Do you want a moment alone?"

I had evolved. I spat at the bodies and said, "To hell with their souls!" Those two dead French bastards had come cowardly under the cover of darkness to kill me. I had won the fight. God was with me.

Events such as that change a man. I was certain on that night that those two French soldiers had come into our encampment with the intention of killing me and other Germans. While looking at them I considered the idea that perhaps both French soldiers would have thrown down their weapons and surrendered if I called out for them to do so. Perhaps I could have shouted a warning and fired in the air. That might have been enough to startle them into surrendering. Perhaps I did not have to kill them and I have always wondered what I might have done if I did not have the previous experience of bureaucratic summary executions at Sachsenhausen and Porajow. Those executions and the tests at Nordhausen had all added to the apathy with which I viewed anyone not of pure German lineage. In our military we were given a red and black ribbon for our first Authenticated Combat Kill. Sergeant Lesser corroborated my shooting despite that he had already fled from the hole when it occurred. Rommel concurred that I was the only soldier in that area and thus, I was awarded the *Authentische Kampftötung* ribbon.

I remember that Rommel was angry, cursing and shouting at his Junior Officers. Word spread that the Wehrmacht Supply column would not reach our position until the following day. I was eating my ration of bread within sight and earshot of the General while watching him pace like a lion. He threw his head back on his shoulders and motioned grandly with a riding baton. He pounded his fists on the map tables, kicked over chairs and demanded to know, "Who in hell is directing this damned war?" He shouted that his armor and troops had been stopped in the middle of the open French countryside, and were more obvious than "a piece of shit on the plate of a bride". Abruptly the General turned and walked in my direction and I jumped to attention when he stood before me. He roared, "Are you the Chief of my police?" Actually, the SS Police was under the authority of the RSHA but at that moment it was not prudent to tell that to the General. I replied that I was. He bellowed, "When the Supply column arrives, fuel and shells will first be dispensed to my tanks before ammunition, water, and food is distributed to the men. Is that clear?" I affirmed it was. He stared at me for several moments as if contemplating whether to shoot me. "Very well!" he snapped. "Shoot anyone that interferes with my order!" As he walked away he added, "And shoot anyone who talks to you while you are carrying it out!" Surely he did not mean that but I understood the importance of his demands.

Late during the next afternoon the Supply column arrived. I directed the fuel trucks to the tanks as ordered and made certain the shells were delivered. The troops became impatient at waiting to receive their parcels and posts from home. Most of them were understanding of the orders issued by Rommel, but as in any group there were those that protested. When the distribution of fuel was completed the trucks began unloading the mail, water, ammunition, and food provisions.

On the following morning we received news from High Command of the Army that 2nd Army Group had broken through at Laon and were pushing south on the city of Reims to establish a bridgehead. Our forces were ordered to advance on Reims ahead of 2nd Army Group and launch a tank and artillery barrage on the city from the north bank of the river. General Rommel walked by me on the way to his tank that morning and ordered, "Get us moving!"

I stood at the head of the column and waved the remaining Panzerjagers forward and directed several halftracks to file in behind them in a "V" support formation. Next I signaled to Rommel's tank and his driver opened the throttle and crept past me. I organized the Mechanized units into their formations, directed the vehicles towing the artillery, launched the 7th Motorcycle Corps, moved the Infantry, and lastly waved the medics, cooks and supply personnel forward. Lesser started his motorcycle and took me to the head of the column.

We advanced at a slow rate of speed in a violent thunderstorm. The weather conditions made it difficult to conduct low level air reconnaissance and because of this, we were forced to rely upon visual observations from the Panzerjager crews and our forward scouts. The column approached the north bank across from Reims approximately two hours after we departed from our encampment. The city was a silent ruin from numerous Luftwaffe attacks. The General staggered the tanks at an approximate distance of 400 meters from the north bank and placed his artillery approximately 400 meters behind the tanks. This created a moveable defensive wall to defend the artillery in the event the French infantry charged our guns.

The German Infantry was given orders to entrench at an approximate distance of 200 meters from the riverbank and all non combative forces such as cooks and medics were sent to the rear behind the artillery guns. As the 7th Motorcycle Corps was an extension of the Army, I found myself crouched in the mud behind hedges just 200 meters from the riverbank. I heard the steady tapping of the raindrops on my steel helmet.

Reims was devastated. The streets were full of rubble and the brown and white buildings stood without roofs, windows, and doors as these things had been blown out during the Luftwaffe bombings. We did not know if Reims was occupied by the enemy, though days old air reconnaissance reports claimed that it was. We saw no movement in the town through our field glasses and the only sound was the rhythmic pattering of the rain.

Our first artillery barrage turned the ruins into a smoking inferno. The wet wood in the town sent thick clouds of black smoke high into the sky as it smoldered. When the first barrage ended there was no counterattack from Reims. Two bridges extended over the river with the one to my right being wider and capable of sustaining heavy vehicles such as tanks. It was apparently used for cargo trucks as the smaller bridge seemed only wide enough to accommodate motor cars, bicycles, and pedestrians. Both bridges were intact. It was logical to assume the French would have blown both bridges if they had evacuated the town. The fact that they remained intact was suspicious.

Moments later we launched a second artillery barrage that further devastated Reims. When our guns fell silent there was yet no counterattack from the French. Our field radios came to life with voices as the Signal Corps relayed orders for a Wehrmacht Reconnaissance Patrol to approach the bridges. Approximately 20 soldiers divided into two groups of 10 and all crouched low with their rifles pointed toward the town as they moved toward the bridges. A soldier near the smaller bridge turned toward us and touched his fists together several times to indicate it was mined. The same signal was sent by the second group. Both units retreated and engineers were sent forward to assess the situation.

They surveyed the wires and explosives for several minutes before French artillery fired at us from the city. The French gunners were firing at will and apparently aimed at nothing in particular on our side of the river. The engineers attempted to fall back to safety but several were cut down by small arms and machine gun fire from within the city. I covered my head as the French shells began exploding around us. The front edge of my helmet was firmly in the mud and my nose was touching the wet earth. I drew my hands over my head for additional protection and remained in that position while waiting for one of the shells to take me from this earth. I do not know how long the French barrage lasted but it seemed an eternity. When the shelling stopped I raised my head to see that trees had been blown in half and smoking black craters had replaced the grass. Approximately one meter on my right was a severed arm inside a Wehrmacht tunic sleeve. A wedding ring was on one finger.

I did not hear the order to assault, but our infantry charged the bridges and tore the detonation wires from the sides. Perhaps the French detonator plungers were wet because the bridges were not blown. Our soldiers endured many casualties while concentrated in tight groups trying to cross the bridges. I had reached the north part of the wider bridge at the same time our troops came to the main road leading into Reims. The French had overlapped the area with heavy machine guns and shot many of our Wehrmacht troops to death. As I began crossing the bridge other soldiers were running past me in the opposite direction to fall back. I never heard any specific orders given during that engagement and I adapted my actions to the behaviors of those around me. I ran back up the hill to the safety of the hedges I previously hid behind.

We traded artillery shells with the French late into the night. I had been summoned to the rear where a field hospital had been created. The Wehrmacht doctors informed me that during the initial infantry assault on Reims, we suffered approximately 50 serious casualties that required evacuation, perhaps 35 treatable casualties and 60 fatalities. The treatable casualties would return to the ranks. We had suffered a loss of approximately 110 men in less than 20 minutes. Of the fatalities, only 16 bodies were at the field hospital. They had either been dead when their comrades brought them to the hospital or died while receiving treatment. The remaining bodies were yet on the bridges, roads, and approaches to Reims. I certified the death cards for the 16 soldiers at the hospital and made my way back to the front. I passed by the artillery guns and through Rommel's Command Post where I learned that 2nd Army Group was expected to arrive at our position on the following morning.

2nd Army Group did not arrive. They had been halted 35 kilometers northwest to await fuel, ammunition, and supplies. They came to our position late in the night. We were delighted to see 2nd Army Group A commanded by Generaloberst von Rundstedt.

Because of the jubilation caused by the arrival, I was ordered to take my Police units to the Command Area to provide security. We had entered into a temporary stalemate with the French in Reims and no shots had been traded for many hours.

I watched and listened as von Rundstedt shouted at Rommel for having ordered an infantry assault into Reims. The Generaloberst had intelligence reports more current than ours and he told Rommel we were not opposed by only French forces at Reims, but that the enemy was accompanied by their British Allies. Von Rundstedt cautioned Rommel to be aware that while the French were completely incompetent at war, the British presented organized tactics and strategy worthy of a cautious counter plan.

The weather cleared the next day and the Luftwaffe began a series of bombing missions on Reims in concert with our artillery barrages. The last mission was flown late in the afternoon and we prepared a full assault. The battle lasted for three days against very light resistance and British snipers. Most of the occupying French and British fled to the ports in the west only to be taken prisoner by the Wehrmacht forces that had previously captured the coastal cities.

On 13 June the French declared Paris to be an Open City and German forces occupied it on the following day. Only light and sporadic resistance was encountered. The French government fled and went into hiding and the retired War Minister of France, Henri Petain, conceded an armistice with the Reich and also agreed to become the representative of the new Vichy government of the country. The French government formally agreed to serve and assist the Reich in all political and social matters. Prior to the formal surrender of France on 22 June, Rommel turned the VII Armored Division to the west to finish off straggling pockets of French and British resistance. I was released from XXV Panzer Regiment on 15 June with orders to report to SS Gruppenführer Felix Lichtman in Paris.

Paris had not been affected by the war. There was a large concentration of German forces making themselves comfortable and at ease in the city when I arrived. French civilians rode on their bicycles, walked their dogs, and conducted business in their shops as if we were mere visitors. After the hell and wrath we delivered to their country the majority of the French people seemed quite joyous to receive us. It was very peculiar.

SS Gruppenführer Lichtman had established his headquarters south of the Seine just over the Pont de Alma bridge on the Quai d'Orsay. I could scarcely believe that I was at Paris in June. I hoped and probably prayed that Paris would be named as my new post. It was much more welcoming and lovely than the wretched town of Porajów, Poland. However, I was soon told by Lichtman that I would have no time to become accustomed to the luxuries of Paris. He represented the RSHA Office of Race and Resettlement and promptly informed me that France contained a population of more than 300,000 Jews and that Heydrich wanted each of them transported to the east. That was the first time I specifically heard the Detainment Facilities referred to by the popular euphemism of "the east". Auschwitz had received its first transport of Polish Jews on the same day Paris was declared an Open City. From what I was told, the Detainment Facility at Auschwitz had been expedited into operational status because its buildings had previously existed as a Polish army barracks and required little maintenance to meet occupancy codes.

I sat across from Lichtman as he reviewed my personnel file and transfer documents. After a while he smiled and said, "Ah, the Blackbird of Porajów. Your reputation precedes you, Lieutenant. I need a man like you here. I have 40 Jewish and French Resistance leaders in the jail at the prefecture. Your orders are to interrogate them and locate all members of their factions." He handed me several documents issued from Berlin. "These are your formal directives. I see Burger has granted you complete personal discretion in these tasks."

The Blackbird of Porajów? I did not like that title. It intrigued me that Burger permitted me full personal discretion as this term held unmitigated meaning. It was the topic of discussion at our meeting one month ago. I knew it meant that I was free to use any means necessary to complete my assigned objectives.

"There is one more thing," added Lichtman. He passed another document to me. "If you are capable of breaking the resistance in Paris, you will receive a transfer to the Office for Jewish Emigrations. The RSHA, Lieutenant? I am honored to know you. It seems you are in good standing with General Heydrich. I trust that you will put in a sound word for me if I assist you at all levels?"

I nodded because I did not know what else to do. "What resources do I have available? How large is my staff?"

"40 SS units and 200 French police. And anything else you may need. I am at your service."

At my service? Those were very unusual words spoken by an SS Gruppenführer to a Lieutenant. Apparently my associations with Burger and Heydrich had impressive influence. "200 French police? How am I to trust them?"

"I know," said Lichtman with an exaggerated understanding. Truthfully, I perceived the impression he did not understand my concern. "It is part of the Reich's agreement with Petain's Vichy government. We are to work closely with the Vichy. It might not be as bad as you think. The French are not very tolerant of Jews."

"What about their own? Am I to expect absolute cooperation from the French when it comes to interrogating and arresting their fellow countrymen?"

"That is the promise we have from Petain," answered Lichtman. "Is there anything you can think of that you need?"

I realized the importance of my assignment and the laudable benefits of its successful completion. The task before me would be brutal but needed to be done if I wished to elevate my personal status in the SS. "Yes," I replied. "Arrange a transfer from Porajów to Paris. I need Waffen SS Oberscharführer Arnulf Schumann."

While awaiting Schumann's arrival I read the files of the arrested resistance leaders and contemplated the methods I would use to gain the necessary information. I also introduced myself to the Captain of the French police, Jérôme Aubertin, and was overcome with suspicion toward his intentions.

Aubertin was a nervous and awkward little man with an amusingly large moustache. His hair was matted and unkempt, and his tan shirt was always stained at the armpits from his profuse sweating. He followed me like a stray hound and constantly mixed German and French when answering me with an annoying, *"Ja, mon Lieutenant"*.

After reviewing his police units in a general formation, I formed the conclusion that perhaps one third of his men were willing to pledge services to the Reich. The remainder seemed willing to accept any orders they were given with the sole intention of not drawing criticism from the SS. This was a reliable historical characteristic of the French. One could always count on them to serve a master because none of them had the spine to resist. Those who did resist, such as those being held in the jail at the prefecture, did not have a spine, but merely possessed no intellect to understand the consequences of opposing a superior power.

I ordered Aubertin to inform each prisoner that they would face an interrogation in the coming days. When Schumann arrived, I showed him the orders issued by Burger and explained the potential benefits if we completed the task in a prompt manner. I made it clear that if I was appointed to the position in the Office for Jewish Emigrations, adjutants would be required for the service. As a Technical Sergeant of the Waffen SS, Schumann had no other reasonable means of being assigned to RSHA duties. He recognized the advantages of being one of my adjutants and was excited by the possibility of elevating himself from the Waffen SS to the RSHA. He pledged unconditional support in the matters before us.

The prefecture building served as the Headquarters for the Paris Gestapo. Chattering typewriters and conversations drifted to a pervasive hush when Schumann, Aubertin, and I entered. The noise and voices slowly resumed after everyone in the reception area had taken a look at us.

A clerk escorted us to the Commanding Colonel of the Gestapo who was pleased by our arrival. He smiled broadly as we took seats in his office and said, "The Blackbird of Porajów. I expected you would be much older." He got comfortable in his chair and asked, "Have you read the files?"

"Yes, Sir."

"I have not had any incidents of partisan activity in Paris, but my office believes the resistance will require several months to organize. My subordinates have interrogated the prisoners but unfortunately have gained nothing but false leads."

"By what means have they been interrogated?"

"Standard means," replied the Colonel. "We beat them. I do not have the authorization to apply more aggressive tactics. I believe that is why you have been sent here?"

My silence confirmed his answer. He stated, "My units have arrested a collection of Jews, some Communists, Bolshevists, traitors, deserters, and political activists. Each of them has a following and some are aligned with each other. Some factions and leaders wish nothing to do with their fellow inmates and regard equal criminals as enemies.

"Have you arrested their spouses and children?' I asked.

"No," responded the Colonel. "I was advised against it because my superiors thought it may strain our relationship with the Vichy government and Mister Petain."

"To hell with Petain and the Vichy," I said. "I want their spouses and children arrested and brought here by dawn. Then we shall see who talks."

Aubertin looked at me with a stupid smile on his face and muttered, "Oh, Lieutenant", as if I should feel shame for using spouses and children as leverage for the interrogations. I ignored him.

I stood to leave the office and reminded the Colonel, "By dawn."

CHAPTER EIGHT
THE BLACKBIRD

I dismissed Aubertin before visiting an outdoor café for a meal. After we took our seats, Schumann looked at me and asked, "The Blackbird of Porajów?"

I was embarrassed. "Yes. That is what they have been calling me since I arrived in Paris. It has to do with that business Göth initiated."

We had a conversation about my willingness to harm the spouses and children of the arrested resistance leaders. I told Schumann I was prepared to take all necessary steps to resolve this matter and receive my appointment to RSHA Headquarters. I had served on the front lines during the invasion and saw many German soldiers torn from this life by French bullets and artillery shells. I had no affinity for the French. Schumann held no reservations about it either. He had witnessed untold horrors in France during the previous war and he saw this as an opportunity to gain personal retribution.

We met Aubertin at the prefecture in the morning and were taken to an enclosed courtyard where the 40 prisoners were standing in 4 rows of 10 under the guard of SS rifles. The order was shouted at them to come to attention and only half of them responded. The remainder stood there with expressions of contempt and mild amusement.

I announced, "I am SS Lieutenant Rolf Schiller." Aubertin translated this as, *"Je suis SS Lieutenant Rolf Schiller, le merle de Porajów!"* I did not require knowledge of the French language to know he introduced me as the Blackbird.

"You will provide answers to my questions. I will be lenient if you genuinely do not know the answer to a question, and honest mistakes on your part will be treated with mild understanding. You will pay for intentional deception and withholding information with your lives."

Some of the prisoners chortled and looked at me as if saying, who is this jester that expects us to cooperate? This laughter ceased when I opened my holster and cocked my Luger. I approached one of the men in the first row who had laughed and pointed my pistol at him while saying, "You! Forward!"

He looked from side to side at his fellow prisoners before taking a few steps in front of the formation.

"What is your name?" I asked.

He responded with a French surname.

Aubertin stepped forward and declared, "Mon Lieutenant. This man is associated with the French Communist Party and its resistance."

"How many men do you represent?" He defied me with silence. I asked Aubertin, "Do we have his family?" He paged through several documents.

"No, Mon Lieutenant."

The French Communist looked at me with a sneer.

I asked again, "How many men do you represent?"

His silence was shaming me before the SS, French police, and the assembly of prisoners. I struck him sharply in the face with the handle of my pistol and heard the crunch of the breaking cartilage in his nose. He staggered three or four steps backward before falling to his knees. He could do nothing to wipe the blood from his face as his hands had been bound behind his back. I stood over him and asked the question again. He spat blood on the ground and looked up at me with hatred. That is when I saw the flesh around his eyes had swollen to a dark purple. When he did not answer me, I became enraged by his insolence and kicked my boot into his sternum. He fell on his side and I shouted the question a final time. When he did not answer I shot him through the head.

I rapidly walked up and down the ranks of the prisoners allowing each of them to view my angry face. They were no longer smirking. I looked at each prisoner in hopes of finding a reason to shoot another one. A facial expression, the way they stood; anything would have fulfilled my desire. I walked back to Aubertin and ordered, "Bring the spouses and children into the courtyard."

He hesitated for a brief moment before carrying out my instructions. Moments later approximately 70 men, women, and children were brought before the prisoners. Panic spread amongst them but the SS guards kept them in check.

I shouted, "All prisoners who do not have family members here are to raise your hands!" 9 or 10 hands went up. "Those with raised hands are to come to the front and center of the formation!" They did as ordered.

On the prompt of my nod, Schumann seized a middle aged woman and pressed his pistol against the side of her head. I announced, "Those without family members will now receive the honor of choosing who lives and who dies." Walking to one of the prisoners, I put my face centimeters from his and shouted, "How many people are in your faction and where are they located?"

He looked over his shoulder at the prisoners behind him but I grabbed his chin and pulled his face back to mine.

"Do not look at them! Look at me! How many people are in your faction and where are they located?"

Once more he looked at the people behind him and I nodded at Schumann who shot the middle aged woman. A cry of anguish came from within the ranks of the prisoners. The man before me looked at the woman's lifeless body and fell to his knees howling in madness and sorrow.

Schumann grabbed an adolescent girl by her wrist and pointed his pistol at her head. I abandoned the blithering prisoner and approached the next in line. "How many people are in your faction and where are they located?"

He immediately complied and the French police recorded his information. All the prisoners complied and reported the names of the of the people in their resistance factions and the addresses of where we could locate them. I detained the family members as hostages until we could collect the resistance members whose names we had been given. I refused to release anyone until my suspicions of French and Jewish deception were assuaged.

Inside the prefecture Schumann and I discussed the fate of the family members. I decided they would be arrested on charters of consorting with criminals. Over the next several days the Paris

Gestapo and SS arrested over 400 resistance members and brought the total of captured French partisans to 534.

This by no means broke the whole of the resistance in Paris, but it was considered a commendable first strike at subduing a subversive population of criminals. We had damaged some of the more powerful partisan units and managed to arrest high level and influential leaders. This placed many setbacks on the organized resistance and provided the Paris Gestapo with adequate time to gather intelligence to prevent future disruptions. It reinforced the point I argued before General Heydrich, Glücks, Höss, and Burger. Immediate action was required to quell additional problems.

I took a telephone call at the prefecture from Captain Eichmann who informed me that my superiors in Berlin were greatly pleased. The Captain told me of his plans to transport the 534 criminals by train from Paris to Troyes, and finally to the Struthof Detainment Facility in Alsace. He ordered me to oversee the transport of the prisoners from the prefecture to an industrial railroad yard in the northern quarter of Paris and to generate a report on my observations of the process and its efficiency. Eichmann stated that the industrial railroad yard was chosen because of its isolated location and urged me to conduct the transfer of prisoners in a manner that did not attract attention from the local population. I was to notify him when we reached the destination.

I had arranged for 5 buses to arrive outside the prefecture courtyard before the overnight curfew was lifted. Each bus was capable of carrying 32 prisoners plus a small contingent of armed SS. Each motorized transport to the railroad yard could carry 160 prisoners and it required 4 rotations to transfer all of them to the gathering point.

My report contained as many details as possible. I itemized the number of MP38 machine guns requisitioned, the number of cartridges for each, the amount of K98 rifles and 5-round clips for each, food and water rations for the guards, liters of petrol consumed by the buses, distance to the railroad yard, and time used for the process. The operation had been quite effective and efficient with no adverse incidents to record. I notified Eichmann with these details.

He told me a train pulling one passenger carriage and five freight wagons had been dispatched from Billancourt to Paris and upon its arrival, I was to load the prisoners in the wagons, board the passenger carriage and generate another report of the procedure during the journey to Struthof. His final instructions were to notify him upon my arrival at the Detainment Facility.

Schumann and the SS guards knew we were waiting for the train but the prisoners had no news of their fate. Though I conducted the transports under the cover of darkness and in the strictest confidentiality, companions of the prisoners rode to the perimeter of the railroad yard on their bicycles and attempted to make contact with their friends. My guards chased them away but by noon a large crowd had gathered outside the yard.

When the train pulled in I ordered my guards to fire over the heads of the civilian assembly and this promptly disbursed them. The prisoners were surprised to see the train as they were certain we brought them to the remote railroad yard to be shot. We loaded 107 prisoners in the first four wagons and placed 106 in the final wagon. I ordered the guards to return to the prefecture and Schumann and I boarded the passenger carriage and sat among a group of wounded SS and Wehrmacht soldiers on their way north for convalescence.

I notated all aspects in my reports as I wanted each to reflect attention to details to impress my potential superiors. Within hours we pulled into the squalid transport facility at Troyes and stopped to take on water. From the passenger carriage we could see hundreds of Jews packed in the courtyard of the facility. All of them were waiting for trains that would take them to Dachau, Buchenwald, Sachsenhausen, Auschwitz, or any one of the numerous ghettos in Poland.

The Jews were a ragged and filthy lot. I do not know how long they had been confined in the courtyard of the transport facility, but the conditions were deplorable. People of all genders and ages walked about in tattered filthy clothes with an exhausted gait. Some looked as if they had been badly beaten. Others were dead on the ground with insects and flies crawling about their bodies. The stench of human waste and decay was unbearable.

We watched the SS patrolling the compound with dogs and harassing the Jews. A row of buildings had been erected across the courtyard and the signs above the doors identified them as the kennel, storehouse, medical office, guard barracks, and latrine. An SS soldier came from the guardhouse with a bowl of water and poured half into a narrow trough for the hounds. A young Jewish woman approached him and though I could not hear what she said, she motioned toward the remaining portion of water in the bowl and touched her throat. The SS guard did not give her a drink, but threw the bowl at her and proceeded to beat her several times with the stock of his rifle until she managed to crawl into the crowd.

Schumann and I shared a laugh. Not because this event was humorous, but because we could not fathom the audacity of Jews. The people at Troyes had been evicted from their homes, driven to the transport facility and were to be placed on transports to take them to labor camps and ghettos. Jews were ordered not to speak to Germans without a prompt. Yet the Jews often refused to obey the most common orders and brought German wrath and ire upon themselves. I sat in the passenger carriage thinking, that foolish woman! How it would have been to her benefit to keep to herself. Thirst was the least of her problems that day.

I never went about my duties with premeditation of harming the Jews or any member of a subjugated populace. My responsibilities often included interrogating these people for matters that concerned the safety and security of Reich forces. I always welcomed and appreciated people that outright told me the truth without wasting my time or lying to me. When someone lied, I adapted to the idea that it was necessary to cause them detriment. I was an officer of the SS with very specific and very important duties. I did not have the time or inclination to entertain word puzzles, half truths, and outright lies during my police investigations. I presented everyone with a fair opportunity, and sometimes multiple openings, to tell me the truth. It really was quite simple. Tell me what I need to know and you can walk away from here with your teeth and limbs intact. Lie to me and I will break your body.

I was well within my legal rights to operate in this fashion. Reich law and German National law provided full leave to the civil and military police to dispense physical pain upon anyone who refused to comply with a legal investigation. I never took pleasure in the application of torture. In truth I considered it a nuisance to exert myself for this purpose. It never had to happen but it often did. What frustrated me about having to do this was that it never would have been necessary in any case if the foolish criminals complied from the very beginning. We did not pull people from the streets arbitrarily for the sake of trying to gain information about crimes and misconduct. If you found yourself in my interrogation room, it was because you had been thoroughly and professionally investigated and the decision was based on evidence that you were a party connected to illegal activity.

We departed from Troyes and arrived at Struthof late in the afternoon. The SS surrounded the train, opened the freight wagons and drove the prisoners onto the platform where they were assembled into a formation and counted. 525 prisoners arrived. 9 had died from asphyxiation inside the freight wagons during the journey.

I telephoned Eichmann from the Struthof railroad station to inform him of the arrival of the transport. He asked, "Were all freight units delivered alive?"

"No, Sir. Nine are dead. Asphyxiation, I believe. Perhaps some from cardiac arrest."

"How many freight units did you place in each wagon?"

"107 in four wagons, 106 in one wagon."

"Good, good."

There was a brief pause before he asked, "In your estimation, Schiller, how many freight units can we pack into a single wagon?"

"I believe we should pack less than 100 in a single wagon, Sir. As noted, nine died during the journey."

"Yes, yes," said Eichmann, "Natural attrition. We allow for that in this department. What is the maximum number of units we can pack in a single wagon?"

I did not know how to respond to this question.

"In the wagons with 107 freight units," asked Eichmann, "could we have packed more? Theoretically, what in your estimation is the maximum capacity?"

"Perhaps 125, Sir, but I would not recommend it."

"If you want to be appointed to this office you will indeed recommend it in writing."

"I understand, Sir."

"We are impressed with your work in Paris," said Eichmann. "Make the recommendation of 125 freight units for each wagon and have the report ready to be presented to General Heydrich. Board the next train from Struthof to Berlin and report to me tomorrow morning."

I watched a group of Jewish workers being marched to the train under the supervision of the Order Police. As the Jews pulled the nine bodies out of the carriages I sat on a bench next to Schumann and began composing my recommendation for 125 freight units to be loaded aboard each wagon.

Eichmann was eager to receive my reports at RSHA Headquarters and immediately assigned clerks to type copies. I introduced him to Schumann and explained the Oberscharführer had been instrumental in assisting me with my duties in Paris. I was anxious to learn of my status and whether I would be permanently assigned to the Office for Jewish Emigrations.

Eichmann instructed Schumann and me to have a cup of coffee while waiting for the copies of the reports to be typed and distributed. We sat on a bench against the wall in the open area of the main office feeling like schoolboys waiting to see the Head Master. The Captain came to us following a very long wait.

"Müller wishes to see you."

Schumann and I followed him into the office of the Chief of the Gestapo and we sat far across the room from Müller's desk.

"534 partisans arrested in Paris," said Gestapo Chief Müller. "That is commendable." He tapped one of the pages and said, "The affair of shooting a French woman seems disproportionate to the investigation. How do you justify the shooting of a civilian who had not been formally accused by the Reich?"

"Necessary coercion to gain the appropriate information from the accused criminals, Sir."

"And what," inquired Müller, "is to prevent the family of this woman from filing civil damages?"

"Forfeiture of legal rights," I answered. "The woman was a blood relative of one of the accused criminals. Due to association with a convicted criminal, the family forfeits all rights to file claims against the Reich and its personnel."

Chief Müller looked at Eichmann for confirmation of my statement. I used the pause to explain.

"Article XXXI, Paragraph 9, Heading II, subsection VI of Reich Civil law. The precedent was established during the Great War in 1916. All enemies of the Republic, and all those related by blood to said enemies, upon legal conviction of the crimes of subversion, sabotage, or any crime so related to rebellion, shall forfeit all rights, legal, civil, and otherwise not stated; to file claims, damages, and restitution against the Republic."

Eichmann nodded and stated, "The law was amended to the Reich under the Nürnberg codes of 1935."

"No incidents with the transport to Struthof?" asked Müller.

"You will see I noted a civilian congregation at the industrial railroad yard in the northern quarter of Paris. There was an obvious breach of security."

"In your opinion, how did that breach occur?"

"I firmly believe the French police disseminated the information."

"The damned French," said Müller. He put the documents together, stamped and signed them. "I see no reason to deny the transfer."

We stood and Eichmann collected the papers from him. We followed the Captain out of the office, ascended a flight of stairs and walked along a corridor. Two black uniformed guards flanked a set of double doors upon which was printed: "Reichsführer-SS Heinrich Himmler". The guards snapped to attention and we entered a very ornate room.

An SS Sturmbannführer immediately ushered us into the office of the Reichsführer-SS and there before me sat Heinrich Himmler and General Reinhard Heydrich. Eichmann handed Müller's approved documents to Heydrich while Schumann and I stood there saluting.

"Sit down," said Himmler in a most inviting tone. He looked at Schumann and asked, "Who is this?"

"I did not authorize you to bring companions to this meeting, Schiller." Heydrich was genuinely annoyed.

"This is Waffen SS Oberscharführer Arnulf Schumann," I replied. "He was an integral part of the successful operations in Paris."

"You refer to the arrest of 534 partisans as a success?" asked the General.

"Do you?" inquired Himmler.

"Yes, Reichsführer, I do."

"Since the occupation of Paris," declared Heydrich, "the Gestapo has arrested 3,000 partisans. How do you grade your operation as a success?"

Politely but firmly I asked, "Have any of your Gestapo agents or SS policemen arrested 534 partisans in less than 48 hours, Sir?"

Heydrich silently stared right through me. Himmler then said, "Tell me about the transport from Paris to Struthof."

I recounted the information in my reports and personally deemed the operation to be another success.

The Reichsführer glanced at the documents and said, "I admire your recommendation for 125 freight units loaded in each wagon. Now we must move on to other business." He looked at Heydrich. "General?"

"What should we do with the Jews, Schiller?" Heydrich sat back as if expecting me to have a complete answer to this problem.

"There are no correct or incorrect answers," said Himmler. "We want to hear your personal thoughts."

"Control them, resettle them, and confine them."

Nobody spoke a word until Eichmann asked, "Are you saying we do not firmly control the Jewish population at the present time?"

"In some cases," I replied. "Mainly in the Detainment Facilities. I can not say we effectively control them in the ghettos."

"And how do you suggest we do this?" asked Heydrich. He was hoping I would say something foolish.

"Force them to want to remove their culture. Nothing is more of an insult than making a people destroy their own identity. It is a direct path to making them submissive. I do not believe Jews should have any associations with Germans. Especially in terms of business and industry."

"The Jews are a free labor force," said Heydrich. "Where do you suggest we obtain labor for the factories?

"We should first employ Polish, French, Austrian, German, and Czechoslovakian criminals. The minor offenders, of course. Did we learn nothing from the last war? Placing Jews on plant floors is a dangerous wager. What is to stop them from sabotaging calibrations or intentionally producing faulty products? The industrialists do not trust them. This certainly strains economic relationships with private businesses. I am certain the civilian populations of the Occupied Zones would be willing to take jobs in German factories."

"Foreign civilians must be paid wages," said Eichmann. "On the other side of this coin, the Jews cost nothing."

The Reichsführer-SS wore an expression of deep concern. Very softly he said, "I am not moved by your argument to replace Jews in the factories." He looked at the ceiling for a brief moment. "You have had close contact with Jews. How do you classify them?"

"Useless," I responded. "Sustaining them as prisoners and as a work force is a drain of Reich finances and resources."

Unexpectedly, Heydrich raised his eyebrows and nodded his head. "So the question remains, Schiller. What is the Reich to do with them?"

"Force them out of Europe. I am certain the Office for Jewish Emigrations can find a suitable location for them. Or perhaps foreign governments will be willing to accept limited quotas?"

"Impossible," said Eichmann. "We have negotiated with foreign governments. South America, North America, Australia, and Asia are not willing to accept shipments of Jews. We have approached the idea of transforming Madagascar into a Jewish colony, but diplomatic negotiations have stalled. Foreign governments are adverse to the notion of receiving Jews."

"Resettling them in Europe is a waste of resources, time, money, and military personnel," I added. "I will also mention the excess traffic placed on the rails because of these transports. If this continues, we will need to increase the transportation budget to repair the stress placed on the railroads, bridges, and crossings."

"And if we can not find a suitable location," posed Heydrich, "What do you suggest we do with the Jews?"

His tone clearly formed my answer. "If we can not find a suitable location for them, I suggest we dust our fields with their ashes. At least their remains will serve the Reich as crop fertilizer."

General Heydrich smiled as his head bobbed up and down in agreement. Himmler inhaled deeply and was also nodding.

"Of all people present in this room," stated the Reichsführer-SS, "You have the most personal experience with the Jews. Your opinions have been heard." He turned to his left. "General?"

Heydrich nodded again. "I think the Office for Jewish Emigrations can find a place for Untersturmführer Schiller."

"And who are you?" asked Himmler. "Oberscharführer Schumann?"

My Junior acknowledged him with a prompt answer.

"And tell us, Mister Schumann," queried the Reichsführer-SS, "How do you feel about the Jews?"

"Bury them all."

"I would like Oberscharführer Schumann to become my personal adjutant," I stated.

"Yes," said Himmler. "I see why."

"Very well," declared Heydrich while stamping and signing the documents. "You will both receive appropriate promotions. Schiller, I am promoting you to the rank of Obersturmführer. Benefits of rank and pay to begin immediately. Schumann, your promotion to Untersturmführer will be considered after a complete review of your service records. You may accompany Captain Eichmann to your new duty posts." He passed the documents to Himmler for his stamp and signature.

We were shown to a spacious office in Eichmann's department that had two desks and a window overlooking a plaza. "I will get you some artwork and flags," said the Captain. "This office is hot in the summer and cold in the winter." He looked at the sparse furnishings. "I will see what I can do. For now, go to the quartermaster on the first floor and draw new collar tabs and patches. He will also give you a housing assignment in Berlin. Fill out the necessary transfer forms and we will see that your field superiors are aware of this. Then send postcards to your family to let them know where you are and how to get in contact with you. Welcome to the RSHA Office for Jewish Emigrations, gentlemen."

While walking to the quartermaster's office I said to Schumann, "Congratulations, Untersturmführer."

"Thank you," he said with a dry tone. "It is my understanding that this is my second nomination for this rank."

I was not aware he knew of the previous appointment that I had denied. "I made that decision with the best interests in mind," I explained.

"Yours, Sir?"

I tersely reminded him that I was his superior officer and that his tone of voice was bordering on insubordination.

Schumann replied, "I accept your decisions, Sir. That is my obligation as a Junior. I may not agree with them, but I accept them. You may rely on my loyalty, Sir."

Despite the uncomfortable nature of that confrontation, I was pleased the matter had been discussed and resolved.

We completed the formalities and were presented with a house on Uhlandstrasse that we were to share. After posting my notification cards to my parents, I was handed my tunic with the new insignia and tabs.

Schumann and I returned to the office to see typewriters and filing cabinets had been delivered along with Party flags and a portrait of Hitler on the wall. Eichmann entered and handed me a small case. I opened it to see the Obersturmführer pips which he affixed to my left collar tab. Stepping back, he and Schumann saluted me with a proud, "Heil Hitler!"

Eichmann took us to his office and we stood before a large map that was affixed to the wall. "The red pins," he said, "denote concentration camps. The blue pins denote ghettos. The question is, how do we effectively transport people from the blue points to the red points?"

"Can we not use the railroads?" I inquired.

"Yes," sighed the Captain, "But many of these rails operate on an alternating directional system."

"Sir?"

"The single rails are open to trains heading in one direction during the day, and then change to accommodate trains heading in the opposite direction at night. If we have to develop a transport schedule around the Reichsbahn, we will never accomplish our tasks."

"What is the premium time to conduct transports?" I asked. "When are the rails most clear from military and commercial traffic?"

"During the days," responded Eichmann. "The Armaments Board wishes to move supply and troop trains under the cover of night because of this business between the Luftwaffe and the Royal Air Force. The Board does not wish to lose trains to the possibility of British air strikes."

"What is the direction most trains follow during the day?"

"East," said the Captain. "But most of our Detainment Facilities are in the north and south of Germany. The ghettos to the east are at full capacity. Globocnik and Frank are demanding a halt on all Jewish cargo shipments being sent to Poland."

"Is it possible to establish more ghettos?" asked Schumann.

"No," said Eichmann, "Not ghettos." He cupped his chin while staring at the map and then looked at us. "Allow me to show you gentlemen something."

We followed him to a chart table on which rested a 1:50,000 scale map of Poland. Certain towns were circled with a red grease pencil. I recognized one as being Oswiecim. "Take a look," he said. "The areas of Oswiecim, Chelmno, Sobibor, Treblinka, Majdanek, and Belzec are being considered as locations for facilities that will be devoted to Special Treatment. We have not received permission from Himmler, Göring or der Führer yet, but I am certain we could sway their decisions with the right reports."

"Excuse me, Sir," I interrupted. "Special Treatment?"

"Yes," he replied, but he did not explain the term. He tapped the circle drawn around Oswiecim. "To date, Auschwitz is the only operational facility. You will go there to perform an assessment of the camp. It is Himmler's wish that you generate a report on the sanitary conditions for the Ministry of Health and Hygiene and project modifications to accommodate a prisoner capacity of 30,000. You will also need to prepare reports for the RAD and Todt Labor Departments; an estimation of building supplies; necessary manpower, and a cost analysis for the general development. I expect the cost will be substantial, so I want you to subtract one third of the total estimate on your final report."

"Excuse me, Sir, but what will happen when the Reich learns the developments will cost more than estimated?"

"I trust they will figure out the budget. Our duty is to see the facility expanded to accommodate Jewish emigrations from Germany and the Occupied Zones." He glanced at his pocket watch and said he could arrange to have us on a train leaving Berlin within the hour. "There is something I should tell you before you go," he said. "While you were in Paris, Himmler appointed Höss as the Kommandant of Auschwitz. I expect you two to put aside your personal differences for the success of these endeavors."

"You can rely on me, Sir."

CHAPTER NINE
AUSCHWITZ

Schumann and I were met at the Oswiecim train station by an SS Hauptscharführer who had been assigned to serve as our driver. My first observation was that the town was isolated in an area of Poland that appeared mostly unpopulated. It gave me a distorted satisfaction to know that Höss had been sent there. As Göth said to me, "Who did you offend to be placed in command of this commode?"

My second observation was that Auschwitz was central to four important railroad lines. One ran south to Korblelów; one southeast to a switching station at Wadowice, and two lines ran east and west just north of Auschwitz.

Northwest of the facility was the town of Katowice which served as a switching station for three additional railroad lines. If the transports were consigned to traveling eastward during optimal hours, Katowice and Auschwitz would be suitable arrival points as both were favorable to accept a high volume of trains from various source locations.

Höss did not exercise the courtesy to greet me inside the camp. Instead he sent his Junior Officer to act as his liaison and serve me as an escort. We started with a tour of the grounds and I learned the population of 10,000 inmates was primarily comprised of captured Polish Army officers, members of the intelligentsia, resistance leaders, and influential Jews.

The facility was in disrepair with little or no improvements made to the prisoner barracks, kitchens, medical ward, and showers. The majority of the improvements budget had obviously been used by Höss to renovate the SS Administration quarters as most of the buildings had new windows, doors, and paint.

There were many problems with the security of the facility including unstable wooden guard towers and ceramic insulators that were either broken or missing from the electrified fence.

Returning to the Administrative complex, a corporal made conversation with the Hauptscharführer and I was told that Höss wished to see me in his office. I prepared myself for an unpleasant confrontation as Schumann and I reported to him.

Höss greeted me casually and stared at the Obersturmführer insignia on my collar. He invited us to sit down and began by saying, "You work for Eichmann now. I can see no logic in perpetuating old grievances. I say, let what happened in the past remain in the past. Let us begin anew."

I returned his handshake and agreed. It was certainly not what I expected from him. Höss shrugged and asked, "How many a code has my facility violated?"

With a smile, I responded, "I lost count. It is my hope that after we discuss them I can count again. Perhaps I will have a lower number then?"

"Is it true?" he inquired. "Do they intend to expand this facility to a capacity of 30,000 inmates?"

"That is Himmler's wish."

"Have you toured the grounds outside the camp? We have found them to be rich with coal, gravel, and other resources." He looked at me with uncertainty. "I know how you feel about Jewish labor, but this is a prime location for industry. Not the small enterprises mind you, but the larger ones. Krupp or I.G. Farben perhaps."

"I do not know if I have the necessary influence to approach I.G. Farben, but perhaps Glücks, Burger, or someone in the Ministry of Economics can author that recommendation."

"Why complicate it?" asked Höss. "This is my facility and I have the right to invite industrialists to establish business here. I do not know how to gain the interest of Krupp or I.G. Farben, but you do."

"I have had negotiations with Krupp at Porajów, but I do not know anyone in the echelon of the I.G. Farben Company."

"What about Göth?" he asked. "I am certain Göth would have a certain level of influence with I.G. Farben."

"This needs to be approved and considered by Glücks, Burger, and the Ministry of Economics," I argued.

"Glücks is occupied with expanding the facilities and building new ones," replied Höss. "If we apply for this through him or the Ministry of Economics it will get tied up in the bureaucracy. However, if we submit the invitation and applications, we can establish this on a private level and state our requirements with the industrial representatives. Once it is all finished, we can present it to the Ministry of Economics, Glücks, or whoever makes the final decision."

I thought about this for some time and realized his suggestion of stating our requirements to the industrial representatives implied personal financial gain.

He inquired, "Do you understand why we may require the advice of Untersturmführer Amon Göth?"

"I want a survey and evaluation of those grounds. I will not telephone or place wires to anyone until I am certain of the resources; the accessibility of them, and the potential amount. I am not going to telephone Göth to have him come here and invest 2,000 Reich Marks to mine 20 pfennigs worth of coal."

Höss was consumed by an expression I had seen before. He was used to getting his way and out here in the middle of this desolation I presumed there were very few people, if any at all, that challenged him.

I was eager to keep the new found peace. "We must not allow greed to be the impetus for a hasty decision. It does not matter who gives us approval. If I.G. Farben decides to come here, you may rest assured that Göth will be involved."

"What if you have Globocnik's approval instead?" he asked. "He is interested in this area. Let him decide. If he recommends that we obtain approval from your superiors we will do as he says."

I agreed to this and placed a telephone call to Globocnik's headquarters in Lublin. Göth answered and when I identified myself, he asked about my health and congratulated me on the promotion and reassignment. I requested to speak to Brigadeführer Globocnik, but Göth informed me his superior was not in the office. I asked for a return call to be placed to Auschwitz and Göth informed me that Globocnik held a very demanding schedule and promised to take up my concerns with him in person. I told him about the natural resources around Auschwitz and our hopes of attracting an industry such as I.G. Farben. I explained that we required surveyors and appraisers to evaluate the area and its resources before proposing the offer. Göth sounded relatively disinterested in the matter but promised he would mention it to Globocnik.

Over the next two days I sorted through inventory and purchase reports to learn the numbers and costs of serving trays, utensils, prisoner uniforms, shoes, bedding planks, medicines and medical supplies, dentistry equipment, food stores, and every last item in the facility. I telephoned several suppliers for each unit and gathered the lowest bids from all. Next I ordered prisoners to measure the barracks and count the screws and nails in each building. I figured the price of glass, thatch; stoves, barbed wire, ceramic insulators, weapons, ammunition and the cost of a garrison triple the size of the current one. I tallied the figures and subtracted one third from the total as instructed. As it was late when I finished, I decided to telephone Eichmann in the morning.

The Captain was excited that I completed the task promptly and efficiently. Despite the subtraction of one third from the total, my figures remained above his projected estimate. He inquired if there were any means by which I could lower the figure by 10,000 Reich Marks and I responded the numbers were final based upon inventory, costs, and that it was totaled using the lowest bids from all suppliers. Knowing it would be tedious, I offered to conduct a secondary evaluation to investigate the possibility of eliminating costs but assured him any change to the total would be minimal.

He appreciated my thoroughness and said another evaluation would not be necessary. He added that the Ministry of Economics and Max Burger would not be pleased with the figures but would have to arrange the necessary funding for the expansion of the camp. He was greatly concerned about budgetary constraints.

Without the knowledge of Höss, I told Eichmann about the possibility of vast natural resources existing around the Auschwitz complex. I hoped that if he dispatched surveyors, I could blame their presence on the idea that Globocnik or Göth had shared the information. In revealing this, I told Eichmann that the Reich could greatly reduce expenses if it made use of the natural resources existing around the complex rather than purchasing or importing supplies.

He inquired about the kinds of resources and I admitted not having an itemized list. However, I told him that Höss spoke of nearly boundless supplies of timber, gravel, stone, ore, lime, and coal. The Captain promised to submit this information to his superiors and instructed me to remain at Auschwitz until he contacted me again.

Höss and I drove to the various deposits of natural resources and the amounts of materials lying on the surface revealed the richness to an untrained eye. Acres of soil were black from the coal beneath the ground and just as many were orange from the deposits of ore. The lime and gravel deposits existed in areas capable of sustaining specific industry and it was then that the thought overtook me that if factories were to be constructed on these sites, Auschwitz could realistically be expanded with subcamps capable of housing 80,000 to 100,000 prisoners. I needed to convince Eichmann to come here and personally see this.

That afternoon I telephoned RSHA Headquarters and the Captain could scarcely believe my assessment. He asked me again and again if I was certain, and I told him the only method to prove my claim was for him to come and see it for himself. Eichmann stated he would convey this information to the Reichsführer-SS on the following morning and contact me with further instructions.

At this time Auschwitz was nothing more than a Detainment Facility of massive proportions. It had long existed as a training center and base for the Polish army and its barracks now served as quarters for the prisoners. While passing time and touring the inmate complex, I learned that several prisoners were familiar with the area from having been trained or posted there prior to the war. I inquired about the resources around the camp and why the Polish had not harvested the materials. A former Lieutenant of the Polish army told me that he knew the land was rich, but the Polish monarchy had prohibited the acquisition of its natural reserves. He could not explain why, and I attributed the decision and his lack of knowledge to the general incompetence of the Poles.

The prisoners were required to work and spent 12 hours each day mending fences, hauling stones, building paved roads, and working the gardens. There was minimal mistreatment of the prisoners in the form of beatings dispensed from guards, but from what I witnessed, this was only in cases when inmates refused to work or disobeyed German authority.

Block 11 existed in the SS Administration complex and had been designated as the Punishment Ward. Prisoners feared this location as the only exit from Block 11 was a direct route to a reinforced and padded wall where they were shot. The padding had been put in place to prevent the deflection of bullets.

The executions at the wall were not an arbitrary matter. Auschwitz contained an elaborate courthouse with Legal Affairs Officers, prosecutors, and a judge. Prisoners who violated the rules of Auschwitz were brought before this tribunal and received a very fair trial. Höss and the subsequent Kommandants argued that the trials often seemed too weighted in defense of the prisoners. In most cases, the inmates were remanded to solitary confinement or subjected to corporal punishment rather than going before the execution wall. Höss complained to me that this demonstrated an aspect of German leniency and toleration for obvious offenders. I regarded this as a contradiction of philosophies for him, because he presented as a proponent of the less harsh temperance promoted by Glücks. Höss admitted that until he had been appointed as the Kommandant of Auschwitz, he never fully agreed with Eicke's institution of a merciless governing of the camps. I could not rationalize this statement because I witnessed his callous administration over the prisoners at Sachsenhausen. In my opinion, Höss had become disillusioned with the prison administration system at a very early time. Rather than tending to each specific problem inside Auschwitz, he preferred to turn a blind eye and permitted his guards to handle these matters with corporal and lethal means.

I agreed with his point that passing violators through the court at Auschwitz with a sentence of solitary confinement or corporal punishment created an element of tolerance and mercy. Höss was disgruntled that Himmler's directives toward the prisoners changed on what he said was a daily basis. He stated that one day Himmler would declare: "We can not work the prisoners for more than 10 hours each day." The following day, Himmler would ask, "Why is production in the camps below quota? The prisoners must work at least 14 hours each day." Himmler said: "We must not beat the prisoners into submission. We must extend German benevolence to rehabilitate them." The next day he would inquire, "Why are the prisoners not adhering to German authority? They must be punished with the harshest means!"

This equaled another prime situation of bureaucrats in Berlin having no real idea of what was happening in the field. I sympathized with Höss but at the same time, realized he had the power to dictate full personal discretion. There was simply no one present at Auschwitz to contradict his will. He was practically cut off from the Reich in southwest Poland and there were no personnel of authority present to monitor his administration. Yet he suffered from the paranoia drilled into our souls by the National Socialist system. Half the time officers could dictate will and discretion without fear of consequences. However, the other half of the time depended on the personal moods of the bureaucrats in Berlin. If they found disfavor in an act committed by a field commander, it might go unpunished due to lack of interest, or you could find yourself before the German High Court pleading for your freedom and life.

I told Höss that in my opinion it was prudent to subject Polish inmates to trials due to international treaties and laws regarding the treatment of Prisoners of War. However, I shared with him that I could find no reason to put Jews before a tribunal. The Jews had been incarcerated because their fundamental existence classified them as enemies of the National Socialist State. In accord with existing laws and Reich policy, any additional violation committed by a Jew after his sentencing was cause for Directive 19. I did not understand why we were not adhering to the codes of our legal system. Why order corporal punishment or solitary confinement? This confusing methodology was a result of the directives that changed daily in Berlin.

Höss was in a very unpleasant mood the next morning and complained that Globocnik had apparently fired his mouth off like a cannon about the natural resources at Auschwitz. When I inquired why he thought this, he told me of receiving notice from Berlin that the Reichsführer-SS, Eichmann, Burger, and Glücks were on their way to inspect the grounds with surveyors and appraisers. I allowed him to believe this as I did not wish to tell him I had informed Eichmann of the reserves.

Moments later his Junior Officer told him that Globocnik was on his way to Auschwitz from Lublin. I maintained my composure and pondered what I would do if it came to light that Himmler's presence was a result of my doing.

By the fate of fortune, the delegations from Berlin and Lublin arrived simultaneously and Höss and I were praised for our proper administration of the situation. Höss still believed that Globocnik notified the RSHA and the truth of the matter was never brought into question between us.

Untersturmführer Amon Göth arrived with Globocnik and though he knew I had informed the RSHA, he exercised restraint. He managed to give me one facial expression that conveyed his displeasure, but later he nodded at me to tacitly say he understood why I proceeded through the proper administrative channels.

During the surveys Göth and I were filling our lunch plates from a sumptuous assortment that had been set out in honor of the Reichsführer-SS. We were alone when he finally said, "You should have trusted me with this."

Before I could respond he added, "I understand why you informed your superiors. I probably would have done the same thing in your position. The RSHA does things differently and I know this. You did what you had to do and I respect that. All hope is not lost. We can yet make this a lucrative experience."

Höss and I were summoned to appear before Himmler. Quietly he said, "This is very encouraging. What are your thoughts for industrial development here?"

"Certainly I.G. Farben and Krupp would recognize the benefits here. Metall Union and Siemens would also do well for us here. The resources are prime materials for armaments construction."

"And the land seems fit for farming, would you not say so?" inquired Himmler.

"Yes, I would, Reichsführer."

That evening we dined in the town and were given a private table inside one of the finer restaurants. Himmler inquired about the management of the potential industries inside the camps and how profits would be calculated.

I recommended that Reich assessors placed a value on each plot of land based upon its market rate plus the estimated worth of its natural resources. The Ministry of Economics could then calculate a table of taxable funds to be levied on each industry that established itself at Auschwitz based upon the initial assessments of the individual plots. As the resources were harvested, the value of the land would naturally decrease, but this could be offset by reassessing the commercial and structural values of the industry upon the plots. The Reich would lease each acre to the industry through bonds drafted by the Ministry of Economics and all titles would be issued by the Reich. Each industry would be required by contract to hire a determined number of RAD or Todt laborers for the construction of its buildings. This would present the Reich with a vested interest in the structures, but all maintenance and operational expenses would remain as the responsibility of the industry owners. These costs would be equalized by the commercial sale of products generated by the corporations at the Auschwitz location.

A standard property management agreement would determine who owned and controlled specific utilities, labor forces, and merchant contracts. The Kommandant of Auschwitz would be ultimately responsible for provisional Reich management of each facility to create collective profit sharing with the SS. As each plot of land would be leased to the industry, the SS Main Department would retain legal rights to oversee operations and production while reserving the right to increase or decrease taxes, amend or institute new laws, and direct every function of industry on Reich property.

The Reichsführer-SS and Eichmann were uncertain of how to respond to this. Max Burger was making written notations about the idea. Höss did not seem pleased by the additional responsibility this would place upon him, and Globocnik appeared unconcerned with such details.

Göth stunned me with his crassness in front of Himmler. "Are you bereft of your God damned senses, Schiller? The labor unions will never accept those terms. Where in hell did you learn about civil law? You will never attract I.G. Farben to this place if you offer them a box of shit in return for coming here."

"His plan is not perfect," said Burger, "But it is a good outline to begin with. Unless you have something more intriguing to offer, Untersturmführer?"

Amon shook his head as if we were all agreeing to make a complicated mistake. "Yes, it is a good outline to begin with, but you will never gain the support of labor union leaders with something like this."

Burger looked at him suspiciously. "I would be careful. Your advocacy for the labor unions could be misconstrued as being in league with them."

"This outline does not contain favorable enticements to industrialists. You are telling them they can come here, but we manage their factories, tax them, and share their profits. How is that good business for them?"

"I am certain the Reich can protect other interests of the industrialists through this plan," said Himmler. "It would not distress me to close down successful factories in other facilities because an industry refused to establish a plant here at Auschwitz."

Burger looked at the Reichsführer-SS. "Make it mandatory to open factories at Auschwitz or close down their plants in other facilities?"

"Of course," said Himmler. "We will not impose these restrictions on plants at other facilities. However, if they refuse to open an additional factory at Auschwitz under these provisions, I am certain we can find the means to make their other contracts void and subject to forfeiture."

I envied Schumann for having the luxury of sitting there without being required to say anything. It surprised me that the Reichsführer-SS was so forthcoming with his intentions to coerce industrialists to establish businesses at Auschwitz. Why, I thought, did we spend countless hours in meetings discussing legal codes, precedents, and civic law when Himmler had the ultimate authority to do as he wished? There was no wisdom to refusing the Reichsführer-SS. Any industrialist who refused Himmler's orders to open a factory at Auschwitz would have all their other assets seized.

Eichmann asked Globocnik, "Have you remedied the situation at the Lublin ghetto?"

"Göth and I were discussing it on the way here," replied the General. "We have a few ideas about how to remedy it."

"I am certain the Blackbird of Porajów has a suggestion," said Göth.

Himmler hovered his fork over his plate and looked at us with a chastising expression. "Gentlemen, we are not on a sports field here. We are officers. Address each other accordingly."

I hoped his admonishment would prevent others from using this title for me. I looked at Göth. "What situation at Lublin?"

"Too many Jews," said Amon. "The ghetto is packed and it is only a matter of time before we have a typhus epidemic on our hands. Most of the residents in the western quarter are already infected with dysentery. It is becoming a real nuisance."

"Have you considered transporting a portion of the population to another ghetto or perhaps a camp?"

Of course," responded Göth. "But where? Frank has put a halt to all transports. There is no place to put these people. The ghetto is not exactly an isolated hold. If a typhus epidemic breaks out inside it will surely spread to the Polish residential areas and the SS administration complex."

Himmler interrupted. "Why have I not been informed of this, Odilo?"

Brigadeführer Globocnik looked firmly at the Reichsführer-SS. "There has been nothing to report yet, Sir. We are investigating precautionary measures to prevent an epidemic."

I did not expect Schumann to speak but he stated, "If you can not resettle the population you will have to liquidate a portion to prevent a potential epidemic."

"Have you considered this as an option, Odilo?" Himmler was acutely matter of fact with his question.

"Frank has advised me to consider that measure as a last resort," answered the Brigadeführer.

Himmler interlaced his fingers and set his hands on the table. He looked at Globocnik as if he was terribly confused by his response. "I have no interest in what Frank advised you to do. I asked if you considered this option."

"Göth and I have discussed the idea, Sir."

"Well," said Himmler with a simple shrug, "If you can not resettle them, you will have to get rid of them."

"How many Jews are we discussing?" asked Eichmann. "A few hundred? A thousand or more?"

"The Judenrat reported twelve hundred ill with dysentery in the western quarter," replied Göth. "That was a few days ago. There is no telling how many more have come down with it since then."

"Enough of this discussion," said Himmler. "Arrange physical examinations for the residents and dispose of the unfit." The

Reichsführer-SS looked at me. "You had experience with this in Poland?"

"Yes, Sir."

"Very well. Return to Lublin with Brigadeführer Globocnik and Mister Göth. You will supervise this action in the ghetto. When it is finished you may return to Headquarters with your reports."

I was put off my meal by those orders. Göth smiled, raised his eyebrows and silently mouthed the word "Blackbird" at me. I wanted nothing to do with the liquidations at the Lublin ghetto. I wanted to return to the comfort of the home I was given in Berlin and quietly work my scheduled hours in the Office for Jewish Emigrations. I was aware my assignment included the role of field liaison, but this particular duty had nothing to do with resettlement. They were ordering me to go to Lublin to kill.

Himmler dabbed his lips with a napkin. "Have any of you gentlemen sampled the desserts here? How is the pie? I am fit for a fresh piece of pie."

Globocnik and Eichmann departed for Lublin in the Staff Mercedes. Göth, Schumann and I were ordered to take the train out of Katowice as our superior officers decided this would give us more time to implement a plan for the partial liquidation of the Lublin ghetto. Schumann kept to himself at the Katowice station. He certainly did not mind being a party to the impending action but he held disdain for Göth.

Amon was a very arrogant and self assured man with a fondness for vulgar jokes, women, cigarettes, and spirits. He was two distinctly different men inside of one body. When in full uniform he was the model SS officer exuding every last one of Eicke's maxims. He was always aware that his uniform and insignia gave him power. He bastardized this authority in many ways such as entering Polish shops and taking whatever he wanted without paying and by stepping in front of civilians waiting in lines to board trains. These were things that no civilized gentleman German would do. However, Göth was an Austrian and I never knew if such behaviors were acceptable in his culture.

I saw the other man inside his body when he settled down in his seat on the train to Lublin. He unbuttoned his tunic and set his hat on a hook and was transformed into the average civil servant. Without his hat and with his tunic wide open, he appeared like a common colleague who could never make decisions over life and death. There was nothing menacing about him in that state. I pondered this for a very long time as I sat across from him in the compartment. He began laughing without any obvious provocation.

"The Blackbird of Porajów," he chortled. "Is that not typical? I do all the work and you get the title and credit." He continued laughing. "The Blackbird of Porajów."

I cautioned, "We are not on a sports field here," hoping my reminder of Himmler's admonishment would end his amusement. Göth laughed harder and slapped the seat. Perhaps he was mildly delirious from exhaustion. It was not as humorous as he believed.

"Was that not perfect?" asked Amon. He became animated and softened his voice to imitate the Reichsführer-SS. "Gentlemen, we are not on a sports field here. How is the pie? I would love to have a piece of pie!" He took himself into a fit of uncontrolled laughter while I stared uneasily out the window. Perhaps I was approaching delirium from exhaustion because I found myself smiling and then laughing with him.

Amon's expression changed and the laughter stopped when he asked, "How do you suggest we do this at Lublin?"

"The same as at Porajów. Ask Brigadeführer Globocnik to order the SS doctors to raise the standards for physical fitness. If he agrees, the prisoners will be marched by and declared fit or unfit. Those marked as unfit will be disposed of."

"What a box of shit!" Göth rubbed his eyes and stretched. "We are talking about twelve hundred or more. Do you know how damned long it will take to hang that many people?"

"Hang them? They were shot at Porajów. I believe this to be the most efficient means for the numbers we are considering."

"Yes," argued Göth, "But Porajów is not part of Frank's domain. Frank will never approve the shootings. The Armaments Board already has him on restrictions. Perhaps you have not heard there is a war going on?"

"What does a war have to do with shooting ghetto residents?"

"You do not understand a damned thing, do you Rolf? The Reich's Blitz on Poland burned up close to two thirds of our damned ammunition stores. Von Rundstedt's folly through Belgium and France did not preserve any shells either. The Armaments Board has ordered no shootings in Central Poland until the munitions factories have restored the reserves to quota. In the meantime, we are permitted to hang them but not shoot them. Is this not organized bureaucratic madness?"

"The Ministry of Health and Hygiene will never permit 1,200 hangings," I said.

"I know this," argued Amon, "And you know this! Do you think Glücks or the Reichsführer will make a concession for this matter? I expect they have already forgotten about it!"

"We must figure on a plan," I said. "Have you heard of any improvements with the mobile gas wagons?"

Göth sighed and stretched out on the seats. "You figure on a plan," he mumbled. "I can not worry about this. It will work itself out when we get to Lublin. It does not matter if we devise a plan. The officers will do it their way in the end."

CHAPTER TEN
THE LUBLIN GHETTO

The Lublin ghetto was much larger than I expected and the only element that set it apart from the buildings all around me was its surrounding wall topped with barbed wire and shards of glass. A gauntlet of three gates served as the entrance to the area. The first was a red and white crossbeam bar that was raised or lowered for traffic. The second was a set of frames strung with barbed wire. These rested on a guiding rail and were pulled opposite of each other to allow access through them, and sandbagged machine gun nests were posted on each side. The third and final gate reminded me of a great set of medieval castle doors. They were approximately 3 meters tall and made of a heavy wood. A great crossbeam locked them in place and it was raised or lowered by a mechanical crank to allow the doors to open outward.

It was cold and rain began to fall as we stood outside the ghetto. Globocnik took us underneath a merchant stall and evicted the Polish proprietor and customers. It was obvious that Globocnik did not have a plan.

Göth shook his head in disgust and said, "Sir, you will need to requisition SS doctors. Twenty perhaps." Amon looked at me for my nod of approval at the number."

"I have six doctors here," replied Globocnik. "Where am I to get fourteen more?"

"There is a hospital northwest at Putawy and one north at Kaztówka. I do not know what else to suggest, Sir. We can start there. You will need to tell them to raise the standards for physical fitness for these examinations."

"I will need authorization from Group D of the SS Main Operational Department," said Globocnik. I assured him that it was not necessary and urged him to tell the doctors what he expected of them. He was pleased to hear I had witnessed medical cooperation at Porajów. He looked at Göth as if Schumann and I were not present. "I mentioned this action to Obersturmführer Scholl. He suggested we hang them in the cellar of the church of Jan Baptysta. It is a large cellar. We may need to dig out part of the floor, but Scholl promises he can hang thirty at a time."

Göth deferred to me with a gesture of his hand and the Brigadeführer looked expectantly in my direction.

"I understand the Armaments Board has placed restrictions on the use of ammunition here, Sir. However, I believe Hauptsturmführer Eichmann can influence the Board to lift the constraints for this action."

He gave me permission to try and instructed Göth, Schumann, and I to perform an inspection of the western quarter of the ghetto, meet with its Judenrat, and determine assembly areas, internal transport points, medical examination stations, and methods for security. Globocnik was firm in stating that we wished to contain the action only to the western quarter.

We entered the Lublin ghetto with a strong force of Order Policemen serving as guards and I immediately observed the peculiar behavior of the residents. Some huddled in packs and carefully pointed out our presence to their companions. A number of them ran off to presumably inform others of our arrival. Most of them watched us cautiously and tried to maintain a normal demeanor while gathered around small heating fires burning in metal barrels.

"The rats have seen the cats," said Göth. "They know something is going to happen. They are not used to seeing officers inside this shit filled burrow."

An elderly man in a frayed coat carefully approached us, and at a distance of approximately four and a half meters he removed his hat and knelt on the cobblestones in the rain with his arms stretched out to each side. We stopped in front of him and Göth asked, "Do you wish to say something you little squeaking rat?"

"Sir, the Judenrat politely requests a meeting with you."

"Yes," retorted Göth. "What in hell do you think I am here for?"

He turned to Schumann and me. "You see this, gentlemen? This is what I have been talking about. This is what they do; coming out here like this to tell us the Judenrat wishes to see us. No, no. We wish to see them. These damned Jews. I am telling you, Schiller, they are not satisfied unless they believe they are controlling us. Even underhanded like this. You see?"

It was cold and raining. I did not have the urge to argue and agreed with him. Göth picked up a small stone and carefully placed it atop the Jew's head. He stepped back, looked at two Order Policemen and said, "If that stone falls, or if he lowers his arms before we return, shoot him."

The Judenrat was crowded with residents lodging complaints but the room immediately became silent and the mob of Jews parted as we made our way into the council room. Five elderly Jews sat there quite nervously as Göth pulled papers from desk drawers and filing cabinets. He did not place them back where he took them from, but dropped each one on the floor. The council members of the Judenrat were not bound to the common practice of awaiting a prompt before speaking to us.

"Sir," said one of the men, "We received no notice of an audit. We are to be given at least two hours notice before an audit."

He apparently believed Göth's inspection of the documents was a formal review. Amon paced back and forth.

"You would have received your damned two hours of notice if this was a damned audit. How many residents of this rats nest are infected with dysentery?"

The Jew pointed to a filing cabinet and received a nod from Amon. He presented a document that Göth glanced at before handing it to me. The reported total had been falsified at approximately 200.

A distant gunshot brought a pause to the room. Amon smiled at me and asked, "Stone or arms?" I shrugged. He gestured to me to continue the meeting.

"Two hundred residents infected with dysentery?" I inquired. "Several weeks ago two inspectors from the Reich Ministry of Health and Hygiene came through here and declared approximately 1,200 residents to be infected. How is it that you report such low numbers?" My contempt for them increased when they did not answer my question.

Göth stood there with his arms crossed and scoffed, "Perhaps Yahweh cured them by means of a celestial miracle."

I extended his derision. "Is that it? Did Yahweh, Jehovah or whatever in hell you heathens call God come down here and cure one thousand Jews by a miracle?"

"Impossible," interjected Schumann. "I imagine lazy Jews pray to a lazy God. I would think Jehovah too much of a sloth to intervene."

The Judenrat elders tried to maintain composure but I saw their rigid posture and curled lips when we outright insulted their pagan theology.

"I will compromise. We will expect 600 infected Jews at the gate in 72 hours. Is this understood?" Göth realized my deception. I would never compromise with the Jews but it was necessary to excuse our current presence in the ghetto. There would be no collection in 72 hours. The liquidation was scheduled for dawn on the very next morning.

"Very well," muttered Göth. "That is why we are wasting time in this damned hole. Why did you send that squeaking rat to us? What in hell do you want now?"

One of the Jewish elders responded there was a problem with the housing assignments in the ghetto. According to his verbal report, the residents were not adhering to the orders of occupying the dwellings allocated to them. Some had willingly traded apartments with others, and some took it upon themselves to relocate to different places when the occupying tenants died. This had created an imbalance for monthly Judenrat census records.

Göth began to speak but I interrupted him. "You have one week to correct this problem or I will burn this disgusting cesspit to its goddamned foundations."

Outside the Judenrat Göth was smiling. "Burn this disgusting cesspit to its goddamned foundations? That was very good, Schiller. Very articulate."

Late in the afternoon we had finished our assessments for the impending operation and retired to Globocnik's headquarters. I telephoned Eichmann and implored him to use his influence to convince the Armaments Board to lift the restrictions for shooting. He gave me permission to proceed with it and promised full support of RSHA Headquarters. The Captain encouraged me to conduct the shootings in a discreet location away from the Lublin area. Göth, Schumann and I studied maps of the local area. There was a forest southeast of Lublin, one northwest at Kaztówka, and another northeast at Poleski. I demanded something closer and we continued to stare at the maps until Schumann pointed to an area that revealed a significant terrain depression. He asked what it was and Göth did not know. When no one in Globocnik's headquarters could explain the mark on the map, Göth dispatched SS soldiers to drive to the location.

They returned to inform us that the depression on the map was an abandoned quarry approximately nine meters deep and with a base circumference of approximately ninety one meters. The guards reported a sloped access road leading into it and confirmed that the location was isolated six and half kilometers west of Lublin. We decided to use the quarry as the execution site.

The next morning we were driven to the ghetto gates before dawn. A mixed battalion of Order Police and SS were assembling under the supervision of officers while an enclosed truck stopped near them. The crew of the vehicle opened the back and fastened chains to barking shepherds and wolfhounds. We noticed lights flashing in the upper windows inside the ghetto and heard whistles and pipes being blown. The Jews were sending signals to each other to announce our presence at the gates.

"It is going to be a very long day," said Amon. "Where are the damned speaker trucks? And where are my damned halftracks? I was supposed to have four halftracks. These damned Jews will die from natural causes before we get this operation started."

Globocnik arrived with the SS physicians and was demanding to know why our soldiers had not yet gone through the gates. Göth was directing traffic and gave the orders to open the gauntlet. Our soldiers trotted into the ghetto wearing greatcoats, steel helmets, and with rifles in their hands. The loud rhythmic crunching of their boots on the cobblestones sounded like a beat pounded out by a drummer. The speaker trucks followed and turned on different streets broadcasting the message: *"Achtung! Achtung! Auf Befehl von der Lublin SS Polizei müssen Sie im Quadrat zusammenbauen!"* Most of the residents obeyed and assembled in the ghetto square as instructed while the Order Police cordoned off the north, east and south quarters.

Many Jews exited the buildings and presented blue work cards to the SS and Order Police with the belief that status as an essential worker would exempt them from the assembly. Our guards were instructed to ignore each *blauschein* waved in front of them. The shrieking of the Jewish women cut through the raised voices of men pleading with our guards and the wailing of the children. The barking dogs, roar of engines, and announcements from the speaker trucks blended with this to create a flood of chaotic sounds. Some of the people were so fearful that they lost their wits and fled. Only Heaven knows where they were running to. This action on behalf of the Jews was considered attempted escape and the guards were within legal rights to shoot them.

The SS searched the buildings in the western quarter but once the Jews realized their belongings were not being scattered and combed through, a subdued state befell them. Our soldiers were searching for people, not contraband.

I saw the council members of the Lublin Judenrat held under guard and they were conversing with Amon. From the gestures, they appeared displeased that we had deceived them. The Jews disrobed in the square and presented themselves to the SS physicians for examination. Those determined to be unfit were not permitted to dress and were told their clothing had to be burned due to lice and infections. They were loaded aboard open trucks with the assurance they were going to a location to be deloused before being admitted to a quarantine unit for seven days of observation. At that time there was nothing in their minds to contradict this. There had been no lethal actions at Lublin until this day.

Schumann rushed into the square and excitedly spoke with the drivers of the trucks. He ran to me and said, "There is a problem at the quarry. Globocnik has ordered you to correct it."

"What kind of problem?"

"I do not know, Sir. But he does not want the trucks to leave the square until it is corrected."

I rode in the gondola of a motorcycle as Schumann drove us to the quarry west of Lublin. Two Blitz Opel trucks were at the bottom with equipment waiting to be unloaded while SS soldiers stood there doing nothing but smoking cigarettes. They discarded them and came to attention when Schumann and I dismounted from the motorcycle. I quickly glanced at each collar tab until I found the Unterscharführer in command. "Why are those trucks still loaded with equipment?!"

"I am begging your pardon, Sir. No one gave us orders of where to set up or told us what we are to do." He looked at the stone walls of the quarry. "This is not a good place for shooting practice, Sir. Do you not think we will get a lot of deflections off the stone?"

Schumann and I exchanged a very troubled glance. I held my poise and struggled to find a way to tell those men what was expected of them. "We have been given orders to dispose of the ill residents of the ghetto. If we do not do this, a typhus epidemic will threaten us all."

"We are to shoot people from the ghetto, Sir?" The question came from a young Schütze. There was an innocence and disbelief in his voice that tested my resolve. The soldiers began to look at each other.

Another soldier asked, "If they have typhus, will we not contract it when they are brought here?"

I could not find a reasonable method to explain the orders and I was not required to. "The people being brought here are susceptible to contracting typhus. We must dispose of the ill to prevent the manifestation of the disease." I pointed to an area where an earthen wall sloped upward. "I want the machine guns put in position facing that mound. The rest of you will form two lines at the base of the access road. Any Jew who attempts to escape must be shot. Any Jew who refuses to stand before the machine guns must also be shot. Each truck will bring twenty people. These groups must be quickly subdued and lined up."

I was stunned by their exuberance. The soldiers began unloading the weapons and setting them into position at the same time a Scharführer appeared at the top of the quarry in a Kubelwagen and shouted, "The Brigadeführer demands action!" I reported that we were ready to receive the trucks.

I sent a detachment of soldiers to the top of the quarry with instructions to receive the Jews calmly and in good spirits. It was important to preserve a tranquil atmosphere for as long as possible. I did not know how the first group of Jews would react when they saw the machine guns and I could not speculate as to how the subsequent arrivals would respond to seeing corpses.

The SS soldiers assigned to this task rationalized it amongst themselves. I overheard one soldier as he spoke to his comrade while unloading ammunition from the trucks. "This is better than roving guard duty," he stated. A soldier near the gun line complained, "The officers should have chosen a day with better weather."

One by one the soldiers looked to the top of the quarry. The first group of Jews straggled down the slope with the SS guards encouraging and reassuring them. The Jews were laughing amongst themselves and making awkward jokes about their nakedness. They reached the floor of the quarry and saw the two MG38 machine guns but had no idea why the weapons were there. I ordered them all to join hands and form a line in front of the guns. Their expressions changed to uncertainty while some covered their mouths and others began trembling. A few believed there was nothing at all to fear and tried to calm the rest.

They obediently walked in front of the guns and stood with their backs to us. I am certain that each then became aware that we were going to shoot them and I was astonished they formed the line so passively. What else could they do but obey? The shame of being naked before a collection of unfamiliar people created a submission for them that numbed their minds, senses, and reactions. The Jews were so debased by being disrobed that none could look us in the eye, and it was much easier for us to kill living creatures that did not so much as acknowledge us.

A Jewish woman began singing seconds before I gave the order to fire. Both gunners expended a heavy volley and the people were transformed into mutilated masses of bloodied meat. A young SS soldier dropped to his knees and vomited from the hideous sight in front of him. A few soldiers were in awe of the gruesome spectacle, and a couple turned their backs to it. The young Schütze staggered to the quarry wall where he pulled off his helmet and let it fall to the dirt. He crouched and began weeping bitterly.

"Stand your posts!" I bellowed. Amon was correct when he stated it was going to be a long day and I refused to tolerate breakdowns in duty and discipline so early into the operation.

The next group was ushered down into the quarry and though they saw the bodies and knew they too were going to die, the reaction was not what I expected.

"Please Sir, let me live! I am from a wealthy family and will give you money!"

"You do not want to kill me, Sir. I will tailor suits for you at the cost of materials!"

"You are making a mistake, Sir. I can sell you land and waive the transfer fees!"

What human being would not offer up all he has in exchange for the precious reward of life?

Even when confronted with the final seconds of their lives the Jews sought to negotiate a transaction. I certainly believed they were beneath primates and equal to vermin. Human beings are capable of exercising a rational thought process to communicate leverage and terms of diplomatic negotiation. Perhaps I would have granted the Jews certain requests and concessions before shooting them had they not haggled for release.

This was the bewildering absurdity of the Jews. They tramped from one country to another using their pagan values as a chisel to fragment the practicalities of civilized Europe. In the early days we accepted, nurtured, and encouraged them. Their icons appeared innocently in our towns and their synagogues emerged in our cities. They refused to learn our language and spoke their filthy heathen tongue in our streets and schools. Our fathers permitted the Jews to perform their unholy dances at our traditional festivals and allowed them to march in our National parades. Our fathers attempted to accept these unfamiliar practices while imparting German culture upon the Jews. But the Jews would not have it. Instead they shoved knives in our backs and charged us a fee for our burial plots.

When the ninth or tenth group was led into the quarry I had no personal objections or moral conflicts with what I was doing. Indeed, it was like eating raw clams on the shell. The first few were very difficult, but the remainder became easier.

The pile of corpses eventually became so high that the bodies of those being shot merely leaned forward against the others. It was impossible for them to fall down any more. At this point I felt nothing emotional and it was somewhat of an epiphany to realize I had become as insensitive as Höss. Because the Reich officially classified Jews under veterinary laws, I adopted the same attitude that I imagined any butcher would have. It is certainly an undesirable duty to slaughter cows in the pen, but it must be undertaken to provide substance for survival. My task was the undesirable slaughter of Jews for the substantial survival of Germany.

We had liquidated approximately 500 Jews in 6 hours. Engineers arrived at the top of the quarry and began placing gas powered generators and searchlights on the perimeter so the shootings could continue through the night. Amon stepped out of a Staff Mercedes and entered the quarry where he stared at the mountain of corpses. He said to me and Schumann, "You two must be hungry and tired. Globocnik has released us for the day. As soon as your relief gets here we can return to headquarters for hot showers and hot food."

We were taking a meal in an aperture near the main dining room when Brigadeführer Globocnik stormed into the room. He violently pulled open the door of a liquor cabinet, took a bottle of spirits and disappeared. No one said a word as we heard his boots thumping up the stairs of his headquarters.

CHAPTER ELEVEN
BLUEPRINTS FOR DESTRUCTION

My plans of returning to Berlin were interrupted by orders from Eichmann that required me to go to the Lodz ghetto to supervise the arrival of 12,000 Jews from Germany, France, and Austria. Despite the number of transports and the volume of freight, the action was successful and with few incidents.

Schumann and I had no sooner entered our office in Berlin to see a large map of Poland pinned to a board. Certain towns and cities were designated by a Star of David and the names of the locations. Opole, Tarnów, Tomaszow, Kraków, Sosnowiec, Kielce, Warsaw, Lodz, Lublin, Radom, Kozminek, Kolo, Glowno, and perhaps twenty or thirty others.

"Welcome back to Berlin," said Eichmann from the doorway. "That is your next assignment," he said in reference to the map. "Each location represents the establishment of a ghetto capable of housing 15,000 to 25,000 residents. In total, these locations will provide temporary living space for approximately 750,000 Jews over the next several years. It is best to think of them as Transit Stations. Once Auschwitz is developed and expanded and several camps like it are established elsewhere in Poland, we will empty these ghettos and deport the residents to the Detainment Facilities. This in turn will provide available living space in the ghettos for new shipments."

He pointed to a ledger on my desk. "The first thing you will do each Monday morning is telephone the SS Chiefs of Police and Security in these towns and cities. They will inform you of weekly fluctuations of ghetto population density. You will subtract these figures from the respective occupational capacity of each ghetto to develop a delivery schedule for the transports. If I am deporting 10,000 Jews from Austria and Germany, you must be able to immediately inform me where I can deliver them. If there is room for all 10,000 at Lodz, I will transport them there. If not, you will inform me where I can deposit increments along a steady eastern route; such as stopping the train to deliver 2,500 at Sosnowiec, then going on to deposit 2,500 at Kraków, another 2,500 in Kielce, and the remaining 2,500 in Radom. This system should give us the advantage to work out the train schedules with the Reichsbahn."

"What if there are not suitable shifts in the ghetto population densities, Sir?"

"Natural attrition, illnesses, food shortages, lack of heat. There will be appropriate fluctuations." He took his eyes away from the map. "May I have your reports from Lublin and Lodz? The Reichsführer is most eager to review them."

Over the next several months Schumann and I developed a color coded system to keep abreast of the situations in the various ghettos. A blue circle around a particular map point indicated available space for 5,000 or more; green denoted 3,000 to 5,000; yellow was used for those capable of containing 1,000 to 3,000; black for up to 1,000; and red indicated a ghetto with no available space.

We also invested much time in the plans for the expansion at Auschwitz. A second camp was to be built on the grounds at Birkenau and it would be administratively designated as Auschwitz II. The development for this site was projected for early 1942 and was expected to spawn a third camp.

During the first months of 1941 I had authored numerous drafts of the contracts the Reich wished to present to the industrialists it required at the original Auschwitz site. Most if not all were returned with instructions to amend this; alter that; add this; and clarify that. By March 1941 all contracts had been approved by Max Burger and were issued to prospective industrialists.

Around this time I was summoned to the office of SS General Reinhard Heydrich. He sat behind his desk and stared at my tunic for a moment. He said, "I sent you through Belgium and France to gain combat experience and you return with nothing but campaign ribbons. By God, Schiller, are you making an effort to offend me?"

I stammered out an apology and assured the General it was not my intention to insult him.

Globocnik was impressed with you at Lublin, Eichmann lauded your efforts at Lodz, and we all know about the transports to Porajów and Struthof. Personally, I am marginally impressed by your endeavors to expand Auschwitz as is the Reichsführer-SS. This is why I sent for you. What are your thoughts about lebensraum in the east?"

"I think we have filled Poland with Jews, Sir. I do not know how the Reich can offer lebensraum to the German people when all the Polish towns and cities have been converted into Jewish prisons."

Very slowly and articulately he said, "Think beyond Poland."

"Russia, Sir?"

"Der Führer is finalizing plans for the invasion of Russia. I am considering who to appoint to Special Action Squads that will follow behind the main combat forces. The responsibilities of these Squads will be to neutralize all enemies in the occupied zones, and I will need a contingent of men with your skills to survey the areas for potential sites upon which we can construct Detainment Facilities and Prisoner of War camps. Much will depend on deporting mass numbers of Jews, Slavs, Ukrainians, and Russians to Poland until the facilities are built. You have knowledge of the rails and transports, and I believe you may be qualified for this task." He rested his elbows on his desk and placed his palms together. "You will still be working for Eichmann, but you will also be working for me. What say you, Schiller? Can I rely on you?"

General Heydrich did not need to ask for your permission, support, or approval. He had the ultimate authority to assign an officer where he deemed fit. The fact that he asked led me to believe he had a plan in mind that had not yet been approved by his superiors. It somehow seemed he required all the pieces to be in place before proposing the idea. As General Heydrich's superiors were Himmler and der Führer, I viewed working for him as an opportunity to advance myself. I told him he could rely on me.

April was filled with countless meetings. Eichmann was not in the office very often and I was left to make improvements to the transport system. Schumann and I continued to collect population density reports from the various ghettos and many times we processed all aspects of deportations to Poland from Germany and the Occupied Territories.

Glücks summoned me to his office quite frequently to discuss business affairs in the various concentration camps. Unique situations were constantly arising in terms of labor, profits, management, and expenses. I referred most of these matters to Burger's assistant for the sole reason of decreasing my personal amount of duties.

Between these affairs I found myself in SS General Heydrich's office to meet with his potential candidates for the Einsatzgruppen Squads. I had no influence on deciding who the General selected, but we used these forums to discuss potential scenarios in Russia. The conversations often centered on reports that the Soviet NKVD was murdering hundreds of thousands of Ukrainians who opposed Stalin. The General agreed with der Führer that a German invasion would be viewed as liberation from Soviet oppression. He also spoke of Bolshevism and the evil Jewish influence in Russia, and believed the Ukrainian Nationals would greatly assist German forces with anti Jewish pogroms. The NKVD constructed massive prisons and work camps, and SS General Heydrich was interested in securing these locations to convert them into German Detainment Facilities and Prisoner of War camps.

During the second week of May I was transferred to Zamošc on the eastern border of Poland. However, my orders first took me to Auschwitz to report on the progress of the construction.

Höss told me that Göth would come to the facility whenever time allowed and that he was usually seen following the engineers from I.G. Farben like a stray hound.

I.G. Farben had agreed to build a factory at Dwory and Auschwitz was to provide 1,000 prisoners to assist with the construction. For the most part, the construction was on schedule and I attributed this to Amon's supervision. I realized the sooner it was built and operational, the sooner Göth would be enjoying illegal profits.

Höss was concerned about Amon's involvement in financial schemes. We had all previously discussed and considered a plan to share monetary gains, but major industries had attracted more attention from the Ministry of Economics. Höss was already meeting with auditors and confided that direct involvement in Amon's plans was a venture drenched in risks. The Kommandants of all facilities were being scrutinized by auditors and Höss was very clear that improprieties would eventually be discovered. He was currently debating the idea of confronting Göth or reporting him to Globocnik.

If Amon was investigated, Höss would subsequently be too. All things taking place at Auschwitz were the responsibility of the Kommandant.

I accompanied the Kommandant on a 10 kilometer drive to the Buna synthetic rubber plant that had been established by I.G. Farben. It was the first functional factory opened by the company on the Auschwitz grounds and Höss was eager to show it to me. I was not interested in the tour of the plant, primarily because I had no understanding of the manufacturing process and because the odor of synthetics was atrocious. Production was slightly below quota, and the representative from I.G. Farben explained this was due to initial operation faults. He lucidly stated that all businesses undergo these problems during the first three months of operation.

While finishing my reports at the main facility, I was distracted by voices and vehicles in the administrative complex. It was discernible that the voices reflected a tone of panic and anger, and I exited the office and walked to Block 11. Kapos were dragging a corpse from the Block into the street and I asked an SS guard what had happened. He explained that several prisoners had been taken to the Block as retaliatory punishment for the escape of a comrade. The guard informed me Höss had ordered that no food or water was to be given to the prisoners until they revealed how the escape was planned and carried out. Either none of the prisoners knew, or if they did know, refused to talk. All had starved to death and the body being dragged out was the prisoner who had held out the longest.

Höss was standing nearby and I approached him to demand an accounting of the situation. Corporal punishment and solitary confinement were considered acceptable and legal penalties, but I was concerned about depriving inmates of food and water. This matter could certainly become a subject of Red Cross and international investigation.

"Are you earnest?" asked the Kommandant. "No one knows this place exists." He openly admitted this method of punishment had been used before and frankly stated he had no plans to revoke it. "What will it matter?" he inquired. "Has your office not informed you of what is to begin here in the coming months? Special Treatment. That is the intended purpose of this place."

I heard Eichmann use this term before but my superior never

explained it. I had a good idea of what the euphemism meant and asked Höss for clarity.

He smiled and shook his head from side to side. "Are some things so secretive that your superiors keep them from you? The Reichsführer-SS has entered negotiations with the companies of Hütte, Schlesische, Hoch and Tiefbau, and Lenz. Do you know what they are to build here? Crematories. It appears that Topf and Sons Company will construct the gas halls that we will use to fill the new crematories. Special Treatment is what it is to be called. The Jews will be taken to the gas halls for Special Treatment."

"Gas halls?"

"That is what they are discussing. My fellow Kommandants have been complaining about the effects firing squads have upon their men." He looked at me for a moment and shrugged. "I do not suppose the Blackbird of Porajów needs an education on the effects of firing squads."

I certainly did not. I was aware that two of my guards at Porajów had emotional breakdowns just days after the actions in the forest. I received word later that one of the afflicted men, a 19 years old Schütze from Heidelberg, broke a drinking glass in the hospital and used it to cut his throat. I also saw the young man at Lublin who walked to the wall of the quarry and wept.

In spite these events, the alleged discussion of gas halls seemed improbable. "Carbon monoxide poisoning is very unreliable," I said.

"The experts seem to disagree with you, Schiller."

I arrived at Zamošc during the first week of June and was assigned to the Police unit of EK5, Einsatzgruppen C. This Group was under the command of SS Standartenführer Otto Rasch. There were several RSHA administrators attached to the main unit and most of us were unclear as to what our roles with EGC would be. Rasch's element was linked with Army Group South and our designated area of operations was soon to be the southern and central Ukraine.

By now there was no secrecy covering the Reich's plans to invade the Soviet Union and none of us knew what to expect. Our Commanders constantly reminded us that Russia had refused to sign the latest draft of the Geneva Convention and this meant there would be no standard rules regarding warfare. Der Führer's *Commissar*

Order had been explained and we had clear directives that all Russian Political Officers were to be executed on sight. Our unit was told that the Russian soldiers were inhuman barbarians who would take great pleasure in torturing and mutilating us if we allowed ourselves to be captured. This warning provided the personal policy for each man that surrender was not an option.

CHAPTER TWELVE
OPERATION BARBAROSSA

O n 22 June 1941, the Fatherland opened its campaign against the Soviet Union. The skies were filled with squadrons of our planes heading east and the ground around us shook from the percussion of outgoing artillery. EGC received orders to stand down and we waited in the rear areas while the Wehrmacht crossed the borders.

Each hour seemed eternal. We gathered around field radios to listen to the units communicating at the front. We had taken the Russians by surprise and our Luftwaffe had succeeded in destroying Soviet aircraft still in hangers and on the fields. Resistance was minimal and the initial reports claimed the Ukrainians were welcoming us as liberators.

Late that evening we were given orders to mobilize and the unit made final preparations to join the fight. However, the orders came to stand down again. We were disappointed but stowed our field gear and regrouped around the radios.

Near midnight we again received orders to assemble and once more our advance column made ready. After an hour or two the orders were cancelled and we paced in the darkness. We listened to the shelling in the distance and heard the roar of propellers overhead. It was a very long night.

On the following morning, the first casualties from the Russian front were brought across the border to Zamošc. The wounded were trucked or carried into our area and separated in rows depending on the seriousness of their wounds. I saw boys and men missing fingers, feet, arms, and legs. Some had such large holes in their bodies that the medics had used leather trouser belts and rucksack straps to keep the innards from spilling out. I saw men and boys so badly disfigured that their own mothers and fathers would never recognize them. One soldier had been burned so badly that his tunic melted to his body and his leather helmet liner fused to his head. Another man sat quietly while packing rags and bandages against the roof of his mouth. His lower jaw had been completely torn away and his white upper teeth glistened with blood.

There was an abundance of medicines but a shortage of doctors. We all did what we could. I helped to distribute morphine and sulfur powder but this was not enough. Hundreds of men died while waiting for treatment, ambulances, and transport planes. This was how we lived for the next three days. On 25 June, EGC received our orders to cross the border into the Ukraine.

Our objective was the city of Lutsk, which according to information from the Wehrmacht, had been captured and secured. Our vehicles first rolled through the town of Ustyluh where we passed mobs of Ukrainian Nationalists rejoicing at our arrival. They threw flowers at us and ran to the sides of the road to hand loaves of bread and bottles of wine to our soldiers. The column braked in the town of Lokachi just west of Lutsk.

Some elderly women in babushkas fell to their knees and looked skyward with tears of joy while their folded hands bobbed up and down with thanks. Others knelt before us and hugged our legs and stroked our boots. They too sat back and looked up at us with hands clutched together in gratitude. The young women gave us necklaces fashioned from flowers and wheat stalks, and the men presented us with lambs, goats, food, and jewelry. Children climbed on our vehicles and marveled at the great machines of war. Many of our soldiers removed their helmets and placed them on the heads of the children.

A group of four or five Ukrainian Nationalists approached an SS Scharführer and began to chatter in the native language. The Scharführer summoned a Corporal who intently listened to the men before looking around and seeing me. He brought the small delegation over and explained that the men told him the Soviet NKVD had come through Lokachi on the night of the German invasion. He related how the Soviets rounded up the village school teachers, politicians, doctor, census taker, tax collector, and priest. According to the account, the Soviet soldiers marched the members of the local intelligentsia into the nearby woods and shot them. When I asked why they would do this, the Corporal translated and one of the men explained. It was said that the NKVD had orders to liquidate all members of the Ukrainian Nationalist intelligentsia because of Stalin's fear they would collaborate with invading German forces to retaliate against Soviet political and social oppression.

I presented this information to the commander of EK5, Sturmbannführer Mohr. He found this to be very curious and consulted with Standartenführer Rasch. I was given orders to investigate this matter and the Ukrainian Nationalists escorted me and a small contingent of SS guards into the nearby woods.

We found eleven bodies approximately 20 meters inside the forest. Most had fallen facedown and the bullet holes in their backs were barely visible beneath layers of fly eggs. The Ukrainian Nationalists pointed to each body and identified it with a name and told us what position the person formerly held in the Lokachi village.

I reported the gruesome discovery to Mohr and he insisted on visiting the site with an SS photographer. Headquarters believed the scene would provide an excellent depiction of Soviet atrocities that could be used as propaganda to incite the Ukrainian people. Afterward, I stood near Rasch who was communicating on a field telephone with other Einsatzgruppen commanders. Our find was not unique. Reports from SS and Wehrmacht units along the border and inside the Ukraine confirmed the discovery of tens of thousands of people murdered by the Soviet NKVD. Rasch conducted many different conversations before he ordered an assembly of officers.

We met in a grove of trees away from the main body of soldiers. Rasch told us that Berlin suspected we would find these horrors in the Ukraine, and Headquarters issued a statement that field intelligence reports confirmed local Ukrainian Jews had assisted the NKVD by identifying members of the Nationalist intelligentsia. It was said the motive for this was Jewish greed and that the Jews had struck a bargain with the Communists in which they would remain free from Soviet sanctions in exchange for assisting the NKVD. Rasch said we were to inform the local people at Lokachi of this and remain passive to any pogrom it might incite.

I believed the statement as the Jews were expert turncoats when it came to preserving themselves and their interests. The SS Corporal stood on the back of a tank and translated this information to the Ukrainian villagers. The people did not seem to be astonished, but rather pleased that the announcement confirmed their suspicions. Voices mixed in the crowd and then erupted into angry demands for justice. Many of the village Jews skulked back inside their hovels and closed the doors while the remainder adamantly objected to the accusations.

The Ukrainian Nationalists looked at us with inquisitive eyes. They were on the edge of vigilante justice and wondered if we would intervene or take matters into our hands. Rasch gave orders for his officers and soldiers to follow him 15 meters away into a field and the Ukrainian villagers realized our indifference to the matter.

Rakes, shovels, and pieces of firewood were seized by the Ukrainians and used as weapons to beat the Jews to death alongside the road. The people forced open the doors of the Jewish houses and dragged their enemies onto the doorsteps where they violently clubbed the life from them. No Jewish man or woman was spared. In the 30 or 40 minutes of chaotic carnage, perhaps 25 Jews were slain. The Ukrainian Nationalists entered a passionate debate regarding the fate of the Jewish children. The local women advocated for the sparing of their lives and many of the men agreed. The children had been rounded up behind the last Blitz Opel truck in our column. They stood there confused and crying with their hands in the air. The SS soldiers began encouraging the Ukrainian Nationalists to shoot them.

A soldier yelled, "Those misbegotten swines will grow up and take revenge on you unless you shoot them now!"

Another soldier shouted, "If you allow them to live, those mongrels will run into the arms of the NKVD and tell lies about you!"

A stocky Ukrainian approached our troops and pointed to the MP38 machine pistol one was carrying. The soldier pulled the charging handle and looked at me and my fellow officers for approval. None of us objected and he gave the weapon to the man. The burly fellow walked to the side of the road, crouched on one knee, and expended the entire cartridge of bullets into the Jewish children. Some of the local men and women fell to their knees from this horror, but most of them radiated expressions of resolute satisfaction. This had been an appalling experience, but the locals regarded it as inculpable justice.

Rasch gave the orders to resume the advance at which the subdivisions of EGC separated and moved toward different objectives. EK5 departed on the road to Lutsk. Now and then our vehicles would pull over and come to a complete stop, or travel on the shoulders of the road to allow our returning medical convoys unobstructed passage. The least wounded leaned out of the trucks and shouted encouraging words to us as we headed toward the front. "To the east in '45," I thought. We had arrived four years ahead of our projected schedule. This was unnerving after I learned how we expended two-thirds of our ammunition stores during the Polish and French campaigns. I could not imagine der Führer would take us onto a battlefront without the necessary arms, munitions, and equipment. I rationalized that Hitler and his High Command would never do such a thing.

The outskirts of Lutsk had been badly damaged during the battles, but the city remained mostly intact. I was still uncertain of our purpose as a unit and believed we were there to bring Occupational Law, order, and stability to the area. I thought our first task would be to review the local prison and the surrounding areas for evidence of natural resources to determine sites where Detainment Facilities and Prisoner of War camps could be constructed. Within one hour after arriving at Lutsk, I was made cognizant of the real purpose of the Einsatzgruppen. We had indeed been sent to the Ukraine to determine construction sites for facilities and camps, but this was not our chief priority. However, law, order, and stability were to be established with brutal force. The real purpose of our deployment in the Ukraine was to arrest and deport a large portion of its Jewish population as forced labor units. We also had standing orders to liquidate all Jews we did not deport.

No one was quite certain how to exercise these orders at first. Headquarters specifically prohibited us from harming the Ukrainian Nationalist population and from meddling in their local affairs. They were very receptive to the burgeoning propaganda that the Jews had an active role in handing over Ukrainians to the NKVD. As long as they believed this, they were instrumental in configuring pogroms against the Jews. This well conceived plan, and the success of the propaganda, paved the roads with favorable local attitudes toward our subsequent actions against the Jews in the Ukraine.

The local inhabitants of Lutsk took us to a schoolhouse to see how the NKVD had nailed the former teachers to the walls of the classrooms. Our final stop was the cellar of a cathedral where several Catholic nuns and priests had been beheaded and mutilated. It was explained to us that the clergy were Italians who recently received approval to come to Lutsk to establish a mercy hospital.

The Ukrainian Nationalists were asking if we could confirm rumors that Jews had assisted the NKVD with the brutal massacres. Sturmbannführer Mohr stated the reports had been substantiated and the locals clamored for justice. Junior Lieutenant Schumann was greatly satisfied to see the bloodthirsty mob calling out for vengeance against the Jews. While the senior officers discussed actions at Lutsk, I made my way to the Communications Post to contact RSHA Headquarters in Berlin. Eichmann was not in his office and this was the first time I spoke directly to Franz Novak. He was equally surprised and pleased to hear about the local reaction to the anti Soviet propaganda and encouraged me to bolster these rumors among the Ukrainian population. Novak inquired about the location of railroad lines leading into and out of Lutsk and requested a general assessment of buildings that could be potentially converted into holding facilities. He took the information but it did not seem promising that anything productive would be done with it. Novak ordered me to take command of the Gestapo units of EK5 and work with the Ukrainian Nationalists to gather a list of local enemies. I was further instructed to search out intelligence documents, weapons, and explosives.

A Ukrainian with the surname of Zabolotnyj was most enthusiastic about assisting me and his use of the German language was most proficient. Inside the Lutsk police station he told me that many Russian soldiers and a few members of the NKVD had attempted to pass themselves off as locals by giving up their uniforms for civilian garments. These saboteurs were harassing and threatening German forces with sniper fire and timed explosives.

Zabolotnyj revealed dozens of names of Jews, Communist and Bolshevist sympathizers. It soon became obvious that he and his comrades were also using the opportunity to name people they had personal differences with in an attempt to settle old scores.

I demanded that all rabbis in Lutsk be escorted to their respective synagogues to retrieve the census records for their congregations. The rabbis were then brought to the police station so I could review this information, generate lists for arrests, and interview them.

The first congregation census contained approximately 1,000 names and known addresses for Jews in Lutsk. I entered the interrogation room where the rabbi had been tethered to a chair. He wore a black suit and a wide brimmed black hat, and a ragged dark beard hung from his chin and touched his chest. The rabbi sat there calmly as I ordered the interpreter to ask him his name.

"That will not be necessary," said the rabbi. "I studied the German language at the University at Hamburg."

"How many members of your congregation have been formerly convicted of crimes?" I inquired.

He shrugged and babbled what he thought to be some form of a clever and profound Jewish riddle. "Men convict men, but only Jehovah may judge them."

I repeated my question with diminishing patience.

"Are you here to collect those who have committed transgressions in the past?" he asked. "Have they not already paid restitution for erroneous acts by being sentenced and shamed? Why do you wish to punish them again?"

"Save yourself from the pain," said the Gestapo interpreter.

I handed the census records to the rabbi and asked the question for the third and final time. "How many members of your congregation have been formerly convicted of crimes?"

The rabbi looked at the list for a moment and then at me. "I am sure I would not know," he answered.

I briefly studied him with anger coursing through my veins. I thought to myself, why must we do this through difficult means? You stupid, Yid! Why do you insist on making me hurt you?

"Very well," I said calmly. The interpreter followed me out of the room and we discussed the various tools we could use to extract the information from the rabbi. We dispatched a soldier to collect a hammer, pliers, and a rod from the Engineering Corps.

Schumann, the interpreter, and I entered the interrogation room with these devices and the rabbi locked his gaze on them. He abruptly turned his head and stared up at the ceiling as if looking away would somehow numb him.

Once more I asked, "The census, rabbi?"

When he did not reply I pulled my bayonet from its scabbard, grabbed his beard, and sawed it off. The rabbi reacted with polite indifference and was cautious not to exude an expression of defiance for fear it would bring about the rod, hammer or pliers. I had hoped that removing his beard; that symbol of Jewish wisdom, would bring him enough humiliation and force him to cooperate.

Schumann grabbed him by the ankle and pulled the shoe off the rabbi's left foot. He took the hammer from the interpreter, pulled his bayonet and placed the tip of it above the Jew's foot. Schumann raised the hammer and shouted, "The criminals, Jew!" Following the rabbi's refusal to answer, Schumann struck the top of the bayonet with the hammer and impaled the Jew's left foot to the wooden floor. The prisoner gasped inwardly with wide eyes, but let out no scream. The Junior Lieutenant removed the shoe from the other foot and took my bayonet from me.

The interpreter looked at the rabbi and calmly said, "End this. Tell us what we want to know. Why endure this pain for criminals?"

Schumann asked the question again but the Jew defied us once more. His right foot was promptly impaled to the floor and this time the rabbi screeched in an ungodly fashion.

I tapped the list and asked, "Perhaps you know of a few criminals now?" The rabbi began to relent but stopped himself and shook his head in the negative.

Schumann brought the hammer down and smashed several toes on the rabbi's right foot which brought out a primordial scream from the Jew. The Junior Lieutenant bashed the prisoner's foot two or three more times.

"Perhaps he needs a moment to reconsider this," I said. We exited the room and discussed a new strategy for the interrogation.

"He is obviously concealing information," said Schumann. "For what other reason would a Jew endure this?"

"Stubborn stupidity," I replied. "The Jews gain a virtuous pleasure by defying us."

"Hang him before his congregation and we shall see who begins talking," suggested Schumann.

The Gestapo had seized and arrested 16 rabbis in the city of Lutsk. I used a field radio to contact my unit commander and suggested this plan to him. He was not opposed to it, but suggested I contact Standartenführer Rasch for authorization.

I explained the situation to Rasch and informed him of my intentions. I was told that EGC had been approved to operate with the complete personal discretion of its officers and that I did not require his permission.

"Sir," I inquired, "Do I need to make applications for the Directive 19?"

"No," replied Rasch. "Just carry out the action."

"Sir?"

"You heard me, Obersturmführer. You do not need my authorization or a formal Directive 19 order. You have complete discretion as an officer of EK5. Do you understand this?"

"Ja, wohl."

I remembered seeing an ancient manor house on the eastern side of the city when we approached. It had a large enclosed courtyard with massive oak trees growing in its center and I determined this would be a suitable place to execute the rabbis.

Schumann and I walked outside the building and stood there in silence for quite some time. The Order Police and KRIPO were hauling Jews and saboteurs up the stairs and into the station. The Junior Lieutenant asked the question aloud that I was silently pondering.

"What does this have to do with Jewish Emigrations, Sir?"

I did not know. Nor did I understand being appointed to a respectable office with specific responsibilities only to find myself contemplating the hanging of rabbis on the Eastern Front. I clearly understood the purpose of the Einsatzgruppen. These were mobile execution squads. They were designed to kill. Nothing more, nothing less.

Sturmbannführer Mohr arrived at the prefecture and made his way up the stone stairs to where Schumann and I were standing.

"Do you have nothing better to do than stand here? Did you not report a plan to execute 16 rabbis?"

"Yes, Sir."

"Has this been completed?"

"No, Sir. Our plan is to conduct the executions in front of the congregations."

"What in hell is wrong with you, Schiller? We are not hosting a circus here for spectators. Hang those bastards in an open area. Along the main street or in the plaza! You will convey the same message if you hang them in a public place. Now do it and then get up to the local prison!"

"Ja, wohl!"

I passed the orders to my subordinates and the rabbis were taken to the main street of Lutsk and hanged from the gaslight poles. Schumann and I saw this as we drove along the avenue on our way to the municipal prison compound.

The Lutsk jail was atop a winding road outside the southern border of the town. Wheat fields were on opposite sides of the lane, and for just a moment while driving through; there was a moment of tranquility removed from the war. This comfort vanished as we approached the open gates and saw SS soldiers standing over a multitude of corpses.

We were saluted as we stepped from the vehicle and one of the troops reported, "Victims of the NKVD, Sir."

"Has Rasch or Mohr been informed of this?"

"Yes, Sir. But they have not been here to see it. There are more bodies inside in the cells, Sir."

Schumann and I toured the prison and estimated the NKVD had murdered 800 Ukrainian Nationalists. The Russians had locked Ukrainians in cells and executed them. Many had been machine gunned in the confined quarters. In other cells it appeared primed grenades had been passed through the bars. There were also several cells where liquid accelerants had been poured through the bars and set aflame.

I told the soldiers to set demolitions in one of the wheat fields to blow two large holes to serve as mass graves. The Jews of Lutsk would carry the Ukrainian bodies to one of the burial pits. When finished with this task, the Jews would enter the second hole to be shot.

So the necks of the rabbis had been stretched along the main street. At that time, and in my opinion, they deserved it. The Jews were a certified enemy of the Reich, but what malice existed between Jews and Ukrainians? Every detail at Lutsk was in perfect alignment with the German propaganda I had heard for years. The Jews claimed to be dispossessed and used this status to gain the benefits of charity and social assistance. They were exempt from enlisting in armies, took advantage of communal programs, and paid less for housing and food than all good citizens. Germans, Austrians, and Czechs paid into a poor tax to sustain the Jews. They claimed no allegiance to any government, nor did they side with any political faction until their hides were threatened. When faced with sanctions and penalties, the Jews chose the alliance of the party with the strongest representation. When all things are finished and when the dust blows away, the Jews gradually return to their dispossessed status, claim exemption, and again stretch out their palms for free coins.

My search for intelligence documents, weapons, and explosives was moderately successful but it generated a list of names beyond what I expected. In an effort to please my superiors I made certain nothing was overlooked. Within one week I had collected the names of approximately 2,500 people including Jews, Communists, Bolshevists, and to my dismay, Ukrainian Nationalists. During a city wide sweep conducted by our KRIPO, SD, and SS units, an additional 7,000 people had been arrested.

We held meetings late into the night to arbitrate the dispositions of some of the people we had arrested. Headquarters was absolutely clear in that we were to take all necessary steps from preventing the implication of Ukrainian Nationalists in subversive plots. However, it was impossible to overlook the facts regarding some of the locals who had been arrested. On one hand, it could be argued that the Ukrainians stored weapons and explosives to counteract the NKVD, but this did not entirely meet logical reasoning. The NKVD had been thorough in eradicating its enemies, and if the Jews were indeed helping the Russians to identify them, the local Ukrainians would not have escaped Soviet arrest.

When I telephoned Franz Novak at the Berlin Office for Jewish Emigrations, he was astonished that EK5 had arrested 9,500 people. I informed him that my assessment of the situation included a reasonable plan to march the prisoners to the railroad stations northwest at Kivertsi, and southeast to Horokhiv and Sokal. Lutsk also had a railroad station but the Wehrmacht had seized control of it with Reichsbahn sanction to transport combat supplies and soldiers to the east. Resource reports confirmed 55 freight wagons in the vicinity and with the occupational capacity of 125 units in each carriage; I estimated we could deport 6,875 prisoners. This would result in a balance of 2,625 unmovable units, and I expected the Office for Jewish Emigrations would authorize Directive 19 for them.

Novak was very hesitant to make a decision regarding this matter. He instructed me to conduct arbitrations for the Ukrainian Nationalist prisoners and promised he would have an answer for me by the end of the following day.

It was quite impossible to conduct a fair arbitration in the cases of the Ukrainian Nationalists. Except for census, employment, and the arrest records, I did not have any pertinent information about the people I was interviewing. I sat at a desk in an office inside the Lutsk police station as the people were brought before me one by one. I watched for physical signs that they were lying to me. Wringing hands, steepling the fingers, crossing the arms, gesturing in an animated manner; all these things were indications of potential lying. I understood der Führer's intentions for the Ukraine at this time and realized the people before me were classified as *untermenschen.* They were not as low or despicable as the Jews, but nonetheless, the Ukrainians were inferior and served no other purpose than a labor force for the Reich. With this in mind, it was easy to adopt the attitude that it was not my responsibility to arbitrate each case in their favor. It was their responsibility to provide reasonable assurance that they were not a threat to German forces or Reich ambitions. If they convinced me of this, I released them. If not, they were put aboard the transports.

Late in the afternoon on the following day, Novak telephoned and ordered me to arrange the transports of 6,875 prisoners to the Bialystok, Lodz, and Kraków ghettos. The final transport would ship 1,000 people to the Auschwitz facility. The remainder of the prisoners were subjected to Directive 19 at the discretion of EK5.

I dispatched Schumann to the Kivertsi railroad station to oversee the transports from that location and I ordered an SS Hauptscharführer to supervise the process at the Horokhiv station. A contingent of SS and Order Police accompanied me to Sokal. We would maintain contact with each other during all stages of this operation. It was very important to me that I impress my superiors at Headquarters as this was the first major action I had been assigned in the field.

When I arrived at Sokal, a Class C locomotive was backing up and pushing five freight wagons against a bumper. The SS enlisted Ukrainians to serve as kapos and each of them was given an armband, hat and truncheon. They formed a long line across from the freight wagons and this human chain curved to cut off an escape at the head of the train. It was hours before we would receive the first delivery of prisoners to be loaded aboard the wagons, but the kapos were very devoted to this duty. These people were a humorous lot to me as there was no consistency in their appearance. They were obese, thin, short, and tall, though each one of them had a most stern expression on his face.

The Class C locomotive arrived twice more to deliver a total of 18 freight wagons and I used a field radio to contact the prefecture at Lutsk to inform them I was ready to receive the prisoners. I addressed my soldiers while waiting for the buses and trucks to arrive. I told them we would begin loading the freight wagons starting at the front and working our way back. The prisoners were to be told they were being resettled in Poland to protect them from Soviet retaliation, and that they would receive housing and work assignments as Reich laborers. Any prisoner who attempted to escape or who was not cooperative with the boarding process was to be seized, taken into the station storehouse and shot. I explained to the men that it was imperative to maintain the pretense that the people were being deported as a labor force.

The Hauptscharführer at Horokhiv telephoned me to report the Wehrmacht had seized 10 freight wagons previously allocated for the deportations. While trying to contact the officer responsible for this, Schumann reported that the Class A locomotive designated to tow his freight wagons out of Kivertsi had been rerouted to Dubno by the Wehrmacht. The Class A locomotive assigned to my transports had just arrived and was coupling with the freight wagons.

I convinced a Wehrmacht Supply officer to return the 10 freight wagons and had them delivered to Horokhiv. The Class A locomotive promised to Schumann had already departed for Dubno and there was nothing we could do except await its return to Kivertsi.

Novak telephoned me and requested a status report just as the boarding process at all three locations began. I told him we had encountered difficulties with the Wehrmacht in that freight wagons and locomotives had been reassigned, but overall the process was on schedule and I anticipated the transports from Sokal and Horokhiv would be underway within hours.

He was adamant that all three transports were to depart simultaneously because the Reichsbahn insisted all railroad switches were to operate with directional coordination. There were too many supply and troop trains on the rails to restructure the flow of traffic and this made it crucial that all three prisoner transports departed at once.

To facilitate this order I was forced to await the return of the locomotive from Dubno to Kivertsi. My troops began loading the prisoners into the wagons at Sokal and this was completed with the unpleasantness of only two or three shootings. The Hauptscharführer reported the success of his loadings at Horokhiv and I telephoned the Reichsbahn to learn the whereabouts of the third locomotive. The train had been delayed indefinitely because of damage on the Dubno rails caused by partisans.

It was a very hot July day and the Ukrainian kapos at the Sokal station became distressed when the prisoners began complaining they could not breathe inside the freight wagons. An Order Policeman inquired if we should open them to provide ventilation, but I ordered him not to do so. I feared that opening the doors would create a terror stricken exodus of the prisoners. Within hours the suffering inside the freight wagons reached a level of madness and hysteria, and the prisoners began banging on the insides of the carriages and pleaded for release. Diabolical screams came out of the wagons and we assumed the prisoners were tearing each other apart in a frenzy of dementia. The Hauptscharführer contacted me about a similar encounter at Horokhiv.

"Sir, the prisoners are suffocating," he said. "I am requesting permission to open the wagons until we can get these trains moving."

"Permission is denied," I responded. "You will keep them locked up."

Within an hour or two the screaming had stopped inside the freight wagons. If it was not for soft moaning and choking gasps, I would have thought all the prisoners were dead. Five hours later the locomotive arrived at Kivertsi and I contacted the Reichsbahn for permission to get the transports underway. I was later informed that of the 6,875 prisoners on the three transports, less than half survived the journey to Poland.

At the prefecture I was shown a series of orders issued by SS General Heydrich that had just reached the forward Einsatz Units. According to the directives, Communist politicians; party officials of all levels; and members of the central, provincial, and district committees and people's commissars, were to be immediately executed. Furthermore, Jews in the party and state apparatus; and other extremist elements such as saboteurs, propagandists, snipers, assassins, and agitators were also marked for immediate liquidation. The order affecting the "Jews in the party and state apparatus" included all the Jews in the Soviet Union.

A meeting of officers was held and Rasch called upon each one of us for situational reports in the Occupied Zone. The 2,625 immovable units had been liquidated and the deportation of 6,875 units was hailed as a success. Our new orders involved moving east to the city of Rovno to establish an SS Police Administration for the Central Ukrainian District. We were advised the city had not yet been secured and we were expected to encounter enemy contact.

An Advance Column of tanks and halftracks crept out of Lutsk on a very humid morning. We followed the main element in Blitz Opels, bouncing in and out of shell craters in the roads. We heard Rovno before we set our eyes upon it. The heavy thudding of outgoing artillery alerted us to the horizon where thick pillars of black smoke spiraled into the sky. As we neared the battle, our planes became visible as they dived from the sky to deliver ordnance. Soon we were on the edge of a hill next to artillery batteries of 88mm and 102mm guns that spit shells into Rovno. The column halted there and we watched the buildings being torn apart and listened to the small arms fire in the city.

Schumann and I stepped out of the truck and involuntarily flinched each time an 88 fired a round. Rasch called a general assembly and informed us that we were not to enter the city until the Wehrmacht reported it as secure. In the meantime we set up a field Command Post to monitor the activity inside the city and we each received ammunition and grenades.

We watched the Wehrmacht march a unit of Russian soldiers out of the suburbs at gunpoint. They arrived at our location and I studied the Russians as this was my first close look at the enemy. Most of them wore dull green uniforms and helmets, except for one dressed as an officer, and two wearing brown wool tunics. A Wehrmacht Sergeant was more than pleased to turn the prisoners over to the SS and he pointed to the two men wearing the brown tunics and stated, "Snipers." He leveled a finger at the Russian in the officers' uniform and added, "Political Officer."

The three were pulled from the group of prisoners and were forced to kneel with their hands over their heads. The officers of EGC consulted with each other for a brief moment before one of them pulled his pistol and shot the snipers and Political Officer. None of the Russians dared to protest as they were certain a verbal objection would bring the same fate upon them. The prisoners were put aboard an empty Blitz Opel under Wehrmacht guard and driven off to the west.

Most of the Russian resistance broke at dawn and Rovno was declared secure despite light pockets of remaining Soviet defenses. Our Commanders issued the orders to enter the town and Schumann and I boarded a Kubelwagen with an SS driver and radio operator. Wehrmacht Field Police were diverting traffic off the main roads through the suburbs due to debris and impassable shell craters. Our driver swung to the south and took us past rows of farm fields, roundhouses, and wells. He maneuvered the Kubelwagen down a clear passage to the east and we were making a steady approach to the main city. The front of the vehicle lifted up from the ground with a loud bang and the glass in all windows shattered in a burst of flames. Schumann's door was jammed shut but mine opened with ease and I pulled him out on my side. We crouched between the wrecked Kubelwagen and a stone retaining wall around a home. The SS driver and radio operator in the front seats were dead.

"What in hell was that?" asked Schumann.

How was I to know? I suspected we had hit a landmine but stopped speculating when bullets tore holes in the front fender of the burning vehicle. I looked behind us to see a small unit of Wehrmacht soldiers who had been alerted to our location by the explosion.

One of the soldiers shouted, "Stay down! We will come to you!"

That seemed sound advice and I was not about to offer an argument. I noticed Schumann was bleeding from his upper chest and right shoulder.

Before I could tell him this, he said, "You have been hit, Schiller." I had not even noticed. There was no pain whatsoever, but I had a deep gash in my right forearm with a piece of shrapnel protruding from it.

The Wehrmacht was upon us. Two men guarded us while others flanked the ruined Kubelwagen and house. Shots were fired as we were dragged back a block or two where medical personnel rushed to us. More shots were fired near the Kubelwagen before a voice shouted, "Clear!"

We were told that a Russian rifle fired grenade had been launched at our Kubelwagen and the soldiers said Schumann and I were very fortunate to be alive. I did not feel so fortunate as the pain in my forearm became excruciating. "Let us do this promptly," said a Wehrmacht doctor. He grasped the piece of shrapnel with a pair of large forceps and grabbed my wrist with his other hand. He pushed and pulled at the same time while I howled in agony. The piece of metal did not come out of my arm.

The other doctors had removed Schumann's tunic and were pouring sulfur powder into his wounds. He sat there quite courageously as they pushed forceps inside two holes in his chest and the one in his shoulder to extract the shrapnel.

I saw the morphine needle moments before it was plunged into my shoulder. The fragment of metal in my forearm was apparently wider at the base and had become lodged underneath my flesh. The doctor said he was going to have to make incisions in my skin to get it out of me. I felt a light pressure on my arm but no pain at all as he cut open my flesh. He removed the piece of shrapnel and filled the wound with sulfur powder and iodine. Sitting there without a care, I watched the doctor bandage my arm before he asked us our names. The injuries had qualified us for Wound Badges.

The Wehrmacht soldiers helped us to our feet and led us to a halftrack that took us to the rear. I insisted that I was well enough to continue the advance into Rovno, but the doctor informed me I would have to wait 30 minutes to an hour before the morphine stabilized in my body. Back at the field Command Post I was laid on the ground and was given orders not to stand for at least 30 minutes.

Schumann and I looked at each other for a moment to

acknowledge how close we came to being killed. "The driver could not have been more than 19 years," he said. "And the radio operator. 25 years, I would suppose."

As the morphine stabilized I was overcome with heat, pain and nausea. I began sweating profusely and regurgitated several times before regaining my composure. Schumann helped me to my feet and we walked to where Rasch and a few other officers were standing and conversing.

"What happened to the both of you?" asked Sturmbannführer Mohr.

"Our Kubelwagen was struck by a rifle fired grenade," replied Schumann.

"Are you both well?" asked Standartenführer Rasch.

"Yes, Sir," I responded.

Rasch looked at Schumann and me as if we did not belong there and said, "Then get your asses into Rovno."

I resented the orders to enter the city because I rationalized the wounds Schumann and I sustained had somehow earned us an exemption from dangerous duty. Moreover, as RSHA officers, we were not classified as combat soldiers nor were we practiced in the skills of battle. It was noticeable that EGC had exclusiveness among its core officers, and men such as Schumann and I, as well as a few others assigned from various departments, were treated as outsiders. All officers attached to an Einsatz Unit had some form of personal association with SS General Heydrich or the Reichsführer-SS. Problems and suspicions arose because none of us knew just how well our fellow officers were connected to these Party Officials. Men like Rasch and Mohr had been transferred from the Waffen SS, and others had been assigned from political offices. My young age and lack of experience made me an easily manipulated pawn, and Schumann's desire to protect his rank of Junior Lieutenant made him the same. Most of the EK5 officers considered our presence in the unit to be an enigma. None of them could understand why representatives from the Office for Jewish Emigrations had been placed in the field and I could not answer their questions because at that time I was not certain of my purpose either. My fellow officers had reasons to be there, but Schumann and I followed aimlessly until orders provided a purpose for us. Orders such as entering Rovno.

We followed a heavily armed group of Wehrmacht soldiers into the suburbs and pressed ourselves up against walls and cautiously peered around corners. Using hand signals, we sprinted by twos across open intersections in a low crouch and took cover behind anything suitable. A feeling of relative safety overtook us as we neared the perimeter of the main city and saw several of our halftrack crews standing by. Some were studying maps while their comrades surveyed the city through field glasses. None of them seemed concerned with any immediate threats in the area and a Sergeant advised us of the situation when we joined them at their vehicles.

"We have secured the northern, southern, and western quarters," he said. "The Soviets have fortified several apartment buildings in the eastern quarter and seem willing to fight to the end. IV Armored has just dispatched three tanks to the area. We have checkpoints leading to the center market square, but be cautious. We have lost more than twenty men to snipers today."

"Has an Administrative Headquarters been established?" I asked.

"Yes, Sir. Just south of the market square. The Officer of the Field Police is there if you need him."

An SS halftrack idled in an intersection with a soldier manning its mounted machine gun in the open back. I suppose he took compassion on Schumann and me because of our fresh bandages and he inquired where we were going. I told him we were trying to reach the city administrative buildings and he offered to give us a ride. There was something very encouraging about the comfort of an armored vehicle so we parted ways with our Wehrmacht escort and boarded the halftrack.

We sat low against the armored sides as the soldier swung the gun back and forth on its mounts. He studied balconies, windows and rooftops for any sign of enemy occupation as the vehicle crept through the shattered streets. It stopped in front of a three or four story building where we got out. Several SS soldiers were coming and going from the building with their weapons shouldered and we assumed the area to be secured.

At the top of the stone stairs I reached for the door as a Waffen SS Lieutenant exited the building. Recognizing our Police insignia, he told us that his troops had captured several enemy documents, maps, lists, and photographs during the initial invasion of Rovno and told us to speak to the Sergeant on Watch inside the building.

I felt a warm spray on the left side of my face before I heard the crack of a rifle shot. I barely saw the SS soldier that rushed up the stairs and forced me through the wooden doors of the administrative building. We had landed on the floor with him on top of me as glass and wood splinters rained down around us. The Waffen SS Lieutenant had also retreated inside the building and took cover behind a marble stair railing. He shouted, "Sniper!"

The SS soldier dragged me away from the open doors and I took cover with him and another enlisted man behind a thick wooden desk. I cautiously peered out the door to see Schumann's motionless body lying atop the stairs. The right side of his face was gone and I had been covered with his blood. I heard another shot and saw the gunner inside the halftrack flinch before firing the machine gun at a building across the street. The vehicle opened its throttle and moved down the avenue.

Moments later several halftracks and three or four tanks arrived before spreading out to surround the building. SS soldiers came from the halftracks and took cover behind the vehicles with their weapons pointed at the windows of the building. I continued to glance at Schumann in the hopes that he would move or show some sign of life. The soldiers left the cover of the halftracks, and at great risk to themselves, took new positions and surrounded the building. A Waffen SS Tactical Sergeant on one knee studied the building from behind a halftrack. He spoke into a field radio while pointing to the third story of the building where several windows were propped open. On his orders, two halftracks raised their machine guns and raked the third floor with a storm of bullets that threw plaster in all directions in a white cloud of dust.

We were too terrified to move inside the administrative building as we did not know if the sniper had been killed by the halftrack bullets or if he was peering through his scope at us. A heavy crackle of gunfire erupted from the windows of the building and forced the SS soldiers to drop behind cover. How, I wondered, did the SS establish a headquarters in the administrative building with enemy snipers directly across the street?

The halftracks responded with another burst of machine gun fire that ventilated the structure. The Tactical Sergeant was shouting coordinates into his radio while keeping one eye on his men and the other on the occupied building.

Several minutes later two halftracks turned their engines and moved approximately five meters in opposite directions before coming to a halt. We heard the loud mechanical screeching of treads and metal wheels in dire need of a good oiling prior to seeing the motorized beast. It was nothing that I had previously seen. The chassis of a tank carried an obtrusive looking turret on the rear its the hull. Extending from it was a massive cannon. It halted at the base of the stairs in front of the administrative building, engaged its right side track and pivoted toward the building across the street before cutting its motor.

"What in the name of God is that thing?" I asked.

"75mm assault gun," said the soldier who pushed me through the door. "That should cook those Russian bastards like sausages."

The cannon lifted with a loud series of metal clicks before it steadied for a moment. The gun fired and the recoil forced the vehicle to lurch backward as flame and smoke exploded from the third floor of the Russian held building. Something clattered across the cobblestones followed by many soldiers shouting, "Grenade!" The explosive harmlessly detonated underneath the 75mm assault gun as it fired another round. When the smoke dissipated we could clearly see inside the third level of the structure. The street had become littered with beds, wrought iron chairs, cabinets, and debris that had been blown out of the apartments by the 75mm.

A white bed linen appeared through a shattered window, and then another was unraveled. Rifles and light machine guns were thrown from the balconies and Russian voices were shouting, "Moy sa-dots! Moy sa-dots!"

"They are surrendering," said the Waffen SS Lieutenant while standing up from behind the marble stair railing.

The SS soldier who saved me shouted at the Lieutenant. "Stay down, damn it! They have not surrendered yet!"

More than a dozen Russian soldiers exited the apartment building with their hands held high above their heads. We slowly got up from behind our cover and watched the SS surround them. "You damned fools," I thought to myself while looking at Schumann's corpse. "You should have shot yourselves." My friend was lying dead atop a flight of stone stairs because of them. They had no idea what I was prepared to do to them for this crime.

"I want them all."

The Waffen SS Lieutenant said, "They have demonstrated criminal subversion as snipers. They are to be shot on sight in accord with the Commissar Order."

"Do not attempt to teach me the law," I said. "Arrest and hold them. I will decide their fate."

He glanced at Schumann's body and nodded. He left the administrative building and intervened with the Tactical Sergeant who had ordered the Russians lined up against the wall of the building. The Sergeant issued directives to have the prisoners shackled and they were led away.

I demanded a full accounting to explain how the SS Administrative Headquarters had come under fire from Russian soldiers. I insisted on knowing what kind of security had been conducted in the area prior to establishing the headquarters and who was responsible for it. To allow enemy soldiers to infiltrate and threaten our area of command operations was an abomination and dereliction of duty.

An SS Sergeant was brought before me while Schumann's body was being carried to a halftrack. I made the man look at the maimed corpse and demanded an explanation for the Russian snipers. I ordered him to give me details of why all buildings surrounding the Administrative Headquarters had not been secured and occupied by SS forces. I asked him question after question without providing him the slightest opportunity to respond. In my opinion there was no answer he could offer. There was nothing that could be said to explain his absolute neglect of duty. I shouted at him that an officer was dead because of his disgraceful dereliction and I had him placed under arrest and transferred to the rear. I authored scathing charters against him and gave my word as an officer that his conduct was not befitting of a soldier of the SS and personally recommended him to be tried before a military tribunal, stripped of rank, and incarcerated in a military prison to perform hard labor.

I instructed an SS Corporal to lead a search of the apartment building for Russian corpses, weapons, and explosives. Minutes later I was shown to an office on the first floor of the administrative building and the desk was covered with captured documents. I moved

them aside and sat down to compose countless drafts of a letter to
Schumann's family. Each one was crumbled and thrown aside as
there were no words to describe what happened. I tried to write that
Schumann had died a soldier's death, but the truth was he did not. He
was spied through a scope, stalked, and shot like an animal by a
hunter. He was killed in a manner of cowardly stealth. I struggled
with depression and anger as I held myself responsible for his death.
The man had survived the fields of the Great War and followed me
into a wretched Ukrainian city where he was outright murdered by a
coward hiding in a window with a rifle.

Hours later the Corporal returned to report his unit found several
Russian rifles, pistols, and grenades.

"Did you find any corpses?" I asked.

"No, Sir."

"I want you to report to the holding cells and learn which one of
those captured Russian bastards killed Junior Lieutenant Schumann."

The Corporal looked at me as if I should know I was asking for
something impossible. His expression indicated that he believed the
Russians would never admit to the deed.

"Use any means necessary," I said. "Beat them to the edge of
death if you must. Then stop and revive them to do it again if you
have to. Do not kill them. Learn which one shot the Junior
Lieutenant."

The Corporal nodded and acknowledged that this was a very
personal matter for me. He left and I sat down at the desk to attempt
to find the correct words for Schumann's family.

On the following morning the Corporal reported to inform me
there had been no success with the interrogations. I encouraged him to
keep trying and then conducted a meeting with the Gestapo, SD and
Order Police units in the city. We discussed the potential existence of
a few anti German factions operating in Rovno and generated lists of
possible suspects.

The city had been declared secure that day and a grand lunch was
prepared as a celebration for the officers. I refused to attend this
function as I believed it was not moral to enjoy myself while
Schumann's body was being laid in a grave. Anger overtook me and I
exited the administrative building and stormed into the holding cells
where I ordered the acting Sergeant to pull the prisoners from their

cells and line them up inside a walled garden behind the building.

16 of them stood in a long line and I walked up and down in front of them several times. I wanted personal revenge for Schumann's death but I did not want to have to kill all 16 Russian prisoners. I asked questions that were relayed through an SS interpreter. "Which of you shot the SS officer?"

There was no admission to this deed.

"None of you dumb pieces of animal shit know who did this," I said. "One of you did. We found no bodies in the apartment building. This means whoever shot the Junior Lieutenant is standing before me now. Tell me, which one of you did this?"

I walked up and down the line and stared at the face of each Russian prisoner. There was something strong in my thoughts that made me believe I would recognize the assassin from the way he looked at me.

"Are you all aware that the illegitimate son who calls himself the leader of your criminal government has not signed an agreement for the treatment of Prisoners of War? This is correct. Stalin; the swine, has refused to put his signature on the pact of conventional conducts. This means your disreputable leader has given me legal permission to treat you in a manner of my personal choosing." I took a wooden truncheon from an Order Policeman and again asked, "Which of you shot our officer?"

There was no response and my anger had taken root. "Fifteen of you are honorable soldiers," I said. "One of you is a lowly coward. I have no misgivings for the soldiers. You faithfully performed your duty and I respect that. However, I can not tolerate cowards."

I paced back and forth until reaching a decision. "Would you not prefer to be taken to a Prisoner Camp where you can work and live in relative security until this war is over? Who among you does not wish to return to your family some day? I decide whether you will go to a camp or die here today. Fifteen of you may go if you tell me who shot our officer."

For the final time there was no response and the anger boiled in my veins. What was proven by such stubbornness? Was their wish to defy me some code of honor among the Communists? I provided them with the opportunity to save themselves and they refused to take advantage of my benevolence. I threw the truncheon aside, pulled my pistol and walked down the line shooting eight of them in their foreheads. I reloaded and shot the remaining eight Russians.

When I turned around to leave the garden I noticed the SS soldiers refused to look at me. Some stared at the ground and others gazed over their shoulders. I slammed the gate open and returned to my office in the administrative building.

Perhaps two hours later the door to my office burst open and an SS Colonel and his adjutant were calling me to attention. I stood there as the Colonel screamed, "Who in hell authorized you to shoot my prisoners, Lieutenant? I will take your goddamned rank! Who in hell are you to interfere with the Waffen SS? You bastard! You son of a swine! How dare you shoot my prisoners before they were interrogated by my intelligence officers! Explain yourself! Explain yourself now!"

"One of those Russians acted as a sniper and shot an SS Junior Lieutenant, Sir. In accord with the Commissar Order, I had legal rights to execute them. I am the acting SS Chief of Police and Security attached to EK5."

"One of them acted as a sniper?!" shouted the Colonel. "Then only one should have been executed! Damn it, Lieutenant! Rovno is not the new nest for the Blackbird of Porajów!"

He stared at me for a very long moment. "EK5?" he asked.

"Ja, wohl."

"I have no time or patience for Heydrich's pets in my forward goddamned areas."

"Perhaps the General would be interested in hearing your opinion, Sir."

He squinted and his face became tight. His black gloved hand clenched into a fist and a finger pointed at me. "Do not fence with me, you little piece of shit. I will shoot you just as you shot those goddamned Russians."

I had enough wisdom to remain silent. As long as the Colonel was aware I served under SS General Heydrich, I was certain no harm or demotion would come to me.

His eyes seemed cemented in place as he said, "In the future you will request my personal authorization before sinking your talons into anyone else. Am I understood?"

"Yes, Sir!"

The Colonel's adjutant stomped a heel, extended his arm and shouted, "Heil Hitler!" Both men abruptly turned and left my office without closing the door. I noticed the clerks in the outer offices staring blankly at me from having heard the Colonel's tirade. Closing the door with all the dignity I could muster, I sat down while trembling.

During the subsequent meetings with the Gestapo, SD, and Order Police, I realized my opinions and suggestions were not being seriously regarded by my fellow officers. They listened to me, but no one openly agreed or disagreed with anything I said. It was as if they had been advised to treat me with a distinct aspect of neutrality.

Days later I received calls from Novak and Eichmann about the confrontation I had with the Waffen SS Colonel. I was told by Eichmann that Heydrich did not appreciate learning that I used him as a shield of protection. He said I represented the RSHA in the field, but was accountable for my own actions. I would receive no support from my office or superiors if I acted outside the parameters of my rightful jurisdiction. Eichmann and Novak were very understanding of the manner in which I resolved the problem of Schumann's death, and I was informed that Heydrich had lauded my decision. It was emphasized that I was to summon personal fortitude to confront officers who objected to RSHA policies and not to hide behind Party Officials.

Novak informed me that I was being assigned to a Surveyors Unit to scout potential locations for Detainment Facilities and Prisoner of War camps. A unit had been assembled at Lutsk and was expected to arrive at Rovno in the coming days. I would become the Acting Officer of this unit and I was to report all favorable findings to the Office for Jewish Emigrations.

In the meantime I managed a diversity of reactions from fellow officers and the men. Half seemed to support the aggressive approach I used against the Russian prisoners and the remainder believed I was a dangerous and unstable man. What none of them took into account was that my decision, whether aggressive or unstable, was in accord with Reich Occupational Law. The division of attitudes about it was not drawn from a single acknowledgement of the law. Officers and soldiers formed their opinions based upon the act itself. Because what I did was legal, the Waffen SS Colonel could shout at me until there was no more wind in his lungs. I could not be subjected to demotion or a military tribunal. Perhaps I breached certain objectives by circumventing the Colonel's opportunity to interrogate those men, but our superiors viewed this as a matter of personal efficiency. The Colonel knew those prisoners were being held and he had ample time to dispatch his military intelligence officers to interview them. As police and security matters were my responsibility, I also had a timely investigation to conduct. It was never a real issue of being demoted or put before a tribunal. The Colonel expressed his anger that I had been more efficient than him. Of course his complaints were received at higher levels and to keep the peace in Rovno, I was being assigned to a Surveyors Unit.

I met this unit a few days later and was surprised at how under strengthened it was. It consisted of 3 halftracks, 4 Blitz Opels, and a Kubelwagen. Of the 48 men, 36 were combat and police units acquired from various KRIPO, SD, Gestapo, Order Police and Waffen SS squads. 12 men were civilian surveyors attached by RSHA Headquarters to the RAD and Todt Labor Services.

The general orders for the unit created more anxiety within me. We were to travel to various destinations and survey each as a potential site for the construction of Detainment Facilities, Prisoner of War camps, forward headquarters, supply depots, and other military installations. Each location had been suggested by SS or Wehrmacht engineers assigned to other units, or had been charted by Luftwaffe pilots. A serious problem existed in that many of these locations were situated in non secured forward combat areas. The matter was further complicated by a lack of reliable intelligence on whether the roads we needed to travel were secured. 36 lightly armed combat troops equaled little more than a Battle Group and it distressed me to travel into hostile territory with so few men.

Our first survey was scheduled to take place northeast of Rovno near the town of Klesiv. The Wehrmacht had encountered a Soviet Rifle Company east of Stepan and the skirmish had stalemated with both forces withdrawing. We were to travel to Klesiv on a road that passed through two towns being held by the Wehrmacht. Kostopil was our first checkpoint, and the second was to be Berezne. It was well known that when we departed Berezne we would be east of Stepan and passing through the area which the Soviet Rifle Company had pulled back to. A German Battle Group against a full Soviet Rifle Company was a situation I wished to avoid at all costs.

I objected to the presence of the twelve civilians as my orders stated that their welfare and safety was my responsibility. They initially seemed receptive to following my instructions and each had been briefed of the importance of this prior to leaving Berlin. The civilians hardly looked the sort to be found in a combat area and there was awkwardness about them that I found to be annoying. It was as if they were trying to stay out of the way of military affairs, yet they sought an amalgamation with it. Rasch signed off on my written orders and I assembled the unit and prepared it to move out.

Two halftracks led the column with the four Blitz Opels behind them and the third halftrack covered the rear. The Kubelwagen was situated behind the second Blitz Opel and in front of the third. I was apprehensive to get inside the car as my forearm yet ached from my last experience inside one. Two civilian surveyors joined me in the vehicle and the one in the front seat was wearing a fine silk business suit. The man who climbed in the back next to me was wearing dress trousers, a white shirt, a black tie, and was carrying a satchel and an umbrella. If not for the uniformed SS driver it would have felt more like I was going on a church outing.

The man in the front seat introduced himself and inquired of the bandage on my arm. He desired to know if I had sustained the wound in combat, but instead of entering conversation with him, I stared out the window. He blathered on and on about how exciting it must be to see the fighting on the front lines and how much of an honor it must be for me to serve the Fatherland. He continued about how gracious all Germans were for the sacrifices and hardships we were enduring on the lines, and he asked a few more times about my injury. I had nothing to say to him. In fact, just what was I to say? Did he wish to hear that I saw men and boys blown apart? Would he find it exciting if I told him about the young German soldier I saw clutching his severed foot and staring at it while crying in shock? Would the man find honor in packing thousands of Jews into freight wagons, shooting Political Officers, and burning civilian villages? Would Germans yet be gracious if they knew these things?

At Kostopil I reviewed the latest reconnaissance reports and learned the road north was open, secured, and in good repair. We reached the ruins of Berezne late in the afternoon and found it to be a series of rubble bunkers that had been fortified by the Wehrmacht. The men there were very dirty and tired, and their Commander informed me that a Russian artillery battery had been frequently pounding them from the east throughout the day. He had very little information about the terrain north of the city except that a Wehrmacht Grenadier Battalion and a Luftwaffe Artillery Battery were holding Klesiv. However, the road from Berezne to Klesiv was declared not open and not secured. The Commander said he could spare a few of his men to operate handheld mine detectors in front of our column, but this was on the condition we halted for the night and resumed our advance at dawn. He felt it was too dangerous to travel a potentially mined road during dusk and night hours and I agreed with him. We moved our vehicles several blocks away and parked them near an old Roman Catholic Church and joined the Commander and his soldiers in the pockets of debris. Fortunately, the Russians must have redeployed their guns because there were no artillery attacks that night.

The Wehrmacht Commander had a change of mind at dawn and refused to allow his men to serve as our escort. Early reports from the Luftwaffe contained information that our pilots sighted Mechanized Soviet Infantry east of the ruins. I called upon my unit to make ready and we began our advance against sound judgment.

Leaving Berezne was easy and somewhat peaceful on a warm and humid August morning. The dirt road cut through fields of wild flowers until we crossed a small stone bridge over a rivulet and continued northeast toward a tree line. The ruins of the city disappeared in the distance behind us as we motored through the narrow forest roads. Abruptly everything appeared to be the perfect ambush point for the enemy to hit us. After a kilometer or two, the lead halftrack stopped and word was passed along our column that we were facing a very unnatural roadblock.

A tree had been intentionally laid across the roadway and this was evidenced from fresh cuts at its trunk and drag marks along the path. The foliage and branches made it impossible to see if it contained mines or explosives. I disembarked from the Kubelwagen and walked to the second halftrack where I opened the radio compartment on its back. Conferring with the lead halftrack crew chief, I advised him that I had seen a similar tactic in the forests north of Francorchamps in

Belgium. There, the Belgian Army felled trees and then shelled the last vehicle in the column to create an immovable roadblock at the front and rear. This left the column exposed to be systematically destroyed by mortars and artillery.

The lead crew chief opened his machine guns on the fallen tree and seconds later two successive explosions threw splinters, dirt and stones into the sky. When the smoke cleared we saw a very navigable crater where the roadblock had been placed. The machine gun bullets had successfully triggered the mines and explosives.

Destroying the roadblock was too easy and there were no consequences. Moments later the birds began singing again in the forest and we could not help but wonder why Russians or partisans would place that obstacle there without hitting us with an ambush. The lead halftrack crew chief very frankly reported that the enemy was baiting us in. He said they were sending us the message that they were in the forest watching us. I ordered him to get us through the woods as quickly as possible but he countered with logical strategy to advance at a minimum rate of speed to detect any other obstacles or mines that may have been set to impede our progress.

I returned to the Kubelwagen where the civilian surveyors were asking questions about the roadblock. I ignored them and watched the men inside the Blitz Opel in front of us as they removed the canvas top and crouched low with their weapons pointing in all directions. Each vehicle followed the one in front of it at a distance of approximately 13 meters except for my Kubelwagen which remained close to the Blitz Opel in front of us. We crept through the forest at a speed of perhaps 25 kilometers per hour while scanning for dangers in the road and enemies in the trees. Despite our caution, the lead halftrack hit a mine nearly 5 kilometers beyond the roadblock we had blown.

The vehicle had its right tread completely torn away in the blast and thus was disabled. The crew stumbled from the escape hatch amidst billowing smoke but they were unharmed and fit to fight. I should have hurried them into the Blitz Opels but we were standing there looking at the damage done to the halftrack when gunfire erupted from a gulch in the forest to our left. The civilian surveyors were pressing themselves against the windows of the Kubelwagen to see what was happening and I saw the driver yelling at them to get down. I crouched behind the second halftrack and pulled the charging handle on my MP40. A thunderous roar of gunfire was being delivered into the trees from the men in the Blitz Opels and both remaining halftracks were raking the woods with their machine guns. I thought about the tires on the Blitz Opels and how if they were shot out, the entire column would be immobilized. I pulled the radio transmitter out of the back of the halftrack again and contacted the secondary crew chief. "Get that goddamned wreck out of the way!"

"Sir?"

"Ram the goddamned thing! Get it off the road! If we stay here we will all be dead men!"

"I am responsible for this vehicle, Sir."

I could not believe what I was hearing under fire. I squeezed the handle on the transmitter and shouted, "It is my call! Get that wreck off the road now or by God I swear I will have you shot!"

"Yes, Sir!"

The halftrack opened its throttle and lurched forward until it hit the disabled vehicle in front of it. It paused for a brief moment before the throttle opened wider to push the wrecked halftrack off the left side of the road.

Once more I used the transmitter. "You are now the lead crew chief. Get us the hell out of here!"

I waited until the first Blitz Opel passed and jumped into the moving Kubelwagen. Suddenly, the idea of more mines and obstacles was not a primary concern. We roared through the forest recklessly until we exited into a rolling meadow. We halted to inspect the men for casualties. Miraculously, none of my men had been injured in the skirmish.

The crew chief of the ruined halftrack approached me while the soldiers reloaded in the backs of the trucks. "Partisans?" he inquired.

"Why do you think so?"

"That was a very disorganized attack, Sir. They got my halftrack with the mine, but all that shooting hit nothing. Russian infantry would have overwhelmed us before we got the wreck off the road."

I contacted Rasch at Rovno to report what I believed to be a partisan attack on the road between Berezne and Klesiv. He was very interested in this news and kept me waiting on the radio while he reviewed maps. Rasch eventually informed me of a nearby village called Redivka and ordered me to hold my position until an element from Einsatzgruppe B, EK9, arrived to investigate. I told Rasch that I was in an extremely hostile area and that it was not prudent to halt my advance. He understood and said that if EK9 did not arrive within two hours I was to proceed to Klesiv.

Perhaps an hour and a half later my spotters identified SS Cavalry Officers approaching from the southeast and moments later the forward element of EK9 was in our midst. Approximately 300 SS soldiers arrived behind them in Blitz Opels, halftracks and on horseback. An SS Hauptsturmführer unfolded a map in front of me and pointed to a small village called Redivka. He said it was a small farming area inhabited by 150 to 200 Ukrainian Communists and Jews. German intelligence had identified the village as a potential partisan base and the Commander of EGB gave orders to liquidate it. I believed this would entail the deportation of its populace at which the communal structures would then be razed.

The SS Captain of EK9 gave orders to hold the German civilian surveyors behind and requested my presence during the liquidation of Redivka. He entrusted his mount to an SS Sergeant and the Captain and I boarded my Kubelwagen. The SS Cavalry galloped westward and moments later we followed them.

Redivka was a collection of perhaps 50 small wooden and earthen homes with thatch roofs and tiny vegetable gardens separating them. Cultivated farm fields were at the western and southern borders of the village, and a few barns and grain storehouses were at the outskirts. The SS Cavalry was riding up and down the main dirt road in the center of the buildings while firing their weapons in the air. Some of the citizens of Redivka attempted to flee but the SS Cavalry halted each escape by cutting their horses in front of the running people. They rounded up the civilians like shepherd hounds as foot soldiers began forcing them into a tight group in the southern fields. Guards formed a perimeter around them and within moments most of the population had been captured.

The SS went from house to house to search for hiding villagers. Now and then shots were fired from inside the buildings and the SS emerged alone. Other times the SS forced men, women and children from the homes and shoved them toward the surrounded group in the field.

Without realization of what was about to happen, I asked the SS Captain, "May I see the map?" He looked at me with an odd expression.

"I need to locate the nearest rail station," I said. It was my belief that the people were going to be deported.

"They are not leaving here," said the Captain.

I noticed several groups of SS soldiers slowly walking into three different barns with rifles at the ready.

The Captain shouted, "Males to the east field! Adolescents and infants to the road! Females stay where they are!"

I stood there while the SS began separating families. The women screamed for their husbands and offspring. The children cried out for their parents, and those who did not comply with the orders were beaten with rifle stocks or kicked. It took ten or fifteen minutes to separate them according to the Captain's orders.

In a very clipped manner the Captain jabbed his finger at the men and then pointed to one of the barns containing SS soldiers. He repeated this mechanical gesture to direct the women and children to barns. The citizens were led inside the buildings in groups of 10 and moments later a volley of rifle fire sounded. Subsequent groups were ushered inside until the walls began to disappear from the steady hail of bullets. Within the span of one hour the entire population of Redivka had been liquidated.

The soldiers exited the barns with mixed expressions. Some men displayed no emotion at all but others appeared as if they were on the very border of madness. The Captain gave orders for the Cavalry to mount, and for the engines of the vehicles to be turned over. He then looked at a group of soldiers and dryly stated, "Fire the village."

I watched the men pull the pins on incendiary grenades and heave them into the community. 10 or 15 devices went off and created a firestorm. As it spread I turned to see the source of a hammering noise above the crackling flames. A soldier on his knees was nailing a flat board onto a post. He lifted it and pounded it into the dirt at the southern end of the village. The sign read: "This is the fate of all partisans and those connected to them."

This incident had been arbitrary. The Captain did not conduct a formal investigation to determine if the civilians had any part whatsoever in the attack on the Berezne-Klesiv road. More disturbing was that no weapons, explosives, intelligence documents, ammunition or local maps had been found in the village. We departed from the smoking remains and made our way back to the rear element of the column where the German civilian surveyors were eagerly waiting to learn what happened.

"Did you find those responsible for the attack?" asked one. EK9 began pulling out to the east. I did not answer the man.

Our journey to Klesiv intensified my anxiety after this action. I believed that the remains of Redivka would serve the Russians as an icon of German brutality and realized that our capture would result in barbaric treatment. Ironically, the incident at Redivka also provided me with a perverted inner peace in that I believed the Russians would not confront or capture us for fear of bringing more reprisals on the local population. I knew the Soviet Rifle Company was out there somewhere and I could not help but feel the occurrence at the village would shock them into tacit and temporary neutrality. Sometimes the pure trauma of an incident like that could lead to a stunned delay of counteraction.

The checkpoint outside of Klesiv was a dreamlike encounter. The Wehrmacht guards looked like the living dead with hollow and sunken eyes. The men were exhausted, filthy and had not been groomed or shaved for weeks. A layer of tan dust coated their uniforms, skin and stubble. I shrunk back from the scab-covered dirty claw that reached through the window of the Kubelwagen to take my identity documents. The soldier closed his eyes and rubbed them, and then stared at my papers for a moment to gather focus. He dropped his hand to his side and loosely held my documents while leaning his elbow on the roof of the car. He rubbed his forehead under the brim of the helmet and sighed heavily. His companions stood behind him with slumped posture and bent knees as if doing everything within human ability to remain on their feet.

He dropped the papers through the window onto my lap and said, "Straight. Cross the bridge to the next checkpoint. They will direct you to the headquarters. Welcome to the throne room of hell, Sir."

Under other circumstances I would have objected to the unprofessional manner in which he spoke to an SS officer, but I would not have been human if I did not exude compassion for those poor Sons of the Fatherland. All I could think of to say to him was a quote from popular propaganda. "One people, one Reich, one Führer."

The fatigued soldier nodded and said, "Yes, Sir."

We advanced through the next checkpoint and were directed through the rubble cluttered streets to a hotel that had been modified as a headquarters. The SS Captain on duty could scarcely believe my purpose in Klesiv. He did not object to the oddity of my orders, but was surprised that the Office for Jewish Emigrations would conduct such business in a hostile and forward area. He showed me several maps and pointed out a few areas that were rich with resources of stone, timber, coal and ore. The Captain said he could not spare men to serve as escorts or guides and cautioned me about partisan attacks and artillery barrages in the zone. I requested accommodations for my men and the surveyors. He gave me an incredulous look when he learned I was traveling with civilians but granted me professional cooperation.

During the next several days we traveled to these locations, set up guard perimeters, and conducted the surveys as quickly as possible. Novak and Eichmann were greatly pleased with our findings but demanded evaluations on the potential establishments of rail and motor transport stations.

The months of August, September and October took us to sites as far west as Yavoriz and as far east as Bila Tserkva near Kiev. During the first week of November we were given orders to return to Berlin to present our final assessments to our superiors.

CHAPTER THIRTEEN
THE INDUSTRY OF DEATH

I t took several days for my superiors to process and read my reports. I was given leave from duty during this time and retired to my assigned home in Berlin. On one particular evening I was visited by fellow officers from the Office for Jewish Emigrations and they encouraged me to join them for a night of revelry in the city. One of the men promised we would raise a glass to the memory of Junior Lieutenant Schumann and this was the only reason I went.

When we arrived at the *Musik-Haus* on Wilhelm Strasse I felt as if I had graduated into a fraternal order. The nightclub was once a public venue but had since become an exclusive location for SS officers and their wives or women friends. It was also a place where single girls of pure German lineage came to meet eligible SS officers. I had just been handed a stein of beer when my comrade, Untersturmführer Lange, introduced me to a young lady called Klaudia Krüger.

I felt very awkward in her presence. I did not know how to conduct myself with proper social grace and I believed I made the fool of myself to her. She inquired of my duties in the SS, but in accord with RSHA policies, I was not at liberty to discuss such matters. This was very fortunate as there was no possible means to tell her what I witnessed, ordered, and personally did. What would that angel have done upon learning I was the devil?

The evening with Klaudia was a magical experience that seemed to happen in a place removed from the realities around us. However, those walls crashed down and my enchanted evening collided with reality when the Gestapo entered the *Musik-Haus* and put a halt to the gentle playing of the pianist. The houselights were turned up and the

Gestapo officers stood there staring at the patrons. They glanced at a photograph in their hands and then pointed to a young woman sitting with an SS officer. The Gestapo briskly crossed the hall, violently pulled the woman from a chair and seized her. They twisted her arms behind her back and one Gestapo officer lingered behind while the others of the contingent escorted their prisoner out of the hall. The remaining Gestapo representative spoke to the SS officer who had been in the company of the arrested woman. The conversation was quiet and peaceful but ended with the SS officer paying the fare, gathering his hat, and leaving with the Gestapo agent's guiding hand on his shoulder. Moments later soft music from the piano filled the hall as the houselights went down and the mood returned to as normal as it could be under such circumstances.

Klaudia and I talked about her employment as a secretary for an automobile manufacturer; about German victories on all fronts, and the state of German political affairs. It was difficult to ignore the fact that a woman and an SS officer had been arrested before our eyes but it was pure madness to speak of it. One did not dare utter a word about such things. A statement as simple as: "That poor woman" could easily be misconstrued by others as a form of concern or an association with the accused. All of us knew better than to put ourselves in such a position. It was better to ignore it. The public doctrine was clear: Serve der Führer, serve the law, serve Germany, and serve the people. It was understood that we as German citizens knew better than to breach the laws or associate with those who did. Unfortunately, that event lit a spark of suspicion inside of me toward Klaudia. I had just met her and did not know anything about her past affiliations or involvements.

We parted ways late that evening at a trolley stop and the next morning I telephoned a comrade in the Office of Racial Affairs to request a basic lineage investigation of her. When I returned to duty at the Office for Jewish Emigrations, foolish male rumors had circulated that I had courted the most attractive lady in the *Musik-Haus* that night. I did not appreciate this as tales of immoral fraternization could hold dire consequences. The time spent with Klaudia had been innocent, but my comrades in the office exaggerated and invented details.

I reported to Eichmann's office believing we would discuss the reports I had authored in the Ukraine. However, he informed me that because I was his subordinate, Klaudia's lineage investigation had ended up on his desk. He told me her flawless German heritage was traced back over four generations and stated the Reichsführer-SS took a very active concern in the romantic interests of all SS members. Hitler and Himmler were intent on breeding pure German children and Mothers Crosses were being awarded to those women serving this aim.

"Do you intend to marry her?" asked Eichmann.

The thought had not entered my mind. I had just met her and certainly believed a woman of her beauty would never have an ordinary man such as me. "I do not know her, Sir."

"Court her," advised Eichmann. "There is not an unlimited quota of women with pure blood. Court her. The Reichsführer will be very pleased to hear of this."

I had heard of many officers who married women of pure blood within weeks of meeting them. The traditional values of love, commitment and mutual attraction had little or nothing to do with such marital unions. Pure German women were encouraged to wed SS men of pure blood. There was somewhat of a social competition between the elite genders to meet and marry. Some marriages were arranged by superior officers so their subordinates could wed into noble families and higher social orders. Klaudia Krüger did not have aristocratic ties, but she was pure in more forms than blood. I used the encouragement of my superior officer to court her and this was something I probably would have not had the confidence to do without his support.

During the month of December there was much talk about an important meeting being organized. Most of us only knew that the Reichsführer-SS and General Heydrich were scheduling the assembly, but the purpose of it was not revealed to the subordinates. Eichmann was greatly stressed by the impending meeting and constantly gave me orders to complete certain assignments only to rescind the instructions and give me new tasks. Most of my work was directly related to the Ministry of Transportation and involved gathering information about scheduling railroad departures from Drancy in France, Westerbork in the Netherlands, Fossoli di Carpi and Rome in Italy, and Berlin.

These transports were intended to carry Jews from these territories to specific points in Poland. My fellow officers were assigned similar tasks and were ordered to arrange transports from Greece, Romania, Bulgaria and the Ukraine.

At times Eichmann would come into my office, review my progress, and order me to cease what I was doing and transfer all my current information to the Foreign Office. He would deliver stacks of contracts and proposals from firms constructing buildings and establishing utilities in Poland, and a day later he would order me to stop working on them and forward everything to the Ministry of Economics before putting me to work again on deportation matters with the Ministry of Transportation. All this time he would threaten to revoke my Christmas leave if everything was not completed on time. The problem was, I did not know what "everything" was, and he never took the time to explain.

The purpose for the impending meeting became evident within two weeks. From the information I had been ordered to gather and process, I only had to look at the maps to realize my superiors were planning the complete and uncontested deportation of European Jewry. All indications pointed to southern and eastern Poland as destination points and I recognized them to be the ghetto locations. I was also processing information to conduct transports from the ghettos to the places Eichmann had shown us before: Auschwitz, Chelmno, Treblinka, Belzec and Majdanek.

I stared at the maps on my desk for a very long time and pondered how it would be possible to contain hundreds of thousands, or even millions of Jews in these areas. There certainly was not enough Order Policemen to enforce the law for such a population. A very nauseating sensation overcame me when I remembered some details on the labor contracts and proposals Eichmann had asked me to review. Pulling them from the piles of documents on my desk, I realized just what was being constructed at Auschwitz, Chelmno, Treblinka, Belzec and Majdanek. The company of *J.A. Topf und Sons* was delivering equipment and materials to *Hoch und Tiefbau AG Kattowitz* for the building of massive gassing halls and crematoriums.

The papers on my desk also included proposals to deliver submarine engines from Kiel, and tank engines from Leipzig, to eastern Poland. "Hallowed Mother of Jesus," I thought. The huge engines were to be used for the mass scale carbon monoxide poisoning of Jews.

Eichmann had been standing in the doorway of my office for quite some time before I noticed him. He read my face and quickly detected that I was aware of the plans being made at higher levels. He closed the door and sat down across from me.

"I wanted to tell you," he said, "but orders are orders."

"We are going to gas them? All of them?" I needed his clarification to prove I had not lost my senses.

"Yes," replied Eichmann. "This is what Himmler and Heydrich are referring to as the Final Solution to the Jewish Question." He thought for a moment and asked, "Who have you shared this with?"

"No one, Sir."

"Good," he responded. "Let us keep it that way for now." He leaned back and said, "Höss previously conducted experiments at Auschwitz using Zyklon B as a gassing agent. It is a prussic acid widely used to exterminate rodents, fleas and lice, but its vaporous qualities have proven effective at killing Jews and Russian Prisoners of War. Unfortunately, Höss did not author a descriptive report. I want you to go to Auschwitz where Höss will conduct a second experiment with the Zyklon B. I want you to observe and report on it to me."

Eichmann stood and opened the door before looking at me again. "The meeting has been rescheduled for January. When your work is completed at Auschwitz, you may take leave to visit your family for Christmas. I trust you will be sharing time with Frau Krüger?"

"Yes, Sir."

"Very well, Lieutenant Schiller. Happy Christmas."

"Happy Christmas, Sir."

It was snowing when I got off the train at the Oswiecim Station and I did not understand why a Facility Driver had not met me. I was about to ask the rail clerk where a telephone was located when I noticed a Staff Mercedes sliding on its brakes in the thin coating of ice that had formed on the road. Its driver approached me hastily and inquired of my name. When I told him, he said that Höss was genuinely surprised by my visit and had just learned of my impending arrival a couple hours ago.

Inside the facility I entered the antechamber of Höss's office where his secretary gave me a hot cup of coffee while I waited for the Kommandant to finish other business. Christmas music spun on a gramophone with a few light pops and hisses, and the office was decorated with red ribbons, festive candles, wreaths, and a tree with ornaments propped in the corner by a window. The light chatter of the secretary's typewriter stopped as the young officer asked, "Have you just come from Berlin, Sir?"

I looked out the window into the falling snow and replied that I had.

"How wonderful for you! I am from Berlin, Sir. I would perform any feat asked of me to be there for Christmas!"

I thought that was ironic. I would perform any feat asked of me to avoid coming to Auschwitz again.

Höss opened the door and spread his arms apart while saying, *"Obersturmführer Schiller! Fröhlich Weihnachten, mein Freund!"* It seemed immoral to return his greeting for a Happy Christmas when I had come to Auschwitz to observe an experimental gassing of prisoners with Zyklon B, but I did.

The Kommandant was confused about my visit and stated he received no information about why I had come. He said construction was proceeding on schedule and as planned, and that Auschwitz II Birkenau was soon expected to be operational. Höss frowned when I told him why I had come and admitted that the experimental gassings he reported had actually been the unauthorized doings of his enlisted men. He explained his men had sealed off the vents of Block 11 and poured a heavy concentration of Zyklon B in the cells out of curiosity to learn what would happen. He also confessed writing and submitting the report in a manner that made it seem he had authorized the experiment. Höss feared potential repercussions if it was found out that his men executed prisoners without his knowledge and authority.

When I asked him to recreate the experiment he looked out the window for a long time in silence. He attempted to avoid the matter by stating he did not have any prisoners scheduled for execution.

That did not seem relevant to me and I explained that these orders came from Berlin and were not my personal directives. I inquired how many prisoners were currently in the hospital ward.

Höss turned from the window and looked at me while realizing there was nothing he could do to avoid the orders. "I do not know the exact number from memory," he replied. "Perhaps one hundred."

"We will use them," I stated.

"It is not that easy, Schiller." He appeared as if he wanted to delay or circumvent the orders but suddenly came to the conclusion it was fruitless. "Yes. I can author the orders, but you will need permission from the facility doctors." He mindlessly readjusted the position of several blown glass ornaments on the tree. "Go over to the hospital ward. I will inform the doctors you are coming and I will send my secretary over there as soon as I complete the orders."

The journey to the ward at F Camp was eerily peaceful in the falling snow. Exiting the car I noticed the female prisoners staring blankly at me from behind the wire fencing of FKL Camp. They had pitiful expressions on their faces and their eyes seemed to register me as an outsider. I did not perceive that they saw me as a German among Jews. It was as if the dead were curious at seeing someone who was alive.

Inside the ward an orderly came to attention and I demanded to see the Chief Physician at once. We retired to his office where I declined his offer of cognac and explained my purpose at the facility. The doctor did not have an adverse opinion about my orders but insisted I spare six or seven inmate patients from the gassing ordeal as he was conducting experiments of his own upon them. He said there were 89 prisoners in the ward and that he was willing to sign them over to me. He also requested to observe the gassing experiment for the curiosity of medical evaluation.

As we talked, I learned he knew Doctor Lutz from Sachsenhausen and I saw he shared a similar personal disposition. Most of the doctors I met had tranquility about their personalities that made them easy to talk to and work with.

The doctor told me about the experiments he was conducting upon the prisoners. He said the procedures were intended to study the effects of hypothermia on the human body and this involved submerging the prisoners in icy vats of water; recording body temperature, monitoring vital signs, and then attempting to revive the inmates through various means such as artificial respiration and warming them under industrial heat lamps. The doctor was certain the Reich could benefit from such studies in learning how to resuscitate pilots who crashed in the icy English Channel and soldiers exposed to the elements on the battlefields.

His telephone rang and after a brief conversation he informed me that Höss's secretary was on his way with the signed Directive 19 orders. The doctor suggested using the delousing hall for the gassing experiment instead of Block 11. He stated the delousing hall had its doors sealed with rubber and once closed, created an air lock. He also said there were thick glass windows in the metal doors which would provide a suitable perspective to view and record the procedure.

When Höss's secretary arrived, I took the Directive 19 order which had been condensed to two pages instead of 89 separate warrants. Höss had taken a blank Directive 19 form and simply typed the names of the prisoners beneath the orders. It was rather basic, but legal by every standard. I asked the doctor how many of the inmate patients were ambulatory and we made the necessary arrangements to transport a small number of cripples to the delousing hall by bus.

The delousing hall was a very unobtrusive concrete building cut into a wall of earth. 7 or 8 stairs led down through a door that opened into the disrobing area with wooden benches along the left and right side walls. At the opposite end of this room was the door that led into the delousing hall.

The hall was capable of accommodating approximately 125 people and it was a large and sterile empty room with an exit door on the far wall. For our purposes that day, the door had been barred shut from the opposite side. All inmates and Russian Prisoners of War arriving at Auschwitz were sent immediately to the delousing hall where minimal amounts of Zyklon B or other pesticides were introduced to the room to kill lice, fleas, parasites and other vermin. Normally, the clothing would be deloused simultaneously in another area and when finished, the prisoners would exit and get dressed again.

The SS Medical Staff conducted the transports of prisoners to the delousing hall in a very calm and orderly manner that day. The inmates were told, and they believed, they were being deloused for hygienic reasons and they went to the hall willingly. They undressed in an organized method and filed through the door into the main chamber. This was not surprising as they had experienced this procedure upon their initial arrival at Auschwitz and had passed through it without harm or suspicion.

Once the last person had gone into the hall, the door from the disrobing room was closed and sealed. We stood in front of the glass window and watched the inmates standing inside the chamber. Some stared at a wire mesh tube with a metal basket that hung from the ceiling and waited patiently for the delousing crystals to be dropped in. An orderly from the Medical Staff emptied a canister of Zyklon B through the opening of the tube on the roof of the hall. When the crystals filled the basket, one of the prisoners shouted, "That is too much!"

Panic spread among the prisoners when they realized the quantity of Zyklon B was lethal. Their breathing became labored and some of them jumped at the basket in efforts to tear it down from its fixture. At approximately 2 minutes, the inmates began grabbing at their chests and throats and a flurry of coughing and gagging began. One ingenious prisoner got on his hands and knees beneath the basket and another inmate stood on his back and grabbed the metal basket. He swung back and forth on it like a primate on a vine until it came loose and spilled the vaporizing crystals on the floor of the hall. Several prisoners attempted to save the others and became martyrs by eating the Zyklon B crystals. This had no effect on the other inmates as the prussic acid and cyanide gas caused instant death to those who ingested it. At 5 to 7 minutes their muscles began to stiffen and contract and their skin turned a grayish blue. Their lips puckered and extended, and their tongues began to poke out like sausages. At 9 to 10 minutes their spirits began to leave their bodies. The screaming faded into gentle moans and within 13 minutes and 35 seconds, all 89 prisoners were dead.

Höss dispatched several members of the Medical Staff who donned gasmasks and walked around the outside of the building. They opened the barred door and entered the delousing hall where they moved several bodies out of their way. They exited and returned with electrical fans powered by a mobile generator. Setting these devices up inside in the hall, they turned them on to ventilate the chamber.

After this we moved approximately 10 meters away to a pergola in a garden that had been turned for the winter season. The Chief Physician of Auschwitz was greatly pleased with the experiment and the first thing I noticed was the mood of the men. They were calm and in good spirits. It was nothing like the disposition I had previously witnessed of the men who had performed executions by firing squad. The Zyklon B poisoning had been very humane and it required no direct group participation. A Medical Orderly emptied a canister of prussic acid crystals through a tube in the ceiling. He did not have to see his victims. He did not have to lower a weapon, contemplate the action, and pull the trigger. It was a very impersonal approach to mass killing that left no obvious mental stress on the participants.

I noted that the entire process, from disrobing until death, had taken 26 minutes and thirty seconds. I was certain this procedure could be improved to 20 minutes, and if larger halls were being constructed according to the contracts and proposals I had reviewed in Berlin, I believed it would be possible to liquidate 800 people every 20 minutes for a total of 2,400 each hour. Allowing for maintenance and body disposal, I estimated the larger gas chambers could operate for a reasonable period of 12 hours. At peak efficiency, a single large gas chamber would be capable of liquidating 28,800 prisoners each day. The main benefit of the Zyklon B gassing method opposed to carbon monoxide was that it did not rely on the maintenance of submarine or tank engines. These devices, as well as truck engines, had been used for the T4 Euthanasia program to dispose of the mentally ill, crippled, and elderly. As with Rauff's experiments at Nordhausen, this technique was very unreliable and the motors required constant and costly repairs. Zyklon B was a clean, efficient, and cost effective method for mass liquidations.

At Höss's office I authored a very favorable report on the use of the gassing agent. I remarked to Höss, his secretary and any person who would listen, that I was deeply impressed by the impersonal effect this had on the SS. In contrast to the shootings, carbon monoxide experiments and hangings I witnessed in Germany, Poland and the Ukraine, the Zyklon B seemed a godsend to the logistical and personal problems of eradicating Jews and criminals. I was so enthusiastic about the idea that I telephoned the Office for Jewish Emigrations and demanded to speak to Eichmann. I was informed he was in the process of leaving the office for the day, but I insisted. He took the telephone call and could not understand my excitement. I told him it was the kind of thing he would have to witness for himself to appreciate. The Reichsführer-SS was already disturbed by the psychological damage being done to SS soldiers by asking them to participate in firing squads. Eichmann asked if I was absolutely certain about my statements and asked me to consider if I was overreacting to the experiment. I pleaded with him to come to Poland to witness the use of Zyklon B. He trusted that I was accurate in my verbal accounting and promised to take the matter up with Himmler after the celebration of the New Year.

I returned to Berlin to deliver my reports and was preparing to leave the office in time to board the last trolley to the train station to begin my leave for Christmas. SS General Heydrich had come to RSHA Headquarters from Prague to attend a few meetings before retiring for the holiday. I was informed that he wished to see me before I departed for my home in Füssen.

As usual, he ignored me for some time as I stood at attention before his desk. He was listening to Wagner as he often did, and signing and stamping documents. After several minutes he motioned to a chair with the tip of his fountain pen and I sat down. Heydrich pulled some papers from a stack of documents on his desk and briefly read them.

"This report from Auschwitz is most intriguing," he said. "Obvious, too. Why not use a pesticide to destroy the largest vermin of them all?"

He put his elbow on the desk and leaned his forehead into his hand. "The Jews," he mumbled disparagingly in an exhausted tone. "We have so many resources tied up in the Final Solution to the Jewish Question. Pesticide, Schiller?"

I began to excitedly tell him of what I witnessed but he waved me off.

"You do not have to persuade me with the idea," he said. "Your report answers most of the questions that get raised with something like this. Personally, I support the use of this pesticide. However, I am not certain it will be approved by other offices."

The General seemed relaxed enough for me to ask a question without drawing criticism. "It is clean, efficient and cost effective. Why would it not be approved?"

Heydrich looked directly at me. "Because Porsche, Mercedes and Daimler build engines. The industrialists will have some influence on whether this method is chosen. Politics, Schiller. That is what it is."

"Engines require costly maintenance and suffer from natural stress and wear," I said. "Doctor Rauff could not perfect his truck at Nordhausen, and the motors being used at sanitariums are constantly being replaced and worked on."

"You do not have to persuade me," repeated the General. "Himmler will be impressed by this method if what you wrote in your report is accurate. If gassing prevents SS men from becoming lunatics, he will see to it that it gets authorized. We are sending other Legal Affairs Officers to conduct similar gassing experiments for comparable reports. If they relate similar accounts to yours, we may have a stronger argument against the industrialists."

I sat there for several moments unsure of what to say.

"Are you taking leave for Christmas?" asked the General.

I responded that I was.

He spit the word out as if it was sour. "Christmas!" He shook his head as if I had disappointed him. "Very well. Off to your family then. Be prepared for a full schedule when you return."

I stood and wrestled with the thought of whether to extend a seasonal greeting to him. Against better judgment I said, "Happy Christmas, Sir."

He signed documents and waved me off with his other hand.

My respite in Füssen was the last time I saw my Father. He was a proud veteran of the Great War and had earned many medals at the battles of Marne and Verdun. He lost his left eye, a portion of his hearing and most of his face at the third Battle for Ypres in 1917. He was a humble and honorable man that sought nothing more than a proud Germany in which to raise his family. Father never spoke much about the war; the defeat of our country being a shameful responsibility that he always carried with him.

Father often forgot common things and my family made polite excuses for his inattentive behavior. The physicians diagnosed his condition as being of advanced age though Father was but 53 years when the doctors claimed this. Other medical experts claimed his condition had been caused by the head injuries he suffered during the war but for all the diagnosis, no one had a cure.

Mother, the proud and stubborn Berliner, was proud of my rapid advancement in rank and the fact that I could genuinely speak of being in the presence of Party Officials such as the Reichsführer-SS, and

Generals Best and Heydrich. She invited many of the local villagers to come to the house for pastries so they could set their eyes upon a legitimate officer of the SS that she called her son.

My young sister, Katharina, was in her last year of school and looking forward to attending the University at Munich to pursue studies in biology and sciences. She too invited friends to stare at me as if I were some great curiosity set on display.

My elder brothers, Jürgen and Lukas, were both assigned to different Wehrmacht units engaged in heavy fighting on the Eastern Front. Neither was granted leave for Christmas, but Mother placed settings on the table for them and before the meal was served, Katharina read their most recent letters aloud.

I departed Füssen a few days before my leave expired to call on Klaudia Krüger in Berlin. Earning the approval and permission of Herr Krüger, I began my courtship of his daughter.

1942

The Office for Jewish Emigrations was in a chaotic state upon my return. Eichmann resumed his habit of confusing me by delivering work to my office, insisting on a deadline, and then ordering me to forego it and begin a new project. All of this work was specifically related to three different but equally imperative matters.

Most of my tasks involved the collection of information regarding train schedules, railroad accessibility, the number of Class A locomotives and freight wagons available in in the Occupied Zones, and the projected timeframe for the manufacture of more. All of these details were recorded and forwarded to the Ministry of Transportation.

I was also occupied with the collection of Jewish census records for Germany and the Occupied Zones. The Foreign Office supplied similar information that they obtained through diplomatic negotiations with the Heads of State of foreign countries the Reich had not yet invaded, or had no plans to invade. Many foreign countries were given the option to allow the Reich to annex them, forge an alliance, or capitulate without being subjected to German military action in exchange for handing over the Jews that occupied those respective areas.

My third roster of assignments included the amending and editing of legal documents, proposals and contracts that were intended to govern the establishment of business and industry at Auschwitz, Treblinka, Majdanek, Belzec, Chelmno and Sobibor. This involved authoring labor agreements, profit disbursements, utility management agreements, industrial administration laws, limits on manufacturing costs, price reductions for salability to military purchasers, and countless minor details.

The availability of natural resources in Oswiecim led to a strong economic projection for Auschwitz. Glücks, Pohl and Burger had persuaded the Reichsführer-SS to consider a mass expansion of the facility and to make it the premier forced labor industrial network of the Reich. At this time, plans were being considered to enlarge Auschwitz, and construct Auschwitz II Birkenau, and Auschwitz III which was intended to be a conglomerate of specific industrial works inside the camp.

Meanwhile, large gas chambers and crematoriums were being constructed to manage the steady schedule of liquidations intended to take place there. The theory being discussed, was the incorporation of approximately 25 or 30 satellite camps around Auschwitz to provide commercial trade, agriculture, textile manufacturing and other goods and services necessary to make the camp a self sustaining enterprise. Each transport of Jewish freight arriving at Auschwitz would undergo a selection process to separate essential and non essential workers. Useful Jews would be put to work in newly developed employment stations or replace laborers that were no longer meeting production requirements or expectations. Those replaced by fresh workers were to be taken directly to the gas chambers with the other non essentials.

During the third week of January, Eichmann requested all my work. I had not been able to complete a good portion of it, but this did not seem to matter to him. The meeting took place in Berlin with a number of industrialists and civilians having been invited. Most of us paced our offices and the halls of RSHA Headquarters while this assembly was engaged.

By the end of the day, none of us at headquarters had heard about the outcome of the meeting, nor had any of the attending officers returned. I retired to my home in Berlin and was very anxious until my telephone rang. The call was from a fellow officer who worked in my department. He did not know exactly what had been discussed at the assembly but his message was clear. "Take comfort and sleep well tonight, Rolf. Our superiors are celebrating. Tomorrow will be a long day of work."

Upon my return to duty at RSHA Headquarters I learned that the meeting had indeed been hailed as a success and that it resulted in the Final Solution to the Jewish Question. The Reich had decided, with support from civilian industrialists and financiers, to proceed with the unconditional eradication of European Jewry. All offices and departments were to devote full resources to the advancement of this aim, and massive deportations from Occupied Zones to ghettos were being arranged. Construction and expansion for Auschwitz, Treblinka, Majdanek, Chelmno, Sobibor and Belzec; now officially referred to in documentation as Termination Stations, was expedited to meet the needs of the new directives.

Hans Frank wished for immediate action inside the Polish General Government. This area was most feasible as no transportation problems existed within the districts and due to Frank's desire to implement the process. I had been assigned to a committee that was responsible for maintaining security in the Polish ghettos. As inmate populations were growing, and were projected to increase further, security violations were occurring on a frequent basis. An organized black market provided numerous items to underground resistance factions inside and outside the ghettos, and it became necessary to disrupt the illegal operations and maintain strict control over the resident populations.

During the month of January, an SS Supply Depot at Radom had been looted by members of the Polish Resistance. In February, over a dozen Jews walked out of the Lublin Ghetto wearing stolen uniforms from the Radom depot. It was argued that the ghetto populations exceeded the manageable control of the understaffed German garrisons guarding them and new methods needed to be devised in order to maintain security.

A major portion of the disruptive actions were taking place in the Lublin ghetto and I was dispatched there during the third week of February to meet with the local officers of the Order Police and SS to assess the situation and propose a solution.

Before departing for Lublin, I attended a conference with Doctor

Bühler, General Heydrich, and several officers from the Office for Jewish Emigrations. It was announced that the industrialists had persuaded the Reichsführer-SS to continue mass gassing operations by means of carbon monoxide. Those of us who witnessed the effects and efficiency of Zyklon B were requested to author favorable reports on its use. These reports would be submitted to Himmler, Göring and Hitler for a reassessment of its benefits. I had no personal conflicts in advocating the use of Zyklon B. It had been officially declared that the Jews as a category had been legally marked for extermination, and General Heydrich and Doctor Bühler shared an interest for the most effective means.

There were many unique international factors that advanced the German plan for the systematic liquidation of European Jews. Before deciding upon the eradication of the Jews, our Foreign Office sought diplomatic solutions with the ambassadors of many international governments. In 1940, The US State Department returned a statement to our Foreign Office that was endorsed by President Roosevelt. In response to multiple requests that the United States of America accept Jews emigrating from Germany and its Occupied Territories, the United States government replied that it already had numerous problems with its wealthy New York Jews, and denied entry based on the theory that European Jews would only provide impetus to consolidate Jewish influence in America. Von Ribbentrop was yet attempting to negotiate with the United States Ambassador when Japan attacked the American Naval port at Pearl Harbor. The Japanese, who had diplomatically assured us they would take no aggressive military action against the United States until May or June 1942, had catapulted the Axis Alliance into a war of global proportions 5 to 6 months ahead of planned schedules. The Japanese attack of 7 December 1941 had not only disrupted diplomatic negotiations between German and United States offices, but had changed America's classification as a Neutral to a direct enemy of the Third Reich.

This was among the last things desired by the Reich at that time. The Russian campaign had resulted in nothing but maps being redrawn with ever changing front lines. Our forces had made excellent progress against the Soviet army, but the first 8 months of the campaign had cost the Reich nearly three times what it projected in resources, men, equipment and ammunition.

Simultaneously, Rommel had gone on the defensive against British General Montgomery in Africa. Our Western Defenses were being strengthened due to our 1940 stalemated air battle with Britain; but the Italian and Greek coasts were widely unprotected. If the American military was to mobilize against Germany at that time, numerous strike points existed as possible landing locations for an invasion force. It was also debated whether the Reich was capable of sustaining a prolonged war on more than one front.

Consequently, this effected German conduct in many different ways. Our Military High Command began looking for weak territories that could easily be occupied for the sake of increasing the range of our borders. Natural resources were to be captured, protected and harvested for the impending war with the United States. In order to equally distribute the stores of food in each area to the German soldiers and people required to occupy them, the populations of the zones needed to be drastically reduced. This resulted in expediting the liquidation of the Jews.

Roosevelt's announcement to the American Congress of 11 December 1941 was full of ambiguous statements. He affirmed the American Declaration of War upon the Reich was in response to a German Declaration of War upon the United States. There had been several incidents in international waters where American and German vessels of war had traded shots. It was never officially determined who fired first, but reports clearly prove a majority of German vessels lost to American Naval and Airplane fire.

The Reich stood to gain nothing at all from a December 1941 Declaration of War against the United States of America. Our manpower and resources were too weak at that time to make and sustain such a declaration. The design of the Reich, at the time the American declaration was made, was to conscript locals from the Occupied Zones and form SS Volunteer Units and train them over the next four to five months. This would have provided our munitions factories with the necessary time to restock the amount of supplies used during the Russian campaign and would have directly coincided with the Japanese agreement to strike the American Naval port at Pearl Harbor in May or June 1942. At that point, the time necessary to mobilize, train and equip the American military would equal additional time for the Reich to prepare for this war. When the Japanese struck months ahead of schedule, it became a political and industrial competition to restock our military in time to defend against an American invasion.

The Americans. All I knew of them was Benny Goodman, King Kong, and Ginger Rogers. Most of us were optimistic that a diplomatic peace could be established between our countries before hostilities escalated. In spite of the declarations, the United States and Germany possessed similar political ambitions. The Americans had liquidated a massive portion of its undesirable Indian tribes and placed the remainder on reservations. Our superior officers debated the difference between an American reservation and a German Detainment Facility. Also, the American Jim Crow Laws established in 1870 were very much aligned to the German Nürnberg Laws. Whereas the United States sought to restrict the political and social abilities of Negroes, we sought the same for the Jewish population. Many of the 1935 German Nürnberg Laws were taken and adapted from the existing American Jim Crow Laws. The United States had a reputation of hooded vigilantes hanging Negroes from trees and its government did nothing to regulate the treatment of its second class citizens. We could not reason why a foreign government would allow these practices in its own country and object to such policies in Europe.

This was the primary discussion among the men on the train to Lublin. What we were told about foreign countries was greatly controlled by our Ministry of Propaganda. There was always a science in finding the truth between the reality of international situations and the information disseminated through the German people by our tainted political viewpoints. The world had been impacted and weakened by the Great War, and while many countries enjoyed a rapid recovery, we believed the 1929 financial depression in the United States had left that country vulnerable and without immediate hopes for prosperity. America was just beginning to see a profitable revitalization by 1939 and though a war would serve as excellent motivation to inspire its industry, Germany and Europe as a whole did not see the United States as a viable competitor in a massive military engagement. Therefore, we viewed the American government's Declaration of War as nothing more than sword rattling and fist shaking.

I had never met an American but I enjoyed the things they shared with and brought to our culture. Many were the days that I ran from my uncle's house in Munich to purchase a New York Hotdog with mustard and sauerkraut. Of course we had to eat them with sauerkraut. What respectable German would not do this? However, when the adults were not around we ate them without the sauerkraut.

There were many American reporters and newsmen posted in our Foreign Office and at various radio broadcast stations during the early days of the war. I had never been introduced to them, but I observed them to be happy and polite people with a very carefree disposition on the world and the events occurring within it. I never viewed them as the enemy and even when I learned of the Declaration of War against Germany by the United States, I could scarcely believe it held merit. All governments knew the true global enemy was the Communists, and we believed that England would rescind its opposition to our forces and that She and the United States would join the Axis Alliance in the combined effort to defeat the Russians. No German could help but believe the United States made this declaration based upon outdated and thin alliances with Great Britain and France; alliances that no longer held beneficial gains in the post Great War world. We understood that a degree of posturing, fist shaking and sword rattling were necessary for the United States government in order to win the support of its people for a war.

All of these events created a marvelous stir in our Foreign Office. The world viewed the Asian races as a shifty and untrustworthy lot. The mysteries of their cultures and their desire to remain alienated from the world provided the core foundation for a potential breaking of the Japanese and German alliance. Our Foreign Office recognized the fact that America was formally at war with Japan and tried to use this as a tool to prompt American diplomats and ambassadors to consider a potential alliance with Germany. The geographic location of Japan and its burgeoning Communist neighbors provided the possibility of a central theater of war. Germany could push on the Soviet Union from the west and America could push on Japan and eventually Russia from the east.

Plans had been discussed for the eventual German invasion of North America, and these designs were to go into effect within two years after the capitulation of the Soviet Union. OKH and OKW had persuaded Hitler to consider the establishment of Wehrmacht and SS bases in the Siberian territory at Anadyr. The goal was to launch a Five Point assault on the Alaskan coast after U-Boats eliminated harbor traffic and defenses at Point Hope, Kotzebue and Hooper Bay. Saint Lawrence and Nunivak islands were to be occupied and captured to establish midway airfields, and the islands of Saint Matthew and Saint Paul were to be captured and employed as midway supply depots.

The Five Point assault was designed to follow a Kriegsmarine naval bombardment to soften SS and Wehrmacht ground landings at Shishmaref, Teller, Nome, Saint Michael and Alakanuk. The Shishmaref and Teller forces would then swing north to cut off and capture the ports of Point Hope and Point Lay with Kriegsmarine and Luftwaffe support.

Subsequent SS and Wehrmacht landings would take place at Pilot Point, Egegik, Kipnuk and Tununak Bay. A Blitzkrieg on the Tok Junction Valley was expected to clear a crossing of the Canadian border into the Yukon Territory where the Reich would establish the first of its North American ghettos at Carmacks.

In 1942 all of this was purely theoretical. Der Führer had a proclivity for long term planning and enjoyed discussing these matters. I had been privy to this information in the Office for Jewish Emigrations as it raised numerous questions about the North American railroad system, both as a transport line for Jewish freight and for the routing of military troops and supplies. I never participated in formal meetings regarding the North American Invasion plans, but they were realistically discussed as a future endeavor of the Reich. While Hitler took pleasure in such conversations, his subordinates were greatly concerned with managing current projects. We were looking to stabilize the situations in Russia, the Ukraine and Poland, not at potential designs to occupy North America.

CHAPTER FOURTEEN
A RETURN TO LUBLIN AND THE UKRAINE

I had grown quite weary of Poland and the problems occurring within its General Government. It seemed fitting that Frank, Fischer and Globocnik should resolve their own matters as they possessed the power and authority to do it. On the other side of this coin, I was constantly in the position of being required to request permission and wasted countless hours applying my methods through proper channels. All superior officers desired that matters in their areas of operation were taken care of in a prompt manner.

Göth was scheduled to meet me at Lublin but I arrived a day or two before him. In the meantime I met with the officers of the Order Police, KRIPO, Gestapo and SD to learn of the many security concerns. Though several problems existed, each was easily traced to the root of the illegal black market activity taking place inside the ghetto. We acknowledged the maxim that wherever Jews existed, trade existed too. My priority was learning where this activity took place, who controlled it, and where the goods were coming from.

When Göth arrived we examined the methods used in our previous procedures to expose the black market activity. In spite of our earlier successes, the market had flourished and become more secretive. Göth pointed out that all postal correspondence and parcels coming into and going out of the ghetto were acutely monitored by Order Police and Gestapo censors and inspectors. The most logical process for the illegal smuggling of goods into the ghetto had to have its core in the Jewish work details permitted outside its walls. Göth took a contingent of SS soldiers to interrogate the local Polish business owners while I enlisted a group of Order Police, SS troops, and dog handlers to serve as my escort into the ghetto.

I recalled Göth's previous words the moment I entered the Lublin ghetto: "The rats have seen the cats." The Jews obviously had no notion that their alleged clandestine activity was so noticeable. Couriers tried to casually make their way down streets to alert others of my presence but I instructed the SS dog handlers to release their hounds upon them. Any Jew who appeared remotely suspicious to me was seized by my soldiers or the dogs. Within a couple hours we had arrested 9 or 10 Jews.

We came upon a column of ghetto residents that spanned three or four to the Judenrat building. This line of people stood in the gutter and the group disappeared inside the doors of the Judenrat. My escort and I traveled on the sidewalk and each Jew tore his hat from his head and bowed as I passed. I could sense the essence of their fear and could feel that they did not dare to look directly at me. At the doorway a Jew shouted "SS", and the gathering parted to give us unobstructed entry.

The interior of the Judenrat reeked of people who had not practiced hygiene for weeks or longer. The speed of typing increased as the Jewish clerks attempted to demonstrate their status as essential workers. My escort and I traversed the first floor and ascended a wooden staircase to the main offices.

Again someone shouted "SS" when we entered, and the room came to a quietness found only in desolate crypts. The five eldest Jews of the council opened a door to a back office and I entered with three SS guards. The Jews sat on both sides of a long table while I took a seat at its head. Two SS guards posted themselves at the door and one stood by the a window.

"The black market," I said. "Do not waste my time by pretending you do not know about such things. Where are the goods coming from and who are the leaders?"

The Jews remained silent but looked at each other as if expecting someone else to make a comment.

"You can not tell me you know nothing about this," I stated. "Certainly all matters come through this office. I am inclined to think the Judenrat is directly associated with this black market in the ghetto. Give me the information I am demanding or I swear under the eyes of

God, every Jew in this ghetto will find himself on a train to Auschwitz by tomorrow night."

One of the Jews pulled his hands close together and lifted his empty palms. "We know about this black market, but we do not know who controls it or where the goods are coming from. We do not want any trouble with you, Sir. We have it good here. We do not want any trouble."

I was amused by the Jew's statement of having a good life in the ghetto. It was not a good life. It was a miserable life without enough food, medicine, fresh water, heating fuel, clothing or adequate accommodations. One of the purposes of the Judenrat was to serve as a council to hear the complaints of the Jewish ghetto residents. Monthly records proved that the majority of officially registered grievances were: not enough food, medicine, fresh water, heating fuel, clothing and adequate accommodations. The council promised their fellow residents that they would take these matters up with governing German forces, but how could I take these complaints seriously when the Jewish elders told me they had it good inside the ghetto?

"You have kapos patrolling the ghetto," I said. "They have not reported anything suspicious or unusual?"

"There has been talk," replied one of the other elders. "Idle rumors." He looked at his companions but each of them stared down at the table. "Some people have food. Some have jewelry."

"You will have a roster of names for me within 24 hours or I promise you each resident in this ghetto will be sent to Auschwitz." Nothing else needed to be said. I exited the office and pushed my way past the crowd of dirty Jews.

Later that evening I dined with Göth at a former Polish restaurant that had been converted to an exclusive SS eatery. He was very quiet and moody which was in stark opposition to his usual boisterous manner.

We drank from our cups in this uneasy silence and he stared at me for quite some time. His eyes studied my collar tabs, shoulder boards, tunic and awards. Next he fixed his gaze on my hands before scrutinizing my face. "You are different Schiller. Are you not? Do you argue with this?"

"How am I different?"

"You are doing what you are told to do. Yes, you make many

decisions but they are very regulated. The decisions you make are perfectly structured. I mean, there is no wrong choice in the decisions you make. There can not be. Everything you do is a result of some higher authority or decree."

Göth's tone of voice seemed eerily removed from his physical presence. It was as if he was speaking from some kind of spiritual dimension. His hands became animated as if he was trying to rationalize his statements either to me or himself.

"I have to make decisions," he said. Göth did not look directly at me. It seemed as if he was incapable of fixing his eyes on me while he spoke. "I do not have higher authorities or written decrees protecting my decisions. No. I am not like you. I am doing this because I have to. Because men like Globocnik and Frank are much too occupied with bureaucratic shit to take just a few short moments to oversee my actions. No. I have to do these things. No one else will do them. I mean, who will do these things? You, Schiller? No. You are much too intelligent to find yourself in my position. I am alone. And now the damned Americans are coming."

I did not know what Amon was talking about or what he had gotten himself involved in, but whatever it was seemed quite severe. "What things?" I inquired.

He lowered his head and began to softly laugh. He looked up at me with a large grin and said, "We have opened a door we can not close. We have crossed into an area from which there is no return." He pointed in the general direction of the ghetto. "Yes, sure! Kill them all! What else can we do now? We have started the liquidations! We can not reverse our policy now. And the damned Americans are coming."

I was just beginning to understand the nature of his lament and wished he would lower his voice. Not all SS men in the eatery knew of such things. "What do the Americans have to do with this, Amon?"

He looked very nervous and raised his eyebrows while saying, "We had better win this war or they will hang us all." Upon this statement he returned to his usual senses. "That was not a defeatist remark," he firmly said.

"I know, Amon." It never entered my thoughts to report him for the many treasonist and defeatist statements he made. Mainly because most of them were stated with a sound basis of argumentative logic.

"They want to give me my own camp, Schiller. A work camp here in Poland. I was hoping for an appointment to Auschwitz but it looks like Höss promised the positions to other people."

"Who wants to give you the camp?"

"It is Globocnik's recommendation. Probably somewhere in southwest Poland. It could be a good thing, I suppose. I will need a Legal Affairs Officer that I can trust."

Every thread of common sense in my being urged me to distance myself from Göth. His financial schemes would bring nothing but ruin and dishonor to my career.

"What did you learn about the black market from the industrialists?" I asked.

"Of course they do not know anything," he answered. "Damned liars. I say we shoot the foremen and see who talks."

"The Judenrat has promised me a list of suspects within 24 hours."

Amon laughed. "A promise from Jews? And what good is that?"

"They know something about the activity," I said.

"Of course they do," interjected Amon. "They are probably behind it. They have probably organized it. Get your list tomorrow. We shall arrest every person on it as well as the Judenrat council members and the forced labor foremen. All of them will go to Auschwitz. I am exhausted from fencing with these fleas. We will deport all of them and start again with new council elders, kapos and factory foremen. If that does not disrupt the damned black market and send a clear message to others, we will have to come back and hang them by the hundreds."

"Amon, we can not arrest the Judenrat elders without proper authorization. They are an established council recognized by the General Government of Poland. The council is a judicial body."

"It is a damned puppet government that does what we tell it to do," said Amon sharply. "Use a telephone and tell your superiors what we have here. Tell them if they want this problem remedied they will have to grant us the power to arrest and deport the council. I am done playing chess with these Jewish bastards and annoyed with having my hands tied by a damned bureaucracy that refuses to acknowledge the facts out here."

We were joined at our table by adjutants from the Order Police and Gestapo. Amon attempted to motivate these men into tearing apart the ghetto to locate the sources of the black market. None of them were eager to agree as everyone knew the logistical problems involved with such a task. Amon relented from the mass search but continued to encourage the men to participate in a brutal search and seizure of those Jews associated with the black market. The more he talked, the more the adjutants agreed and after some time, so did I. Göth struck upon the point that many ghettos were the hives of illegal activity and Jewish treachery. He convinced us all that our efforts could establish the protocol for future ghetto security measures. This was the very reason I had been dispatched to Lublin but until Amon made his speech at the table, I had no viable plan to construct these aims. The conversation became an analytical and professional discourse on enforcing SS Police authority and it was determined that I would gather the list from the council and we would then interrogate the kapos who patrolled the ghetto. Afterwards we would conduct forceful seizures of all those who had been implicated, arrest the Judenrat council, and confiscate all industrial firms whose forced labor units were involved.

Taking control of the industrial firms was perhaps our boldest gesture in this plan but Amon reasoned the Reichsführer-SS would not mind as the confiscation would result in a complete forfeiture of assets to the SS. Himmler's recent interest in controlling the V-2 rocket works at Peenumünde, and his desire for the civilian scientists working there to become members of the SS, demonstrated his willingness to convert private businesses into SS industries.

That night we ordered a lockdown of the entire ghetto and prohibited work details from traveling outside its walls on the following days. The industrialist leaders went into fits of rage about the damage this caused to production quotas and they immediately notified Berlin to complain about it. Amon requested that I delegate our position to my superior officer and Eichmann relayed the information to the Reichsführer-SS. Himmler approved our plan to seize any business whose forced labor units were involved in the black market scheme and we were given direct authority to proceed with our designs.

At the appointed time on the following evening I met with the Judenrat to receive the list. They inquired about the lockdown and were very mindful that we were planning something beyond what we were willing to tell them. This had no bearing on my position as I owed no Jew an explanation for any action committed on behalf of the Reich.

Göth, me, and several adjutants from the Gestapo and Order Police interviewed the kapos at a warehouse inside the ghetto. The kapos were always a curious source of entertainment for us. They were Jews who were traitors to their own kind and they comprised a puppet Jewish police force inside the ghetto. Most of them had previous criminal records or some kind of grudge against their fellow Jews. In exchange for enforcing order inside the ghetto, they received better accommodations, extra food rations and additional liberties. They were exempt from most restriction rules and could freely traverse the interior of the ghetto whereas the regular residents were confined to certain districts or quarters. They wore a hat with the Jewish Star of David upon it, and a matching armband and breast patch. The kapos carried truncheons and quite often used them to fulfill their own desires for vengeance.

They were very eager to assist us but often strayed from the points of the investigation to report other lawbreakers in the hopes we would add their names to the list of those we intended to punish. Göth demanded that they remain committed to the efforts at hand, but I was interested in hearing about the other offenders as I believed it created profiles of potentially dangerous criminals who were capable of usurping German authority. I did not trust the idea that apprehending those involved with the immediate black market scheme would bring about a cessation to the trouble. Jews had a proven propensity for criminal behavior and eliminating the problem at Lublin was no assurance that it would not be reborn in a month or two. I pressured Göth into allowing the kapos to report all Jews in the ghetto who were worthy of suspicion or who participated in delinquent criminal behaviors.

The kapos could not explain the system of communication used by the Jewish ghetto residents to inform each other of impending German actions. They admitted there was a Jewish intelligence network inside the ghetto and that much of the information they acquired was gathered from conversations overheard in the factories or while marching to work. Newspapers, radios and communication devices were forbidden in the ghettos, but the kapos assured us that such items existed and that most had been built using parts stolen from various industrial work sites. This encouraged Göth since an illegal acquisition of Reich, private, or industrial property was a security violation attributable to the firms from which the parts had been stolen. This would certainly advance the grounds and causes for forfeiture of the industrial plants to the SS.

The Jewish policemen reported that there were a series of observation points inside the ghetto such as steeples, bell towers and apartment buildings that were used by residents to monitor German activity outside the walls. We had witnessed this during a previous search and had heard the whistles and saw flashing signal lights. The kapos revealed the names of Jewish residents who served as spotters, signalers and watchers at these locations. I would conduct their arrests while Göth sought permission from Globocnik to raze the buildings being used for these purposes.

There was credibility in the reports from the kapos as the names they submitted harnessed a degree of consistency fit for the crimes. Most names we received were Jewish forced laborers inside the Siemens factory where technical parts were available for pilfering. This would account for the allegations of radios and communication devices existing inside the ghettos. The primary smugglers were forced laborers at locations that were either remote or virtually unguarded because of low level risks. It proved that Jews could not be given any amount of trust under any circumstance whatsoever.

The kapos informed us of the many different means by which items were successfully smuggled into the ghetto. Following our discovery of their previous crude system, the Jews constructed an elaborate network to ferry contraband inside the ghetto. One method involved the Jews who washed, polished and performed general maintenance on the SS police vehicles at the Lublin motor yard. They promptly learned which vehicles were designated to perform patrol duty inside the ghetto and strapped items such as food, batteries, knives, ammunition, and sometimes handguns, underneath the chassis. Once the vehicles were inside the ghetto, Jews would create a planned commotion to force the crew of the vehicle to exit and tend to the situation. While the matter was being resolved by the SS, a crowd of Jews gathered around the vehicle to hide those collecting the items that had been fastened underneath it.

I asked for a general list of the kinds of items being smuggled into the ghetto and the kapos said they had heard of food, medicines, knives, handguns, rifles, grenades, ammunition, explosives, batteries, wine, beer, cigarettes, jewelry, fine clothing, porcelain, technical components, maps, and petrol.

These items indicated a highly effective black market and one that could not solely operate from one side. I directly interrogated the kapos about their knowledge of outside sources lending assistance to the scheme. They became nervous, and all but one went silent. The kapo who talked told us that he had witnessed Order Policemen at the gates that waved certain Jews through without patting them down for a search. It was mandatory that all Jews returning from a forced labor detail were to be thoroughly searched before returning inside the ghetto and the kapo and his companions knew and understood the gravity of this allegation. As they had provided sound information for my investigation, I promised no harm would come to them for this revelation. A few of the others nodded and admitted to witnessing this. The kapos identified the accused German Order Policemen by physical description and the days and guard shifts they worked. The only information about sympathetic industrialists was an accusation made against the Siemens Company in that the Jewish purchaser illegally adjusted the stock inventory totals so that stolen components would not be noticed.

After the interrogations, Göth prepared the plans for the search and seizures inside the ghetto while I relayed all of this information to my superior officers. Novak told me that he would convey this progress to General Heydrich at his headquarters in Prague.

Globocnik had returned to Lublin on the following morning and we advised him of the situation before civilian industrialists began demanding explanations for the imposed halt to production. The General informed Hans Frank and within hours, Staff cars carried SS and Gestapo delegates into the city. Göth submitted numerous ideas until Globocnik settled upon one. Amon escorted me to a table and laid out his hand drawn maps. "I hope you approve of these plans," he said with a smile.

"Why is my approval necessary?" I asked.

Amon replied with a tone of satisfactory spite. "Because you are in charge of this shit. Globocnik has named you to lead the search and seizures." He laughed in an evil way as if he had urged the General to take the responsibility off him and place it upon me. "I will be working for you, Sir." He uttered the word "Sir" with a mocking emphasis.

I was frustrated and angry, and when Göth saw this in me he abandoned his sarcasm and became civil and concerned. "You know, the General admires you, Schiller. If you do this correctly and efficiently it could benefit you."

There was a seriousness in his voice; one that I had learned to heed. "How?" I inquired. I wanted complete understanding.

"Reassignment," suggested Amon. "Perhaps a promotion. Globocnik is under pressure from Hans Frank because he has not found a collection of dependable officers to resolve these matters. If you impress Globocnik, you will impress Frank. That has to have some reward, no?"

Once again I played directly into the will of Untersturmführer Amon Göth. The man had a remarkable way of enforcing his spirit upon people in a manner that always made one feel that it was strictly for your own benefit. Nothing could have been farther from the truth. Amon served himself and put a distance between his personal ambitions and any action that did not serve his private goals. How he existed as a respectable officer in the SS was an enigma in itself.

Amon began explaining his plans and I could not believe what I was looking at and hearing. Globocnik had approved a complete military saturation of the ghetto using 1,600 soldiers of the SS, Order Police and Wehrmacht. Snipers were to be posted on rooftops outside the ghetto with orders to shoot any person attempting to flee over the walls. Mounted machine guns and halftracks were to provide cover on the main roads inside the ghetto and a specialty squad of demolition engineers was assigned to destroy the buildings being used as Jewish observation and signaling points.

The Jews were to be taken to gathering points at the town square and market area while house to house searches were conducted. It was expected that this operation would draw out the elders of the Judenrat to lodge complaints with Göth, me or Globocnik, and once they showed themselves they were to be immediately taken into custody. Finally, all soldiers had been given total authority to shoot those who resisted, attempted to escape, or refused to cooperate.

We entered the ghetto with a great show of force but of course the Jewish spotters and signalers had announced our presence and intentions to all residents. I was aware this provided an opportunity for the criminals to hide their contraband but we had authorization to tear the districts apart to search for what we knew existed.

Amon and I established a Command Post in a ruined park across the street from a row of former shops and businesses. Early into the operation I received word from the Gestapo that the industrialists outside the ghetto, and some of their civilian staff, had been successfully detained without incidents.

The clatter of sporadic gunfire sounded in distance. "Jesus," said Göth with an air of amused surprise. "The men are shooting them already."

I was shouting at the SS radio operators to set up my communications equipment. The men were connecting wires and installing batteries but none of it was prompt enough for my satisfaction. I repeatedly asked Göth if all Squad Leaders had been furnished with a copy of the arrest roster. I demanded to know why none of the Squads had reported on their progress of apprehending the criminals, and was signing documents and requisition forms for the equipment we were using. SS soldiers with dogs ran by in one direction and moments later ran by in the opposite direction. Halftracks circled blocks, a unit of Order Policemen loitered at the end of the street and two Wehrmacht soldiers were smoking cigarettes near me in the park. I was shouting horrible curses, kicking over chairs, and shouting into the radio transmitters for reports from my Squad Leaders.

One of the units reported they had located a supply of cigarettes and a large sum of money under the floorboards beneath a bath tub in one of the apartment buildings. I requested the address and then ordered the engineers to detonate explosives in the apartment. Göth shook his head and said, "By God, Schiller. You do not want to set off charges inside the building, do you?"

I reminded him that I was in charge of the operation. I understood what he meant that night at dinner when he said he was exhausted from fencing with these Jewish fleas. I was angry and damn all, I was going to demonstrate who held the ultimate authority over the Lublin ghetto that day.

The engineers asked for confirmation to wire explosives in the apartment. "Blow the damned thing," I replied.

We heard the explosion and Göth covered his eyes with his hand and muttered, "Jesus, Schiller."

Gunfire had become more frequent and the Squads began notifying me of positive identifications and arrests of those on the roster. A procession of Jews was being marched from the side streets onto the main thoroughfare that passed between the ruined park and the shops. The SS, Order Police and kapos drove the Jews along with repeated blows from their rifle stocks and truncheons. Now and then a shot was fired followed by screams. The chain of Jews would halt momentarily and then adjust its direction around the corpses lying in their paths.

Within hours I was receiving reports of numerous discoveries of contraband. Weapons, printing presses, a couple of radios and other critical devices had been located. I ordered the presses to be demolished but instructed my soldiers to transport all remaining illegal items to a collection point near the ghetto gates. Each time a discovery was reported I requested the address and dispatched the engineers to wire, set, and detonate explosives where the items were located. Globocnik called me on the field command telephone to inquire about the multiple explosions and I precisely reported what I had ordered. I told the General that if the Jews misused the living spaces we provided them with, those apartments should be rendered useless. Globocnik hailed my tactic and extended his permission.

I was informed that the members of the Lublin ghetto Judenrat had been apprehended in the market area. Hours later the Squads reported excellent progress in seizing the majority of those listed on the arrest roster. Other criminals were being collected by the SS and Order Police as they performed a forced registration at the market and town square gathering points.

Late in the afternoon most of the Jews had been contained in designated locations while the building to building searches continued. Along with the discovery of more contraband, clever hiding places for Jews had also been located. Fires had broken out and spread from my orders to detonate explosives inside the apartments and buildings where illegal items were discovered, but nothing was done to douse or control them.

A horse drawn kitchen wagon was brought into the park and I ate a meal while the engineers and Signal Corps began connecting searchlights to gas powered generators. When Göth saw this, he pointed to them and said, "This is why I hate these damned searches. They go on all night."

Many hours past midnight my soldiers had arrested the majority of the Jews listed on the criminal roster and the structure searches were being called complete by the Squad Leaders. A train was on its way to Lublin from Naleczów. In the morning it would be loaded with the apprehended Jewish freight and routed to Auschwitz.

Göth and I retired to Globocnik's headquarters and briefly discussed the plans for the following day. We decided we would first inspect the collection of contraband items to determine which devices might have come from local industries. Once this was ascertained, I would author the documentation for forfeiture and Reich seizure. We were also required to collect the written reports from all Squads and sign off on each to complete the operation.

On the following morning I was informed that Amon had departed Lublin and was on his way to Czestochowa. I believe this was a calculated action on his behalf as it left me responsible to individually sign each report from the ghetto search and seizures.

More of Amon's words came back to me from the unusual dinner conversation we had shared. I was affixing my signature to documents that identified me as the Executive Officer of the action and though the reports contained accounts of methods considered legal by Reich law, I realized such matters could very easily be misconstrued by an enemy as acts of aggression.

I individually signed reports accounting for 52 Jewish residents of combined ages and genders who were shot dead during the forced procession to the gathering points. I signed another that accounted for an additional 26 Jewish residents shot dead while attempting to escape. Other documents related my personal orders to wire, set, and detonate explosives in areas identified and designated as residential dwellings. I put my signature on a collective arrest roster for 244 Jewish criminals and 7 members of the Lublin ghetto Judenrat. The final document I signed was the order for the train carrying the prisoners to depart from Lublin later that day. It would go west to Kielce and then southwest to Jedrzejów and Kraków before arriving at Auschwitz.

As I looked at those documents and my signatures upon them I realized that I had helped to open the door Amon spoke of. The one we could not close. I realized that my finger had dipped into the dirt and drawn a line behind me. I was now irrevocably committed to the Final Solution to the Jewish Question by name and deeds. God help me indeed if we lose this war.

These actions and their results became more profound when I set them aside and began authoring the report Heydrich had requested before I left for Lublin. Once again I wrote of the benefits of Zyklon B and its efficiency, and I used formal language on the document as I knew it would go before Hitler, Himmler and Göring. I completed the report in Globocnik's headquarters and handed it to a motorcycle dispatch rider to be delivered to SS Command at Kazimierz Dolny where it would be relayed to Berlin. By the end of the day I had transported 251 Jews to Auschwitz and encouraged their subjection to Zyklon B.

Previous to this I had done exactly what Untersturmführer Göth had said. I had made each of my decisions based on laws, precedents and operational guidelines that were established by my superiors. I had previously participated in searches, trials and executions, but I was not the superior officer in those matters. I had been one of many tools and at that point a valid argument could have been offered that I was dutifully following orders. In spite of following orders, I believed there was accountability for my actions and decisions in those previous matters. However, I felt any repercussion upon me would be lessened by the fact that I was not the proactive force in those affairs. But, now I had conceived and issued the orders. Now my accountability had gone to the forefront.

This is not to say I believed any criminal act had been committed on behalf of the Reich, nor did I feel guilty of unlawful participation. The laws of the Reich were very clear and I had acted well within the parameters of legal command. My personal position on the Jews at that time was something I strictly kept to myself. I certainly understood and agreed with the need to remove the Jews from German culture, society and politics. However, I was an officer in the Office for Jewish Emigrations and I was foolish enough, for a very long time, to believe my department had the goal of emigration in mind. At some point, perhaps in 1940, emigration ceased to exist and was replaced with forced deportation. The direct name of our office became a general matter of semantics. By 1942, emigration and forced deportation equaled the unconditional extermination of the Jewish population of Europe.

Months prior, when Schumann and I looked at the maps in Eichmann's office and saw the numerous ghettos, we both believed the goal was emigration to Poland. At various meetings we discussed the classification of Jews as essential and non essential workers and this resulted in arguments over what purpose Jews had within the German Reich. Many officers and industrialists argued that the Jews were to serve as a free labor force for Germany, but the Party loyalists countered that the mere thought of a Jew having any place whatsoever in the Reich was seditious.

Of course we knew of the Termination Stations, but this was explained to us in a manner that suggested the non essential workers were to be exterminated to conserve resources for the German people and our war effort. The T4 Euthanasia Program was theoretically aligned to the principles of the Termination Stations in that all Germans suffering from poor mental faculties, advanced age, crippling physical conditions and terminal illnesses were to be executed for the conservation of valuable resources. The execution of non essential Jews therefore, was not a primary concern when relatives of Reich Party members, officers, soldiers, and German citizens were also subjected to a similar fate for non essential beings.

All of these matters were surrounded by a highly protective shield of secrecy that kept the stark truth from most people. My Father's declining mental condition resulted in his being admitted to a hospital near Munich in 1942. My family received a letter from the hospital stating that Father did not respond to medicines or treatment and that he contracted pneumonia and died in May. I did not learn until 1956 that Father's condition marked him for the T4 Program and that he received a lethal and intentional phenol injection to his heart. Not in May 1942, but eleven days after he was admitted to the hospital in February. Visitations were conveniently denied to my family under the excuse that Father was resting in a ward full of contagions. It took three months before my family learned of his death of which the date had been falsified by the Medical Office. There was no funeral to attend. My family and I simply received the news that Father had died and was buried on the grounds of the hospital. Thousands of German families received similar news. Many years later it was discovered that headstones marked empty graves at the hospital cemetery. In truth, there was no cemetery. The bodies had been cremated and the ashes disposed of in fields and ponds.

I attempted to clear my orders to leave Lublin and return to Berlin but Eichmann dispatched me to the SS Tactical Command Headquarters at the city of Mariupol in the Ukraine. The SS and Wehrmacht were capturing Russian soldiers by the thousands and these prisoners required transport to Sobibor, Auschwitz and Belzec. Partisan and battle damage had disrupted the railroads and I was being sent there to rectify and expedite the process.

A Storch airplane flew me from Kaztówka, Poland to Nikopol, Ukraine. We descended with the Dnieper River to our right and I could see how much the war had altered the landscape below. I was greeted by a delegation of high ranking officers on the airstrip and they treated me with courtesies fit for royalty. A Citroen car had been decorated with Party flags and this was to be my ride into Mariupol which was approximately 200 kilometers east across the Dnieper.

There was a mood of anxiety among the combat soldiers at Nikopol and heavy gun emplacements and machine gun nests were pointed across the river. Large pockmarks and shell craters dotted the area and a field hospital was full with recently wounded. The officers explained that Nikopol had not been completely secured and that an ongoing battle had raged for control of the city's bridgehead across the Dnieper.

"What is the tactical situation east of the river?" I asked.

"Heavy fighting south of Zaporizhzhia and north of Melitopol," was the reply.

I looked at the maps and saw that in order to reach Mariupol I would be required to travel directly south of Zaporizhzhia and directly north of Melitopol.

"And you wish for me to make this journey in that Citroen? With the flags and markings? Which one of you has this great desire to see me killed?"

They realized the error of marking the car and immediately ordered enlisted soldiers to remove the insignias. I would receive an escort of 4 halftracks, 150 infantry, 2 SDKFZ armored cars and 3 Panzer IV tanks.

"I would prefer to make this journey in one of the armored vehicles."

The officers explained the benefits of the speed of the Citroen and the fact that it was a smaller and more maneuverable vehicle that would be harder to hit with mortars or artillery. This made no difference to me. A single Staff car in the middle of an armored column meant only one thing: an officer was present. I elected to make the journey in one of the halftracks which had more maneuverability than the tanks, but thicker armor than the SDKFZs.

We crossed the Dnieper River at 0330 hours and made unimpeded progress under the cover of darkness. At sunrise the vehicle commanders began conversing on their radios to point out potential dangers and ambush points in the surrounding terrain. Now and then an ME 109 would soar over our heads, circle briefly, and return to the west.

Outside the town of Kuibysheve we were waved down by a group of ragged Ukrainian adolescents. They told us Russian soldiers occupied Komysh-Zoria just east of Kuibysheve and urged us to alter our direction northeast to Rozivka, or south to Chernihivka. The Ukrainians were evenly divided in their willingness to assist German forces, but this helpful alliance was beginning to waiver under the shadow of the mass executions and destruction of Ukrainian villages being carried out by the SS. None of us could be certain that the Russians were indeed at Komysh-Zoria and for all we knew, the children were sending us into the jaws of an ambush at either of the suggested alternate destinations.

Our Column Leader requested Luftwaffe reconnaissance and following a rapid flight by an ME 109, it was reported that Russian trucks and soldiers were indeed spotted on the ground at Komysh-Zoria. We waited for the pilot's report of ground situations to the north and south. Eventually he informed us that Rozivka was temporarily secure but he spotted a Russian Rifle Company 15 to 20 kilometers east of the town. His survey of Chernihivka was favorable in that the nearest Russian forces were located approximately 35 kilometers south at Zelenivka. We gave the children chocolate and hard candies and rerouted our column south to Chernihivka.

We passed this southern destination as a heavy downpour of rain began to fall, and turned east to continue onward toward Mariupol. Outside Volodarske the road before us erupted into fountains of earth that threw muddy soil high over our heads. The SS infantry staggered themselves in the drainage ditches on both sides of the dirt path. The column came to a complete halt and the noise from the idling motor of the halftrack filled the narrow compartment.

Our vehicle operator began cursing the SDKFZ driver in front of us and the Panzer IV crew behind us, telling both to move their vehicles out of the way and form a defensive gauntlet. There was too much foolish conversation between the drivers and commanders.

"Did anyone see anything?"

"Were those mines or mortars?"

"What direction did those strikes come from?"

More shells detonated around our vehicles while the drivers and commanders continued their confused discussion. The concussion from the shells rocked our halftrack back and forth on its struts. I squeezed through the narrow carriage and looked at the frightened faces of the men inside the vehicle with me. I pushed my head into the forward compartment and shouted, "Scharführer! Get these vehicles off this damned road at once!"

I was not a combat officer and I had no real authority to tell those experienced vehicle drivers and commander what to do, but one thing seemed certain. As long as we remained idle on the road we were stationary targets.

The Scharführer called the lead tank on his radio. "What is the problem up there? Why are you not moving?"

The response was prompt. "I have a shell crater in front of me that is the size of the Harz Valley. The ditches are too steep on either side. We are going to have to reverse onto solid ground."

Orders were relayed to put all vehicles in reverse and one by one we began to back up. The SDKFZ in front of us lost its traction on the right side and rolled off the road into the drainage ditch crushing several SS soldiers taking cover there.

The downpour was greatly complicating matters as it was turning the slush and ice into an impassable quagmire of mud and water. The treads and wheels on our vehicles were throwing this sloppy mess in all directions and we were sinking in the divots we were creating.

More explosions banged around us and the voice of the commander in the lead tank came over the radios.

"I just took a hit," he said. "My drive shaft is disabled. I am giving orders to abandon my vehicle."

Another voice called the airstrip at Mariupol to request Luftwaffe support. It was denied as the weather was too inclement to permit planes to take off.

The driver of our halftrack opened the throttle but we felt no movement of the vehicle other than the shuddering caused by spinning treads.

"That is all I can do," he shouted back to us. "We are stuck and not going anywhere. Abandon the vehicle. Single line. Use the rear escape hatch."

While waiting for the hatch to be opened I heard another one of our vehicle commanders calling Mariupol to request armor and infantry support along with two prime movers to free our stuck vehicles from the mud.

Outside it was nearly impossible to walk. The slush and mud was up to our shins and each step almost sucked our boots off our feet. The temperature of the pouring rain was just enough to create a thick fog around the battlefield and we had no visibility beyond 13 or 14 meters. Now and then we could hear a metallic thud before Russian mortar rounds exploded in our vicinity.

It was a hellish feeling to be blinded by fog and rain on the steppes of the Ukraine with the enemy knowing our position. There was nothing we could do to fight back as we had no logical reasoning of where the Russians were. The commanders debated our choices and they were evenly divided on whether to remain at our current position or move. Any man who lost an armored vehicle had undeniable hell to account for it. This greatly influenced our commanders to remain with their vehicles, but that choice was being overcome by the brutal fact that the Russians had marked our location. The fog was growing thicker and visibility had now been limited to approximately 9 meters. It seemed sound to use the cover of the fog to evacuate the area. The argument to this was that we did not know where the Russian mortar crews were or how heavily reinforced they might be. An evacuation of the immediate area could lead to a procession straight into enemy hands.

The armored commanders pressed their case that the guns on their vehicles were yet serviceable and provided adequate defenses to our current position. The infantry leaders argued that outgoing rounds from tanks and halftracks could very well slice our soldiers to pieces in a crossfire caused by the blindness from the fog. Two Waffen SS Lieutenants were studying a map in an effort to find a suitable location to move to. Other officers and enlisted men were reviewing maps of the local area to try to determine the most probable position of the Russians.

Mortar rounds dropped on us intermittently and the only warning we had was a few seconds of a sizzling noise before they impacted. Most of us tried to take cover near the vehicles and we were all soaked through to our flesh with mud and water.

After another attack, I noticed a Corporal holding a map near the two Waffen SS Lieutenants. He was waiting for a pause in their conversation but they paid him no heed. I asked the Corporal if there was something of value he had to say.

He pointed to a small hill on his map that was approximately one quarter of a kilometer to the south. "That is where the Russians are, Sir."

I looked at his map and given the vastness of the area around us, told him his decision seemed quite arbitrary but that I was willing to listen to how he formed his conclusion.

"I served with mortar crews in Belgium and Poland, Sir. The shells being fired at us are coming in at an angle, not a straight downward drop."

I was impressed. "How can you be certain of this?"

"The sound, Sir. Mortar shells only hiss like that when they are fired from an acute angle. My guess, Sir, is that the enemy mortars are set at an outgoing angle of 18 to 22 ½ degrees. That would be a perfect tube discharge from an elevation. An outgoing direction at 45 or 58 degrees would launch the shells upward in an arc. We would not hear them cutting through the air because they would come in on a dead drop."

I interrupted the two Waffen SS Lieutenants and they were equally impressed with the Corporal's assessment. A reconnaissance patrol of 25 or 30 men was assembled and I offered to lead them with the Corporal at my side. It seemed better to be outside the immediate kill box than to stand there and wait for more mortar shells.

Fear overtook me when the vehicles disappeared in the fog behind us. It was very easy to lose sight of the members of the patrol in the fog and staying tightly grouped was also dangerous. An enemy machine gun emplacement or a single mortar round would have taken all of us from this earth.

As we came closer to the elevation we could hear the distinct discharges from the mortar tubes. The Corporal nodded. "The mortars are certainly set at an angle of 18 to 22 ½ degrees."

The top of the hill was covered in fog and the Russians launched five or six shells every ten minutes. They could not be attempting to hit anything as they could not see what was out there. They knew we were using the road and were therefore saturating it with harassment fire. I used the radio to inform the vehicle commanders of our discovery and I requested an additional twenty five men for the assault.

My request was denied. SS Tactical Command at Mariupol had authorized an assault with the unit I had led there, or we could wait for a break in the weather at which a medium Luftwaffe bomber would be dispatched to remove the hill. I was informed that our troops had moved away from the stranded vehicles in the main zone of concentrated fire and were relatively safe. However, we had lost two halftracks to mortar shells in addition to the disabled tank and the crashed SDKFZ.

The SS never promoted the idea of free thinking until a situation like this arose. Superior officers might authorize an assault such as this, but unless the objectives were clear, they would not directly order it. No one knew what was on top of that hill. It could have been a few light mortar crews. It could also have been a few light mortar crews supported by heavy machine guns and tanks. Our superior officers, who sat in the comfort of warm, dry offices many kilometers away from this situation, enjoyed the benefits of potential political gain. They took the position of authorizing the assault. This meant that if I chose not to take that hill and our vehicles were destroyed on the road, I would be accountable for not leading the attack and my superiors could argue they encouraged the assault. If I ordered the attack and it was successful, the superior officers pinned it to their service records as a tactical victory. This is to say that I was conveniently put into a position that required independent thought in a military that discouraged it. It was a careful scheme to displace superior officers from being implicated in a potential debacle and it placed all the responsibility firmly on my shoulders.

I asked the Corporal, "If you were up on that hill, how would you defend your position?"

He thought for a brief moment. "Two or three medium machine guns. Each would have a two man crew. Rely on at least 6 men applied to machine guns up there, Sir. I would also use riflemen. No less than 10. I am hearing at least four mortars up there so I would estimate 4 men to each crew. We are looking at approximately 32 Russians up there and perhaps an officer, doctor and communications crew. A safe approximation would be 40 to 45 Russians, Sir."

I pulled my squad together and gave the orders to take the hill. We would divide into two evenly numbered squads and flank it from the east and west. I gave specific instructions to saturate the top of the elevation with grenades prior to a gun assault. I also issued directives to be careful of the crossfire we would create from attacking at opposite sides.

As we began our laborious ascent up the muddy hill I swore I heard my Mother's voice asking, "Rolf! What in the Holy Heavens are you doing?"

Indeed what was I doing? Climbing up the side of some damned soaked and muddy hill in the middle of the damned Ukraine. Putting myself closer and closer to Russian guns and for what? One people, one Reich, one Führer? No. Not that day. I was climbing that hill in hopes of sparing my comrades down on the road. I did not want to do it, but in combat you are forced to do things you would never normally do or ever aspire to do. I was so terrified climbing that hill that I can not reason how I did it. I managed to come within less than 2 meters of the top before I pulled a grenade from my belt. It slipped from my trembling hands before I could prime it and I watched it slide down the muddy hill. The men followed my lead and we threw a dozen or so grenades.

Chaos followed the explosions and Russian voices shouted in a dead panic. We maneuvered our way to the precipice and pressed ourselves into the slush and mud. There were four mortar crews, two medium machine guns and five or six Soviet riflemen. We quickly overtook them and they instinctively fled toward the other side of the elevation where our other squad appeared and cut them down.

I walked to the center of the captured Russian fire base as if I was some sort of conquering hero and sat down on a Russian ammunition crate. My men enjoyed looting the dead of their watches, rings and personal items. The Corporal must have been standing before me for quite some time until I noticed him.

"Sir," he said. "Do you wish to notify the column?" I looked up and saw he was next to a radio operator who was offering me the transmitter. I could not even form words at that point. I mustered all the resolve in my being to maintain composure in front of the men but I felt like shouting, crying and cursing. So many emotions were filtering through my brain about the events that just transpired. We had been successful and I should have been jubilant about it. However, I had jeopardized the lives of my men, and Russian bullets had been fired directly at us. It was only by the grace of God that my men and I had not been wounded or killed. How do you find triumph or elation in this? How could I look at the slaughtered Russians and be moved to celebrate?

As the weather cleared we established an observation post on the hill to monitor activity around us on the steppes until our prime movers and support arrived from Mariupol. While waiting, I authored a recommendation of promotion for the Corporal. The vehicle commanders had gathered around to inspect the dead Russians, photograph the bodies and rejoice over the victory. The units from Mariupol arrived in the early evening and towed our vehicles out of the mud. We resumed our advance late in the night.

I was grateful to arrive at Mariupol as the city was well fortified as an outpost. The Waffen SS officers said they were honored to meet me and hailed my assault on the elevation. I accepted the praise because it would have been discourteous to do anything other. I was given a nice hotel room where I lost myself in the first hot bath I had in weeks. On the following morning I met with a Waffen SS Colonel and his Staff to discuss the transport of Russian Prisoners of War out of the Occupied Zones.

Before the conversation began, the Colonel presented me with documents and new collar tabs. By the order and recommendation of

Brigadeführer Odilo Globocnik, I was promoted to the rank of Hauptsturmführer. That bastard Göth had been accurate with his prediction that my work at the Lublin ghetto would be rewarded. I was in disagreement to the promotion but I dared not decline it. Promotions meant more responsibility and the ability to make critical decisions over life and death. I believed that my role in the Final Solution had thus far been minimal. I knew that the Office for Jewish Emigrations would place great burdens upon me in the field and that my new tasks would require brutal resolve to very difficult situations.

The Colonel informed me that many problems existed in maintaining security over the railroads. Partisans and Russian forces had been detonating bridges, tunnels and switching stations to disrupt our flow of supplies to the east and no sooner was the damage repaired when it occurred again elsewhere.

It seemed logical that the disruptions in the Occupied Zones were the direct work of partisans. However, as we experienced west of Mariupol, the front lines were constantly shifting. We held the bridge over the Dnieper at Nikopol, and Mariupol 200 kilometers east, but what lied in between was a virtual No Man's Land. German and Russian forces were desperately clinging to small towns and rural villages across the landscape.

The Colonel pointed to Rostov-on-Don on a map and explained that this city was our most powerful stronghold in the east. It was by all accounts a fully operational Reich headquarters and city inside the Ukrainian state. At that time approximately 7,000 Russian prisoners were being detained there and were awaiting transport to facilities in Poland. OKW and OKH had become deadlocked in arguments with the Ministry of Transportation about how the rails should be used. Military High Command demanded free passage for the distribution of critical supplies and the Ministry of Transportation wanted to take advantage of a minimal break in the fighting to transport the prisoners. The Colonel could not answer if the resources existed for such an operation. He had no information on the number of freight wagons or Class A locomotives available for such an operation.

Complicating the matter was the fact that Russian forces knew their comrades were being detained at Rostov-on-Don. It was believed that 7,000 veteran Russian soldiers might be realistic motivation for the Soviets to launch an assault on the city. High

Command demanded that Rostov-on-Don was to be held at all costs and part of ensuring the safety of the city was to eliminate it as a potential target. This meant the immediate evacuation of the 7,000 prisoners in order that the Russians would not attack Rostov-on-Don in the attempt to free them.

Before resolving this matter it was necessary to address the 3,600 Soviet Prisoners of War being held in Mariupol. My superiors in Berlin were adamant about deporting the prisoners to Sobibor and Belzec in order to keep them out of military circulation. Potential dangers existed in the possibilities of air raids or artillery assaults that might blow apart the walls of the detainment areas in Mariupol. 3,600 Russians running free in a German held city was something everyone wished to avoid. Logistically, it was not feasible for the Russian army to launch an assault against Mariupol. In spite of shifting battle lines, the approaches to the city were well guarded and defended. This did not prevent Soviet aircraft or artillery guns from being a factor.

I spoke with representatives from the Ministry of Transportation and managed to forge a temporary peace between that department and OKH and OKW. I assured them I could organize the transports within 10 days using 29 freight wagons each loaded with 125 Russian units. Two Class A locomotives would be capable of pulling the wagons and I proposed two transports: one with 14 wagons and the other with 15. The Office for Jewish Emigrations was pleased with my projection but limited me to 4 days to organize the transports.

One Class A locomotive was requisitioned from Novoazovs'k and I obtained the other from Taganrog. Within 72 hours both were on the rail platforms at Mariupol and the freight wagons were being connected. The Waffen SS Colonel came to the platforms to inspect the process and asked if the Russian prisoners would be loaded according to rank. I had no idea what he was talking about, but the Colonel insisted it would not be proper to force Russian officers to share freight wagons with enlisted men. He prattled on about proper military customs and courtesies being enforced and I was of no mind or mood to listen to him. It was cold and raining, and my sole purpose was to load the Russian prisoners and get the trains out of Mariupol.

There were not enough Order Policemen to escort the prisoners from the holding facilities to the rail platforms and I was forced to request Waffen SS soldiers for this task. The Colonel was interested in bickering about loading enemy officers and enlisted soldiers in the same wagons and stated he would only grant me Waffen SS troops on the condition that I met his expectations for the loading process.

The Russians were untermenschen by political definition. They were equal to Jews and other undesirables by the classification laws of the Reich, and Stalin's refusal to sign the Code of Conducts removed them from being treated with military customs and courtesies. In my opinion I did not care if a Russian General was forced to share a freight wagon with the Company cook. I was angry that I had to waste time placing telephone calls to Berlin to request the assistance I needed from the Waffen SS. Curiously, my superiors were not enraged by the Colonel's unwillingness to help me. On the request of my superiors, I handed the telephone to the Colonel who listened with resignation. He disconnected and apologized to me and promised all the assistance I needed.

I loaded the wagons within 6 hours and the letters "P.O.W" were stained on the roofs and sides. This international abbreviation would prevent aircraft from strafing the trains and it would prevent partisans and enemy forces from attacking them on the ground. The trains departed Mariupol 8 hours ahead of schedule.

My work at Rostov-on-Don was less complicated as I received the full support of the Waffen SS. The city had a large industrial belt and though most of its factories had been destroyed, the transportation lines were in good repair. Situated on a river, its previous commercial output greatly depended on a complex railroad system and most of the freight locomotives and wagons had escaped extensive damage. During the third week of March I had organized several transports containing over 7,000 Russian Prisoners of War and more than 1,300 Jews to Poland.

The following weeks required my presence at a series of meetings at Rostov-on-Don. The assemblies were attended by Waffen SS and Wehrmacht combat officers who demanded a compromised usage of the railroads. Most of them complained that they could not fight the war when shipments of supplies were being diverted and halted so that my department could use the rails to transport Jews. It was another bureaucratic deadlock over what departments had control over what resources. As far as I was told and concerned, the deportation of Jews and Russian prisoners was a matter of priority. I understood the need to ship war supplies to the front but I did not make those decisions. I did as told and performed my duties to the best of my abilities.

Several officers from the Einsatzgruppen were present at these meetings and they asked questions of me that I could not answer. The Einsatzgruppen and I served the same departments in Berlin and we all answered to the same superior officers. The Einsatz Commanders at Rostov-on-Don embraced the opportunity to speak with me whom they regarded as a field delegate from Berlin.

They told me of the mass liquidations they were carrying out by firing squad on almost a daily basis. Each unit had one or more Legal Affairs Officers assigned to it, and the responsibility of the lawyers was to make certain the executions were completed in a legal manner. According to the Einsatz Commanders, many situations arose during the mass liquidations that were not specifically governed by Reich Law or Occupational Law. The Legal officers were supposed to intervene and allow the executions based on legal precedent or deny the killings based on lack of one. However, pressure from Berlin often superceded the authority of the Einsatz Commanders and the legal officers, and the men carrying out these deeds were left wondering if any legality governed their actions at all. The Einsatz Units were rapidly becoming rogue killing squads governed by no direct authority.

I conveyed this information to Berlin and was directly assigned to accompany Einsatzgruppe D as an observer. On or about 5 April 1942 I followed this unit north of Mariupol to the town of Andrivka.

The orders of Einsatzgruppe D were very common and simple. They were to round up the local Jews and dispose of them in a forest west of the town. I was surprised that there was no tactical search of the buildings for intelligence documents, maps or weapons. Nothing of the sort transpired. Einsatzgruppe D entered the town and immediately began seizing the Jews based on physical characteristics, census records, and a number of dubious reasons.

The SD and Waffen SS members of EGD became engaged in an argument over who was to perform the menial task of setting and wiring demolitions in a creek bed that was to serve as a mass grave. The SD claimed they had provided the last trench and the Waffen SS maintained that the Jews should be made to dig the ditch since they were the ones who were going to occupy it. The KRIPO and Order

Police began escorting groups of Jews toward the edge of the forest in a very calm and orderly manner.

I stood near the EGD Commander, Standartenführer Otto Ohlendorf, while observing the activities of his unit. He was complaining about the Special Action at Andrivka and talking to no one in particular about how his Einsatzgruppe should be operating well within Bessarabia or the Crimea rather than north of Mariupol. I directly asked him what kinds of unusual legal matters arose during such actions.

"Be patient," he replied. "You will learn soon enough. There is always something that complicates these matters."

The Waffen SS detonated the trench in the creek bed and the sudden explosion brought about the startled screams of the Jewish women and children. Four or five Ukrainian Nationals had wrenched the arm of a Catholic priest behind his back and were pushing him toward members of the SD. A conversation ensued between them that seemed confusing from the gestures being made.

Ohlendorf watched this before saying, "I believe that situation could benefit from your expertise."

I approached the group and firmly inquired, "What have we here?"

The Ukrainian Nationals pushed the priest to his knees as one pointed to him and shouted, *"Er ist Johanne der Baptist!"*

One of the SD soldiers looked at me. "Sir, they say the priest has falsely converted Jews to the Catholic religion. They claim he hides Jews and has helped many to escape the territory."

Ohlendorf joined us and inquired about the nature of the problem.

"They call him John the Baptist, Sir," I replied. "He fancies himself a converter of Jews."

The Standartenführer studied him. "A Catholic priest assisting the Jews?" He nodded and asked me, "What are we to do?"

"Put him with the Jews. The law regulates the fate of all enemies and those connected to them."

"And what evidence do we have of his crimes beyond the accusations of peasants?"

I instructed the SD to escort the Catholic priest to the collection of Jews and then asked Ohlendorf, "Do you honestly maintain that there is some semblance of a judicial system out here?"

"No," responded the Standartenführer. "But that is why you are here. A Catholic priest, Hauptsturmführer? What would the Foreign Office say about this?"

"Very well. I will pull him from the line to be spared."

"I would not recommend that now," said Ohlendorf. "You can not reverse your decisions in front of the Jews."

Members of the Order Police and Waffen SS began vomiting. Ohlendorf smiled and nodded. "Now come the requests to be excused from duty due to illness."

I looked at those suffering from the sudden sickness but could not figure what brought on the condition.

Ohlendorf explained. "They soak rotten cabbage in their canteens and mix mustard with the water. They drink it an hour or two before the scheduled actions. Stahlecker has reported the same problem with his men in EGA. Blobel shoots the men in EGC that do this."

"And you, Sir? What do you do?"

"I do not shoot my men, Hauptsturmführer. These are good men. A bit exhausted perhaps, but they are good men."

The Oberscharführer of the SD units approached us. "Sir," he said to Ohlendorf, "We are ready to assemble the shooting squads."

"I am deferring command of this action to Hauptsturmführer Schiller." He crossed his arms and fixed his eyes on me. "I am certain RSHA Headquarters can collect the most accurate information by personally overseeing an operation like this one. It is better to experience the logistical and legal problems firsthand. Undoubtedly your superiors will gain better insight into these matters from your personal experience."

The Oberscharführer put his attention on me. "Sir, we are ready to assemble the shooting squads." He pointed to the men regurgitating in patches of melting snow. "Should I excuse them from duty, Sir?"

I stared at the ill soldiers, cast my eyes over the collection of people scheduled for execution and locked my gaze on a pregnant Jewess.

"Sir! Am I to excuse those men from duty?"

"No, Oberscharführer. Assemble a shooting squad with those men."

He looked at me for a moment before sprinting off to relay my orders. Ohlendorf showed no emotion but I could hear the ill soldiers protesting that they were not fit for duty. The Oberscharführer responded, "You are soldiers, damn it! You are not fit because you are drinking the shit-water that you make! The Hauptsturmführer has ordered you to gather your rifles! To the trench! Now!"

One of the sickened soldiers slowly approached me and explained that he was married and a father of three. He pleaded that he could not discharge his rifle at women and children. He appealed to Ohlendorf but the Standartenführer informed him I was in command.

"There are no women or children here," I said. "There are only Jews; enemies of the Reich and German people, Rottenführer."

He looked at Ohlendorf as if I were some bystander. "Sir, you know of my family! You know I can not do this."

Ohlendorf replied, "Because of your family I have not previously ordered you to do this. This does not mean you can not do this. It is your duty, Rottenführer, and the Hauptsturmführer has given you orders."

An argument erupted near the edge of the forest and I immediately went to investigate its source. A man with blonde hair was trying to convince the SS that he was not a Jew and that he had been consigned to the line because of a petty land dispute with his neighboring villagers. Even the Jews next to him were reinforcing his claim, but the man did not have identity documents to prove it. He did not have the physical appearance of a Jew but this was not sound basis to release him. As Ohlendorf stated, I could not reverse SS decisions before the people.

The situation began to get out of control. The Catholic priest was advocating for the man's release, the man was arguing his case, people shouted for and against him, our soldiers were regurgitating, and it began to rain.

An Untersturmführer came to my side and asked, "Are we doing this today or not, Sir?" He had a wry smile as if he believed a Field Liaison from the Office for Jewish Emigrations could not possibly manage such circumstances.

"Where is Standartenführer Ohlendorf?" I asked.

"He has departed for Mariupol, Sir. He ordered me to tell you that he expects your After Action Report by this evening."

"Are the gun squads ready?" I inquired.

"They have been ready," responded the Untersturmführer.

Knowing that Ohlendorf had gone, I pondered the idea of releasing the Catholic priest, the blonde haired man and perhaps the pregnant Jewess."

The Jews shifted their claims that they too had been falsely accused by Ukrainian Nationalists; children began crying, and I was losing my patience and composure.

"It is raining," pointed out the Untersturmführer.

There were approximately 150 Jews of all genders and ages lined up at the edge of the forest. "How many gunners do I have at the creek bed?"

"A standard squad," replied the Junior Lieutenant. He knew that I did not know the numerical total of men and there was sarcasm in his answer. I leveled an impatient gaze at him and he stated, "Twenty, Sir."

"Get the Jews moving in groups to fifteen," I ordered. "Reserve five gunners for the coup de gras."

He relayed my orders to the SD who took fifteen Jews aside and forced them to remove their clothing.

A group of Ukrainian Nationals came from the village and held approximately twelve people under guard with rakes, shovels and axes shouting, *"Mehr Juden! Mehr Juden!"*

One of the captives appealed to me in perfect German. "Sir, none of us are Jews. We are livestock and produce vendors from the village of Vilovik. This is a grudge held against us by the people of Andrivka!"

He blathered on about events last winter and how the crops at Andrivka had not produced a bountiful harvest. He claimed the village of Vilovik was also below quota for food and was forced to inflate prices of livestock and produce sold to the people of Andrivka. I did not care about any of this.

The SD had not moved the group of fifteen Jews into the forest to the creek bed but instead stood there talking with them. The Catholic priest was now advocating for the blonde haired man and the people from Vilovik; the rain was becoming heavier, and one of the Ukrainian Nationals was waving a tattered Jewish prayer shawl before me and stating it was the property of one of the Vilovik people before me. The collection of Jews began to argue for their release and the Untersturmführer watched all of this with a smug expression that tore me from my senses.

I took the MP40 from my shoulder, pulled its charging handle and sprayed the group of people from Vilovik with bullets. Each one of them fell dead in a patch of watery snow on the Ukrainian steppes and all voices went silent. I shouted at the SD to get the Jews moving. They complied at once.

The pregnant Jewess walked by me with her hands on her distended womb. Dark curls extended from her babushka and while passing, she dipped her head with a sorrowful and resigned expression. Her jade green eyes stared into my soul for a brief moment and she lightly spoke in German, saying, "The highest form of wisdom is kindness."

I followed the Untersturmführer into the forest and we made our way toward the sounds of the systematic gunfire. We stood near the trench and watched the Jews enter it in groups of fifteen. Men, women and children were shot on my orders. The pregnant Jewess, naked except for the babushka on her head, was assisted into the ditch by others. She cradled her swollen belly until the bullets took her from this life.

When the action was completed, the Ukrainian Nationalists were forced to fill the trench with earth. EGD departed the area to the southeast and I returned directly to Mariupol hoping to have words with Ohlendorf. When I arrived I learned he had left to join his unit. New orders called for my immediate return to Berlin and while in flight I composed the After Action Report requested by Ohlendorf. I would present it to my superiors and as far as I was concerned, they could pass it on to the Standartenführer. I authored a very adverse report and detailed the intentional illnesses of the men, the lack of discipline and order, and the confusion and mental stress upon the soldiers. Though not appropriate for this particular document, I authored an addendum to it on the efficiency and impersonal use of Zyklon B.

CHAPTER FIFTEEN
THE RAGING FLAMES OF DESTRUCTION

At RSHA Headquarters Berlin, I requested a private meeting with Eichmann to relay my accounts of the Einsatzgruppe D action at Andrivka. He was greatly concerned by what I told him and informed me that the Reichsführer-SS was personally against the widespread use of firing squads. Eichmann stated that the Reich, and especially our department, was entering a new segment for the Final Solution to the Jewish Question and that firing squads would no longer be a suitable means of extermination for the vast number of Jews intended for Special Treatment.

Over the next two weeks I prepared reports for the Ministry of Transportation regarding the railroads in the Ukraine. During the first few days of May I was personally summoned to Heydrich's headquarters in Prague. The directives were different than most I had previously received. I was requested to bring formal civilian attire and the invitation extended to Klaudia Krüger.

I arrived at Hydracny Castle at Prague in full military dress uniform and Klaudia looked like the subject of a formal painting. Heydrich had certainly chosen a very lavish headquarters and once inside, I saw that it rivaled the most ornate buildings back in Berlin. The interior of the castle smelled of freshly cut flowers and I marveled at the decorations while being escorted up a grand flight of stairs to the General's office. Klaudia was taken to private quarters.

When I was shown through the doors, Heydrich acted in a manner I had never known before. He stood and walked around from his desk and shook my hand instead of waiting for a salute. "Hauptsturmführer Schiller," he said approvingly. "I trust your journey was comfortable?"

"Indeed, Sir."

He walked to a large pair of open windows and stared out over Prague. "Look at this," he said.

I joined him at his side and admired the full and sweeping view of the Czech landscape.

After a few moments he looked at me. "I read your report on the action at Andrivka. I also read your addendum." He paused for a moment.

"The behavior at Andrivka was not civilized German conduct," I said.

"Did you expect it to be? War is ugly and brutal; you should know that by now. We all must do our part no matter what it demands of us." He walked to his desk and sorted through several documents.

He asked, "Did you know a Waffen SS Rottenführer Kerbaugh?"

"The name is not familiar, Sir."

"He knew you," said Heydrich while handing me several documents. The first was an application for Kerbaugh's Death Card. The other papers were his service records and the last page was his handwritten suicide note composed two weeks prior in the Ukraine. As I read Kerbaugh's letter, I recognized from its contents that he was the married man with offspring who objected to shooting Jewish women and children.

"Himmler has had enough of this," said the General. "The reports from all Legal Affairs Officers have convinced the Reichsführer to move forward with Zyklon B gassings at Auschwitz, Majdanek and Chelmno. For now, carbon monoxide will be used at Treblinka, Sobibor and Belzec. Höss has been requesting an evaluation of the selection process for Jewish freight arriving at Auschwitz II Birkenau. Auschwitz III Monowitz is expected to be formally operational on 1 June. The realization of the Monowitz complex is a direct result of hard work by men like you, Schiller."

He returned to the window and inhaled a deep breath of the fresh air. "I believe that the physicians at Auschwitz are being too lenient with their assessments of prisoner fitness. It seems an unusually high quota is going into the barracks and to work details. Höss is reporting complications with the gas chambers and crematoriums, however, mechanical and structural inspections have proven all to be fully operational."

He pulled a chair out from behind a pedestal table with an ivory chess set on it and sat down. He motioned to the other chair and I took a seat. "You know Höss, do you not?"

"Yes, Sir."

"In your opinion he is a good man? An honest man and a reliable officer?"

"Yes, that is my opinion Sir."

Heydrich moved a pawn forward on the board and asked, "He is a family man, is he not?"

"He has a wife and children." I moved a chess piece.

The General rapidly countered my move. "Did you ever observe him to have affinity for the Jews?"

"Never, Sir."

While waiting for me to select a chess piece he sat back and asked, "Why would a Kommandant with seven gas chambers and three crematoriums not use them?"

I looked up to realize he was expecting an answer. "I am afraid I do not know, Sir."

"But you will learn the reasons for this," he stated. "That is why I have called you here. You will dispatch orders directly to Höss from my headquarters."

Heydrich stood and returned to the window again. "Do you play tennis, Schiller?"

It seemed to be another one of his displaced questions. "I have played tennis, Sir, but I do not think of myself as an able competitor of the sport."

"We shall see," he said. "You will find adequate attire in your quarters. I will expect you on the court within thirty minutes."

Laid upon a table next to the bed in my private quarters was a set of white SS sports attire. I donned the outfit and felt so commonly civilian standing there in the sumptuous room. The General's staff showed me the way to the outer court where Heydrich was practicing a tennis serve that made me nervous simply by watching it.

The General permitted me the honor of the first serve and several fouls drew prompt derision of my abilities. He was a most accomplished sportsman and though I managed several scores against him, I lost all of three matches. Heydrich was smiling at the end of the games and congratulated me on a competitive effort. "Wear formal civilian attire for dinner this evening. As my guests, you and Frau Krüger may make use of the horses and stables."

While riding on the castle grounds, Klaudia believed that such occurrences happened frequently during my service. She playfully chastised me for being humble and not boasting of my personal relationship with SS General Reinhard Heydrich. I did not tell her that I had no personal relationship with the General. I also did not tell her that I could not begin to imagine why he had summoned the two of us Hydracny Castle. My belief was that Heydrich had grown suspicious of Höss, and knowing of my former interactions with him, wanted to look me in the eyes while I answered questions. The physical action of dispatching me directly to Auschwitz from his personal headquarters would also apply psychological pressure to Höss, especially if I was inclined to tell him about the enjoyment and generosity the General provided me with as his guest. Höss would logically assume that I was close to Heydrich and perform the duties demanded of him out of fear I would author adverse reports about his management abilities.

There was no personal relationship between myself and Heydrich. I recognized that I was being used as a tool to promote the General's intentions. However, I did not mind this as news of being his personal guest would do nothing but bring me honor and respect.

Klaudia and I dined with General Heydrich and his wife and children. There was no mention of the war or our personal duties at the dinner table. After the meal we retired to a sitting room for cognac and Heydrich took a violin case from atop a bookshelf and opened it in front of me.

"What is your opinion of this?" he asked.

I looked at the old violin and recognized its shape. "A fine Stradivarius, Sir."

"It is more than 200 years old," said the General. "It is a 1705 Stradivarius."

"How does one obtain a 200 year old Stradivarius?" asked Klaudia. "Certainly instruments like this must be sought after and prized."

"They are," stated the General. "This one was given to Brigadeführer Globocnik after his men found it in some stinking Polish-Jewish apartment in Warsaw. The Brigadeführer presented it to me."

Heydrich removed it from the case, placed it under his chin and softly played a solo from Mozart. We sat there for a couple hours sipping our spirits and listening to the General play music fit for gods.

Following a breakfast the next morning I entered Heydrich's office, received his directives for Höss, and thanked him for his generous hospitality. Klaudia and I departed from Hydracny Castle and were driven to the railroad station in one of Heydrich's Staff cars. She boarded a train bound for Germany as I boarded one to Poland.

It is necessary to define Auschwitz as it was at that time. Initially, Auschwitz was established as a Detainment Facility to contain Poles. The first inmates were Polish military officers, civil, religious and political leaders; cultural figureheads such as scientists and artists; members of the Polish intelligentsia and resistance leaders and partisans. This Detainment Facility was named Auschwitz and it operated exclusively as a prison for political enemies. Legal executions occurred there by means of firing squads and hangings but there never existed a gas chamber at that location. In 1941 the Detainment Facility was officially designated as Auschwitz I.

Auschwitz-Birkenau, or Auschwitz II as it was designated in the Reich Detainment Facility System Administration, is the location rightly associated with mass gassings. This facility officially went into operation in 1941 and was primarily reserved for Jews and Russian prisoners of war.

Auschwitz III-Monowitz contained the industrial and commercial enterprises of the Auschwitz camp system including the synthetic rubber plant at Buna. Eventually, Auschwitz would contain over 40 satellite camps in its system including Janinagrube, Babitz, Plawy, Sosnowitz, Kobior and more than 35 others. The subcamps were separate from the main complexes at Auschwitz I, II and III but operated under the management of the Kommandant of Auschwitz. However, the inmates of the subcamps were not subjected to the protocol of confinement found in the three primary complexes. To explain this, the subcamp at Sosnowitz was a Labor Facility owned by the Reich and managed by the SS but, it was leased and directed by the Berghutte-Ost-Machineworks Company where it employed approximately 900 prisoners to manufacture artillery weapons and shells. Janinagrube was leased and directed by the Furstengrube GmbH Mining Company and it employed approximately 1000 prisoners for the collection of coal. The prisoners employed by leasing companies were primarily exempt from execution due to exclusive securities purchased and maintained by said companies. A leasing company stood to benefit from the employment of Jewish prisoners in that Jews received no wages. However, the leasing company was bound to pay a fee to the Reich Ministry of Economics for each Jew it employed on a daily basis. I believe the fee was established at a minimum of six Reich marks and increased to perhaps eight or ten Reich marks for Jews with special skills. As the Ministry of Economics received a fee for each employed Jew from the leasing company, the Jew technically became a protected property interest and as such, was exempt from summary execution. If a protected property interest was maimed or killed the leasing company was authorized to file damage claims with the Reich Ministry of Economics for compensation.

Conversely, Babitz was a farm integral to the food supply for the three main Auschwitz complexes and it was managed and directed by the SS. Approximately 200 inmates were employed at Babitz with no wages paid to them and no fees provided to the Reich Ministry of Economics.

Of course this is a very basic overview of the Auschwitz Detainment Facility system and its administration. However, this should provide the basic information necessary to demonstrate that Auschwitz was a series of three primary complexes and approximately 40 subcamps. The sole Termination Station was Auschwitz-II-Birkenau. Many inmates came forth with the claim they were imprisoned in Auschwitz and with that statement comes the general assumption they were subjected to abominable horrors at the hands of German keepers on a daily basis. Those that survived Birkenau are the only people with legitimate claims. Auschwitz I and Auschwitz III-Monowitz were not Termination Stations and the inmates of these Detainment Facilities, while subjected to brutal confinement conditions, were not exposed to arbitrary beatings, summary executions and illegal deprivation of provisions. It is true that prisoners of Auschwitz I and III were subjected to execution for critical violations of Detainment Facility regulations, but each of these facilities had its own internal courthouse wherein such matters were arbitrated by professional lawyers. The majority of legal cases submitted, wherein execution of the offending prisoner was warranted as justifiable punishment, were commuted to corporal punishment and carried out by a term of administered lashes. Corporal punishment replaced most criminal death sentences at Auschwitz when SS Gruppenführer Richard Glücks had succeeded Major General Eicke as Inspector of Concentration Camps. Whereas Eicke promoted no tolerance or mercy toward prisoners, Glücks replaced that philosophy by imposing strict penalties on SS Guards who brutalized and mistreated prisoners. Göth once jested that, "With Glücks running the system we can kill them but we can not mistreat them."

This time when I arrived at the Oswiecim Station there was a delegation of Auschwitz Junior Officers waiting for me with a Staff car. During the ride to the Detainment Facility I pondered how much to tell Höss about the nature of my visit. It was clear that Heydrich regarded him with a mood of suspicion but I could not figure if the General was concerned with the operation of Auschwitz II Birkenau or Höss's loyalty. I reasoned there was no logic in discussing my perception of Heydrich's feelings toward him because if he was later questioned and cornered, he could easily reveal that I warned him. This would rattle the level of trust I had established with Heydrich and there was no sense in damaging it.

None of this seemed to matter as Höss instinctively knew why Heydrich had sent me. After greetings and handshakes we sat across from each other and before inquiring about the reason for my visit, Höss said, "You can inform your superiors that the problems with the gas halls and crematoriums have been remedied."

I asked because I had to. "What were the problems?"

"Defective seals in chambers I and II. The lift in Crematorium II was broken and Crematorium III failed structural inspection."

"I do not suppose you have the maintenance orders and inspection reports."

"Not in my office, but I can provide you with them."

Höss meant that he could generate them to reflect what he had just told me. "They will not be necessary. Your word as an officer will suffice."

Nobody, including Heydrich and the Office for Jewish Emigrations, wanted such paperwork. Primarily because most superior officers acknowledged that Höss was delaying the inevitable and did not want to be the party responsible for encouraging him to increase the quota of gassing exterminations to its maximum efficiency. It was better not to have the alleged paperwork because all documents were subjected to a required degree of processing. This created several problems. One being that his reports would be falsely generated to reflect what he told me and this discovery would eventually be made. It was a daunting task for our superior officers to find men suited for the tasks of managing the Detainment Facilities and no one wished to replace Höss. Another problem was that the Reichsführer-SS was not enthusiastic about the existence of paperwork that detailed the Special Treatment taking place at the facilities.

I looked directly at him. "To be clear, each chamber and crematorium is operational?"

"Yes. Each is operational."

"What of the selection process?" Before I could continue he interrupted me.

"I have been forced to overcrowd the barracks and assign larger work details because of the malfunctions with the chambers and crematoriums."

I knew that was an excuse and not a factual statement. "Never mind the previous problems. All things are now in working order, correct? I have been requested to oversee each chamber and crematorium operating at maximum efficiency. When can this begin?"

"Perhaps a week or two," stated Höss. "They are planning to divide shipments of more than 50,000 Slovakian Jews between my facility and Majdan Tatarski. I suspect most of Koch's Jews will be put in the ghetto at Lublin rather than his facility at Majdanek. That always seems the course. Send them all here! Why frustrate other Kommandants with these problems? Send them to Höss!"

There was rich sarcasm and aggravation in his tone of voice. "Have you received any word from my office or the Ministry of Transportation on the numbers you are to receive here?"

"The Ministry of Transportation does not advise me of the numbers, Schiller. They only ensure a steady procession of trains through my gates. And word from your office? If you do not know the numbers expected to arrive, how am I to know?"

"Berlin wishes to see immediate results," I said. "What is your estimate on the number of expendable units confined here?"

Höss sighed, shrugged and began rubbing the sides of his head. "Perhaps 3,000."

"Including Russian Prisoners of War and Poles?"

He slowly walked to a filing cabinet and pulled several rosters to tally the numbers of useless units in the facility. "Approximately 7,500. 3,000 Jews, 1,500 Poles and 3,000 Russians."

"Inform your staff that Berlin wishes the execution of the 7,500 no later than tomorrow afternoon." He nodded without emotion.

"When do you expect your next shipment to arrive?"

Höss looked at the clock on the wall and responded, "Two hours. Austrian Jews, I believe. More Russians are expected to arrive later this afternoon."

"Numbers?"

He took a roster from his desk. "1,400 Jews and 3,450 Russians."

"I wish to observe the selection process, the registration, and the Special Treatment."

"If you will excuse me," said Höss curtly, "I have much work that needs to be done."

I made my way to the Judenrampe approximately thirty minutes before the arrival of the Austrian Jews. SS guards were assembling along this platform with shepherds and wolfhounds and each dog had a metal muzzle over its snout. I watched as some of the guards tested the devices by releasing a metal catch on the top. When the catch was pushed, the spring loaded muzzle instantly expanded and dropped to the ground.

Kapos arrived under guard and began moving wooden ramps into place to accommodate the disembarking procedure from the freight wagons. More guards appeared and finally the SS Medical Staff and doctors arrived. I told the Chief Physician that I would not tolerate leniency for the fitness standards of the arriving cargo.

The dogs began growling moments before we heard the whistle of the train announcing its arrival. A red spotlight was turned on in the signal tower. The locomotive slowly entered the facility with many freight wagons in tow. As it came to a halt the Jewish kapos moved the wooden risers in front of the wagon doors to form an even passage onto the Judenrampe. The SS surrounded the train and more kapos formed a human corridor between each wagon and the Judenrampe to prevent any of the new arrivals from escaping from the disembarkation process. The SS dog handlers stood nearby to provide additional security.

The SS Squad Leaders blew whistles after the train came to a complete halt and on this signal the kapos began slamming back the locking arms on each wagon. The doors were slid open and the cargo units stepped out onto the wooden risers with bewildered expressions. There were many similarities to the arrivals I witnessed in Porajów in that the Jews were dressed in fine clothing and hats. The women clutched their purses to their breasts as if some great risk existed they would be stolen.

A voice repeated the same message through an amplified speaker: *"Achtung! Achtung! Reisen den Wagen ab! Treten Sie auf die Plattform in einer regelmäßigen Weise!"* The people heeded this order to exit the freight wagons and step onto the platform in an orderly manner.

The new arrivals immediately surveyed their surroundings with suspicion. Some Jews attempted to ask the kapos where they were, but the inmates knew better than to respond. It was easy to identify the Jews of prominence as they were dressed in absolute finery. These people searched out officers and made demands to learn of their whereabouts.

Those officers and enlisted men that responded took great amusement in confounding the Jews who asked about the location. One officer replied, "You are now guests of the Reich in the finest spa in all of Europe!"

The selection process began with separating the arrivals into two lines. Women and children were put into one and men in the other. The groups were then marched from the Judenrampe to the gates of the main compound of Auschwitz II Birkenau where the doctors and Medical Staff promptly gave each Jew a visual evaluation. The people were again separated based on physical fitness. Some doctors motioned one way or the other with their thumbs and others did it with a nod of the head to either side. The process was very quick and efficient with approximately two-thirds of the arrivals being marked for Special Processing.

Höss had come to the platform and walked about the area performing inspections of the various stages of the arrival. He seemed to have the need to satisfy himself that everything was being done to my approval. I met him near the gates and he shook his head from side to side.

"All of this today," he said. "And next week I am to receive shipments from Ravensbrücke and France. Two thousand more."

The gates opened and the SS led the prisoners into the camp. Höss walked a few paces away and I followed him. "Is this all there is to it?" he asked. "They send them here to me, and for what?" He pointed to the words above the gates: *Arbeit Macht Frei.* "Work makes you free," he scoffed.

Trucks were waiting inside the main compound and several soldiers spoke to the crowd through conical megaphones. "Your luggage and belongings will follow. Please board the trucks. You will be taken for delousing and then you will each receive a barracks assignment and work card."

Most of the people obeyed but there were a few who could not rationalize being taken from their homes, being placed upon a train and arriving at an unknown location. Most of them did not even know they were in Poland. The general belief among them was that they were somewhere inside Germany.

A prompt registration occurred inside a barracks that the SS garrison referred to as the Isolation Station. It was walled off from the main camp and completely out of view from the other inmates. Names, occupations and countries of origin were recorded before the prisoners were marched in groups to Bunker I. They entered the building without arguments and waited to be deloused. 20 minutes later they were dead. Kapos ventilated the bunker to remove the Zyklon B before extracting the corpses.

This process went on for several hours with each group of prisoners silently entering Bunker I. The first transport of Russian Prisoners of War arrived and the Soviets were being separated on terms of fitness. Those not healthy were placed aboard trucks and driven to the Isolation Station to await their time to enter Bunker I. In a period of 4 hours we had gassed approximately 2,100 prisoners without the slightest incident and without drawing the least bit of suspicion from them. The kapos systematically ventilated the chamber and loaded the corpses onto horse drawn wagons at which they were taken to two crematoriums to be disposed of. The clothing was taken from the disrobing room and loaded into a covered Blitz Opel parked near the entrance. No sooner had Bunker I been ventilated, cleared of corpses and hosed to remove body fluids when the next group of prisoners arrived. The SS Medical Staff was tremendously efficient in carrying out the methodical executions. I remained at Auschwitz for a couple weeks to oversee the systematic liquidations of several freight shipments.

On the morning of 28 May I was awakened in the predawn darkness by a heavy pounding on the door of my quarters. An enlisted man stood outside with a very disturbing expression on his face. "The Kommandant desires to see you immediately, Sir!"

I dressed while pondering what urgent matter was worthy of disturbing my sleep at such an early hour. There was a noticeable tension in Höss's office. His secretary and adjutant stood by a desk with anxious expressions. One of them said, "The Kommandant is waiting for you."

Entering his office, I noticed that Höss looked pale and distressed. He gestured toward a chair and I sat down. He drew in a very deep breath and folded his hands on his desk. His expression was grim as he said, "General Heydrich was attacked by partisans in Prague yesterday. No one has much information at this time, but the General's state of health is said to be unfavorable."

I could not believe what I had heard. "Attacked?" It was all I could manage to say in my astonishment.

"Witnesses stated that partisans threw an explosive device underneath his car. The General suffered shrapnel wounds. That is all I know."

I requested permission to use his telephone to contact the Office for Jewish Emigrations at RSHA Headquarters Berlin. Most of my superiors could not be located but I managed a few words with Theodor Dannecker who confirmed the attack on SS General Heydrich but he would not share details of it. He also said that Heydrich was in a state of critical physical condition.

Höss and I sat there in silence while thinking of how such a thing could have happened. There was no fathomable answer.

"One thing is now certain," said Höss. "Dead Czechs will line the streets of Prague."

"How could this happen?" I asked.

"If partisans can get to Heydrich, imagine who else they can get to," replied Höss.

"He will make a full recovery," I said. "He is of strong constitution. He will be well and walking soon."

"That will not prevent the streets of Prague from being filled with dead Czechs."

"Let them hang. They have earned that fate."

Höss looked at me for a moment. "And where does this event leave you and me? Are you to remain here? Are the General's orders for you still in effect? Who do you answer to while he is convalescing?"

I exited the office and returned to my quarters where I sat on the bed and thought for a very long time. Perhaps one hour later I placed another telephone call to Berlin to confirm that my current orders were still in effect. They were not. I was directed to return to RSHA Headquarters immediately. Höss was not displeased to see me leave.

The train pulled into the Berlin Station near midnight and I went directly to RSHA Headquarters were the lights were burning brightly in all windows. Novak was in the Office for Jewish Emigrations and I asked him for information about the attack on General Heydrich.

Novak shouted at me in a rage and demanded that I concern myself with duties fit for my rank and to cease my attempt to involve myself in affairs that were not mine. I considered the incident with Heydrich to be very much within my affairs and tried to explain the orders the General had given me. I told Novak that I suddenly found those directives rescinded without appointment to new responsibilities.

Novak calmed his demeanor from the anxiety this had brought upon all of us. "Go home," he softly said. "Report for new duties in the morning."

It was difficult to do that. I walked about the halls of RSHA Headquarters and inquired about the details of the incident from any person who had a familiar face. Many who I questioned did not know, and those who did were forbidden to speak about it. Eventually I went home and placed several telephone calls and achieved the same results.

Early on the following morning we were called into a meeting and told that SS General Heydrich had been riding in an open car when he was cowardly ambushed by partisans lying in wait. The physicians sent reports that declared Heydrich had sustained wounds from grenade shrapnel, and that pieces of the automobile tore into his body from the blast. It was said that the General was in and out of consciousness.

On 4 June 1942 SS General Reinhard Heydrich succumbed to his wounds. Within 48 hours a new and more extreme policy went into effect against the Jews. Until Heydrich's death, the Foreign Office had been greatly concerned with international opinion toward The Reich's treatment of European Jews. However, when the General died, there ceased to be an analytical process to the resettling of our enemies and a policy of indiscriminate destruction followed. It was no longer a matter of deporting 1,000 or 2,000 Jews from Vienna to Mauthausen or Ravensbrücke. It then became a subject of transporting tens of thousands of Jews to Auschwitz, Belzec and Majdanek. The intended purpose was not rehabilitation or work forces. It was extermination.

Aktion Reinhard was ordered by Hitler and implemented by Himmler and Eichmann. This operation, named after the late and great General, demanded the deportation of all Jews in Germany and the Occupied Zones to Auschwitz, Belzec, Sobibor, Chelmno, Treblinka and Majdanek. Each of these locations was specifically designated as an *Aktion Reinhard Camp*. To make the necessary space available to hold the Jews, the Polish ghettos were to be emptied and their occupants sent to one of the *Aktion Reinhard Camps* for Special Treatment. The ghettos were to be refilled and if they again exceeded occupancy quotas, they were to be cleared out repeatedly in the same manner.

I was overcome by a mood that was noticed not only by my fellow officers, but by my superiors as well. In June, Eichmann came into my office, closed the door and sat down. He informed me that my new orders involved the creation of additional rail stations along the most frequently used deportation lines and that I was to choose locations to construct rail yards near these points to house additional locomotives and freight wagons. He told me I would have complete cooperation from the Ministry of Transportation and that any resistance from that office was to be reported immediately. Eichmann assured me he would personally mention any bureaucratic objections to the Reichsführer-SS.

The orders were just what I needed. I had not passively accepted the death of General Reinhard Heydrich as an unfortunate incident of the war. I can not say that the General and I shared any common bonds, but my experience at Hydracny Castle had created multiple feelings within me and created many possibilities. I believed that a tiny spark of familiarity had emerged during that visit, and though I was aware he used me as an instrument to investigate Höss, I also realized he could have chosen any officer for that task. However, he had chosen me which reflected a level of trust and confidence in my abilities. At that time I felt a burgeoning of my career and believed that if I impressed Heydrich with my work at Auschwitz, more personal assignments would follow.

It must also be stated that Heydrich's demeanor toward me at Hydracny Castle was different than I had previously experienced. I stood next to him at a window overlooking Prague and during that moment there was absolutely no distinction between General and Captain. We were two men enjoying a view. It had been an honor to move chess pieces against him and even though we did not finish the game, I matched strategic wits with General Heydrich. We played tennis together and he smiled in good sportsmanship while making amusingly competitive remarks about my style and form. I sat in the General's library with Klaudia Krüger and listened to Heydrich the Virtuoso as he privately played his violin for us. Were we friends or companions? No. I am certain, as any person who knew the General would be, that he calculated such courtesies in the effort to pacify me into agreeing to be used for his services. I knew this but I certainly did not object to it. Private circles were forming throughout the Reich and it was considered an honor to be a member of one of them. Each group had a reputation of being somewhat of a prestigious knightly order. The Reichsführer-SS had his circle; Müller, Kaltenbrunner, Röthke, Eichmann, Höfle and Globocnik had theirs. Heydrich's was considered one of the elite as it was well known he trusted very few people.

The morning of 10 June 1942 saw RSHA Headquarters devoid of most superior officers. They returned from high level meetings later that day and we received the information that the Czech village of Lidice had been completely liquidated and razed as a reprisal for General Heydrich's death. Approximately one week later the Gestapo and SS had located the partisans responsible for the attack. They were holed up in the basement of a Czech church and were holding out against our forces. It was not long before they were overpowered by German justice.

By August I had established rail yards and stations in Poland at Gniezno, Wielun, Radziejowice near Warsaw, and Bydgoszcz near Chelmno. I also established a station and yard at Wieliczka to serve as a waypoint to accommodate transports on their way to Auschwitz from Russia and the Ukraine. I had consolidated the Polish rail system into a series of routes that connected to ghettos along three or four central lines. Transports carrying Jewish freight units from the Ukraine and Russia were thus capable of delivering portions of their manifests to several ghettos along a westward route. This prevented mass arrivals and overcrowding issues. A ghetto accepted and registered the maximum number of units before the train departed to deliver another quota to the next ghetto connected to the line. When the trains were empty, they were rerouted to the east along a different line to collect Jews from subsequent ghettos that had been marked for delivery to the *Aktion Reinhard Camps* for Special Treatment. The transports ran smoothly and daily from the far western reaches of the Polish General Government to points east in Russia and back again.

Due to the collapse of Russian forces at Kharkov and Millerovo, I was dispatched to Rostov-on-Don to consolidate and adapt its rail system to transport the thousands of Soviet prisoners being taken during our campaign against Southern Russia. I was familiar with the Rostov Oblast and Mariupol transportation systems from previous work in the areas and therefore was best suited for this task. I was flown to Rostov-on-Don during the final week of August.

By the time I arrived, the XVI Panzer Division and Army Group South B had established positions along the Volga river in preparation for the massive assault on the city of Stalingrad. A complete German victory was expected to occur there and this projection required accounting for tens of thousands of Russian Prisoners of War.

There was not much for me to do at Rostov-on-Don during the first days I was there. The Office for Jewish Emigrations asked me to perform trivial tasks which mainly involved the authoring of reports about the rail lines that contained little or no practical value. I was told that my work at Rostov-on-Don would more than likely be suspended and that I would instead be dispatched to the Volga with Army Group South B to establish a major transport facility near Stalingrad to process the expected prisoners. I received my orders to move to the Volga River on 5 September.

CHAPTER SIXTEEN
STALINGRAD

The city had been relentlessly pounded by Luftwaffe air raids during the previous weeks. Stalingrad had been turned into a maze of rubble and smoking ruins. I was in the company of many Wehrmacht officers who were genuinely surprised by the nature of my presence. They informed me that the engagement at Stalingrad would be a prompt and certain victory as the Russian forces were mainly comprised of Worker Militias and women. The Soviets were only capable of supplying and reinforcing by crossing the river south of the city and our Stukas and Messerschmidt fighters controlled the skies. It was akin to shooting fish in a barrel as our planes dived in sortie after sortie to eliminate the Russians attempting to cross. The Wehrmacht had effectively backed the Russian soldiers up to the bank of the river where our artillery saturated the pockets with a deadly hail of shells.

The Soviet 62nd Army was our main adversary occupying the ruins at that time. The Wehrmacht Commanders acknowledged the strong defensive positions established by the Russians but figured without steady resupply, the enemy would be forced to surrender. We all were very optimistic.

I was told that the Wehrmacht could not spare escort troops to protect me and that I would be forced to command a combat team inside the city. Once the enemy had capitulated and Stalingrad was secured, I was assured full cooperation from Wehrmacht engineers to assess damages and rebuild damaged railroad stations. I was told this would occur within ten days to two weeks.

I drew ammunition and grenades from the Supply Company while my Kampfgruppe was being assembled. Many things were issued to me including a medical bag, field food kit, blanket roll, rucksack, additional pairs of socks, a compass, map and radio. I could barely manage the load of items in my arms let alone figure how to carry it all into battle. My Battle Group consisted of 40 Wehrmacht soldiers who all seemed quite excited to be under SS command. A young man from the Signal Corps took the radio and agreed to remain by my side at all times. Another young soldier; a large Prussian whose comrades called him *"die Elche"*, came to me and requested the map and compass. I handed the items to him and realized why the men called him The Moose. He stood approximately 198 centimeters and weighed perhaps 118 kilograms. He was slow of wit but extremely skilled in matters of war.

From our position we could see the pilots inside our ground-attack aircraft as they skimmed overhead to assault various Russian positions. We were amused at the prospect of facing Worker Militias and women. Was Mother Russia so desperate that laborers and females were required for her defense? The Wehrmacht was complaining that there was no honor in fighting such an enemy and we truly believed Stalingrad would be appended to the Reich within two weeks.

I moved my Kampfgruppe through the outer fields containing grain elevators and silos. Sporadic machine gun and small arms fire came from inside the city but it did not seem to be aimed at anything in particular. There was a Pionier Squad approximately fifteen meters ahead of mine and they were following the advance of a halftrack. Midway across the grain fields two landmines detonated under the feet of the Pionier Squad. One of them shouted back to my unit with the news their doctor had been hit. I had no medical personnel with me and I relayed the orders back to our Tactical Command Post with my radio.

"Do not move," was the reply. "We are dispatching engineers to inspect the minefield."

Despite the two Forward Pioniers striking mines, it had not entered my thoughts that we were in a minefield. I gave the orders for my men to pull their bayonets and trench knives to probe the ground in front of them. All of us including the Pionier Squad had become motionless and the halftrack idled in front of them. Russian sniper fire began eliminating the Pioniers. After each shot, we heard the distressed shouts of our wounded and the curses of their comrades. I called Tactical Command to advise them of the situation and they were resolute at sending the engineers into the field.

Moments later artillery shells began dropping on the Forward Pionier Squad before they were arced and walked back toward our position. I shared the information with Tactical Command and I was given the orders to move into the city. We were not to fall back under any circumstances.

I shared the news with my Squad Leaders and though no one was particularly fond of the idea of running through a minefield, the idea of lying motionless under an artillery barrage was equally distressing. The order was given; whistles were blown, and we charged forward at a full sprint. When the Pioniers saw us coming from their rear, they too stood and sprinted toward the rubble at the outer confines of Stalingrad.

We reached a blown out department store where I assembled my unit and counted off. I had lost four men during the charge. Tactical Command was pleased to learn we breached the outer defenses and made it to the streets. I was told to take my unit several blocks south to join a VI Army assault line.

I had previously been inside destroyed cities but Stalingrad was a place like none other I had encountered. Very few buildings had been spared from obliteration and in some places the rubble was piled so high that one could climb it and enter buildings through second story windows. The stenches of sulfur, gunpowder, charred wood and the dead was overpowering. Approximately two blocks into the city we took heavy fire from a petrol filling station across the street.

Two of my men primed panzerfausts and launched shells into the structure. The blast ignited the remaining petrol in the tanks and rich orange flames sent clouds of dark smoke spiraling into the sky. Believing this had neutralized the opposition; I gave the orders to move forward and ran my troops directly into a heavy wall of machine gun fire from the station. The Russians held out as long as they could inside the inferno before dashing out to escape. We promptly cut them down in a storm of rifle and machine gun bullets and cautiously continued our advance. I had lost another two men.

I reached the Wehrmacht Assault line and reported to the officer with 34 soldiers. The defensive position was a long line of stacked earth, sandbags and household items consisting of sinks, infant carriages, automobile doors and anything else that could serve as a blockade. It had all been placed at the edge of the sidewalk in the gutter. A few 37mm cannons were interspersed throughout the line and approximately 350 VI Army troops were in place. A row of burned out buildings was to our backs and at that moment no one was shooting but there was a tense mood present among all.

The Line Officer, who was a seasoned Lieutenant, told me he was very relieved to know the SS was at Stalingrad. I informed him that as far as I knew, there were but a handful of us in the area of operations and that our role was more administrative than for combat purposes. He told me that he would need my absolute dedication to combat operations and I assured him I would exercise professional leadership.

The Lieutenant pointed to the ruined park in front of his line and told me that heavy Russian forces occupied the buildings across the streets. There were hundreds of corpses in the park, mainly civilians and women. That, he said, was the remains of the Worker Militia that continued to launch suicide assaults. He also stated that another attack was imminent.

"Why have you not moved forward to take those buildings?" I inquired.

The Lieutenant looked at me as if his answer would be improper. From his expression I realized the civilian militia was more of a problem than he expected.

Whistles blew from across the street and at once the Wehrmacht engaged the bolts on their rifles, primed their MP40s, and crouched behind the defensive barrier. A Russian voice echoed through a megaphone and the hair on the back of my neck stood out.

The Lieutenant said, "Take cover, Hauptsturmführer."

I crouched behind the barrier as a long whistle sounded across the park. This was followed by a barbaric roar of human voices as the Russians launched a full assault at us from the opposite buildings. Our gunfire created a solid reverberating thunder that slammed into the human tidal wave approaching us. Our MG42 machine guns discharged thousands of rounds and our infantry supported this with more lead. The Russians did not retreat, nor did they reach our defenses. The slaughter lasted for approximately fifteen minutes before the last rounds were fired.

More whistles blew from inside the opposite buildings. "They are calling up the next units," said the Lieutenant. "They have been doing this all day."

One of our soldiers shouted, "Lieutenant! Nine dead. Eleven wounded."

"They seem content to think they can slowly decimate us like this," said the Line Officer. More Wehrmacht soldiers arrived and took positions behind the barrier. He used his radio and requested artillery support on coordinates that matched the location of the enemy buildings. To my surprise his appeal was denied. He must have seen the curiosity on my face because he explained, "Our situation here is not critical or desperate." He smiled with disbelief.

"Can we call for tank support?"

"If they will not grant us a few artillery shells, they will certainly not commit tanks to our defense."

Ten minutes later another series of whistles were blown, followed by the same Russian voice through the megaphone. The Wehrmacht instinctively took their positions and waited for the long whistle that sent another wave of Soviet women and Worker Militia at us. Each German soldier contained his shooting to his particular field of fire and again the assault was stopped cold.

More Wehrmacht soldiers arrived during the afternoon and they were followed by stores of ammunition and fresh water that was passed up and down the line. Three or four more Russian assaults took place until darkness fell over Stalingrad.

That night male and female Russian voices shouted horrible curses at us from the opposite buildings. A voice broadcasted in German from a Russian speaker telling us that the Soviet Army and people had no plans to surrender. The message promised us safety if we surrendered and warned that if we were captured in battle, the Russians would take great pleasure in flaying the skin from our bodies. The voice told us that Hitler was finished and that he did not care for his troops. He had sent us to Stalingrad to die inglorious and unnecessary deaths. This was Day One for me at Stalingrad. Whereas the Commander at the Volga promised victory in ten days to two weeks, we had gained but four city blocks during the first twenty four hours.

After several more Russian suicide assaults over the next few days, we were given artillery and tank support. The Wehrmacht line had been reinforced to nearly 1,500 men and it moved another two or three blocks south into Stalingrad before being stalemated by heavy Russian forces. At the end of the two week time projection for victory, my Squad had been reduced to 27 men and we had gained 10 city blocks.

Near the end of September my unit was reinstated to 40 soldiers and we were ordered to strike out toward the center of the city where Russian tank factories were still producing armored vehicles. We were to meet up and work in tandem with other roving German units to secure the industrial belt and destroy the enemy munitions plants.

The cold weather had become noticeable during the final week of September. My unit made slow progress as we were forced to fight from house to house and street to street. Every doorway, alley and shop was defended by pockets of Soviet resistance. The Russians employed an excellent strategy of consolidating and tightly grouping their front line units in areas that split our infantry. This resulted in many German units being separated and forced to fight on their own.

The Soviets continued to detonate piles of rubble and shattered walls to impede the progress of our tanks. In the very few lanes that our tanks and halftracks were able to move forward, the Russians sighted and destroyed them with anti tank guns positioned on balconies and rooftops. Soviet spotters relayed our positions to their artillery gunners near the river and we found ourselves under constant fire and often unable to move. My unit had still not reached the munitions factories by the first days of October. The Russians continued to use the rubble as a maze of carefully planned defenses and they only appeared to quickly strike at us before disappearing in the labyrinth. We called this tactic *Rattenkrieg* because the Soviets came up out of the ruins like a pack of rats, unleashed hell and chaos upon us, and then scurried away before we could launch a counterassault.

When we established contact with other German units in the area we learned that the roads leading to the munitions factories had been mined and zeroed by Russian anti tank weapons and machine guns. No direct approach was possible and the Luftwaffe attacks had been reduced by Flight Command due to the successes of Soviet anti aircraft batteries. We took a concealed position inside a burned out restaurant and continued surveillance of the factories. Within four or five hours we watched a newly manufactured Russian T-34 tank roll off the production floor and straight into the battle. The tank had not been primed, painted, or given markings. It was a massive assortment of welded and riveted armor plates rattling on its chassis. My men suggested hitting it with panzerfausts before it reached a position capable of inflicting terrible damage upon our troops.

I was concerned with charting its progress over the streets as the tank's commander swerved here and there to avoid mines. I promptly drew the pattern on the wall of the restaurant with a grease pencil and once it passed I gave the orders for my panzerfaust crews to hit it from behind.

The shells struck the rear motor compartment and immediately disabled the tank. Its turret began to rotate to the rear before another accurate panzerfaust shell struck the pivot rim and bent the cuff, making it impossible for the cannon to spin left. The T-34 attempted to rotate its turret to the opposite side but its cannon could not clear the remains of a wall. My panzerfaust crews hit the rear motor compartment again and we saw white smoke pour from its hatches and ventilation tubes. The tank opened its throttle and heavy black smoke curled from its engine compartment before something mechanical loudly snapped inside. The motor died and moments later the rear escape hatch opened. Before the Russians appeared, one of my soldiers fired a perfectly aimed panzerfaust shell into the hatch. The blast set off the ammunition stored inside the tank and in the powerful explosion that followed, the turret dislodged from the chassis and landed next to the destroyed hull in the street. My men rightly celebrated. Destroying a mechanical beast of that size was equal to felling a rhinoceros with a knife. We all shared that moment of pride.

I marked the coordinates and began calling Tactical Command on the radio to request artillery strikes on the active tank factory. A Russian heavy machine gun blew holes through the wall of the restaurant and hit four or five of my men. The sun was going down; my men were badly hit, and I knew I could not evacuate them or get medical help here during the night. Two of the wounded were sobbing in uncontrollable pain. *Die Elche* peered through a hole in the wall and tried to spot the machine gun.

"Bastards," he mumbled. "I will wager they have it placed in that storehouse, Sir." I began to position myself for a look but flinched back when more bullets ripped through the wall. I noticed that *die Elche* did not move. He kept his eye pressed against the small hole.

"Yes. I am correct," he said. "It is in that small storehouse to the right of the factory. I saw its muzzle flash."

I looked through a hole in the wall, saw the tiny storage shed and pulled back to safety as if the Russians knew I was looking at them.

"Should I take it out, Sir?" *Die Elche* seemed very stoic and confident that he could do it.

There was too much static interference on the radio and I could not raise Tactical Command.

"Yes. Take as many men as you need."

Die Elche pointed to two men. "You and you. Come with me."

They exited through the kitchen in the back of the restaurant and set off to flank the machine gun. In the meantime it fired another burst through the wall. I took the medical bag off my shoulder and began sorting through its contents and reading the labels. The wounded man closest to me was hit so bad that there was nothing I could do for him. He had ceased moaning as shock had settled over him. His eyes darted from side to side and occasionally he looked at me and said, "Why did this happen to me, Viktor?" I do not know if Viktor was his friend or brother, but I said nothing while he called me this. The poor young man was at the gates to eternal sleep and was only waiting for the Angel of Death to come and collect him.

I looked at my remaining men and gave an order. *"Laden Sie und bereiten sich vor!"* At once they put fresh ammunition cartridges in their weapons, engaged the bolts and pulled the charging handles. "When *die Elche* destroys the machine gun position we are going to move up this road and take the tank factory. I want my Squad Leaders to study this drawing on the wall. It is the same route the tank followed out of the plant. I want to get up to those doors and take the factory. Be careful you do not get caught in crossfire! Watch for enemy positions! Remain in groups of two! Does any man have a question?"

A crackling barrage of rifle fire and several grenade blasts drew our attention outside. The Russian storehouse next to the factory was in flames. Moments later, *die Elche* and his companions burst through the kitchen doors into the restaurant.

"On my orders," I said. I surveyed the area to make certain

Russian forces had not arrived to investigate the attack on the storehouse. "Follow me!"

When we took to the road we saw the light impressions from the tank treads and safely followed them to the entrance of the factory. My soldiers flanked both sides and pulled open the doors. Behind the sparks of welding torches were more than a hundred armed Russian soldiers. There was a pause of disbelief on both sides before they leveled their weapons at us and we exchanged a horrible burst of gunfire.

My men scattered in retreat and I could never blame them or hold them as cowards for doing this. We were clearly outnumbered 4:1 and I held myself responsible for not conducting proper reconnaissance of the objective before leading the assault against it. As my men fled they triggered mines and tripwires that set off explosives in the streets. The Russians gave chase and I found myself running through the streets of Stalingrad under the flicker of flames and through patches of total darkness. Twelve of us managed to stay together and we smashed through the door of a small bakery and surprised a small group of Worker Militia. We traded shots and were fortunate enough to eliminate them without sustaining casualties.

I grabbed the transmitter of the radio and had a clear channel to Tactical Command. I gave them the coordinates of the factory and our 88mm guns opened from near the banks of the Volga. I explained our current situation to the Wehrmacht Commanders but I could not be certain of what direction we had retreated in. I believed we had gone back toward our lines but pockets of debris had forced us to change our direction. Tactical Command ordered me to reinforce and hold my position until morning light.

Die Elche and a few men inspected the building to make sure it was clear of additional Russian forces and we found the entrance to the basement. We entered the dark hold and lit our tiny cooking candles to provide light. I positioned two MP40 gunners at the bottom of the basement stairs with firm orders to shoot anyone who came through the upper door. We settled along the walls on the floor and listened to the distant rumbling of artillery shells. Now and then a motorized vehicle roared by outside but we could never discern if it was ours or theirs. Late in the evening we heard an accordion in the distance accompanied by Russian voices signing with it.

The temperature dropped that night and we did not have adequate winter clothing. The men began complaining about the cold and I studied their faces as they huddled against the walls of the cellar. Underneath the outlines of the helmets I saw young and fearful faces breathing into their hands for warmth. I tried to maintain decorum befitting of an officer and though I too was cold, I dared not show it.

In the morning we used the compass to orient ourselves and followed the directives issued from Tactical Command to make our way west of our position to link with a Wehrmacht unit. We moved cautiously and with precision as German and Russian shells rained down around us. We traversed a narrow alley that opened into a large four way intersection. We paused near a small retaining wall to study the windows and rooftops around the area. It was at that moment that the gray skies released the first flakes of snow.

The sounds of gunfire became louder as we advanced to the west and we assumed this was a sign of the unit we were to link with. After making progress along a few more streets we came into a pitched battle being fought for control of a plaza. Broken and pocked statues and fountains were in the center and we easily spotted our forces to the north and Russian soldiers to the south.

A heavy Soviet machine gun on a wheeled carriage was decimating the buildings being used as cover by the Wehrmacht. *Die Elche* was aiming his rifle at the enemy gun crew but at 68 1/2 meters without a scope, an accurate shot seemed improbable. He pulled the trigger and the Russian gunner fell to the ground like a wet sack of flour. He adjusted his aim while engaging his bolt and fired again. The Russian assistant gunner dropped. The Soviet spotter took cover behind the carriage but *die Elche* eliminated him with a perfectly aimed bullet through the wheel spokes.

After *die Elche* removed the enemy crew, the Wehrmacht who had been pinned down by this weapon charged into the plaza. Our soldiers moved up to the fountains and monuments and took cover in the market stalls. More Russians made attempts to seize the carriage gun, but *die Elche* killed all Soviets that got close to it.

There had been a noticeable shift in the battle and Russian resistance became heavier. Rifle fired grenades rained down on our troops but the Wehrmacht solidly returned equal kilograms of lead. German grenades bounced underneath the carriage gun and when it was destroyed, we broke out from the side street and joined a group of Wehrmacht soldiers behind a large stone fountain in the middle of the plaza.

A Wehrmacht Feldwebel immediately focused on my collar tabs. "The SS!" he exclaimed. "By God am I happy to see you. Where is the rest of your battalion situated, Sir?"

"In Berlin," I replied. "I am a Legal Administrator from RSHA Headquarters."

"God help us!"

The Soviets began sealing off the roads to the north and flanked us from the west. A volley of machine gun bullets chipped stone off the fountain we were hiding behind. A T-34 rumbled down a side street and spun its turret to align a shot against a monument behind which seven or eight Wehrmacht soldiers were taking cover. The Feldwebel and I shouted at the men to warn them, but our voices were drowned by the steady thunder of gunfire. The T-34 unloaded its barrel and the monument exploded in a hail of concrete and plaster. Our panzerfaust crews attempted to counterattack the tank but to do so they had to expose themselves to enemy fire. Each of our anti tank crews was cut down by Russian bullets.

The Feldwebel used my radio to contact his superiors. He shouted out the situation, and his demand for permission to withdraw from the plaza. I heard an officer order him to remain in position and fight. Reinforcements were promised but it was impossible to know if they would reach us in time.

The T-34 fired another shell into the plaza and it destroyed one of our sandbagged MG42 crews.

"We have to fall back to the buildings," said the Feldwebel. I told *die Elche*, my radio operator and the remainder of my men to get ready to move on the Feldwebel's orders. We waited, returned fire, and waited longer. It was an eerie feeling to cower behind that fountain with bullets and shrapnel filling each millimeter of space around us. If we stayed where we were, it was logical that the Russian bullets or tank would eventually find us. Moving a centimeter in any direction meant intersecting paths with the bullets and shrapnel. I resigned to the thought then and there that I was a dead man. When one realizes that life as you know it can realistically cease within seconds, you come to a plateau of understanding and acceptance. You simply resign yourself to the absolute fact that you are dead. Even though you may be breathing, walking and talking, you acknowledge that all things around you are existing for a limited time. In this realization, nothing matters. Nothing will change in response to what you do.

When the Feldwebel gave the order to move, I ran toward the buildings behind us without the slightest care of being shot. When we entered the structures we took cover and used a moment to collect ourselves. That was when I noticed *die Elche* clutching at his back. His eyes looked distant and his head grew heavy on his neck. I saw that he had taken two bullets in his back. He was dead within minutes.

A ferocious storm of Russian artillery shells slammed into the plaza. One could not see the buildings across the way for the veil of smoke, flames and percussion flashes. A great tan and gray cloud of dust arose and swept through the broken windows of the building we had taken cover in. It was impossible to breathe and we coughed and choked with burning lungs. There was no logical reasoning that any man could survive this barrage and it was clear to us that Ivan was willing to sacrifice himself if it meant destroying us as well. It was as if he defiantly said: "We will die with you today. You are of limited numbers but we are infinite."

We felt our way along and pressed through a hole in the wall into the street behind the building. Russians leapt from doorways, windows and from behind piles of debris to briefly shoot and force us to take cover. When we emerged to return fire we learned they were gone. It was the strategy of the Russian *Rattenkrieg.* How can you fight the enemy when you do not know where they are?

Eight of us worked north through the debris in hopes of finding a defensive line. The snow had coated the ruins and we kept a cautious eye on our surroundings. A check of our equipment revealed we were down to our last few cartridges of ammunition and our canteens were almost empty. Many of the men had discarded their rucksacks and blanket rolls to reduce weight and increase running speed and endurance. Those of us who had rucksacks were the only people carrying food rations. All of our supplies would have to be used sparingly and wisely.

We moved in an alternate staggered position with each man taking cover behind anything he could find. Once secure, the lead man moved to a new position while every man moved up. We were spread with four men on each side of a street when machine gun fire raked the area and killed our pathfinder. Several rifle fired grenades erupted in the midst of our positions and my squad of four men entered an apartment building through its blown out doors. The squad on the opposite side of the street was pinned down and valiantly fought it out until they were destroyed by Soviet machine gun fire.

Either the enemy did not see us enter the building or assumed they killed us all. The battle for Stalingrad seemed to go quiet around us for the moment. That is when we became aware of Russian voices coming from inside the various apartments. Field telephones were ringing and from the tone of the voices, we realized we had entered a Russian Forward Headquarters.

The entry corridor extended approximately 17 meters with closed doors on each side. In the center was a staircase leading upward and at the end was a hole blown through the wall. The two Wehrmacht soldiers and the Feldwebel looked at me for orders and only one thing seemed rational. If the Russian infantry at the end of the road had witnessed our withdrawal into the apartment building, they certainly would have notified their comrades inside of it and we would not have had time to stand there and contemplate our strategy. This meant that exiting from the same doorway was not an option. If the enemy was still in position, I did not want to give them the opportunity to alert others of our position. I pointed to the hole in the wall at the opposite end of the 17 meters long corridor and slowly led the way to it.

Hearing the Russian voices just centimeters behind the walls and waiting for any one of the doors to open was a sickening feeling. We did not run as our heavy footfalls would have given them notice of our presence. Instead we cautiously traversed the corridor and pointed our weapons at each door we passed.

We made it to the end and looked into a broken courtyard with the remains of a swimming pool and a retaining wall around it. Two knocked out Panzer IV tanks and one of our shattered halftracks burned at the southern side. It was a wide and open area with another apartment building to the north and a row of ruined homes on the opposite side. The prefecture and apartment buildings were solid structures and seemed to be excellent positions of enemy occupation. The destroyed homes were therefore our best source for cover but reaching them meant a full sprint across the open courtyard. We could not stay where we were and I led the run with the three men close behind.

We entered a narrow two story house and the Wehrmacht soldiers pulled open the cabinets and cupboards in search of food but found nothing of use. It was growing dark and the sounds of battle had intensified in the streets around us. My radio operator had been killed on the other side of the Russian Forward Headquarters and it was impossible to contact fellow units in the area. With our close proximity to the Russian stronghold, I figured we would be relatively safe from artillery bombardments and I gave the orders to secure the upper floor of the home. When this was done I chose a bedroom window that overlooked the courtyard to be used as a sentry point. I divided guard shifts among myself and the men and decided to hold out through the night. Despite the distant shelling and gunfire I managed to fall asleep.

I was awakened by the Feldwebel who informed me our guard had spotted a group of Russians who exited the Forward Headquarters and were approaching the homes through the courtyard. I saw them by the swimming pool and they were making a direct approach to our position. They held their weapons loosely in their hands as if expecting the area to be reasonably secure and I gave the order not to fire. We heard them enter the rooms below and they talked while rummaging through the cabinets and cupboards the same as we had done.

Footsteps on the wooden staircase made us freeze in terror. The Feldwebel and I pressed ourselves against the floor on the opposite side of the bed while one of our soldiers squeezed himself into an armoire and another hid behind an oak storage chest. We saw a sweeping flashlight beam and heard the footfalls come closer. The Russian stopped in the doorway of the bedroom, quickly shined his light over the room and left to continue his inspection. When they found no useable provisions, they exited the house and continued their search elsewhere.

I was awakened again and saw gray light streaming through the window. The Feldwebel tried to explain why he disturbed me but before he could form his words I heard the rumbling of engines and the shouting of Russian voices. I peered through the window and saw several T-34 tanks and Soviet halftracks amassing in the courtyard with approximately 150 heavily armed enemy soldiers.

A young Gefreiter looked at me with fear in his eyes. "What do we do now, Sir?"

I pressed myself against the wall and cautiously glanced at the activity taking place below. The Russians were laying communication wires and digging defensive emplacements to protect their headquarters area. They were reinforcing the zone with armored vehicles and heavy machine guns and we were in the middle of it.

A bulldozer and maintenance equipment arrived with a squad of Soviet engineers and they began filling in the swimming pool with rubble and earth. We could hear shelling and gunfire in the distance that revealed the battle had been confined to areas far from our position. We were technically behind enemy lines in a Russian controlled area. I pondered the idea of surrendering but would do so only on the condition the Soviets gave my three subordinates full quarter. Without a signed code for the treatment of Prisoners of War, and with rumors about what the Russians were doing to captured SS officers, I sank deeper into the resolution that I was a dead man. Ivan could torture me to death if he so wished as long as my three juniors received fair and appropriate treatment.

"They are coming this way," said the Feldwebel. We could only observe them for a brief moment without risking being seen by the Russians in the courtyard. It appeared that an officer and several men were approaching the row of houses we were hiding in.

"They are reinforcing," said the Gefreiter. "They will surely occupy these buildings, Sir! What are we to do?"

"We need to break out or surrender," stated the Oberschütze.

The Feldwebel took control of his men. "Steady and calm. Keep your poise, men. All is not lost here."

I glanced at him and we shared an expression of resignation. The Oberschütze and Gefreiter had faith in us but we had no reasonable plan for defense.

Several Russian ZIS-32 trucks delivered another hundred or so well armed enemy soldiers into the courtyard.

"Damn it," muttered the Gefreiter. "They are all over this place, Sir!"

"Keep your poise," reminded the Feldwebel.

Again we heard voices on the floor below us and the sounds of boards and debris being moved around. Moments later we heard the same voices and noises from an adjoining house.

"What is on the opposite side of this house?" I inquired. The Feldwebel and I picked our way out of the bedroom and across the hall into a bathroom. The blown out window gave us a view of several streets full of destroyed buildings. Plumes of smoke spiraled into the sky many blocks away and for the first time, that destruction encouraged us as we knew our comrades were positioned there.

"That area makes for a prime sniper field," said the Feldwebel.

I took the field glasses from my case and raised them to my eyes before the Feldwebel slapped my hand away from my face. "Are you mad, Sir? Cover the lenses with your other hand! Snipers will mark the reflection!"

He was correct and I was grateful for his combat experience. I cupped my hand over the lenses and studied the terrain before us. I spotted the rear of a Russian halftrack protruding between two buildings but there was no activity around it. "Is it disabled?"

I pointed it out and handed the glasses to the Feldwebel. "I am not certain," he replied. "There does not seem to be any movement around it though."

"If the headquarters is behind us, they will certainly reinforce and protect this area," I said. "We will have to attempt to break out here."

"Can we wait until it grows dark?" asked the Feldwebel.

There was too much activity to risk moving out at that moment. I gave the orders to hold in the bedroom and cautiously monitor the activity in the courtyard.

Hours later, God provided our opportunity by granting us swirling winds and heavy snow that halted the activity in the courtyard due to white out conditions. The Oberschütze and Gefreiter were elated by the decision to move out and the Feldwebel and I were silently grateful for the change in the weather.

Once we reached the lower level we made our way out through the main door of the house. The Feldwebel was the only man with a heavy overcoat and the cold numbed our muscles and made each step laborious. The swirling snow was heavy and it mixed with walls of lighter snow being blown off rooftops. We were forced to maintain contact by holding onto each others sleeves or risk being lost. I opened my compass several times but moisture had collected inside the glass and the needle had frozen. We walked blindly through the snow until we reached a set of ruins near the Russian halftrack. The front of the vehicle was gone, presumably to a mine. We briefly looked inside for salvageable equipment but it had been stripped by its crew.

Without a compass, and without the sun to provide directional assistance, we followed the walls of the buildings on what I assumed to be an eastward course. Our only orientation was the increased volume of shelling and shooting and we made our way toward it.

We took cover inside ruined buildings long enough to warm our hands and regain our breath. The cold was so oppressive that our lungs ached each time we inhaled the frozen air. Stopping for even a few minutes could have been a disaster to our circulatory systems, but the physical need to shield ourselves from the wind and snow took control over common medical sense.

Suddenly we saw the battle in a hellish and surreal display. Several blocks away from us the wall of snow lit up from the flashes of artillery shells detonating behind it. We felt the ground reverberating under our feet and loose pieces of rooftops slid free and crashed down around us on the streets. We primed our weapons and approached this mystical light show until we heard voices calling out above the gunfire. Each step we took did not seem to take us across the threshold of the flashing wall of falling snow. It seemed that somehow the wall was impenetrable or moving away from us though I knew this to be impossible. At last I heard beautiful words shouted out in German. *"Goddamnit you son of a swine! Get your ass moving and bring me more ammunition!"*

I shouted, "SS and Wehrmacht coming out!"

Moments later the voice responded. "Well then get your asses out here!"

We moved through the flashing wall and were suddenly in an area with perfect visibility. Raging flames to the north and farther east melted the falling and blowing snow and we saw the VI Wehrmacht dug in along a prime assault line. The MG42 gunner was surprised when he saw I was an officer. "I meant no disrespect, Sir."

If circumstances were different I may have chastised him for the insubordination, but under those conditions I could have embraced him.

"Where is your Superior Officer?" I asked.

"About four blocks to the south," he responded. "In nine or ten pieces."

"Who is in command here?"

"How should I know, Sir? Our troops scattered when Ivan hit us with halftracks and tanks yesterday. I think there is a Medical Stabsfeldwebel three blocks south at the church."

"Who is commanding this operation?" I demanded.

"Does it look organized, Sir? We are trying not to lose control of these roads. There might be an officer to the rear. Is that not always where most can be found?"

His insubordination was starting to chip away at my patience when his assistant gunner arrived with more ammunition. They reloaded the weapon and commenced firing into the buildings ahead of them.

I moved to the rear with my three men and managed to locate a Wehrmacht Oberleutnant in a tailoring shop. He had pinned maps to the wall and was discussing the operation with a staff of enlisted men. The officer brought them all to attention when I entered and he seemed to believe I was there to take command. He also seemed grateful to give it to me.

"RSHA Administrative SS," I said. I always detested the puzzled expressions I received for making this statement in a combat area. "I need to contact my office in Berlin."

The men looked at each other with politely surprised features. "Communications are out," said the Oberleutnant. "We have been sending runners and motorcycle dispatch riders to the rear to relay orders."

"Do you have a clear passage to the rear?" I asked.

"It is relatively safe, Sir. We have lost two runners to snipers. None today. Probably because of this weather, Sir."

"I need to reach the rear for RSHA business. How soon can you furnish me with a runner?"

The Oberleutnant looked at his pocket watch. "Approximately fifteen minutes, Sir."

While waiting, the Feldwebel, Gefreiter and Oberschütze were given orders by the Oberleutnant to take positions on the assault line. I never knew their names or saw them again.

A motorcycle reached the Command Post and the rider delivered his orders and was directed to take me to the rear. I sat in the sidecar as he slowly maneuvered through the hellish weather and avoided pockets of debris and shell craters. By evening I had returned to the Rear Command Area along the bank of the Volga River.

A Wehrmacht General was surrounded by an entourage of advisors and Staff personnel. Junior officers manned the radios and gathered reports from the front lines inside Stalingrad. None of the forward communications seemed promising. While I was standing there, several units pleaded for permission to fall back and when the orders were denied, they were senselessly slaughtered. Several units reported that they had been completely encircled and others announced their intentions to defy directives and surrender.

I requested to use one of the radios to contact a relay to Berlin but was told all communications to the west had been cut. A Wehrmacht Major handed me an overcoat and gloves while pointing to my collar tabs. "It would be wise to cover them," he said.

The SS was despised by the Russian Army and my tabs made me a prime target. I told the Major of my urgency to contact Berlin and he advised me to board one of the trucks making its way to Pitomnik Airfield. He mentioned that the communication lines had been severed to the west and suggested sending a message from a radio aboard one of the Medical Evacuation Aircraft at the field.

He pointed out the direction of where the trucks were located and I trudged through the snow stopping only to gather more ammunition for my MP40. When I came upon the vehicles I was appalled by what I found. A convoy of 25 or 30 open Blitz Opels was in a line facing west and each was stacked with our frozen dead.

I spoke with the Transportation Officer and he granted me passage in the lead truck. I entered the cab and sat next to a Wehrmacht Obergefreiter who was chewing on a lump of tobacco as the windshield wipers brushed the snow off the front window. The heating vents were more then welcome and I noticed the soldier staring at the left side of my helmet while I warmed myself. There was no Wehrmacht decal where he expected to see one and he realized there must be runes on the opposite side of my helmet. He smiled in a relieved manner and stated, "Thanks to God that the SS is with us at Stalingrad!" I allowed him to revel in his newly found morale and did not tell him that only a handful of SS was present.

Pitomnik Airfield had been temporarily closed down due to the inclement weather. Field crews were busy chipping the ice from the propeller shafts and wings of the planes as our truck pulled alongside a mountain of frozen German corpses. Several tents emitted the glow of lanterns and generator powered bulbs, and I was informed it was the field hospital where our wounded were being treated. The driver directed me to a ravine along the runway where a series of wooden bunkers had been erected. He explained they served as the command offices and quarters for officers. I identified the communications post from the numerous aerials protruding from the roof and entered the bunker.

The men came to attention but I waved them off. I told the Wehrmacht Communications Officer of my need to contact Berlin and he demonstrated the uselessness of the radio by twisting its dial to show me every channel was nothing but static. The short range frequencies to the Volga and inside Stalingrad were working, but nothing could be transmitted to the west. I requested his assistance in using one of the radios aboard an aircraft and he explained that it would be no use to try. He said the aircraft radios were effective at communicating with other pilots on the same frequency, but that the air to ground capacity was diminished due to the weather. My only remaining option was to send a personal message with a pilot, but this too would have to wait as all flights were grounded until there was a break in the weather conditions.

The Luftwaffe and Wehrmacht personnel at Pitomnik Airfield seemed to have a more realistic perception of the events taking place at Stalingrad. They had monitored the forward communications and very few troop reports had contained promising news. I warmed myself by the stove and had a cup of coffee while listening to the transmissions from the front. Our troops were being overrun, decimated and destroyed in the city. Ivan was willing to engage in a full assault to draw us into battle and then destroy us and his own forces with an artillery barrage. The General and his Staff at the Volga were requesting reinforcements and continued to thin out the outer defensive perimeters by moving men from those locations to the front.

I was given a tin of hot food which I ate greedily. Afterward, the officers stretched out on the wooden planks of the bunker and composed letters and played cards. I gave orders to wake me in the event communications were restored to the west.

The activity in the bunker awoke me on the following morning and I was first informed that there had been no change in efforts to contact Berlin. Adding to our complications was the news that another storm front was combining with the one currently dropping snow on us. The temperatures outside had dropped to -6 C. By afternoon it had risen to 3 C and the snow turned into frozen rain that crusted the landscape with a layer of thick ice. During the evening the temperatures dropped again and heavy, wet snow blanketed us.

I passed the time composing letters and wondering when it would be possible to get our postage off the ground and to Berlin. I had played enough hands of cards for one life and the insignificant conversations in the bunker had stressed my patience. It was not wise to go outdoors but each of us did this now and then for as long as we could tolerate the cold. It was the only method to gain a few moments of privacy.

Near the end of October a line had been reestablished to Taganrog but it went no farther west. We received an official report that partisans had used the past several weeks to capture thousands of kilograms of our supplies en route from Taganrog to Stalingrad. An SS Sturmbannführer was bellowing through the radio that he was trying to enforce the codes of Führer Directive 46, but the weather had prevented him from locating the partisan bases. He demanded Luftwaffe reconnaissance flights to assist him but these were denied because of the weather.

The officers in the bunker had accurate information that accounted for more than 50,000 German soldiers killed at Stalingrad since the advance against the city commenced during the final weeks of August. Supplies, fuel and reinforcements were not reaching the front and there was a rumor that Chief of General Staff, Kurt Zeitzler, was urging der Führer to reverse his "no withdrawal" directive. Hitler remained stubborn and continued to announce that German forces would not be driven out of Stalingrad.

During the first days of November I was able to relay a message to Berlin that detailed my current situation at Stalingrad. Hours later I received the reply that only the wounded were to be evacuated. I was instructed to return to the front lines and report directly to General Friedrich Paulus for orders.

I stepped into the cold to see that our dead had been stacked like cord wood to provide wind breaks and serve as defensive barriers around the airfield. The ground was too frozen to bury them so it was decided to put the bodies to use as obstacles. A convoy of trucks delivered more and after they were unceremoniously unloaded, I climbed in the cab to be driven back to the front.

General Paulus had turned the tide of battle and had managed to successfully capture two thirds of the city over the past several days. I reported to him for orders and he assigned me to lead a unit of Wehrmacht Grenadiers from the center of the city to the outskirts of Gumrak Airfield. Paulus was convinced that wrestling Gumrak from Soviet hands would eliminate the advantage and influence of Russian air power from the battle.

I boarded a halftrack to be taken to the unit and while passing through the shattered streets I wondered what we were fighting for. What value did the city hold in its complete state of destruction? The Wehrmacht had captured and destroyed most of the Russian munitions factories and as it stood then, we were fighting for a set of ruins. I realized it was a critical and strategic location for the security of oil fields in the region, but Höth and von Manstein had not made tactical progress toward capturing them.

In the center of the city I took command of 12 riflemen, 6 soldiers with panzerfausts, 4 with MP40s and a 4 man MG42 gun team. My Junior Officer was a Wehrmacht Unterfeldwebel by the name of Saltzmann. He informed me that during the first week of November, they had experienced very little contact with Russian forces and that it was the general belief the enemy had fallen back to prepare for a counterassault. He also told me that the southern sector of Stalingrad had been badly damaged by our 88s, but there was a lack of reliable intelligence regarding Soviet emplacements in the area. We would have to fight our way through the southern sector of the city and link with mechanized infantry to launch the assault on Gumrak Airfield.

The snowfall had increased and the temperature had dropped to approximately -15 C. Very few of the soldiers had been adequately equipped with winter clothing and had resorted to taking extra socks and tunics from our dead. Our ammunition reserves were low but considered sufficient for the task at hand. The water inside our canteens had frozen and we needed to eat snow to hydrate ourselves. None of us could remember the last time we bathed, shaved or wore clean clothing.

We advanced into the southern sector on or about 8 November in the middle of a heavy snowfall. For the first time in weeks Stalingrad was quiet except for the crackling of fires that burned out of control and the sounds of buildings collapsing from subsidence. We passed the last Wehrmacht checkpoint and continued onward for another 6 or 7 blocks where a Russian machine gun nest sprayed our path with bullets. Approximately 20 meters in front of us were a few market stalls serving as the only logical cover for the enemy gun crew. I ordered panzerfaust shells to be fired into the structures and when the smoke cleared we saw one Russian soldier dragging his legless body away and another staggering in a daze who was missing his left arm at the shoulder. My riflemen emerged slowly to make sure the machine gun nest had been eliminated and when confident of this, they pulled their trench knives and finished off the wounded Russians to conserve bullets.

Past the market was an industrial belt with several sets of railroad tracks, warehouses and grain silos. Each structure had gaping holes in its walls and appeared to be unoccupied. Most were on fire and we approached what looked to be a chemical factory with great caution. The railroad tracks were behind it and massive freight wagons and locomotives had been blown off the lines and laid on their sides. Saltzmann and I discussed our advance and as Gumrak was east of the city, we decided to follow the railroad tracks in that direction. The ruined buildings, freight wagons and locomotives provided excellent cover for us as we moved in a staggered formation.

The warehouses and ruined trains disappeared behind us after an approximate march of 205 meters. Earthen embankments rolled back on each side of the tracks and a small wooden station was cut into the northern wall. We stopped to survey the location from afar before sending four riflemen to investigate. They approached slowly and within 14 or 15 meters they signaled it was clear. I gave the orders to move the squad up and once in front of the station, sudden sounds forced us to our knees in the snow. We swung our weapons toward the station and were astonished to see a group of 4 or 5 children kicking a soccer ball onto the tracks. One of the children ran out and retrieved his ball only to look up and see us on the tracks. His head moved back and forth as he studied all of us and then he simply smiled and ran off to continue playing with his friends.

Saltzmann and I halted and tried to use our frozen compass to no avail. From our estimation and from map references, we realized we could ascend the southern embankment and travel through a small wooded grove to reenter the southern sector of Stalingrad. We were very aware that the children could pose a threat to our presence if they were to inform others, and we were leaving fresh tracks in the snow. It seemed safe and logical to abandon the railroad lines.

That short walk through the wooded grove was the only moment of peace and silence for me at Stalingrad. The fir and pine trees seemed to shield me from the horrors that existed all around us. Each one of us seemed mesmerized by the tranquility but was jolted from it at the perimeter of the tree line. A few roundhouses, sheds, wells and farm fields laid between us and the southern sector of Stalingrad. I sent a 4 man reconnaissance team to the edge of the first roundhouse and they waved us forward.

Saltzmann kept the field glasses on the buildings along the edge of the urban area across from us. The 4 man team sprinted to a shed, surveyed the area, and moved south to a well before waving us forward.

The buildings looked to be in fair repair and at the well I used the radio to contact the mechanized infantry we were supposed to link with. I was informed that they were engaged in heavy fighting at a railroad crossing 2 kilometers to the west. I transmitted to the Rear Command Post for intelligence reports on the buildings in front of us. An officer stated that he had no information on the occupational status of the structures. I said I was going to give the orders to halt my unit until the mechanized infantry had broken out from the railroad crossing battle, but a Wehrmacht Colonel instructed me to move forward and secure a hold in the southern sector.

Saltzmann and I studied the buildings in front of us looking for one with unimpeded entry that was soundly defensible. The distance from our position at the well to the buildings was approximately 27 meters of open space. If we were to come under fire, I made it clear that we were not to fall back. The limited cover in the fields could clearly be marked by Russian spotters for enemy artillery units.

We selected a two story home as our gathering point and on my orders we sprinted toward it in groups of 5. I joined the first assault team and approximately midway across the field the Russians unleashed hell upon us. I could hear the bullets snapping through the air and saw them churning up the snow around us. I could see muzzle flashes from the windows of the house we had chosen as a gathering point and was greatly confused of where to lead my men for cover. I squeezed the trigger of my MP40 and fired indiscriminately toward the buildings while in a full sprint. I saw two or three of my men go down before I noticed a narrow alley between the buildings and changed my direction to lead my men into it.

Several soldiers began bashing at a wooden cellar door until it splintered off its hinges. Enemy whistles were blowing and Russian voices were shouting out orders. We entered through the smashed door and made our way through a dark storage area and up a wooden staircase. We paused at the door and when we heard no voices, we pulled it open and poured into the living room of a small house. Gunfire erupted from the kitchen and as I pressed myself against the frame of the door I saw a Russian grenade slide between my feet and bounce down the stairs. The blast was deafening and the screams of my wounded soldiers were horrible. Lanterns, tables and furniture were torn apart in the exchange of gunfire.

The shooting from the kitchen decreased and we heard the sounds of the Soviets falling back. We threw several grenades in their direction and after they detonated there was an eerie silence. It was too dangerous to assist our wounded and because our position was known, I issued the order to exit through the back of the house and continue moving.

Rifle fire opened up on us the moment we ran into the street. The freezing cold stung our faces and made our lungs ache but we had to keep moving. Soviet fragmentation grenades landed on all sides of us from upper story windows and the only means to avoid their lethal blast was to attempt to outrun them. I led the advance though I had no idea where I was taking my men. At last we seemed to distance ourselves from the Russian fields of fire and we took cover inside a brewery.

A count revealed I had lost twelve men between the fields and our current location. I used the radio and learned the mechanized unit had broken through at the railroad crossing and was on its way to link with us. Intelligence reports had marked a bridge near a bell tower west of our position that was not capable of sustaining our armored vehicles. We were ordered to cross the bridge and hold our position until the mechanized unit arrived.

We cautiously emerged from the brewery and made our way toward the bell tower. Approximately two blocks east of it I was inadvertently spun around on my feet before I heard a rifle shot. At once a searing pain tore through my shoulder before another sniper bullet ripped through my left thigh. Every muscle in my body gave out and I landed facedown on the frozen street while watching my men scatter for cover. I heard several of them shouting.

"Is he dead?"

"Did they kill the Hauptsturmführer?"

I could not feel the cold, but the gunshot wounds to my left shoulder and left thigh felt as if someone had poured burning gravel in the holes. I wanted to sit up; examine the wounds, flex my arms and legs and make certain I was not paralyzed. I also knew that if I moved it would indicate to the sniper that I was still alive. I remained motionless despite the agonizing pain and wondered, why have my men not returned fire at this cowardly sniper?

I briefly caught a glimpse of Saltzmann in a doorway and I blinked my eyes at him. He nodded to acknowledge me and began studying the rooftops and windows around us. The pain began to subside and the sounds around me seemed very far away. "Good God," I thought. "Is this what it is like to die?"

At once the pain returned and I began convulsing until I uncontrollably soiled myself in the street. I grew very weary and the pain no longer mattered. I wanted so badly to sleep in the middle of that frozen hell.

I saw the back of a pair of boots in front of my face and saw the form of a Wehrmacht soldier disappear inside the doorway next to Saltzmann. "That cowardly bastard," I thought. Why had he not assisted me?

He had. His daring run across the street baited the sniper into firing a round at him. Saltzmann's team unloaded MP40s, rifles and panzerfausts into the upper floor of a building. Moments later another soldier dashed across the street while two others dragged me into the doorway.

I heard Saltzmann telling me to stay awake and someone else mentioned that the freezing weather had caused my blood to quickly coagulate in the wounds. Saltzmann jammed a hypodermic needle full of morphine into my belly. He opened another one; explained it was to prevent sepsis infection, and injected me again.

Saltzmann posted a rifleman as my guard and promised he would come back for me. He led the assault team across the bridge to link with the mechanized infantry. I was overcome with guilt for having left my wounded soldiers on the field and in the small house.

The rifleman lifted my head each time I closed my eyes. "Do not die," he said with an encouraging smile. "Think of the effect it will have on my service record! I can not be held responsible for a dead SS officer!" I asked him his name. He told me. I carry guilt for forgetting it.

I do not know how long I laid in that doorway before medical personnel from the mechanized unit arrived to treat my wounds and collect me on a litter. I was put aboard a halftrack and rushed through the checkpoints to the north. We stopped once or twice to take on more wounded.

The doctors in the halftrack connected a wire with an exposed end to a large battery. Whenever I began to lose consciousness they touched it to my chin to jolt me awake. On a litter next to me was a badly wounded Wehrmacht soldier with numerous rags and bandages stuffed inside his open chest cavity. The doctors had stopped working on him. He was dead.

Eventually the halftrack stopped and the rear hatches were pulled open. My litter was carried into a field hospital and placed atop sawhorses. Voices were shouting out, "SS! Priority! Priority!"

A doctor loomed over me with a bloodstained medical gown and surgical mask. "Where are you from, Hauptsturmführer?"

"Füssen."

I awoke next to a burning hearth in a ruined house with several other badly wounded officers. My shoulder had been bandaged and my left leg had been splinted. Two or three officers had obviously died from their wounds and laid there in state. I was nauseous from the ether and my wounds felt as if someone was pounding on them with a chisel.

Doctors and orderlies entered the structure and checked us for vital signs. The dead were casually carried out while the physicians monitored pulses and used their stethoscopes to listen to our heartbeats.

One of the doctors began changing the dressing on my shoulder and it was the first time I saw the wound. "You are very fortunate," he said to me. He explained that the down angle of the sniper's fire had probably saved my life. The first bullet had entered underneath the clavicle in my left shoulder and had lodged in my pectoral muscle. If it had been two centimeters higher it would have shattered the bone. Fifteen centimeters toward center would have put the bullet in my heart.

The second bullet had grazed the femur in my left thigh and tore my vastus lateralis muscle and left an exit wound the size of a walnut in the back of my thigh. The femoral artery and vein had been missed by less than half a centimeter. My prognosis was encouraging and the doctors assured me I would walk again and regain full use of my left leg and arm. The most promising news was that the injuries qualified me for a triangular medical evacuation tag. This was the only item that granted a soldier authorized passage out of the Stalingrad pocket. I was to regain my strength over the next several days and then be placed aboard a Ju88 Transport plane as soon as I was stable enough to be moved.

The doctors apologized for not having more pain medications and anesthetics for us. Each wounded officer that was capable of speaking declined our share of medicines and ordered the physicians to dispense our portion among the enlisted wounded. They offered to bring us bottles of schnapps and vodka but we insisted that too was to be distributed among the injured subordinates.

After lying in that house for approximately one week we were startled by a hellish artillery bombardment of our rear area. Medical orderlies practically broke down the door as they rushed in, picked up our litters and trotted outside with us. The landscape was nothing but explosive geysers of earth and flames. My litter was placed inside an ambulance with five others before the doors were slammed shut and it began to move. The passenger in the ambulance began lashing down our litters to prevent us from sliding about in the vehicle. "What has happened?" I asked.

"Full Russian counterattack, Sir. The 62nd Soviet Army reclaimed parts of Gumrak Airfield and several tank and artillery divisions have flanked us from the east."

"Several?" I inquired. "How many exactly?"

"I do not know, Sir."

We eventually pulled into Pitomnik Airfield where Ju88 Transport planes were waiting in a line with propellers spinning. We had not outrun the artillery barrage but it did not appear the airfield had been accurately sighted by the enemy. Shells exploded but not near prime targets or the planes.

I leaned up on my elbow and looked out the windshield to see an endless line of Blitz Opels and ambulances filled with our wounded. With each shell that exploded I felt more confined and helpless inside the vehicle. At last the rear doors opened and orderlies distributed the triangular medical evacuation tags.

"Help me out of here!" I ordered. I wanted to be anywhere except in the back of that ambulance.

"We do not have permission to move you, Sir."

"Damn it soldier," I shouted. "I am giving you permission! You will assist me out of this vehicle or by God I will have you arrested and shot!"

They pulled my litter from the vehicle and removed a pair of crutches hanging inside the ambulance. I could only use one crutch under my right arm and I believed I was a pathetic sight as I hobbled toward the front of the vehicle column.

Two doctors seized me and one said to the other, "He is SS." They escorted me from the line of trucks to the airfield where I was placed on another litter and carried inside a Ju88 Transport plane. I was taken deep into the tail of the aircraft where I was lashed down. I could see through the bulb housing of the tail light to my left and I watched the activity taking place on the far side of the field. Behind a bunker of stacked bodies, two soldiers crouched with their rifles pointing to the east. A group of comrades joined them at the position but even from my vantage point inside the plane I could discern that something was amiss outside at that bunker. I watched two soldiers place their hands under the arms of one of the crouching soldiers. At once they lifted his frozen and lifeless body in its crouched position and set it at the flank of the bunker to provide additional coverage. They set the other frozen crouched solider at the opposite end.

Orderlies covered me with greatcoats and wool blankets as more wounded were crammed aboard the plane. I saw men with faces that had been rotted away by frostbite, young men with bloodied bandages covering the stumps of arms and legs, and the stench of gangrenous wounds was forcing me to gag. The side door of the Ju88 was closed and seconds later the propellers spun at a higher revolution. The aircraft lurched forward several times before gaining a smooth advance. We turned around at the end of the runway and I saw Pitomnik Airfield was under a heavier barrage. The plane gained speed and I felt weightlessness as it lifted into the air. I recognized landmarks below and saw an endless convoy of trucks carrying more wounded toward the airfield. The Volga River appeared and I saw the twisted, smoldering mess of Stalingrad one last time before the pilot banked the aircraft west and headed out of the zone. Moments later the assistant pilot stood in the doorway and shouted, "You are going home!" He stood there as if expecting us to rejoice. No one made a sound.

Hours later we descended and touched down on a snow covered airstrip. Fuel trucks drove out to meet us and began filling the tanks of the plane. The assistant pilot announced we were in the Ukraine and would be taking off for Poland when the refueling was completed. Soon we were airborne again and late in the night we began our approach to Zamošc, Poland. We were unloaded and separated on the airstrip. Partially mobile patients like me were put aboard buses and transported to the train station. We were a frightening sight to the Wehrmacht soldiers heading toward the front. There was a mood of optimism and relief among the wounded but we dared not speak.

At the station I watched the resolve of the wounded men waiting for trains to take us to various hospitals. A soldier missing one leg read letters to a comrade whose eyes were covered by a bloodied bandage. A young man laced the boots of a friend who had lost both arms. Some men embraced comrades who wept bitterly and there was no dishonor in this.

A train entered the station and the Order Police flanked the doors of the passenger carriages and cleared paths in front of each. More wounded were evacuated from the train though I do not know where they had come back from. I saw that many of the injured soldiers wore the tabs and insignia of the II and V SS Divisions. When the wounded had been taken off the train, surgeons and doctors exited with exhausted expressions. A few of them sat on the platforms to rest. Each was stained with blood and sweat. The floors of the carriages were hosed and a sea of watery blood ran down the boarding stairs and onto the tracks. Moments later we were given permission to board.

The train reached Warsaw at dawn and we were once again put aboard buses and driven to a convalescence hospital just outside the south wall of the ghetto. My superior officers and family was notified of my injuries and I began four months of physical recuperation.

Klaudia Krüger had taken temporary residence in Warsaw in December and was instrumental in assisting me with recovery. I petitioned her father for permission to have her hand in marriage and with his blessings; I applied for the authorization from SS Headquarters in Berlin. Upon my release from the hospital, we traveled to Füssen where Klaudia and I married on Sunday, 21 March 1943.

CHAPTER SEVENTEEN
SPECIAL TREATMENT
APRIL, 1943

I returned to duty at RSHA Headquarters Berlin and was not prepared to see the city in its current state. So many critical events had taken place during the war while I was convalescing that I literally exited the hospital to a different Germany.

The Soviets had retaken Leningrad just two weeks before Field Marshal Friedrich Paulus surrendered the entire VI Army and all German forces at Stalingrad on 2 February. During this time United States bombers attacked us at Wilhelmshaven and Düsseldorf. We had also given up Tunisia to the enemy and our Axis Allies had evacuated the Solomon Islands in the Pacific and abandoned the fight for Guadalcanal. During the first week of March, British bombers attacked Berlin. Two weeks later a bomb was found on der Führer's plane and suspicion was growing against every officer on Hitler's staff.

Blocks of Berlin had been destroyed by the British air raids, and the Fire Police had cordoned off the ruins. Blackout conditions had not yet been instituted as a mandatory policy and the will of all Berliners had been strengthened by the attacks.

I reached RSHA Headquarters and was shown to Eichmann's office to wait for him. Moments later he appeared with a kind smile. *"Guten morgen, Hauptsturmführer! Wie ist das Bein und die Schulter?"*

"Good morning, Sir," I replied. "The leg and shoulder are healing well, thank you."

He sat behind his desk and adjusted some papers. "I assume you have been informed of the current state of affairs?"

"I believe so, Sir."

"Have you been informed of the situation in Warsaw?" He recognized my blank expression.

"We had a minor revolution in the ghetto," he explained. "It appears conditions are prime for another uprising. Hans Frank and Globocnik are greatly concerned about the intelligence they have gathered about this matter. We are conducting a meeting later this morning to discuss countermeasures. Educate yourself on the matter by reading the reports in your office and attend the meeting."

As I stood to carry out the directives he said, "I am pleased to have you back here."

I thanked him for the kind remark and retired to my office. The reports echoed the very things I had said to the late General Heydrich a couple years ago. It was impossible to monitor the activities of the ghetto residents, and without strict control to eliminate the black market, the Poles and Jews in the ghetto were believed to be armed and organized.

The meeting was attended by several Waffen SS officers including Brigadeführer Jürgen Stroop. Each officer expected that a second revolt was imminent but believed it could be easily managed and controlled. Himmler had issued directives that authorized extreme force to crush the slightest of rebellions in the ghettos.

At the end of the assembly I was awarded the Close Combat Clasp, Infantry Assault Badge in Silver, and Iron Cross for my deeds at Stalingrad. I did not believe that any of my actions were deserving of medals, but nonetheless, Eichmann pinned them to my tunic. I wished Heydrich was alive to see me wearing the decorations.

On 14 April another assembly was convened to discuss the process of liquidations at the Termination Stations. Each gas chamber and crematorium was functional at Auschwitz and RSHA superiors were distressed that the facility was only subjecting 4,700 Jews to Special Treatment each day. The numbers at Majdanek, Sobibor, Treblinka and Belzec were considerably lower, and gassings had been temporarily suspended at Chelmno until the facility could be refitted with technical modifications and upgrades.

I argued that the plausible reason for the unsatisfactory number of dead was due largely in part to the fact that other facilities were employing carbon monoxide poisoning. The gassings were taking place in the compartments of trucks, small halls, and buildings that were not capable of housing large numbers of Jews. I strongly urged the immediate construction of at least one gas hall, comparable in size to those at Auschwitz, to be constructed at each Termination Station until the problem could be properly assessed.

Eichmann agreed but said Himmler was greatly concerned about the recent debacle at Stalingrad and the current westward push of the Soviets. The Reichsführer-SS had ordered former Einsatzgruppen Commanders to excavate previous killing pits and burial fields throughout the Ukraine for the purposes of exhuming the bodies for disposal. Every bone and thread of clothing was to be found and pulverized or burned with special equipment to prevent the Soviet Army from discovering the mass graves.

I asked Eichmann, "If what we have done is legal, why devote resources to destroying the evidence?"

He looked at me as if I should have known better to ask such a question. He closed a file and said, "No one expects the world to understand German reasons for this ugly business."

His statement was a contradiction of many things I believed in. We had all been following our orders and issuing directives based on the idea that we were the supreme governing force in Europe. To destroy evidence of German activities, to wit: the mass executions of the Jews; seemed to imply a level of complicity in questionable actions. I never felt culpability of criminal activity, nor did I ever believe that our operations against the Jews were by any means illegal. Everything I had done was outlined with legal precedent and clearly laid out in the codes of Reich Law. Why would we concern ourselves with world opinion?

"I am sending you to Belzec," said Eichmann. "I want you to inspect the method of Special Treatment there and report on it. If I can persuade Himmler to construct a gas chamber at Belzec I should be able to convince him to build more at the other facilities."

I dreaded the thought of traveling to Belzec as it was situated inside the Lublin District and it more than likely meant I would be forced to confront Globocnik. These thoughts were very accurate as I saw the District Commander's Citroen parked outside of the Kommandant's office when I arrived.

I entered the office to find Göth, Globocnik and Christian Wirth engaged in a jovial conversation that they continued without so much as acknowledging my presence. There was a short pause before Amon announced, "Look who has come to join us."

Wirth and Globocnik looked at me with absolute disdain. It was the first time I had met Wirth, and his clammy and limp handshake was repulsive.

"What does the RSHA want with me now?" he asked. "I have been entertaining Legal Affairs Officers for two years here. What is this about? Am I in violation of electrical or building codes?"

"No, no," said Amon while putting an informal hand on Wirth's shoulder. "Schiller would not come here for such trivial matters. Would you, Schiller?"

"No," I replied firmly. "I have come to witness your Special Treatment process for purposes of evaluation."

Wirth pursed his lips and squinted at my medals. "Special Treatment," he hissed with disgust. "Why do you people refuse to call it killing? I am sure this word would be more to the point and space efficient on your reports."

Göth and Globocnik chortled at Wirth's sarcasm. The Kommandant looked at Globocnik and asked, "Why do they bedevil me with these things, Odilo? Who wishes this ire upon me?"

"You should not blame Schiller," said Amon in my support and defense. He walked to my side and put his hand on my shoulder. "He is one of us. He realizes the need for what we do out here. I am certain he could make things easier for you."

"How?" asked Wirth while pouring spirits for Globocnik and himself. "How could you possibly make things easier for me? Do you know what goes on here?"

"He does," said Amon still speaking for me. "You should see what this man has done for Höss at Auschwitz. I am telling you, Christian; you could do with a gas hall here. Schiller can make that happen for you. Give him a few moments of your time and an open mind."

Wirth stared at Amon for a few moments and then motioned for me to sit down. "I manage to keep my prisoner population at quota," he said. "This is because I am using carbon monoxide. Your department should know the size and capabilities of this facility. The RSHA would naturally expect me to house more prisoners if I had more efficient means to dispose of them. This leads to problems when those elements are not functioning at full operational capacity. Suppose the chamber has a leaky seal; shipments of gas crystals are delayed, or the crematorium clogs. What then? I will continue to receive prisoners with no place to house them and no means with which to gas them. If I am correct, the Ministry of Health and Hygiene still frowns upon this."

I chose my words carefully. "Let us say that certain developments in the east have expedited the need to dispose of our prisoner population."

Each of them fixed his gaze on a different object in the room as if avoiding the truth that the Soviets were pushing toward our borders.

Göth cautiously asked, "Would the prisoners arrive here with their luggage and valuables or would those items be confiscated before they boarded the transports?"

His question gained Wirth's attention. I replied, "The luggage would remain behind at the station to provide more freight space in the wagons. Portable personal valuables such as watches, jewelry, money, and fine clothing would of course arrive on the possession of each inmate."

Amon moved his index finger back and forth through the air. "And who would collect these items?"

"Those matters are the administrative decisions of the Kommandant."

Göth and Wirth exchanged a quick glance and I know they recognized an opportunity for financial gain.

Wirth nodded and asked, "How may I accommodate you, Hauptsturmführer?"

I detested men like Wirth, Göth, and Otto Koch who made a mockery of the prison administration system and manipulated its policies to fill their pockets. There was a limitless amount of corruption on behalf of many of the Kommandants but it was foolish and dangerous to my career to report such matters. The corruption was so widespread that it involved many different people on as many different social, political and military levels. For instance, reporting Göth's illegal activities would have meant exposing Globocnik. This in turn would have involved Hans Frank to some degree. My personal uncertainty was how my superiors would receive the news of Frank's involvement. In my mind there was a very even chance that the Reichsführer-SS would assist Frank by officially denying or covering up the allegations. Where would that leave me? Would I become known as a troublemaker for high ranking Party Officials? Would my reports of corruption and illegal activities cast me out of the RSHA? I was apprehensive to report these matters to Könrad Morgen who officially investigated corruption in the prison system, let alone directly to Eichmann and the Reichsführer-SS.

In a sense, this made me as self serving as the men I claim to have detested. I said nothing and allowed the corruption to continue in order that the adverse reports would not have a negative impact on my career. I convinced myself that such matters were not my concern. They were the responsibility of men like Morgen. This is why so many of us Legal Affairs Officers were disliked by Camp Kommandants. They never knew where we stood and what our intentions were.

Wirth's operation was an organized but inefficient process for Special Treatment. I joined him at a building he called *"Der Manor"* where the Jews disrobed and were escorted along a long corridor through a set of doors and into the back of a truck. The Jews were calmly told they were being taken to delousing baths on the opposite side of the camp and they had no reason not to believe this. Once inside the compartment of the truck, the doors were closed and the motor was turned over. They were gassed by piping the carbon monoxide into the rear.

I composed my report in a garden and recommended the gas chamber to process a larger number of Jews. I ordered a mechanical inspection of the truck motor used to generate the carbon monoxide and included the details of its deteriorated condition to advance the idea of the hall. Steady maintenance on motors equaled less time for the Special Treatment of Jews. In my report, I urged Eichmann and the Reichsführer-SS to personally inspect Belzec to witness the current process. I specifically closed the report with: *"The continued use of the carbon monoxide vans denies opportunity to liquidate a greater number of Jews."*

My report would have been futile if I did not propose a location to build the chamber. My superiors were known for demanding reports and reviewing them, but then doing nothing about them because the author did not propose all possible solutions. It took a very long time before I realized that when I was dispatched to generate a report, I was the driving force of that particular bureaucratic process. I am convinced that my superiors hardly knew any specific details of what was actually taking place at the camps or in the field. Even when my superiors personally visited and inspected these facilities, they only saw and noted what they wished to acknowledge. And, during these inspections, the Kommandants went to such lengths to fool my superiors with proverbial *smoke and mirrors* that RSHA officials departed the facilities thinking all was well and questioning me about why I had authored oppositional notes in my reports. Many times I wanted to shake Eichmann or the Reichsführer-SS by their shoulders and shout, "Look beyond the smoke and mirrors! See the truth!"

This caused me a great portion of personal concern when I combined the general ignorance of my superiors with Eichmann's statement about disposing of evidence in the east. In the Spring of 1943 I was greatly worried that perhaps my superiors knew exactly what was taking place in the camps and in the field but that they perpetuated a false ignorance to claim disassociation to it. After all, my name was on the factual reports and my signature was on each document requesting that the maximum number of human executions take place in each of these facilities. I was indeed the driving force behind these particular bureaucratic processes and if, as Eichmann said, the world did not understand German reasons, the world would have a marvelous collection of documentation to hold me personally accountable for it.

The future of Germany and the Reich was a very realistic question in 1943 though it was an impossible subject to discuss. Defeatist remarks would land me in a military prison or Detainment Facility and there was no means of knowing who one could trust to share such a conversation with. The bomb found on der Führer's plane had created an almost physical veil of suspicion that each person had to wend through. Innocent statements were frequently taken out of context and many high level officers found themselves explaining such remarks to

Gestapo officials.

Perhaps my Father was the only man I could have had such a discussion with, but he had died from pneumonia the previous winter, or so I believed at that time. I knew it would have been possible to discuss these matters with Amon Göth but this would have enslaved me to his criminal will. Had I refused to participate in his schemes subsequent to such a conversation, he could have easily used my remarks as an influential Sword of Damocles.

In my assessment, a portion of the Belzec vehicle compound could be used for the construction of the gas chamber. It fit the specifications for the necessary dimensions and was close enough to *Der Manor* to not disrupt Wirth's original process. I returned to Wirth's office where he, Göth, Globocnik and two other men were well into a bottle of spirits.

Wirth motioned to an older man with a dark mustache. "This is Mister Göckel, the manager of the new arrivals. Tell him how your proposed idea will work."

We discussed the present use of the railroad spur leading into Belzec from the main Tomaszow line and his current methods for processing new arrivals. He informed me that most portable valuables were stripped from the Jews by the Gestapo at the Rawa Ruska station before the train arrived at the facility. Wirth wished to know if and how my plan could prevent the Gestapo seizure of valuables at Rawa Ruska, and how we could circumvent Gestapo interference at Belzec.

Before answering this question I demanded to know the identity of the other man in the office. He was introduced as SS Scharführer Rudolf Kamm, the overseer of prisoners and work details.

I explained that the presence of a gas chamber at Belzec would classify the Termination Station as a priority destination and that all trains routed to the facility would receive right of way. There would of course be security inspections and temporary halts due to rail traffic congestion along the way, but I could personally assure Wirth the trains would arrive at Belzec without the cargo being accosted or stripped of valuables. To my knowledge, the stop at Rawa Ruska was primarily a maintenance matter where the locomotive took on water. The Gestapo used this to their advantage to pick the freight clean and this was neither an official or unofficial measure. This process had to be completed at some stage of the journey so no interference or investigation had been conducted into the matter under its present circumstances. Filing a motion that specifically requested the removal of portable valuables at the Belzec station would have raised suspicions, so I suggested rerouting the trains around Rawa Ruska to Belzec. I could file this under a number of reasons that would never be questioned. I could call it reducing traffic on a military line, reduced maintenance, expediting priority freight, or something else that would go without notice.

The Gestapo occupied small houses and offices at the Belzec station and Wirth's appropriation of valuables would be threatened by their presence. I suggested that along with the proposal to construct the gas chamber, we also file a proposal to renovate the station to accommodate expedited and priority freight. Under this guise we could move the Gestapo offices to another location inside the camp and reduce the number of agents present at the arrival point. I clearly stated the details of this security would strictly be the jurisdiction of Wirth.

Each of them looked at Göth to see if his criminal mind approved of my proposals. He nodded his head slowly and Wirth then asked for the copy of my report so that he may endorse my recommendations with his signature. After he signed it, the report was given to a courier and taken to Berlin. We placed a telephone call to RSHA Headquarters to announce the success of the meeting and Wirth confirmed his approval to my superiors.

My new directives sent me from Belzec to Sobibor to report on the activities of Kommandant Fritz Stangl who had ignored numerous RSHA requests to file progress accounts on the activities taking place there. Stangl had filed nothing but numbers of Jews and Soviet Prisoners of War executed, but my superiors were interested in learning about the efficiency of the gas chambers installed there. Treblinka and Majdanek were scarcely capable of processing the numbers of Jews being sent to each facility and my Commanders wished to learn if it was feasible to divert freight shipments from those locations to Stangl's camp.

Sobibor appeared more primitive than any of the other facilities I had visited. It was approximately a 425 by 610 meters enclosure with barbed wire, wooden fences and guard towers bordering its perimeter. The entry area housed a railroad spur and the administrative buildings and living quarters for the SS. It had been originally constructed to contain Soviet Prisoners of War captured during the Eastern Campaign, but in January or February of 1943, the Reichsführer-SS had issued an order to convert it into a Detainment Facility and Termination Station.

Stangl was very receptive to my visit and he exuded a sense of pride in his work and assured me I would find everything to be at proper levels of satisfaction. He escorted me into the first camp which contained the workshops used to service the SS personnel. Tailors, barbers, metalworkers and leather smiths performed services and crafted goods without much supervision. I never felt safe at Sobibor because the prisoners were given much leave to travel about the open areas with a very small number of guards overseeing them.

The second enclosed area was completely obscured by a barbed wire fence that had been packed with tree branches, shrubberies and foliage. Stangl explained that this was the area where the inmates disrobed before being escorted through *der Schlauch* to a small building where their hair was shaved off before entering the gas chamber. *Der Schlauch* was nothing more than a narrow open corridor hemmed in by foliage and fences but it was effective at preventing escape. The inmates who passed through this tube were told they were being deported to another camp such as Terezin.

The third enclosure was constructed deep within a grove of trees and contained a large brick building that had been partitioned into three separate gas chambers. Three tank engines were mounted on a base outside the building and these motors pumped the carbon monoxide inside. Each individual gas chamber was approximately 4 ½ by 4 ½ meters and Stangl told me a single hall could accommodate 150 to 175 Jews. Approximately 75 meters north of the brick building were specially dug mass pits where the bodies were burned on petrol soaked pyres.

Stangl reported that he could process a maximum freight of 20 wagons in a period of 2 to 3 hours if the engines providing the carbon monoxide were operating at peak performance and so long as there were no delays in the unloading, disrobing, and shaving processes. I was pleased with this information as it was a statement of great efficiency. However, as most Kommandants were reporting longer durations for Special Treatment, I was bound to test Stangl on his quoted performance.

On the following day I witnessed the arrival of 20 freight wagons at the Sobibor facility and was impressed by the calm and expedient manner in which the prisoners were processed. With an average of 150 prisoners in each of the three gas chambers at a time, Stangl had successfully liquidated approximately 2,340 Jews in a span of two hours and ten minutes.

I had not seen such incredible efficiency before. Höss had not even demonstrated such marvelous competence with his technically superior facility at Auschwitz. I asked Stangl why he had failed to submit progress reports to RSHA Headquarters and he quite frankly told me that he had intentionally omitted them because he believed he would draw attention to himself with his exclusive efficiency. It was indeed logical to assume that such facts and figures would thrust Sobibor to the forefront of discussions about expansion. It was also sound to presume that Stangl's successes would earn him a transfer to another less competent station for the purpose of improving efficiency. Stangl was quite content with his assignment in eastern Poland as it provided him with a relative liberty from constant inspections and visits from superior officers. I was obligated to report his successes but assured him I would recommend his continued supervision of the Sobibor facility.

On 14 May 1943, the Office for Jewish Emigrations was again beset by one of those anxious moods that put all superior officers in turmoil. Theodor Dannecker, who had temporarily returned to Berlin from his office in Bulgaria, leaned inside my door and asked, "Have you heard, Schiller? The entire *Afrika Korps* surrendered in Tunisia. Goddamned Italians! That is what we get in return for permitting their incapable 1st Army to control our 5th Panzer Division!"

Later I learned that the surrender of the *Afrika Korps* had taken place on the previous day. In spite of the news on 14 May, I could not be distressed. This was the same day I received the news that my wife was pregnant.

Losing North Africa and the Soviet push to the west had tremendous influence on the operations of my department. Previously, the Reich treated its military and political problems with a mood of encouragement. It was said that certain things were delays to the overall progress of the system, but each could be overcome.

Following the surrender of the *Afrika Korps*, an urgent mood prevailed and we were instilled with the impression that our superior officers had reason to believe our plans were coming apart at the seams.

A Croatian Catholic Archbishop was publicly imploring Pope Pius XII to maintain a firm defense over 240,000 Jews who had converted to Catholicism to avoid being transported to the Detainment Facilities. Radios were announcing that Berlin was finally *Judenfrei* and parades were being organized to celebrate the deportation of all its Jews. Meanwhile, the Allies were conducting parades of their own through the streets of Tunisia to observe their victory over the Reich. Propaganda was being spit out of all governments faster than either side could manage and the global political situation plunged into crisis.

During the final week of May, nearly 1,000 United States bombers destroyed our city of Dortmünder. Göring's Luftwaffe had done very little to counter the Allied bombing raid and many of us began to ponder the future of Germany.

June 1943

The first day of the month ended with disastrous news that the Luftwaffe had shot down a British passenger plane flying from Lisbon to London over the Bay of Biscay. Our Intelligence Agency gathered information that the event would cause international outrage not only because of the destruction of a British civilian plane, but also because an American born actor, Leslie Howard, was killed in the incident.

On 10 June, perhaps partially in response to this unfortunate event, the Allies began bombing our cities on a steady basis during both daylight and night hours. I sent my wife south to Füssen to live with my mother and sister as that particular area had been greatly spared from the Allied air raids.

On the following day we attended a meeting conducted by Reichsführer-SS Heinrich Himmler at which he announced orders to liquidate all ghettos in Poland. The inhabitants of each were to be transferred to the Termination Stations for Special Treatment. I was personally assigned to the unit that would conduct the liquidation of the Bialystok ghetto.

My unit was not immediately dispatched for this task but was held in Berlin to plan and organize the action. We conducted meetings three days per week throughout the month in which we reviewed maps, census records, rail lines, availability of resources, and potential destinations based upon the quotas each Termination Station could accept at a time due to the extraordinarily high volume of shipments.

I was also assigned as a liaison to the Ministry of Transportation to make certain the mass deportations from the ghettos operated in an efficient manner. OKH and OKW were constantly sending officers to question me about any potential disruption Himmler's plans may have upon the transfer of military supplies and soldiers to the Eastern Front.

We were in a meeting discussing the maps of the Bialystok ghetto when air raid sirens pierced the air. We immediately ran from the conference room and joined a congestion of humanity at the main staircase. Most voices were calm and there was no excited shoving. The procession began moving in an orderly fashion and I noticed Eichmann standing by one of the pedestal rails acting as an usher to move people along.

Upon reaching the first floor we heard guards shouting that the bunker beneath the headquarters was full. The remainder of us filed out the main doors and followed each other to the nearest bomb shelter. All of us were looking toward the skies for the bombers and a sinking feeling was deep in my stomach. We had no sooner reached the entrance of a shelter when the *Ganz Klar* sirens sounded and we quietly returned to our respective offices. It had been a drill.

We practiced this routine many more times over the next couple weeks but we never became complacent in our belief that Allied bombers were not over our heads. Düsseldorf, Hannover, Bremen, Hamburg and Hildesheim had been bombed while we were conducting drills. Berlin itself had been attacked before and in spite of increased Luftwaffe fighter patrols, we knew the Allies could hit it again without much effort. Midway through the month the Royal Airforce inflicted major damaged upon our V2 Rocket facility at Peenumünde. We were left with the distinct belief that the Allies could reach and bomb anything they so desired.

At the end of the month Himmler declared that all units assigned to liquidate the ghettos were to expedite their plans and submit them for his review no later than 15 July. My unit had generated what we thought to be an effective and efficient plan. It was mostly based upon my experiences at the Lublin and Porajów ghettos, and as Globocnik had been placed in charge of the ghetto liquidations, I felt confident our plans would be accepted. The Gauleiter of the General District of Bialystok, Erich Kock, insisted that Globocnik had no formal jurisdiction in his area of operations and his official complaint postponed the commencement of the operation. While it was delayed and being sorted out on an administrative bureaucratic level, Eichmann assigned me tasks that involved the deportations taking place during the liquidations that had been initiated. I arranged hundreds of transports to Auschwitz and Chelmno and consciously tried to avoid taxing Stangl with additional duties. It was my hope to transfer the bulk of the Bialystok ghetto inhabitants to Sobibor as I knew Stangl's process for extermination would promptly meet the needs of my unit.

We had just received official word of a Soviet advance against our positions at the Kursk in the Ukraine when the air raid sirens were sounded. There was more of a noticeable urgency during the procedure and whereas men previously walked to the staircase, they were now running. I heard the propellers of short and medium range fighters soaring over the building, and by the time I was halfway down the stairs, the distant thudding of bombs came to my ears.

The guards again announced the headquarters bunker was full and we spilled into the streets to see our fighter aircraft skimming the rooftops of Berlin. Civilians were standing and staring up at the skies with mindless expressions of disbelief. The Luftschutze was attempting to move the crowds toward the shelters but a mood of chaos had taken over. People began screaming, wailing, and even cursing at the skies. I maintained my composure in this madness and followed the crowd into a shelter.

Civilians and military personnel were crowded into the dimly lit haven and apart from the crying of infants, every person held their breath and was silent. The explosions seemed far off but now and then the lights would flicker in the bunker. I was left to wonder, if this was happening in Berlin, what was happening over Füssen? I convinced myself that my home village contained nothing of strategic military value and that it would not be considered an Allied objective. The devil then spoke to me in my mind and said things such as, "The Allies would bomb Füssen to clear it as a base of operations for their military!" and, "Füssen is an unprotected target! Why would the Allies not bomb it for the sole reason of eliminating it?" The bombs never came close to our shelter but when the *Ganz Klar* sirens released us, we could smell smoke and sulfur.

Most officers at RSHA Headquarters were concerned with damage reports throughout the city of Berlin. I learned the raid had mostly been confined on our industrial plants in the western quarter of the city. Simultaneous Allied air raids had been conducted on Stendal and Wolfsburg. Other reports gradually came in that the Allied bombers had attacked Stuttgart and Augsburg. I desperately tried to place a telephone call to Füssen but the wires were jammed by soldiers, officers, and civilians who were also attempting to learn the fates of their loved ones. I managed a wire communication to our Munich Headquarters and was informed that nothing south of that city had been attacked. Füssen had been spared.

10 July 1943

The Americans and British landed at Sicily. There seemed no hope to sue for peace with the United States. By God, if they take the Italian mainland they could capture Naples, Rome, Florence and Venice. That would give them a straight advance toward Austria and put them in the Fatherland at Füssen. High Command assured us that the invaders would be thrown back into the sea. I heard that United States General Patton was in Sicily. We heard his name before in connection with the battles against Rommel in North Africa. We heard he had a reputation of being crass and somewhat of a cowboy. He was the last person we wanted on our continent.

The Russians had us confounded and on the defensive in the east. On 12 July the Soviets destroyed our Armored Division at Prochorowka. On the following day we lost the battle at Kursk where approximately 2,900 of our tanks were destroyed.

Our department was quiet except for the chattering of typewriters. The mood was very grim and it almost seemed a crime to speak a single word. The air raid sirens and frequent trips to the shelters disrupted our days but I managed to submit our final plans for the Bialystok ghetto liquidation on 15 July.

There was no immediate response from the Reichsführer-SS and so we each toiled at our assigned duties until the orders came down. Near the end of July the Americans flew more than 250 bombing raids over Hamburg during the day while their British counterparts bombed the city by night. The Allies used incendiary bombs to destroy our factories and docks. The ensuing firestorms murdered more than 40,000 German civilians.

I maintained as much contact as possible with Klaudia and my family. They assured me all was well in Füssen but inquired of the situation at Hamburg. I told them there had been a few air raids. Propaganda had greatly controlled the situation and kept it from the public. How could I tell my loved ones that more than 40,000 citizens had been burned to death or blown to pieces?

My unit received its orders to travel to the Bialystok ghetto on 10 August. Globocnik would be waiting for us and together we would coordinate the liquidation. I was somewhat pleased to know I would not encounter Amon Göth there as Globocnik had rewarded him with his own Detainment Facility at Plaszow.

I was granted four days of leave and on 6 August I walked through the door of the family home in Füssen and into the arms of my wife, mother and sister. They asked about the war and I assured them we were winning it. They did not know any better as they were gullible victims of the propaganda machine that controlled them. The government was not able to stop its citizens from talking about the destruction and death at Hamburg and we treated this subject carefully.

On 7 August I had come down the stairs in the morning to the wonderful scent of cooked sausages and fried eggs. I was distressed to see a Staff Mercedes stop in front of the house and my heart sunk at the thought of having my leave revoked. I exited to the wooden porch and saw the passenger walking toward me with a packet of sealed documents. He lifted his right arm and said, *"Heil Hitler! Der Führer verlängert Lob auf Jürgen Schiller. Jürgen starb für das Vaterland."*

He gave me a firm nod and returned to the car and I stood there watching it drive away. Klaudia came outside and noticed the mood that had overcome me. She asked what was troubling me and I told her.

"My brother Jürgen is dead."

I sat on the stairs of the porch and opened the documents.

According to the papers, Jürgen had been shot during the battle for Kremenchuk near the Dnieper River on 3 August. While retreating to the river his battalion was ambushed by a Soviet Rifle Regiment and my brother was fatally struck by shrapnel from a Russian grenade.

Mother did not cry when I told her this news; at least not in the presence of me, my wife and my sister. Her mood had changed but she went about serving breakfast as if things were normal. After the meal she placed a black candle next to Jürgen's photograph on top of our Telefunken radio.

I walked into the back garden and sat underneath the large oak tree that Jürgen and I climbed as boys. While reading the letter from his Battalion Commander and looking at the photograph of his grave near the Dnieper, I could hear my mother's voice shouting in my mind at Jürgen and me for climbing the tree. I looked around the garden where we trampled Mother's vegetable plants with our soccer ball and looked at the small brook that we pushed each other in regularly as children. I bitterly cried for Jürgen, the men at Stalingrad, and for the reckless abundance of death choking Germany. I realized the Angel of Death was everywhere and no person was safe from his touch. What had befallen you my dear brother? What had become of you my dear Germany, now the giver and receiver of the touch of death? Oh how I questioned God and the existence of good. How I pondered and feared Final Judgment and how my brother's death made me feel insignificantly mortal.

He used to call me *die Kröte*, and while this infuriated me as a boy, I never minded and actually looked forward to him calling me *the toad* when I was older. I would never hear this again nor enjoy one of his disgusting jokes. He was laid in a hole and forsaken by God near the Dnieper River. I reasoned that he was killed for a noble cause and while doing his part to rid the world of Communists and Bolshevists. I certainly did not wish for my child to be born into a world controlled by Jews, Communists and Bolshevists. The struggle we were caught up in was a necessary one. But how very unceremonious and outright disrespectful it was to receive such news from a common courier. If Hitler truly extended praise to my brother, let der Führer stand before me and say it. Do not send me a damned clerk.

I departed from Füssen to Munich on 9 August with promises to be careful. Late on the following day I arrived at Bialystok and assembled my unit. Globocnik called several meetings over the next few days and we reviewed the maps and our plans. On 13 August a battalion of Ukrainian Auxiliary Police arrived and Globocnik set the date of the action for 15 August.

CHAPTER EIGHTEEN
LIQUIDATION OF THE BIALYSTOK GHETTO

On the night of 15 August the SS, Order Police and Ukrainian police surrounded the ghetto. The Bialystok Judenrat was informed by the Gestapo that the residents of the ghetto were to be relocated to Lublin. Globocnik was informed that the Judenrat council members were very suspicious of German intentions but the word was disseminated among the inhabitants to prepare to be moved on the following day.

Throughout the night I organized the arrival of trains to be used as transports at the Jurowiecka Station and at the Czysta Crossing. By 0800 hours on 16 August, tens of thousands of Jews were obediently making their way from their homes to the gathering point on Jurowiecka Street. The trains were scheduled to transport the Jews to Treblinka and Majdanek. Over the following days I would direct several to Auschwitz and Sobibor.

Just before noon I heard shouting and saw the SS bringing their weapons to the ready. A Tiger Tank rolled through the ghetto gates followed by two halftracks. I was informed that the Jews had risen in an armed revolt and were shooting our soldiers near Smolna Street. Panic erupted among the Jews on Jurowiecka Street, and that quickly, our months of planning had dissolved. The Ukrainians were beating the Jews into submission and the Order Police and SS opened fire on crowds of men, women and children. An SS Scharführer was grabbing my arm and shouting, "Sir! Get out of here!"

An armored car stopped several meters away from me and swung its turret back and forth while searching for combatant Jews. I began making my way toward Globocnik's Command Post when rifle shots rang out and rounds bounced off the armored car. I instinctively took cover behind it as the turret pivoted and its two machine guns destroyed the second story floor of an apartment building. Moments later I was covered with petrol and my right sleeve was on fire. The Jews had thrown a lit bottle of fuel at the armored car. The Scharführer doused my sleeve and pushed me down in a crouch.

"I told you to get the hell out of here, Sir. Why do officers never listen to us? Keep your head down or those Yids will blow it off. They do not much care for us, not to mention officers, Sir."

The Scharführer pointed to the Tiger which was now approaching us in reverse. He smiled and said, "I think this is about to get very interesting, Sir."

The Tiger swung its cannon toward the building and blew the roof and walls apart. It fired two more shells until the entire upper story was a burning frame of wood and plaster. The armored car sped off and the soldier escorted me to Globocnik's Command Post.

The General was in a furious rage. "Goddamnned Yids!" he bellowed. "No quarter! No quarter! Get their stinking Jewish asses on the trains and take them to the camps! Goddamned Yids wish to challenge me? Damn them! Damn them all!" Globocnik ordered the Ukrainian Police Leader to take a portion of his battalion to seize the elderly and sick Jews in the ghetto. On Globocnik's orders, the Ukrainians were to take them to a secluded area of the ghetto and beat them to death.

Globocnik looked at me. "What in hell are you doing at my Command Post? The Order Police and Ukrainians have the deportations under control." He pointed at the Infantry Assault badge on my tunic. "Get your ass in the ghetto and crush this damned rebellion!"

I assembled a squad of SS soldiers and trotted into the ghetto with them. We followed the sounds of shooting and realized the seriousness of the situation when we came across one of our armored cars burning on its side. The Jews had wired demolitions at key crossings and used their knowledge of the ghetto terrain to gain an advantage. However, they were poorly and insufficiently armed and displayed no formal or organized training.

On the corner of Jurowiecka and Fabryczna Streets we were pinned down by rifle and pistol fire coming from a series of shops and an apartment building. While I had my head down and was pressing myself against a wall for cover, I heard a young Schütze's voice with a tone of astonishment. "Mary Mother of God. Look at that!"

I saw eyes widening and jaws going slack before I peered around the corner and saw that the Jews had defiantly hung crudely sewn flags bearing Stars of David from a few windows.

An Unterscharführer said, "I am ready to die, for now I have seen everything!"

I could not believe it. My men could not believe it. We would certainly never tell Brigadeführer Globocnik about this. Then a rain of vulgar insults was shouted at us from the Jews in the windows.

"You are begotten of dogs!"

"Your mother is a Jewish whore!"

"Hitler is a pig's ass!"

Now and then indiscriminate small arms fire forced us to take cover. My men had started to laugh as this was something we never before encountered and certainly nothing we ever expected to confront. We were safely behind cover but there was nothing we could do at that precise moment.

The Unterscharführer said, "I do not think I can write of this in a letter to my mother." We shrugged and looked at each other in disbelief. I saw a soldier with several rifle fired grenades hanging from his belt.

"Decorate those flags for me, Oberschütze."

He was more than happy to comply and he attached the fixture to the end of his rifle. He laid prone on the ground and crawled to the corner on his elbows. Taking aim, he fired his weapon and we heard the explosion. "That should have made a mess in their great room, Sir!"

Suddenly the insults stopped and a heavy burst of small arms fire pelted the intersection. The Unterscharführer was shaking his head in confusion. "If we stay here the Yids will use all their ammunition by shooting at nothing."

The Oberschütze had loaded another grenade on the end of his rifle and again crawled forward and discharged his weapon. "Oh, shit!" he yelled with a smile. "I took part of the roof off, Sir!"

"Do you have an incendiary?" I asked.

"Just one, Sir."

"Put it through the front door."

"*Ja wohl!*"

The round set the building on fire just as I hoped it would. I ordered each of my machine gunners to spray the shop fronts with three full belts. I used this suppression fire to move part of my men across the street and into an abandoned structure that gave us a clear view of the burning apartment building. The smoke was billowing out of all windows and through the gaping hole in the roof. We saw the form of a Jew who leapt from a third story window to escape the flames. To our amazement he stood up and began limping toward cover before our machine guns cut him down.

More gunfire came from the shops and we returned our own volley. I used the radio to inquire of the availability of armored vehicles and was relayed to a halftrack a block away on Biala Street. I related our situation to its Commander and moments later it rolled down the street, crossed the intersection, and smashed through the wall of the shops with its machine guns firing. Jews were scattering from their demolished hold and our guns brought them down in the rubble. More leapt from the windows of the apartment building and some attempted to flee through the flames in the main doorway. After perhaps one hour, the burning building subsided under the grenade and fire damage and half of it collapsed. We slowly moved into the intersection as the threat had ended.

Farther along Fabryczna Street we encountered another squad of SS who had apprehended more Jewish resistance fighters. The SS lined them up against the wall of a bakery and machine gunned them. Captured weapons and grenades were being thrown into the back of a Blitz Opel and my unit was still talking about the audacity of the Jews who hung Stars of David from the windows.

By nightfall my unit returned to the ghetto gates and Globocnik was still pacing and cursing at his Command Post. I learned that none of the transports had departed from the Bialystok ghetto because the registration process had been delayed due to the uprising. Tens of thousands of Jews were still being held at the gathering area at gunpoint. The Order Police and SS had also found numerous clever hiding places being used by Jews throughout the ghetto. Globocnik demanded every Jew be accounted for and ordered my unit to report to the field kitchen wagons for a meal and then to join the building to building searches.

I was exhausted as were my men, but Globocnik was firm in his directives. We heard sporadic gunfire and a few heavy explosions from inside the ghetto while we ate. After the meal I assembled my unit in formation and we marched along the dimly lit streets. We joined a squad of Order Police and entered a large apartment building. Our battery powered torches threw eerie and suspicious shadows inside the dwellings. We opened cabinets, armoires, cupboards and storage chests but did not find any Jews hiding in them. Other soldiers struck the floorboards with the butts of their rifles while listening for inconsistencies with the noise to reveal hollow holds. We took each step very cautiously as we knew some of the Jews were armed and we could be walking into an ambush.

A nervous voice carried down the corridor. "Oh, shit! Oh, shit! I found some!" My small squad followed the voice to where a young soldier was holding his rifle on three or four Jews crouching in a dark corner of a bedroom. More SS entered behind us and a soldier immediately discharged a long burst into the Jews from his MP3008 machine gun.

A Stabsscharführer berated the soldier who pulled the trigger. "You ass! We have orders to take them to the registration point! What in hell are you thinking? You are fortunate you did not hit any of us with deflected bullets!"

The soldier silently accepted the admonishment with an expression of contempt and anger. He exited the apartment without taking his eyes off the Stabsscharführer.

"Damn it," mumbled the Sergeant Major. "Check those Yids for intelligence and continue searching!"

He looked at me and asked, "Do you allow this kind of behavior?"

"Continue searching," I said with the coldest tone I could manage.

Throughout the night we found Jews hiding beneath floorboards, inside false walls, in the ceilings, and inside sofas that had the inner stuffing removed. At approximately 0330 hours my unit was relieved and I exited the ghetto to sleep.

I was awakened a few hours later on 17 August and on Globocnik's orders, I proceeded to the gathering point where the registration process was beginning. The rebellion had not been crushed and many SS and Order Police squads were engaged in heavy fighting on Wazka and Fabryczna Streets. Tanks and armored cars had been dispatched to those areas but the fighting was too close to the

Jurowiecka Station to proceed with the deportations. By afternoon more fighting had erupted near Smolna Street and we deduced that the Jews were attempting to break out of the ghetto there and flee into the nearby forest. Globocnik reinforced the opposite side of the Smolna wall and fence with SS troops, tanks and halftracks.

The Jews at the assembly point were very cooperative, subdued and obedient. They were very aware that the resistance fighters were more of a threat to their welfare than we were. Globocnik had ordered the hangings of several hundred Jews from the gathering point to serve as a visual deterrent to the resistance. It did not have the desired effect. The general belief was that the Jews knew they were all marked for death and that they wished to die fighting us.

On the evening of 17 August I oversaw the loading of the first transports at the Czysta Crossing. In the early hours of 18 August, the first trains departed for Treblinka. During the course of the day the Jurowiecka Station was secured and I began loading transports there. By evening I had shipped approximately 3,200 Jews to the Treblinka Facility.

During the second day of the transports, the SS had confined most of the remaining resistance fighters in a fortified building on Chmielna Street. The structure was surrounded by tanks, halftracks, armored cars, and SS and Order Police units. It was leveled under a storm of repeated gunfire and over the following days the last of the Jewish fighters took their own lives or died ingloriously by our guns.

On 24 or 25 August, the Bialystok ghetto had been liquidated and approximately 11,000 Jews had been transported to Treblinka, Terezin, Majdanek, Auschwitz, Poniatowa, Sobibor and Blizyn. For this I received a Meritorious Service medal.

CHAPTER NINETEEN
THE SHIFTING TIDE

More of Berlin had been destroyed by Allied air raids and blackout conditions had now been imposed. While conducting the action at the Bialystok ghetto, our forces at Kharkov had been defeated by the Russian Army. There was very little hope of preventing a Soviet advance on Kiev but OKW and OKH had reinforced the bridgeheads along the Dnieper River to prevent this.

By 1 September five Italian Divisions surrendered in Albania and this greatly threatened our control in that region. The Danes had also declared a national strike against the Reich and ceased production of armaments and goods necessary for our war effort. Our Foreign Office and Ministry of Economics imposed harsh penalties against the Danes and in response to these measures, the Danes managed to scuttle most of their naval vessels in the harbors.

We were losing control of the war and Europe. On 8 September, Italy surrendered to, and formed a partnership with the Allied Forces. A couple days later our forces occupied Rome and prepared to fend off the inevitable Allied offensive.

At this time many military and RSHA departments were being relocated in Uelzen, Neuruppin, Brandenburg and Tangermünde in an attempt to conceal them from Allied intelligence. The air raids were devastating Berlin but the Office for Jewish Emigrations remained at its location because Eichmann and the Reichsführer-SS deemed our work to be too important to have it disrupted by relocation. Throughout September we organized transports and deportations out of all the Occupied Zones to the Termination Stations. At the start of October, the British had captured Naples.

During the second week of October our forces met the American 5th Army in battle at the Volturno River in Italy. OKW and OKH were confident that the Americans would not last long in the Allied European Campaign. It was said the Americans were very aggressive, but also reckless and disorganized. They were not adept at fighting close range battles and were known to unleash a wasteful barrage of artillery shells on the smallest German patrols. They were observed to be a very timid and cautious opponent. Our Panzer Divisions, Grenadiers and Infantry had tremendous successes against them in Southern Italy.

The Soviets were still pushing west and had succeeded at taking the city of Smolensk from us. Most of our Eastern forces had fallen back to defensive positions at the Dnieper River, but our counterattacks at Lubny and Pavlohrad had created a north-to-south pincer that encircled the Russian 89th Army. Eliminating this opposition would have allowed us to capture vital fuel supplies south of Poltava.

On 13 October our former ally, Italy, formally declared war on us. Three days later on 16 October we captured the fuel stores at Poltava. We had also stopped the Americans in their tracks at the Volturno River in Southern Italy. Optimism for victory flourished once again.

The Office for Jewish Emigrations was a steady site of activity. The Danes had refused our demands for the deportation of their Jews and offered staged political and partisan resistance when we forced these measures upon them. Hitler personally ordered the deportations during the middle of September, but the Reichsführer-SS and Eichmann had no success in implementing the plans. The Foreign Office was stalemated and Danish armed resistance brought civil, political and social unrest inside Denmark. In the course of one month we managed to deport approximately 250 Danish Jews from Copenhagen. Hitler personally made it clear to Eichmann that he was very displeased with the lack of progress our office had made. Der Führer asked Müller and Kaltenbrunner to apply steady pressure on us.

A critical event at Sobibor had compounded the problems for our office. Stangl had been replaced by Franz Reichsleitner and on 14 October, approximately 400 Jews and Russian Prisoners of War completed a well planned rebellion and escaped from the facility. More than two dozen SS personnel had been killed during the operation. In response to this and to pacify Hitler, the Waffen SS implemented the apprehension of all Jews in Rome. This in fact did very little to spare Himmler and Müller from der Führer's anger over the events in eastern Poland.

Our efforts to deport the Jews of Rome met stiff verbal opposition from Pope Pius XII, but he did not impose political or economic sanctions against the Reich, nor did he do anything to halt the transports from Rome to Auschwitz.

During this time our Intelligence Office gathered credible information that tensions were being forged between the Allied Nations and the Soviet Union over what their particular war aims were. American and British leaders began squabbling with Soviet controllers about military objectives and plans. This was another mark of confidence for us as we believed the Allies were diplomatically fighting each other more at conference tables than us on the fields.

I began sleeping in my office and only seemed to exit for meals and air raid sirens. Toward the end of the first week of November the Soviet 1st Ukrainian Front drove our forces out of Kiev in the Ukraine. Our combat units fell back to the Zhitomir Line and dug in on a wide front.

On 10 November I was again dispatched to Auschwitz to witness the promotion of Höss to Chief Inspector of Concentration Camps. I was to personally inform his successor, Kommandant Arthur Liebehenschel, of the demands that the Reichsführer-SS, Eichmann, and the Office for Jewish Emigrations would be placing on him.

I was pleased to see Höss promoted and was satisfied that Glücks had been officially removed from the prison administration system. Höss always held a very practical attitude for management, and his experience at Auschwitz designated him as the most qualified expert on the Detainment Facility system. Himmler had become weary of the mistakes and excuses offered on a daily basis by Glücks, and the unfortunate breach of security at Sobibor had sealed his fate. This change in the administration meant that I was now subordinate to Höss but our past differences never surfaced in our contact and communications. He was an advocate for the Zyklon B process and he recognized that I knew and understood the benefits and efficiency of the program.

His first set of orders for me required a personal visit to Amon

Göth at Plaszow. Too many reports had been filed regarding Amon's extensive cruelty as the overseer of the facility, and as the former Kommandant of Auschwitz, Höss had directly been the victim of Göth's schemes and corruption. Höss ordered a Gestapo seizure and audit of Göth's accounts and files, and I was to travel there in the middle of this inspection.

Plaszow was frozen when I arrived there and my Staff Mercedes parked next to several other vehicles bearing the flags and insignia of the Gestapo. Göth was expecting me and seemed aware of the potential consequences he might be facing. We sat in the great room of his villa where we sipped cognac and made small talk before he addressed the true nature of my visit.

"What in hell is this all about?" he asked. "The Gestapo is auditing my ledgers and not telling me a damned thing. Have I done something wrong? Have you come here to arrest me?"

"I am not here to arrest you," I assured him. "There have been reports, Amon. Illegal killings and the misappropriation of Reich finances."

Amon chortled. "Illegal killings. Perhaps Berlin has not noticed that I manage an *Arbeit Lager* here. This is a damned work camp, Schiller. A few kilometers from here at Auschwitz they can put thousands of Jews to death because they are too elderly, young, sick, or incapable of working and this is not illegal. I shoot a Jewish inmate who is standing around not working and this is illegal? What is the difference? Explain this to me."

I could not explain it to him. Of course I could have quoted laws and policies but it would have turned into a circular discourse.

"This is all because of Höss, is it not?" he inquired. "Höss is angry with me because I rarely agreed with him. Is that it?"

"I believe you have provided Höss with an infinite number of reasons not to trust you, Amon."

He took his gaze from me and stared at the ceiling and walls before looking over his shoulder. "These walls," he said with a frightening tone of seriousness. "These walls have eyes and ears. They watch and listen all the time. Let us take a walk."

"Are you mad? It must be -6 C. outside."

He stood and walked to a clothes rack where he donned his overcoat and hat. He handed mine to me and picked up two leashes. I followed him to a room joined to the kitchen where he tethered his dogs before we exited through the front door and walked around the house and into the Plaszow facility.

The prisoners stood at attention and removed their caps as we walked by them. "Tell me the truth," said Amon. "What is to become of me?"

"I do not know. Höss has asked me to look into things here."

"What things in particular?"

"The illegal killings, the misappropriation of Reich finances, and the misuse of Reich property and resources."

"Just what am I accused of?"

"You have not been formally accused of anything, Amon. I am here to determine if there are grounds to accuse you."

"Why did Höss send you? Why did he not send Morgen?"

"It is my understanding that Höss does not wish to inaugurate his tenure as Chief of Concentration Camp Inspectors with unpleasantries. If the situations here are manageable, I suspect you might receive a written reprimand in your personnel file and nothing more. If the situation is discovered to be beyond such measures, I am afraid Morgen will have to be notified."

Amon stopped in his tracks and looked at me. "How can I make this manageable for you?"

I explained the nature of the problems to him. "You have sponsored some very lavish parties in your villa, Amon. You have paid for these gatherings with funds that were supposed to be used for the management and maintenance of the Plaszow facility."

"No one has complained about these functions," interrupted Göth. "People come, have a good time and tell me they can not wait until the next one."

"And no one would have complained," I explained, "If you did not shoot at prisoners from your balcony during the functions, and if you did not physically beat the inmates in front of your guests. The people you have invited are not used to seeing this treatment. Most of them acknowledge that it happens, but all people do not possess the same fortitude and constitution for it that we are forced to have."

"They should," said Amon. "It is not fair that we should have to experience this on a daily basis and other people do not have to see it at all."

"It is not a matter of fairness. It is a matter of good politics and sound behavior."

"Now the Blackbird of Porajów is educating me about good politics and sound behavior."

"Amon, Du haben ein Leben wie ein König hier!"

"You call this the life of a king?" he asked with noticeable agitation.

"What would you call it, Amon? You fill your pockets with money from the Reich and private industrialists; you take the portable values of your inmates, you host stately functions in your villa, and you kill prisoners for sport and amusement. People are complaining about you, Amon. Very influential officers and civilians have made noise about this."

"You know what happens in these facilities, Schiller."

I waved him off. "You do not need to explain yourself to me. I need to know if I have your word that these activities will cease. If I author a neutral report with your promise of positive reform, you have to honor it."

"I promise you I will honor it."

I braced myself for the answer to my final question. "Should I be concerned about the auditing of your ledgers?"

"No," he assured me. "The Gestapo is not looking at the real books. There is no cause for alarm. Everything they are looking at will appear to be legal."

"Will they match supply, requisition, and economic reports in Berlin?"

"They will be mirror reflections of the ledgers in Berlin."

We returned to his villa where the Gestapo auditors asked to speak with me. I joined them privately and they explained that though they were suspicious of Göth's records, they found nothing that could be used against him. They assured me a close examination would be conducted between his ledgers and those in Berlin but that for the moment, Amon was not being chartered with criminal actions. I departed Plaszow and authored the report of my findings when I returned to Auschwitz. Afterward, I conducted my first formal meeting with the new Kommandant.

Liebehenschel seemed the typical bureaucrat who wished not to be bothered with the details of the mass exterminations taking place in his facility.   He spoke of grandiose plans to manage Auschwitz I, Auschwitz II Birkenau, and Auschwitz III Monowitz as three separate complexes with an emphasis on industrial production. I believed this was a beneficial aim, but reminded him of the demands from my office to make certain the gas chambers and crematoriums received priority maintenance in order to operate at maximum efficiency. Liebehenschel acknowledged this but was not eager to speak of it. He asked many questions about the paperwork and prisoner rosters, and demanded to know who to send them to and if he should preserve copies. I answered his questions and stated he would be required to hold copies of all documentation, but he insisted on sending all his files to the Central Office in Oranienburg. I saw no potential problems with his wish to do this, but I inquired of his reasons.

Liebehenschel admitted concerns about the Russian advance and openly stated he believed it would be prudent to store all paperwork in a more secure location. What I perceived him to actually mean was that he desired all documentation to be kept in a place where it could not be immediately associated with him in the event Auschwitz was overrun or captured by the enemy.

There was no immediate threat to western Poland and Liebehenschel's remarks could have been interpreted as defeatist. However, I was astute enough to lend compassion to his concerns, especially after Eichmann's desire to dispose of evidence farther east.

On or about 18 November I stepped off the train in Berlin as air raid sirens were sounding throughout the city. Our short and medium range fighters were flying over the rooftops and at once enemy bombs began fragmenting the buildings around me. Glass, wood, plaster, mortar, concrete and stone were landing on the railroad line and the roof of the station. The very ground shook beneath my feet and there was no semblance of an orderly procession to the shelters. People screamed, violently pushed, and trampled each other like cattle during this panic.

Anti aircraft guns sputtered flak shells into the sky from around the train station. The *Hochs Hotel* took a direct hit and shattered lumber flew end over end through the air. Telephone poles were splitting in half from the percussion of the bombs and live electrical and overhead trolley wires were severed and snapping like live snakes in the streets. Soldiers and civilians had clogged the roads in a chaotic attempt to flee structures and it was impossible to move in any direction. There was no priority given to military personnel as it was a matter of basic human preservation. Insignia, rank, and political status had no bearing on the frightened crowd.

Bomb after bomb whistled through the sky to provide numerous explosions that sent debris and shrapnel in all directions. Fires had started throughout the city and the flames and smoke made our predicament worse to contend with.

We slowly made progress on the street along the station and some people tried to rush into burning buildings to pull their loved ones from the infernos. I do not know how many corpses I stepped over and how many craters and piles of debris I avoided. A bomb landed in a *Bier-Garten* and the percussion sent me and the crowd I was with toppling over from the shockwave. We were consumed by a cloud of dust and smoke and many of us were disoriented from the blast. I grabbed at a pain in my left thigh and immediately felt wetness. My hand was covered with blood and a long splinter of jagged wood was imbedded in my leg. Two civilian men helped me to my feet and a woman placed my hat on my head. The men dragged me through the streets and into the basement of Saint Mary's church. It was crowded with military and civilian personnel and a doctor was fetched to tend to my wound. The explosions ended outside as he began to examine me.

"You do not have excessive bleeding," he said. "You are fortunate the splinter missed your femoral artery."

I had heard that before in regard to the Russian sniper's bullet that struck me in the same place. He cut the fabric of my trousers and wrapped the wound while leaving the fragment embedded.

The *Ganz Klar* sirens sounded and two Luftwaffe soldiers supported me under each arm as I was escorted to a makeshift field hospital several blocks away. As an SS officer I was marked as a priority patient. The doctors assured me that there was a risk of sepsis but I declined immediate treatment and ordered them to tend to others.

I laid under tattered blankets that smelled like smoke and wanted to close my eyes to avoid the scene around me. German children wailed in pain with their little hands, arms, legs and feet blown off. Women walked about in a daze with their hair burned off and blistered skin. A beautiful adolescent girl held bandages to the right side of her face and when the doctors pulled them away to examine her wounds I saw the glistening white of her cheek bone, jaw, and forehead. Her right eye and that half of her nose was gone. Men stood about with their silk suits fused into their flesh from burns. An elderly gentleman with one arm pulled a small cart containing the bodies of two little children. These scenes temporarily disappeared when the wind sent thick clouds of smoke through the hospital and when I closed my eyes from the sting of the sulfur and black powder in the air. Eventually I was treated and moved indoors to a hospital that had been set up inside a restaurant.

The splinter had been removed and the wound was stitched. I was again fortunate to suffer no immediate muscle damage or sepsis. I sent a Wehrmacht soldier to RSHA Headquarters to report my status and location to my superior officers. Everyone was speaking of the massive damage inflicted upon Berlin and it was made known that it had been caused by British bombers. I attempted to learn the fate of Füssen and was told the air raids had been concentrated in the north at Berlin, Hannover, Magdeburg and Dessau.

With the assistance of a cane, I entered RSHA Headquarters on the following day. Eichmann was on his way to Berlin from Vienna and in the meantime we held several meetings to discuss the Protective Custody Policy being implemented by our department. This procedure was not new, but had recently been amended to circumvent foreign diplomatic opposition to our forced deportations of Jews. The new policy contained legal provisions that gave the RSHA full and unconditional power to seize people deemed as enemies. No specific conditions were applied to the classification of these potential enemies and those apprehended under the amended Protective Custody Policy could lawfully be deported to a Detainment Facility without formal arrest documents or trials. The new provisions also denied any possibility of appeal to those arrested under this amendment. The RSHA had exclusively exempted itself from applying any formal judicial process to enemies of the Reich.

Eichmann arrived during the first days of December and we conducted several meetings with him to discuss numerous acts of sabotage committed by the Polish underground movement. In eastern Poland, factories, warehouses, fuel depots, airfields and railroad lines were being destroyed regularly by partisan groups. The same was happening in Italy, Holland, Belgium and France. At a time when the production of war supplies was critical, we were being sabotaged on a wide front. Several German soldiers and officers had also been arrested in connection with these groups as well as for dereliction of duty and desertion. Der Führer ordered Directive 19 for anyone associated with these treasonist activities.

The Polish underground had adopted a new strategy of executing their fellow countrymen who assisted the Reich. We had worked very hard to establish a neutral working relationship with the Poles and the underground had been extremely effective at instilling fear in those who now aided us.

The underground directly targeted the work of our department. Railroad tunnels and bridges on the lines to the Detainment Facilities were being blown on a regular basis and our engineer battalions sent to repair them came under constant fire. We implemented a series of mass reprisals but this only served to strengthen partisan resolve.

When Heydrich died there were many questions of who would fulfill his duties. Müller and Kaltenbrunner attempted to consolidate Heydrich's functions and offices, but Himmler used his ultimate authority to keep those two in check by appending the responsibilities to his own office. Himmler was a brilliant administrator but he had a tendency to issue orders and directives without establishing contingencies for potential setbacks and complications. I can not state that this was entirely his fault as der Führer was constantly placing seemingly impossible demands upon him.

Eichmann announced that our days as RSHA Department Administrators were all but over. Our combined efforts had established a perfect logistical and technical system for the deportations and processing of Jews and Reich enemies. A skeleton crew was being assigned by Himmler to maintain these measures from the office, and each of us was to be assigned to a particular geographic region to physically expedite the deportations of Jews and enemies in our particular area. I was certain my expertise would send me back to Poland and probably somewhere very near Auschwitz. Therefore, I was very surprised to learn that Himmler and Eichmann had decided to dispatch me to Paris.

Before leaving for my new assignment I was briefed in several meetings by Hauptsturmführers Alois Brünner and Klaus Barbie, both of whom had extensive knowledge and information of the French underground and Jews from previous experience. Most of the assemblies were conducted in Barbie's office which appeared more like the bedroom of a child with soft paintings depicting cats, dogs and horses placed on the walls between Party symbols and portraits of Hitler.

Brünner began each of the meetings with the same phrase. "No circumstances exist under which you may trust the French." This was not old school anti French sentiment. It was a warning that the French had perfected a lethal system of interaction with our forces posted in Paris. The French welcomed us into their cities and accommodated our troops with the finest foods, wines, goods and services available. For two years our military adjusted to a comfortable level of complacency and raised its quantity of trust and interaction with the French population. The French had calculated and scripted their contact with us to gain vital information and prove themselves as a passive populace. The masterminds behind the sabotage in France were discovered to be French men and women who were highly trusted in our political circles. Brünner insisted that there was no such thing as an innocent French person. He told me to regard all of them, even elderly women and children, as potential saboteurs and spies.

Brünner had managed the Transit Facility at Drancy and had extensive knowledge about the transportation system in France. He stated that things ran smoothly and recommended the deportation points at Amiens, Orléans, Troyes, and Besançon to be used for expediting priority freight east to the camps. French political criminals were to be routed through the points at Châlons-en-Champagne, Metz, and Dijon on their way to facilities inside Germany such as Dachau and Buchenwald. The Reich had promised certain conditions to the Vichy government and still wished to honor most of them. This is the reason French political enemies and members of ruling French Houses were granted preferential treatment and lesser sentences.

Barbie detested the fact that Brünner was adhering to prior diplomatic agreements forged with the French. He stated that the French had demonstrated opposition to the Reich and its goals, and therefore, no select quarter should be provided to any Frenchman. I agreed with Barbie and claimed my unison with his philosophy based upon what I had seen and learned from so called trusted members of Polish City Councils and Judenrat officials.

Brünner understood but said he could not alter the policies that were in effect due to their enforcement being demanded by Himmler, Müller and Kaltenbrunner. I could not envision an effective measure of German police control over the French if I was bound to offer preferential treatment to select members of the population.

I discussed this matter with Eichmann who was sympathetic to my opinions, but who claimed he could do nothing about it. I implored him to take up the matter with Himmler and he assured me he would. Several days before departing for Paris, I was summoned to the Office of the Reichsführer-SS.

Himmler seemed quite happy and carefree as he instructed me to sit and requested if I would like a cup of coffee or tea. I accepted the coffee which was something I would never have done before, but for some reason at that time, rationalized that I deserved it. There was something very satisfying about watching the Reichsführer-SS prepare my coffee with sugar and cream. I never took my coffee with sugar and cream but wanted to watch Himmler do something for me after I spent the past several years doing everything for him. He handed me the cup on a saucer and sat behind his desk.

"Eichmann tells me you have opinions about how things should be done in France," he said.

"I disagree with preferential treatment being offered to certain political criminals and offenders who are members of the Vichy government."

"The subject of politics is much like an egg," he stated.

I was suddenly reminded of the vagueness of Heydrich's questions and statements by that remark.

"It is very fragile," said Himmler. "But if prepared and cultivated properly, it can be brought to absolute perfection. France is an egg right now and it appears its shell has been cracked. We can repair this damage and again bring about perfection, but this must be done by preparing and cultivating its politicians to our needs."

"France is a rotten egg," I stated. I noticed his eyebrows lifting but was reassured by his appreciation of subordinates speaking their minds to him.

"Continue," he said with interest.

"High Command is certain the Allies are preparing an invasion at Calais. I do not know the intelligence details of when this invasion is expected to come, but one only needs to examine the current state of affairs to emphasize the fact that we must conduct our business with the Jews and our enemies in an expedient manner."

"Are you voicing concern about the capabilities of the Reich?"

That was a very dangerous question.

"No, Reichsführer. I am concerned about any matter that might delay or disrupt the process of my work." I sat back and tried to sound as confident as possible. "If the Allies land at Calais they will be pushed back into the sea. But this will disrupt my work by clogging the rail lines with supplies and soldiers necessary to crush the enemy. I am being sent to France to crush a different enemy. As High Command will demand no delays to its process of crushing the Allied enemy, I believe I have the same grounds to demand no delays to the process of crushing enemies of the Reich."

Himmler stared at me for several moments before saying, "You are indeed a loyalist, Schiller. I am impressed with your devotion and enthusiasm." He nodded before sipping his coffee. "I will send word to the Chief of the Paris Gestapo that your work is to be unimpeded in that zone. Do what you must, but curtail aggression toward French political criminals. Arrest and deport them, but do not provide reason for diplomatic catastrophes. Is this understood?"

"It is Reichsführer."

"Enjoy Paris, Hauptsturmführer."

December 1943
Paris

I was greeted by Jérôme Aubertin, the Captain of the French police I had encountered during my last visit to Paris. His use of the German language had not improved and he pretended that he was very happy to see me again. He informed me that the former Colonel of the Paris Gestapo had since been promoted to Brigadeführer and we reported to his office.

The Brigadeführer shook his head from side to side behind his desk. "The Blackbird returns to Paris," he mumbled. He examined my transfer orders and read from his own collection of documents.

"Himmler has ordered me to not interfere with your work here, but I am bound to enforce certain policies dictated by Müller. We have had some incidents of open rebellion and sabotage, but these events must not be misconstrued as organized resistance. They have primarily been the work of splinter groups who worked with Poles and Belgians."

"What has become of those responsible?" I asked.

"You will be quite pleased to know that we hanged each one of them."

I was not certain why this news was supposed to please me beyond his confused assertion that I had a brutal reputation following me from Porajów. "What are the current problems?"

He handed me a thick stack of documents that listed the unresolved matters in Paris. I paged through the reports and read the charters aloud. "Theft of explosives and weapons, theft of food supplies, theft of radio and communication equipment, snipers, destruction of roads, bridges and vehicles." I looked at the Brigadeführer firmly. "If these incidents are not the mark of organized resistance, what is?"

He did not answer me beyond stating the crimes were nothing more than what was to be expected in an Occupied Zone.

"This is not a frontier zone," I said. "Perhaps these things may be expected to occur in an outpost region, but this is Paris! What buildings have been searched in efforts to locate the stolen explosives, weapons and supplies? What has been done to eliminate the snipers? Why has reverse magnetic tracking equipment not been used to locate the stolen radios and communications equipment?"

I paged through the documents and noticed that none of them had clerical stamps indicating that they had been forwarded to RSHA Headquarters Berlin. I brought this to the Brigadeführer's attention and inquired about it.

"These are internal matters that are being addressed by my units and the KRIPO," he replied.

I pulled a document dated from June 1943 regarding the theft of food supplies from an SS depot on the Rue de Rivoli. "Show me the progress reports connected to this matter."

The Brigadeführer shifted uncomfortably in his chair. I privately noted the name of the enlisted KRIPO agent who had signed the report. It made no sense that the KRIPO would investigate the matter as it involved the theft of military supplies.

"Are you capable of providing progress reports for any of these incidents, Sir?"

"In some cases I am not required to generate corresponding paperwork, Hauptsturmführer. You should know that sensitive paperwork can create sensitive issues, especially in an area such as Paris."

"How is it that a crime occurring six months ago has not been resolved?"

"I assure you that it has been resolved," he answered.

It was obvious that a direct confrontation with the Brigadeführer would bring about unfavorable results. I falsely told him that I accepted his reply and imparted the orders of Himmler that he was to directly notify me of all future criminal reports.

I exited his office and made my way to the KRIPO offices on the Rue des Petits Champs. The demeanor of the men clearly indicated they had been forewarned of my arrival and I requested to speak with the enlisted soldier who had filed the six month old report about the theft of supplies from the Rue de Rivoli SS depot.

We spoke privately and he voiced his devotion to his duty but stated he had been requested to not speak with me regarding the matter in question. He said the Gestapo Brigadeführer was capable of making things very difficult for him if he answered my questions.

I told the soldier that the Brigadeführer was the least of his worries. I made it known that the soldier should fear me and the potential hell I would unleash on him and his family if he did not cooperate with my demands.

He relayed a most incredible account of the Brigadeführer's lack of concern for many of the crimes taking place in and around Paris. The soldier acknowledged that it made no sense that members of the KRIPO, SIPO and Order Police investigated military crimes while the Gestapo, SD and SS relatively investigated nothing at all. He was very nervous but told me that the problems with the Paris Gestapo did not stop there, but extended to morale matters such as the overlooking of promotions and awards. He said the men were frustrated under their current commander and that they feared any form of complaint about him would be met with his personal wrath upon them.

I ordered him to place his statements in a written report and I notified Berlin that I was conducting an investigation into the corruption within the Gestapo Office at Paris. Barbie was very interested in this news and promised his support in the event my allegations were confirmed.

Over the next few weeks I conducted private interrogations of various German Police officers and soldiers. The reports from each of them were consistent enough to consider formal charters against the Paris Gestapo Office.

On 23 December I was given leave to join my family in Füssen to celebrate Christmas and the New Year. I was ordered to return to my post in Paris on 3 January 1944.

Füssen seemed far removed from the war and the political events that reshaped most of the cities. Klaudia was nearly impossible to embrace because of the swelling of her seven months pregnancy. Mother was distressed that the war had aged me and because I had lost so much weight. She decided it was her duty to stuff me with sausages, cheese and bread to keep me fit. My sister was the first to notice my black Wound Badge had been replaced by one made from Silver and I told them of the reason and the injury I sustained during the air raid on Berlin in November.

They asked many questions about the progress of the war and as always, I confirmed the information from our Ministry of Propaganda that we were winning it. I told them that I had been assigned to Paris as a Police administrator and that my duties were boring and routine. I never told them about my role in the deportations and liquidations of the Jews and enemies of the Reich.

My brother Lukas entered the house on 24 December and he also wore a Silver Wound Badge. He had sustained injuries while fighting the Americans south of Monte Cassino at the end of October. Lukas had convalesced in Munich and was promoted to the rank of Medical Oberfeldwebel. I saw in him what Mother claimed to see in me. He looked many years beyond his age.

Lukas was excited to learn I had been assigned to Paris as he had received transfer orders to a Wehrmacht Regiment posted at Rennes. We spoke of trying to coordinate our future hours of leave to get together for drinks and merriment in France.

JANUARY 1944

Klaus Barbie met me in Paris on 3 January and implemented the official removal of the ranking Gestapo officers in the city. He took the position of Chief of the Paris Gestapo and expressed the displeasure of Himmler, Müller and Kaltenbrunner at having learned of the inefficiency of their entrusted subordinates. I was told the Reichsführer-SS was greatly pleased with my work and that Müller had recommended my promotion to the rank of Sturmbannführer. However, this did not materialize at that time and I always suspected that Sturmbannführer Eichmann denied it because the rank would have placed me as his equal.

Barbie assured me that I had Himmler's complete authority to implement a merciless campaign against French partisans and with each step of my investigation I exposed more complicity on behalf of French politicians.

During the middle of January my units located what we believed to be a partisan base located west of Paris in a small farming village called Nouvelles Fermes. Surveillance proved a rash of unnatural activity in the area including the presence of well dressed French civilians gathering in a barn on the northern edge of the village. Jérôme Aubertin introduced me to a lovely young French woman named Noémi Rousseau who was extremely loyal to German interests in Paris. She shared a relationship with a Wehrmacht Lieutenant and had successfully worked as an operative for the Gestapo and KRIPO during former investigations.

Over the following weeks she successfully breached the underground organization at Nouvelles Fermes and confirmed the storage of stolen German weapons and supplies at the barn.

During a scheduled meeting of the underground resistance at the barn, I surrounded the village with SS and Order Police units. The French decided to fight us but we had rapidly defeated them with several incendiary devices that set the barn on fire and ignited the stored explosives within. The few partisans that escaped death were arrested and taken to the Gestapo prison on the Rue Mazarine.

One of the underground leaders was a man of 30 or 35 years who proudly identified himself as *Le Renard.* "The fox," I scoffed as he was bound to a chair. "Do you call yourself this because you are sly?

Because you are cunning and elusive?" I inquired of his formal name but he refused to tell me.

Two Gestapo officials entered the room carrying wooden boxes which they set on a table in front of *Le Renard*. They opened them to reveal a collection of pliers, scissors, serrated blades, hammers, nails, rods, and saws.

"This can be very easy and painless," I told him. "Reveal the names of all those associated with your partisan activity and I promise you confinement."

Jérôme Aubertin translated that *Le Renard* said he would welcome death over the sins of being a traitor. This was very disconcerting and it angered me. I took a heavy 15 centimeter rod from the box and slammed it against the wooden table. Each person including the two Gestapo officers reeled from the sudden noise.

"Your name," I demanded.

"*Votre nom,*" translated Jérôme Aubertin. "*Dites-lui votre nom!*"

"*Le Renard,*" replied the criminal. I struck him sharply on his left clavicle with the thick metal rod. I saw that I broke the bone when a lump had swelled under his shirt.

"*Votre nom!*" shouted Jérôme Aubertin.

Again he replied, "*Le Renard*" and again I brought the rod down on his shattered clavicle.

"*Arrêtez la douleur. Dites-lui votre nom,*" said Jérôme Aubertin. He was encouraging the man to end the pain by revealing his name.

There was a sharp knocking on the door and an Order Policeman requested a private conversation with me. I joined him in the hall where he revealed that a simultaneous interrogation of another partisan prisoner had revealed the true name of *Le Renard.*

I entered the room and stood before the broken man. "Gilbert Jourdain," I said. He instinctively looked up at me. "You see?" I asked while Jérôme Aubertin translated. "Your resistance movement has crumbled. Your fellow countrymen are crying for mercy and revealing the names of those involved. Join them in this revelation of truths and I promise you will receive medical treatment and confinement."

Jourdain grimaced and said, "*Allez à l'enfer vous bâtard allemand.*"

Jérôme Aubertin looked at the floor and translated. "He said, Go to hell you bastard German."

I struck Jourdain in the mouth with the rod at which his blood and teeth lodged in his throat. The partisan coughed and struggled for breath until he spit two teeth onto his lap.

"Strip his clothes off, soak him with water, and chain him out in the courtyard for a few hours to think about this," I ordered.

The other investigations had provided many details of the underground activity in and around Paris. Barbie was pleased with the amount of intelligence we had gathered from a single raid.

Hours later, Gilbert Jourdain still refused to speak with my junior interrogators and I ordered his arms drawn behind his back and for him to be suspended from them while he thought about my offer to comply.

After my evening meal I was informed that the dead nude body of Noémi Rousseau had been found in an alley along the Rue de Lille. She had been brutalized and stabbed numerous times. The reports stated that every inch of her body had been slashed except for her face. The French partisans responsible for this wanted us to know who she was and send the message that they too knew who and what she was for us.

Jourdain refused to comply and Barbie insisted I shoot him through the head. I told Barbie that Jourdain was a valuable source of information and that I felt certain we could extract it if we continued to apply physical pain to him. Barbie did not want to wait and ordered the arrests of Jourdain's wife and children with the plans of subjecting them to torture in front of Jourdain's eyes.

While searching for Jourdain's family over the next few weeks, the Frenchman was continuously beaten to the point of death, revived and given time to recover, then subjected to the process again. Eventually his family was arrested near the Parc de La Villette and brought to Gestapo Headquarters. Upon the promise of torturing his wife and daughters, Jourdain relented and provided us with valuable information about the French underground movement in and around Paris.

On 16 February I returned to Füssen after receiving news my wife had given birth. I can not describe the wonderful feelings and elation that embodied me when I held my infant daughter for the very first time. These feelings and emotions are things that only other parents know. We named her Hannalore. Over the next several days cards and gifts arrived from my superior officers and comrades. I made promises to her that she would grow up in an ideal world and have all the opportunities and possessions that I never had. I would provide protection, guidance and love during her journey through life. I wanted to personally end all threats against Germany and give her a perfect world. Those two weeks with Hannalore, Klaudia, my Mother and sister, were so far removed from the war.

By March 1944 we had gained control over much of the partisan activity in and around Paris and my efforts to maintain steady transports out of the zone had deported most of the Jews and civil criminals.

Paris was taking on the form of a fortified city. Panzer Divisions and Mechanized Infantry were arriving daily and there was no longer a question if the Allies were going to land at Calais. It was now a matter of when this was going to happen.

Our Ministry of Propaganda did very well at extolling the accomplishments of our military and was still praising our month old effort of stopping the Allied attack at Anzio. Being away from Berlin and officers who knew the truth had helped me to believe in the optimism being preached.

The Russians had since crossed the former Polish border in the east and we had lost Monte Cassino in Italy to the Allies. Our defensive lines at Calais were being reinforced due to Luftwaffe reconnaissance over England that revealed a massive concentration of Allied equipment. It was believed that the invasion was being prepared for the spring to correspond with favorable weather conditions in the Channel.

By April we had succeeded in deporting all known Jews from Paris and I had received personal accolades from the Reichsführer-SS though most of the credit for this task was bestowed upon Barbie. I did not mind because Barbie was the sort of officer who delegated his tributes upon those who helped him gain recognition.

The month of April was a series of unusual occurrences in Paris that raised my suspicions. Partisan attacks took place and we arrested the guilty saboteurs with very little effort and no resistance. Those responsible for the attacks openly admitted their guilt and involvement, and even Jérôme Aubertin was disbelieving of the ease and efficiency with which the guilty exposed their crimes. Barbie was pleased by the numbers and statistics we were reporting to Berlin, but he refused to listen to my argument that we were being distracted and diverted. I believed, but could not prove the French resistance was keeping our Police involved with diversionary tactics to take attention away from a more menacing plan.

There was an unusual quiet in Paris during the month of May and I managed 12 hours of leave to travel to Rennes to meet with my brother Lukas. We had enjoyed a fine meal and a few drinks when all personnel were suddenly ordered to report to their duty stations. Back in Paris, Barbie informed me that the Allied Forces had broken through our defenses at the Gustav Line in Italy. American and British troops were pouring into the Liri Valley and it seemed there was nothing we could do to prevent this. RSHA Headquarters had issued new directives for all offices and it was made clear that we were to expedite the liquidation of Jews in the western territories. My department was to concentrate its efforts on the deportation of Dutch Jews from Holland.

I arrived in Westerbork a few days later and found myself in the center of a debacle. The SS had managed to conduct a few transports out of the region before I arrived, but no one had adhered to any form of protocol. The Westerbork rail station was littered with ruined freight wagons and Dutch corpses, and a young Corporal told me it had all been left behind by an SS Sonderkommando unit that conducted a very chaotic and brutal deportation process. I had inadvertently acceded to the responsibility of organizing work details to clear the bodies, remove the damaged freight wagons, and clear the station area for additional deportations. During the next few weeks my units searched the nearby towns and villages for all remaining Jews. By 1 June I had deported approximately 750 Dutch Jews to Auschwitz.

While completing my work at Westerbork I received official word that German forces had evacuated Rome and pulled back to defensive positions in northern Italy. Allied bombers were now frequently taking off from southern Italy and raiding areas in Germany and Poland while using Russian held airfields to land, refuel, and rearm before returning for more bombing raids on their way back to their origination points. Füssen had now become a target. On 2 or 3 June I received more official news. While fleeing to safety in Munich, my

Mother, sister, infant daughter and wife were killed when an American bomb struck the road next to the bus they were riding in.

I became useless in Holland. I became useless anywhere. I fought the urge to put my Luger in my mouth, pull the trigger and join my family. I took it from my holster several times and primed the weapon with every intention of shooting myself. I cried enough tears for one hundred lifetimes yet found a reason each time not to pull the trigger. Everyone was concerned about temporarily removing me from my duties so I could grieve. I requested permission to return to the family home with my brother Lukas, but this was denied. His unit was being held in reserve for the impending Allied attack at Calais. Eichmann extended the offer for me to come and stay with his family in Vienna. I refused his offer. I requested more duties and demanded to remain in the field. On 5 June, RSHA Headquarters assigned me to Police administrative duties at an office in Paris.

CHAPTER TWENTY
THE ALLIED INVASION OF EUROPE
6 JUNE 1944

I was awakened from a sound sleep in a hotel room on the Rue de Rivoli at approximately 0200 hours. Telephones were ringing in adjoining rooms and I heard voices in the corridors. There was a distinct mood of concern in the tone of voices and before I could dress, my telephone rang. It was Hauptsturmführer Fritz Stammler from the Office for Jewish Emigrations in Berlin.

"Rolf," he said with an incredulous tone, "What is happening there?"

"I am afraid I do not know. People are talking in the corridors. It is impossible to sleep. Every telephone in the hotel is ringing. What have you heard?"

"Massive Allied air traffic over southern France," he replied. "We have received reports of Allied planes over Cherbourg, Montfarville, Nonant and Gerrots."

"It must be a bombing campaign, Fritz. I pray we knock each bastard crew out of the sky."

"The Luftwaffe spotters at Gerrots and Montfarville have reported parachutes. There has been minimal bombing."

"Do you think the Allies intend to bomb Paris, Fritz?"

"No. OKW and OKH are confident this is a diversion to draw our forces away from Calais." He paused and I heard him talking to his comrades in Berlin. "Contact me with any developments you learn of."

I dressed and exited my room into the corridor. Nobody seemed to know what was happening. I made my way to the Police

Administration Office and placed a telephone call to my brother's unit at Rennes. I was not able to speak with him, but an enlisted soldier told me there had been confirmed sightings of parachutes at Gerrots, Montfarville and Valognes.

The city of Paris was usually quiet under night curfew conditions but these events had brought every officer from his sleeping quarters. Barbie was conferring with officers from our Intelligence Division but even the Abwehr was confused about the events taking place. He ordered me and several others to place telephone calls and wire communications to coastal SS and Order Police departments. We divided them by sector, and I placed a call to Saint-Laurent-sur-Mer. The Order Police confirmed heavy Allied air traffic but said most of it was coming over the coast to the east at Graye-sur-Mer, Luc-ser-Mer and Ouistreham. I was also informed there had been reports of ground contact at Creully and Bucéels.

One of my comrades placed the telephone on its cradle and called out to Barbie, "SS Police at Isigny report the town is full of Allied paratroopers!"

"Status report?" asked Barbie calmly.

"SS Police at Isigny reports it is like shooting fish in a barrel, Sir!"

I received a similar report and relayed the information. "Allied paratroopers are on the ground at Creully, Sir. Situation is under control."

Other reports were declared:

"Ground contact at Bayeux, Sir!"

"Allied paratroopers are coming down over Blay, Sir!"

Klaus Barbie placed one hand over the telephone that directly connected to the Wehrmacht Headquarters in Paris and rubbed his chin with the other. With a heavy sigh he picked it up, dialed two numbers and placed the amplifier to his ear. Moments later he said, "This is SS Police Headquarters, Paris. I have received numerous reports of Allied contact at coastal locations and inland."

While Barbie answered a battery of questions with either "yes" or "no", my comrades and I discussed the possibility that we were experiencing the early stages of the inevitable Allied Invasion.

Barbie placed the amplifier back in its cradle and addressed us. "OKW and OKH believe these attacks are diversions to pull our defenses away from Calais." He issued new orders that directed each of us to travel to the Normandie area for intelligence gathering and observation. I was dispatched to Montfiquet which was approximately 20 kilometers south of the coastal town of Saint-Laurent-sur-Mer.

We heard that General von Rundstedt ordered two full Panzer Divisions to be moved from Calais to Caen but OKW denied the directives with the belief it would weaken our defenses at the main location of the invasion. There was much talk at the airfield about what was happening and there were as many theories as there were people discussing it. I boarded a Feiseler Storch aircraft with several comrades and we were off the landing strip in minutes.

At approximately 0430 hours we could see marking rounds being fired through the sky in the distance off the right wing of our Feiseler Storch. The running lights on the planes being attacked indicated they were large bombers or transports. Our Luftwaffe set one of the enemy planes on fire and we watched it speed to the earth in flames.

We landed at Litteau airfield where I was promptly escorted to a car that sped north to Montfiquet. An office had been prepared for me and there was a delegation of officers and soldiers waiting to speak with me.

A Waffen SS Lieutenant placed a container the size of a hatbox connected to a small parachute on my desk and curiously stated, "It is an Allied machine gun, Sir." He opened the device to show me that it was divided with an upper and lower compartment. The top half contained a concave metal tray with a hole in the center. The lower half was weighted to ensure its proper landing position and contained a live battery to which was connected to two exposed filaments soldered to a copper plate. The filaments ran through 15 small metal tubes on each side of the box that were packed with gunpowder. The Lieutenant explained that the upper compartment was packed with a block of ice and when it melted, the water funneled through the hole in the concave tray and created an electrical reaction on the copper plate. The filaments heated from the battery and sent a charge through the 30 gunpowder packed tubes which went off with the loud simulated sound of a machine gun. He reported these devices were confounding our soldiers all over the coast.

"Trickery?" I asked. "The Allies are resorting to trickery to confuse us?" This bolstered the theory that the attack was a diversion.

"This is not the only device confounding our soldiers," said the

Lieutenant. "The Allies have been dropping percussion bombs that are controlled by timing devices." He looked at me while rubbing his hands together. "There are also the figurines, Sir."

"The figurines?" I inquired.

The Lieutenant ushered in a Wehrmacht Corporal carrying a figurine that was approximately 100 centimeters tall. It was connected to a parachute and dressed in a green wool uniform.

"These figurines have been coming down from the sky all night. It is impossible for our men to discern these things are not real in the darkness. Real paratroopers are landing in the areas we are vacating in order to chase these things."

"Figurines, simulated machine guns and timed percussion bombs?" I asked. None of this had the mark of an actual invasion. I placed a telephone call to Barbie in Paris and informed him that the situation along the Normandie Coast was mainly comprised of novice Allied deception. He had received similar reports and so had OKW and OKH. No one seemed very concerned about the activity taking place and all attention was focused upon Calais.

The air raid sirens that had filled the air were being methodically turned off. There had been some bombings reported but very few targets of strategic or military value had been hit. Barbie ordered me to travel 8 or 10 kilometers north to Noron-la-Poterie to interview several French partisans being detained in the prison there. He wished for me to learn if the saboteurs had any knowledge of the Allied activity.

Noron-la-Poterie was a series of checkpoints and security that delayed our progress at first. At approximately 0515 hours I entered the municipal French prison and conducted an interview with a partisan called Julien Durand. He insisted he knew nothing about the events taking place in spite of my revelations that the Gestapo knew signals were being broadcast to the French underground by means of the BBC radio network. During this interview I received word that one of our Luftwaffe anti aircraft batteries located approximately 5 kilometers northwest at Le Molay-Littry had engaged in ground gun combat with a unit of American paratroopers. They had taken two prisoners and I issued orders to have the Americans brought to me at Noron-la-Poterie.

I conducted the second interview with another French partisan called Bernard Bonnet who paced excitedly inside his cell in defiance of my orders to remain motionless. He anxiously shouted, *"Il se produit! Il se produit! L'invasion est venue!"*

My interpreter could scarcely translate his terrified ramblings but I was informed the man was shouting, "It is happening! The invasion has come!" The partisan was frightened that the Noron-la-Poterie prison would be struck by bombs and that he would die in his cell. He begged us to move him to a safe location.

I had interviewed hundreds of prisoners prior to him yet he was the first to exude such honest terror. I allowed myself to believe he was telling the truth and relayed the information to Barbie's office in Paris.

At approximately 0530 the American prisoners had arrived from Le Molay-Littry and were placed together in a cell. I employed four Wehrmacht Order Policemen and a Wehrmacht translator to accompany me to interview them.

The translator turned the key in the lock and threw the door open. He entered with two Order Policemen and I remained in the hall with the others. The translator shouted in English, "On your feet!"

Leaving the two Order Policemen in the corridor, I entered the cell and immediately noticed that both American paratroopers locked their eyes on my SS collar tabs and suddenly gave each other a fearful glance before staring at the floor. It was well known to us that the American propaganda machine had undertaken great efforts to convince its soldiers and citizens that the SS embodied sadistic brutality. I used these horrible American lies and rumors to my advantage.

I immediately selected the older and stronger looking of the two Americans and called the Order Policemen from the hall to come in and seize him. I exited the cell with them while the translator made a great noise unlocking an adjoining cell. The two Order Policemen escorted the older and stronger American prisoner out of the block while I entered the vacant adjoining cell. The younger and weaker American prisoner could hear me but he could not see me.

With convincing rage I shouted to no one, *" Was geschieht heute morgen? Beantworten Sie mich! Was geschieht heute morgen?"* I waited several seconds to make the young American prisoner believe his comrade refused to answer me. I pulled my Luger and fired a single shot into the straw mattress.

Returning to the occupied cell, I saw the American prisoner was trembling and holding back tears. He genuinely believed I had executed his friend and he stared at the pistol I still clutched in my hand.

I stepped toward him, raised the pistol and shouted, " *Was geschieht heute morgen? Beantworten Sie mich! Was geschieht heute morgen?* "

He brought his hands up in front of his face as if the motion would somehow stop a bullet. I had no intentions of shooting him and was surprised when his knees gave out and he fell to the floor where he urinated in his trousers from fear.

My translator spoke to him softly in English until the American said something in return to him. The translator waved me into the corridor where he leaned close and said, "The American has said the Allied invasion of Europe has commenced."

I heard the Wehrmacht Order Policemen taunting the prisoner for having soiled himself in the cell. No one had insulted me on the frozen streets of Stalingrad when the same unfortunate situation had befallen me and I went inside to end the mockery. I told the translator that I could not believe the statement of the American. It was too convenient if the Allies were in fact attempting to draw our defenses away from Calais. At approximately 0550 I began a more subdued interrogation of the prisoner.

After perhaps 10 minutes of questioning we heard a steady low rumbling tone in the distance. It was not intermittent and the oddity of this noise caused us all to share an inquisitive glance. The lights began flickering and all telephones inside the prison started ringing. An SS soldier appeared in the doorway of the cell and caught his breath before stammering, "Hauptsturmführer Schiller! You have an urgent telephone call from Paris!"

While making my way to the telephone I avoided SS and Wehrmacht soldiers running throughout the building in a great panic. Someone shouted, "The Allies are shelling our coastal defenses from the sea! Our communications post at Vierville-sur-Mer has been knocked out! I can not raise our artillery batteries at Huppain!"

More confused voices shouted out with dread:

"Our observation post at Saint-Aubin is reporting more than a thousand Allied vessels in the sea!"

"Our barracks at Lion-sur-Mer has taken a hit!"

I picked up the telephone and heard Klaus Barbie shouting, "Schiller! What is happening on the coast?"

"I am not certain, Sir. It has taken the appearance of a great diversion. The Allies are using figurines, blanks and timed explosives to confuse us here. One of the French partisans claims this is the start of the official invasion. A captured American paratrooper confirmed it."

"Relay your information to Tactical Command at Calais!"

"Ja wohl!"

As the telephone operator plugged the lines into the control board, more reports were shouted out from the Communications Personnel.

"Our defenses at Manvieux report heavy shelling!"

"Our 88 batteries at Langrune have been destroyed!"

I was connected to a Waffen SS Colonel at Calais who seemed very calm in spite of the situation on the Normandie coast. I reported the damage and circumstances to him and added more as they were shouted out.

"Stand down," stated the Colonel. "We have confirmation from Luftwaffe Reconnaissance that the bulk of the Allied equipment has not departed from England. Allied tanks and artillery are still on the fields over there. We are certain this is a diversion on behalf of the Allies."

I was patched to RSHA Headquarters Berlin and managed to find Fritz Stammler at his desk. He told me he had not gone home on the previous night.

"Fritz, the Allies are shelling the hell out of the Normandie coast. What are they saying about this at the office?"

"Half of our superiors believe it is a diversion and the other half believes der Führer should dispatch at least two or three Panzer Divisions out of Calais to Normandie."

"Why has der Führer not done this? Our positions on the coastline are being destroyed as we speak!"

"Der Führer is sleeping, Rolf."

"What?!"

"Eichmann said der Führer took a pill to help him sleep and gave orders not to be awakened unless a dire crisis arose."

"This is a goddamned crisis!"

"The Staff Generals agree, Rolf. But no one wants to wake der Führer if the attack is indeed a diversion."

"What should I do in the meantime?"

"If I were you," said Fritz, "I would get the hell out of there!"

I telephoned Barbie's office and explained the opinions in Berlin. He stated that he wished for me to remain at Noron-la-Poterie to interrogate additional Allied soldiers that were captured during the ensuing attack. I advocated for my return to Paris in the name of RSHA duties and Barbie agreed to permit me to leave Noron-la-Poterie, but I was not to return to Paris. He ordered me to SS Police Headquarters at Falaise to collect intelligence as it was reported.

My driver reached Falaise at approximately 0620 hours and I entered the SS Tactical Command Headquarters. I thought der Führer had died. High ranking SS officers stood in front of a wall of radio communications gear in complete silence with somber expressions. Some cupped their chins in their hands while others shook their heads from side to side. Six or seven radio operators turned their dials to monitor communications from all the coastal positions.

Static interfered with many of the transmissions but most of them were panic stricken broadcasts and terrible warnings.

One broadcast was a caution from a soldier to his comrades and we only heard it because the man had continued to press his transmitter in the panic. With explosions in the background we heard him screaming at his unit to abandon their post: *"Gehen Sie hinaus! Gehen Sie jetzt hinaus!"* At once there was silence. No more static and no more voices. A few officers removed their hats to pay silent tribute to the dead.

"Holy Son of Mary!" said a Waffen SS Lieutenant Colonel. "We are being slaughtered like cattle out there!"

Another radio crackled with a terrified voice. *"Verbündet Landungboote! Verbündet Landungboote! Hunderte von ihnen!"*

At once many more voices issued the same report of hundreds of Allied Landing Boats making their way toward the beaches.

"This is not a diversion!" stammered the Waffen SS Lieutenant Colonel. "They are coming ashore! Get me a line to Calais!"

At approximately 0640 hours we heard the first devastating report from our troops at the Normandie coastal defenses: *"Verbündete Soldaten auf den Stränden! Ich wiederhole! Verbündete Soldaten auf den Stränden!"*

"Jesus, Son of God!" muttered a Waffen SS Major. "They are on our goddamned beaches!"

Approximately 10 minutes later the first encouraging reports came to Tactical Command from the coastal positions.

"Erster Sektor! Feind wird enthalten!"

"Did you hear that?" asked an elderly Waffen SS Brigadeführer. "Sector One has contained the enemy advance."

"Zweitens Sektor! Feind wird enthalten!"

"Drittens Sektor! Sicher!"

"Viertes Sektor sicher! Feind wird enthalten!"

"Fünftens Sektor sicher!"

"All Sector Defenses are secure and containing the enemy," said the Waffen SS General. "Now, if Admiral Dönitz is correct, the incoming tide should drown these Allied rats in the lee of the seawall."

The Allies ceased the naval bombardment once their troops had come ashore. Our machine gunners and artillery crews had tremendous success against the invaders at all five of the designated landing zones and our mines and obstacles on the beaches greatly aided our defenses. We listened to reports about the Allied Landing Boats foundering in the swirling currents and running aground in the shallows approximately 27 meters from the beaches. Our mortars and artillery were destroying the abandoned crafts and the Allied soldiers who were using them for cover.

By 0730 hours reports were coming in that the waterline was nothing but an endless row of Allied wreckage and burning debris. It was said to be so congested at the waterline that the second assault wave of Allied Landing Boats could not reach the beaches. The tide was rising and Admiral Dönitz's prediction was coming true. Our spotters reported that Allied soldiers were leaping over the sides of the Landing Boats and being dragged to the bottom of the sea from the weight of their equipment. The enemy soldiers pinned down in the lee of the seawall either tried to escape the rising tide and were cut down on the beaches by our machine guns, or drowned when the tide overtook them.

At 0800 hours the 736th Wehrmacht Infantry was reporting great successes against the British at Colleville. The 352nd Wehrmacht Division was requesting permission to move from Saint-Laurent-sur-

Mer to Colleville to help destroy the British, but the Commanders of the 736th Infantry reported the situation to be secure.

Allied Destroyers had taken advantage of the rising tide and moved within a few hundred meters of the shoreline to fire their massive guns into our coastal defenses. Many of our units reported that they were falling back to reinforce other positions and the Allies noticed the abandoned posts. Radio traffic stated that Allied forces were moving toward our vacated positions and our Line Officers issued directives for soldiers to use the elaborate trench system to reoccupy the areas to surprise and fight off the Allied advances.

The next two hours bolstered our optimism as all defensive sectors confirmed that while the enemy had inflicted considerable losses upon us, we were holding our positions and containing the attack.

At approximately 1400 hours the 352nd Wehrmacht reported to OKW and OKH that the British attack had been thrown back into the sea. It was the first time we rejoiced in the Tactical Command Communications Headquarters. As the tide receded, more landings took place on four of the five beaches and the Allies were unloading tanks that were reported to be smashing through our obstacles. By 1500 hours the Allies had broken through several points in our defenses and were said to be working their way inland in a disorganized manner.

Near 1630 hours the Allies launched a major suicide offensive against our defenses from the beaches. One by one our positions were abandoned or captured. At 1800 hours our forces were falling back to inland positions and reporting that the Allies had established several beachheads and were unloading equipment under our artillery fire that was now pounding the beaches from inland batteries. The 352nd Wehrmacht issued a correction to its previous report of victory and announced the British had overrun our lines and were advancing on Colleville-Louvieres-Asnieres.

At 1930 hours the Brigadeführer of the SS Tactical Command Headquarters issued orders to all German forces on the Normandie coast: Abandon the defenses and regroup at the designated inland defensive lines.

The Allies had successfully landed at Normandie.

On 7 June approximately 150 American, British and Canadian

Prisoners of War were brought to Falaise. Hundreds more had been taken to other locations for preliminary interrogations before being placed on transports to Prisoner of War facilities inside Germany.

Our soldiers were also coming back from the coast to regroup before joining units at the inland defensive lines. Five or six Wehrmacht soldiers recognized my SS Police insignia and ran toward me with great anxiety.

"Mein Haupsturmführer! Ich bitte um Erlaubnis, mit Ihnen zu sprechen!"

"Permission granted," I responded. "What must you tell me?"

They related an account of having been inside a bunker behind the mainline trench works on the coast and watching a unit of twelve comrades surrender to the Americans. They told me the Americans disarmed the Wehrmacht; ordered them into a trench, and shot them from the ground above. The men gave testimony that the dozen Wehrmacht soldiers had clearly surrendered in terms with the Geneva Convention. To my knowledge, Germany and America agreed to honor the codes of conduct listed in the document.

"Are you capable of identifying the leader of this American unit?"

The majority stated they recognized the sleeve insignia of the American from the packet of enemy rank identification cards issued to each German soldier. They informed me the illegal shootings were carried out under the orders of an American Sergeant First Class.

"Are you capable of recognizing this American Sergeant First Class by facial features if you were to see him again?"

"Ja wohl!"

"What of the other Americans? Are you capable of recognizing them as well? Did you notice their ranks?"

They replied with an assortment of details that I recorded on an official report. We identified the location of the illegal killings by referring to a map and though I believed nothing would come of it, I personally wished to bring the American criminals to justice. I had promptly become weary of their murderous tactics of bombing our cities and slaying our civilians. I would not tolerate lawlessness in combat from our forces or theirs. Fearing the Wehrmacht report to be unsubstantiated, I asked if the men had any kind of physical evidence to corroborate the story. One of the men took twelve Wehrmacht identity disks stained with dry blood from the pocket of his tunic and set them on the desk.

Of the 150 Allied prisoners brought to Falaise, perhaps 80 were Americans. I ordered them into a general assembly and ordered the 10 or 12 Sergeants First Class among them to step forward. I permitted the Wehrmacht soldiers who reported the illegal killings to inspect the Americans for members of the illegal execution squad at the coast. The soldiers studied each American but informed me none of those responsible for the shootings was present among them. I had certainly expected the Wehrmacht soldiers to select random enemy troops for the sake of retribution. However, I was greatly pleased with the honor and integrity shown by our young soldiers.

Two days later the American army had captured and occupied the high ground in the Cerisy Forest while another of its Divisions rolled through the Aure and took positions along the Elle River. Der Führer had released Panzer Divisions from Calais, but the delay in deploying these units had been costly to us. Waffen SS Colonel Kurt Meyer was having great success against the Americans with his XII SS Division and though he was recording victories, each came with a major expense of German lives.

In the east the Soviets had opened a powerful offensive against the Finnish front designed to establish an eventual advance against the Fatherland through Denmark in the north. On 9 June 1944, the Soviets were approaching Germany from the east and north, and the Americans were approaching south from Italy and west from France. We were effectively caught in a war on all four fronts.

Der Führer seemed very content to continue operations in Yugoslavia, Albania, Greece, Bulgaria and Romania while our country was slowly being surrounded. It made no sense to us and suddenly defeatist remarks were regarded as potential truth and not treason. At this time in the war we did not regard the Americans as a serious opponent. There were too many logistical complications involved in their sustaining of a war effort against us. Our U-Boats were sinking tons of their supply vessels in the Atlantic and along the British, Canadian and American coastlines. Allied efforts to develop technology to detect our U-Boats had produced moderate results. However, it had been effective enough to send my dear cousin Ernst and his crewmates to the bottom of the Straits of Gibraltar when a British vessel dropped depth charges on U-392 in March of 1944.

The Russians were our main concern as the country hosted a population of millions and had a direct land route to Western Europe. Our Ministry of Propaganda often referred to this struggle in terms of the classical historical battles fought centuries ago. We were told that we were the civilized culture engaged in a war of preservation against the barbarian hordes. We believed this.

On 14 or 15 June I received a telephone call at Falaise from Eichmann. He was irate that Barbie had dispatched me from Paris to the French coast and ordered my immediate return to RSHA Headquarters Berlin. I did not need to be told a second time. I handed my open reports and investigations to the Falaise Gestapo and boarded a train to Germany.

I attended several meetings at Headquarters wherein we discussed the activities at the Detainment Facilities and Termination Stations. It was made clear that very few Selection Processes were taking place anymore and that many prisoners were being marched directly from the trains to the gas chambers.

Eichmann demanded that I travel to the Majdanek Termination Station to oversee the intentional destruction of its gas halls, gas vans, and the exhumation and removal of all bodies. The Soviet military was advancing toward the facility and the Reichsführer-SS wanted all evidence of our activities there to be removed.

CHAPTER TWENTY·ONE
HASTENING THE FINAL SOLUTION

I arrived at Majdanek on or about 20 June to find its Kommandant and most of the Administrative Staff gone. The majority of prisoners had been taken west to Auschwitz and I was to arrange the final transports for the remaining inmates.

As I passed through the gates I heard the steady crack of rifles and pistols inside the facility. Following the noise I saw that the SS garrison had lined up a hundred or so prisoners in the Appellplatz and were systematically shooting them. A Scharführer approached and asked if I had come from Berlin. I confirmed this and asked to be taken to the Officer in Command.

"That is me," he said. "The last of the officers left here several days ago."

"Why do prisoners remain?" I asked. "Why have they not been transported to Auschwitz?"

"I tried," he responded, "But no one will provide me with trains. My rank does not carry the required authorization for them."

"How many prisoners are here?"

"2,000. Perhaps 2,500."

"How many men do you have in the garrison?"

"One hundred and five, Sir."

He escorted me to the armory where there was more than the required amount of explosives to detonate the gas halls and vans. Unfortunately, none of the men in the garrison had experience with demolitions and we did not know how to wire and set the explosives. I asked, "Have any of the bodies been exhumed and pulverized?"

"Hell," said the Scharführer with exasperation, "The Special

Equipment has not come from Lublin. It was supposed to be here days ago."

"Have you requested it again?"

"Of course, Sir. But my rank does not carry the required authorization for priority consideration."

We entered the Kommandant's Office and I picked up the telephone to find a dead line. I slammed down the transmitter with frustration. Sensing my boiling rage the Scharführer said, "I will see if the line has been cut or if the generator powering it needs more fuel."

I ordered him to instruct the remaining prisoners to begin exhuming the bodies of the executed inmates once the telephone line was repaired. In the meantime I inspected the facility and made written notes of the features that required demolition.

The crematoriums had been cold for days and the depositories beneath them were filled with ashes. Partially burnt corpses laid on the racks and it appeared the *Sonderkommandos* operating them had simply abandoned their duties and walked away without completing the cremations. Standing there amidst the foul sweet odor of burned flesh I was overcome by the memories of conversations and plans to commit these acts in the name of a *Reines Deutschland*. The charred and shriveled bodies on the racks, the mounds of ashes in the depositories, and those buried in the mass graves throughout the facility seemed a necessary endeavor in the name of a Pure Germany. Now I had been ordered to dispose of the evidence much like a common killer burns his bloodied clothing and casts the murder weapon to the bottom of a pond. Eichmann had stated a year ago that the world would not understand German reasons for this ugly business. Standing in front of the open ovens at Majdanek I believed him. I was not certain that I understood the reasons for our comprehensive annihilation of the Jewish population.

I was informed that the telephone was operational and returned to the Kommandant's Office to placed a call to Lublin. I was told the Special Equipment was there, but no engineers were available to transport it to Majdanek. Globocnik could not be found and I was in the hopeless position of trying to express my urgent need for this equipment to a clerk whom I could not reveal details to. I resorted to humbling myself by placing a telephone call to Amon Göth at Plaszow. He was the only person I knew that had influence on

Globocnik's staff at Lublin. It greatly bothered me to request a personal favor from him, but in order to entertain the wishes of the Reichsführer-SS, I had no other option.

Göth was very reluctant to help me and promised to do so only if I agreed to address the current matters taking place at his facility. He would not give me details about the issues he spoke of and I was under the distinct impression that he refused to mention them over an open telephone line. I promised my commitment to his matters and he in turn agreed to release the Special Equipment from Lublin.

I placed several telephone calls to RSHA Headquarters Berlin and inquired about Plaszow while waiting for the delivery from Lublin. Several RSHA officers advised me it was best to avoid questions about the current events at Plaszow but no one would tell me why. I eventually spoke with Fritz Stammler who informed me Göth had been placed under official investigation and had been accused by the Gestapo and Könrad Morgen of corruption, cruelty and misappropriation of Reich finances. This sent a chill through my veins as I knew Göth would not go quietly before any German court. He was the sort of man who would accuse those around him of contributing to his delinquent behaviors and sponsoring his illegal activities. My dealings with him had mostly been in marginal terms of the law, but I personally gained illegal profits from him through the structure and implementation of my suggestions at the Auschwitz and Belzec facilities.

The engineers arrived with the Special Equipment on or about 25 June. The machines consisted of massive conveyor belts and generator powered devices designed to crush bones. We could hear the Russians shelling our positions to the northeast and there was a great sense of urgency to complete the tasks at hand and fall back to Kazimierz Dolny. I spoke with two engineers who were adept with demolitions and we devised a plan to wire the gas halls, crematoriums, armory, and a few other integral buildings.

I received a telephone call from RSHA Headquarters in the midst of this activity. Further orders demanded that I was to search the clerical, administrative, Kommandant's Office and prisoner barracks for any documents that had been left behind. I was directed to burn every scrap of paper we found. Now and then Luftwaffe fighters would soar over our heads to the east. For the many we saw going in that direction, none returned.

While wiring the demolitions in the gas halls, one of the members of the prisoner *Sonderkommando* approached me informally and announced that before his incarceration he was a civil engineer who had assisted in the construction of the Obra dam in eastern Poland. He observed we were using a primer fuse cable made of coiled cord and informed us that unless we intended to blow the gas chamber immediately, the primer fuse cable would fail.

One of the Wehrmacht engineers was quick to agree with him and the prisoner explained that weather conditions in western Poland at that time of year were not favorable for the use of coiled cord fuses. He said that condensation and moisture would dampen the primer fuse cable and cause it to smolder and this would create the perilous situation of having to send a man inside the building to cut and reconnect it. I had planned to wire the structure and detonate it on the following morning.

With this advice, I gave the orders to immediately blow the Majdanek gas chambers. We cleared the area and the engineers connected the fuses and pressed the handles on their plungers. The walls were destroyed and the roofs collapsed.

The Special Equipment had been set into action and the SS garrison joined the prisoners in the grisly task of loading the exhumed bodies onto pushcarts at which they were taken and dumped onto the conveyors. The bodies were taken along the belts and deposited in a large fire. Once the flesh and organs were burned away, the remains were pulled out with rakes and hooks to be pulverized by the other machines.

The stench was overpowering and I was cursing the former Kommandants for the large number of prisoners each had executed. I had not been required to count each exhumed body and though I thought of walking away from the gruesome spectacle, I was bound by legal process to observe the action. There was to be no looting of any corpse found to have money or jewelry. Any items of portable value were to be inventoried and transported to the SS offices at Warsaw.

I was very surprised by the manner in which the SS garrison and prisoners worked together during the task. There seemed to be no animosity at the time and I attributed this to the perverted sense of pleasure gained by the inmates from watching their German and

Ukrainian Auxiliary captors being forced to share the same gruesome duties. The soldiers assigned to guard duty kept their weapons shouldered rather than pointed at the prisoners. Doing so would have been pointless. If there was an incident, shooting into the crowd would have claimed as many Germans and Ukrainians as inmates.

This truly was a most curious experience. Jews pointed to pushcarts and equipment and Germans and Ukrainians followed the requests to bring the items to them. I had never before witnessed a German working by the side of a Jew or following the orders of one. It was understood that the Jews had more experience at such grisly duties as we had put them to such tasks over the past several years. There was even a morbid humor shared by the inmates when a German or Ukrainian exhumed a body in extremely bad condition. The Jews would laugh at the soldiers gloomily as if saying; "Now you see what you have done and what we have had to endure!"

On or about 1 July, Höss had telephoned me to inquire about the progress I had made. I informed him the gas chambers had been blown but we were still uncovering and destroying thousands of bodies. I requested more laborers to expedite the process and he promised to send 1,000 inmates from the Radom ghetto. Höss told me that Liebehenschel was preparing to exterminate the prisoners inside the Family Camp at Auschwitz and requested that I attend the gassings to ensure legal protocol was enforced because the approximate 4,000 units were women and children. I told him that Eichmann and the Reichsführer-SS had dispatched me to Majdanek and that I would need an official release from my duties signed by either of those two.

He was not pleased but could not overrule higher orders. He instructed me to blow the crematoriums and inquired about the current location of Russian forces.

"Telephone me tomorrow," I said, "And you can personally speak with the Russians."

He did not find my comment to be the least bit whimsical. I informed him the shelling to the east was getting closer.

Höss stated he would send me 500 laborers in addition to the 1,000 he had already promised. I was to expedite the destruction of evidence at Majdanek and then transport the remaining prisoners and garrison to Auschwitz by train, buses or by foot if necessary. I was to suspend all arbitrary executions at Majdanek to prevent the slowing of my tasks at hand.

I had the crematoriums wired and detonated as Höss ordered. Days later the transports arrived from the Radom ghetto and an uproar ensued when their duties were explained to them. The Jews from Radom were not accustomed to the work that I demanded of them and they quickly noticed the small number of SS guards attempting to maintain control of the 3,500 prisoners. I promptly ordered guards into the towers to man the machine guns in preparation for a rebellion.

Most of the Radom Jews refused to take part in the exhumations and some began picking up stones, rakes and pieces of cordwood as weapons. I stood between two guard towers and maintained visual contact with the gunners in each. The SS and Ukrainian Auxiliary Police had separated themselves from the crowd as voices were raised and curses were shouted. I had no choice when several stones were thrown at my garrison units. I brought my hand down to signal the orders for the tower gunners to open their weapons on the crowd. The shooting lasted for several minutes and when it was finished; approximately 300 Radom Jews were dead. This subdued the crowd of prisoners which went begrudgingly about their ordered tasks. I did not consider this an arbitrary execution that conflicted with Höss' orders. I regarded it as a matter of preserving the safety and security of Reich forces.

By 15 July the shelling was close enough to send vibrations through the ground and walls. It was impossible to report on my progress as the Jews and SS garrison continued to exhume thousands of bodies throughout the fields in the facility. I ordered a group of SS soldiers to go through the barracks and pull up floorboards and knock out walls to discover any place wherein prisoner diaries or written accounts may have been hidden. We were pulling down posters with Facility rules, information placards, and building signs. All of these items and any documents found in the structures were thrown in several large fires. The metal signs were sawed into pieces.

On 19 July two transports arrived at the Majdanek station. I had been given no notice of the trains but the Transportation Officials operating them presented me with orders from RSHA Headquarters stating that I was to load as many prisoners as possible on them. The garrison and I were to board the passenger carriages at which we would be taken to Auschwitz for reassignment. The orders also stated that I was to forego the destruction of evidence at Majdanek and shoot all prisoners not able to be placed aboard the trains. We were to evacuate the area immediately to avoid the Russian advance.

Both trains contained less than 10 freight wagons each and I managed to load approximately 2,200 freight units aboard the transports. I managed to secure a convoy of buses and trucks from the motor yards at Majdanek, Lublin, Poleski, Naleczów and Putawy to evacuate an additional 600 prisoners. Once all the trains and vehicles were loaded, I supervised the SS garrison as we marched the remaining 400 Jewish inmates to the eastern edge of the facility and shot them. We evacuated the vacated Termination Station during the early hours of 20 July 1944. Four days later the Soviet Army discovered and entered the remains of Majdanek.

The trains stopped to take on water at the Kielce station before turning south toward Auschwitz. When the trains arrived at the Kraków station late in the day, we learned that a bomb had exploded in der Führer's Headquarters in East Prussia. We were told that Hitler had addressed Germany after the attack and declared that God had spared his life in order that he may lead the Fatherland to victory.

Most men on the trains and at the station rejoiced at this proclamation and thought it to be wonderful news that Hitler escaped death. Those of us who thought otherwise pretended to rejoice. We also learned that Field Marshal Rommel had been seriously wounded several days previous when British airplanes attacked his open car. It was said he was convalescing in Germany.

What alarming but curiously encouraging news all of this was. Our High Command was no longer impervious to the dangers of war. Hitler and Rommel had both been victims of attacks and I entertained the idea that a neutral peace could be agreed upon to spare Germany from complete destruction. Of course any peace agreement would have to be a negotiated settlement as surrender was no longer an option for German Officers. We had tasted that bitterness in 1918 and would not subject the Fatherland to such humiliation again. I hoped that our Party Officials and diplomats would consider the forging of a neutral and mutual withdrawal of all combat forces. Concessions would naturally have to be made for such an agreement and in my feeble diplomatic reasoning, I believed the Allies and Russians would be willing to accept the territories they gained through military conquest and leave us be with the areas we had taken. Oh what simple and innocent thoughts these were. I failed to acknowledge that we had launched a campaign of war against the world; not from a naïve perception, but because one can not see this as an injustice when you are part of the machine doing it. I firmly believed in the reasons and philosophies of our campaigns and never questioned the necessity of what we had done. I expected international governments to recognize German motives for war and therefore believed a mutual withdrawal of forces could be agreed upon. This is not to say that Eichmann's words did not yet haunt me. There was the matter of what we were doing to the Jewish population. Would international governments recognize this as a German necessity? Or as Eichmann stated, would the world fail to recognize German reasons for such ugliness? It did not matter to me at the Kraków station. I believed I had operated under valid laws and within legal procedures.

The only encouraging news was that the English Channel had been hit by the most violent storm in decades. The weather had dashed hundreds of small Allied boats to pieces and beached hundreds more. It also destroyed part of the beachhead and greatly hindered their attempts to resupply. The II and XII SS were immediately deployed to the area to take advantage of this opportunity.

Our forces had also managed to entrap the American army in the French city of Saint Lô. It was my understanding that we were employing the tactics used against us at Stalingrad. The Wehrmacht had turned the rubble and ruins of Saint Lô into a strategic maze of offensive and defensive positions. Our soldiers would strike quickly and disappear into the debris.

I wandered about the Auschwitz Administrative buildings over the next few days along with the former members of the Majdanek garrison. I had placed several telephone calls to RSHA Headquarters but was unable to reach any of my superiors. Each time I was told they were in conferences and would contact me with new directives.

Liebehenschel did not seem to mind my presence at the facility and he often approached me to discuss the industrial and management matters of the camp. He showed me pencil sketches of new buildings he had conceived and asked my advice about utilities, staffing, and construction codes. After perhaps one week of waiting for orders, the Kommandant informed me that he required the presence of a Legal Affairs Officer at the facility hospital.

I entered the ward of the Chief Physician to find several SS orderlies and inmate assistants. There were two adolescent Jewish girls sitting on a gurney eating candy while their legs happily kicked back and forth. The SS orderlies summoned their superior and moments later I was face to face with the Medical Director of Auschwitz.

He introduced himself as SS Doctor Josef Mengele while warmly shaking my hand. He asked me about the state of the war in eastern Poland and we made small talk about the tragic attempt on der Führer's life. I followed him through the large ward which contained a few patients. The majority of its beds were empty.

He spoke after reading a few charts, consulting with his orderlies and checking the status of the few patients. "I have orders to liquidate the *Zigeunerfamilie Lager* on 2 August. The Central Office has issued Directive 19 for the 2,908 inmates." He looked at me and then out the window as if something was troubling him. "I would like to remove 11 names from the Directive 19. Is this possible?"

"I am afraid not," I replied. "If the Central Office has authorized the Directive 19 there is nothing that can be done to alter the roster. They are very particular about their paperwork and records."

"Why now?" asked Doctor Mengele. "Why must Kommandant Liebehenschel elect to liquidate the *Zigeunerfamilie Lager* now?"

"You do not wish for the liquidation of the Gypsy Family Camp?" I asked. Mengele looked at me as if he thought I suspected he was sympathetic to Gypsys.

"They are all prostitutes and thieves," he said in accord with traditional propaganda. "But there are eleven Gypsys that I need."

"Research?" I inquired.

"Research with limitless possibilities. The eleven I need are prime specimens. An albino, two sets of identical twins, four with birth defects, a midget, and a female giant."

"I can not take them off the list if the Central Office has authorized it."

"Can not or will not?" asked Mengele with a tone of arrogance. I gave him a firm look that brought an apology from his lips.

"I am sorry, Sir," he replied. "This is very important work. I will type the release forms and submit them. I will do all the necessary paperwork. You only need to sign the documents, Sir."

I did not tell him, but I was finished signing documents that related to such matters. Especially when I detonated Majdanek and made a chaotic mess of the grounds and left thousands of bodies lying in open graves to be found by the Russians.

An SS Medical Assistant interrupted us to announce that I had a telephone call from Berlin and that I was to take it in Liebehenschel's office.

The Kommandant vacated his own quarters and closed the door behind him as I took the telephone. It was Eichmann.

"I trust you left no traces of evidence at Majdanek?" he asked.

"I did not have the time, resources, or manpower to complete the task, Sir."

There was a very long pause before Eichmann asked, "What of the chambers and crematoriums, Schiller?"

"Demolished, Sir."

"And the remains of the inmates?"

"Thousands were left exposed and in the fires, Sir."

"Give me a personal estimate of how many were left exposed."

"Perhaps 6,000 or more, Sir. That does not include the numbers we did not have time to exhume."

There was another pause before Eichmann asked, "You do realize this could be disastrous for us?"

I wanted Eichmann to come forward and tell me what he feared. I was exhausted with his cryptic method of speaking in vague terms and metaphors. I answered him with a naïve devotion to duty. "How could it be disastrous for us when it was all completed within the legal codes of the Reich, Sir? Why would it matter that the Russians discovered it? Does not the same fate lie in store for every Communist and Bolshevik?"

He did not answer the question. Eichmann inquired about the efficiency of Auschwitz and I told him doctors were squabbling over prisoners for research and that there was an objection in the name of science to the liquidation of the Gypsy Family Camp. He ordered me to oversee this action and to remain at Auschwitz to direct the arrival of 70,000 Jews from the Lodz ghetto on or about 15 August. He specifically stated the entire transport from Lodz was to be liquidated under my supervision. When completed, I was to return to Berlin.

Liebehenschel and Mengele were waiting for me when I exited the

Kommandant's Office. Both argued a very strong case for the sparing of the 11 Gypsys for medical research. Whereas I had been apprehensive to sign documents that committed eleven inmates to scientific experiments, it now seemed a small and insignificant matter in light of the 70,000 Lodz Jews I had been ordered to gas. I changed my position and told Mengele to draft the paperwork.

Liebehenschel was thrusting design plans in my face and I tore them from his hands and set them on his desk. "There is nothing left to design," I said sharply. "Dispatch your engineers to the gas chambers and crematoriums. I want each inspected. I demand that any necessary repairs are made at once. I want an inventory of the number of canisters of Zyklon B in stock and I no longer wish to be bored with your administrative delusions!"

That evening I dined with Doctor Josef Mengele and was treated to a personal discourse of his absolute medical genius. He explained the various experiments he had been conducting on Jewish inmates and I was most intrigued by the details he offered about the tests regarding conjoined twins and hypothermia.

On 28 July the Soviets took Litovsk in the Ukraine while the Americans captured Coutances in France. Both armies were now pressing on us like a vice from opposite directions. Several days later I supervised the liquidation of the Gypsy Family Camp and worked closely with SS Medical Personnel as we carried out the gassings of 2,897 men, women, and children. We completed this task and retired to an evening meal where we were informed of a massive rebellion taking place inside the Warsaw ghetto.

Liebehenschel and Mengele were talking about administrative and medical matters while I stared at my plate. I pondered if I was the only officer in the Reich at that time who was genuinely vexed by the military progress being made by our enemies. The war had shifted into an incomprehensible series of orders and objectives immediately following the assassination attempt on Hitler. At once, der Führer lost confidence in his Staff Generals and began dictating the war according to his personal wishes. His ideas had not seemed sound since ordering the total withdrawal of our forces when he had Moscow surrounded and was weeks from taking the Soviet capital. For reasons of personal pride and arrogance, Hitler directed a full assault against Stalingrad in an effort to humiliate the Soviet leader whom the city was named after. Now, Panzer Divisions and Infantry Regiments were being sent from one location to another without any real effective strategy being considered. Germany was in complete disarray.

Near the end of the first week of August our forces launched its first successful counterattack in over a month. The SS and Wehrmacht moved against Allied positions at Avranches and inflicted heavy losses on the enemy. The attack provided our forces with momentum and gave our units time to resupply and reinforce.

On 14 August the transports began arriving from Lodz and this increased the prisoner population total to well over 100,000. There was no place to house the freight so I immediately began the extermination process. The Lodz Jews were made to disrobe in an open area and were told they were being taken for delousing showers. To facilitate the processing of the bodies and to avoid mechanical stress on the crematoriums, I had several large pits excavated and soaked with oil and kerosene in which a large portion of the 70,000 expected corpses were to be burned. Approximately 250 Lodz Jews were seized by Liebehenschel and Mengele; given numbers, and escorted into the camp to perform specialty work. I supervised the extermination of 70,000 Jews in a matter of 96 hours.

The day after the liquidations, an organized uprising in Paris erupted while the Soviets launched their Balkan offensive against our positions in Romania. While preparing to leave Auschwitz I received a visit in my quarters from Amon Göth. He was visibly stressed and very angry.

"What in hell is going on, Schiller? What have you done to me?"

"Amon," I replied quite cautiously, "I have done nothing to you. What are you speaking about?"

"What am I speaking about?" he asked. He nodded his head with a very cold and accusatory smile. "I am speaking about the report you filed about me during your last visit to Plaszow. You promised an entry of positive reform."

"I upheld my promise, Amon. What has happened?"

"They are relieving me of command, Schiller. The Gestapo is considering filing formal charters against me. They are talking to former guests at my functions and my prisoners as well." He looked through me. "Did you have something to do with this?"

I replied slowly. "Amon, where is the logic in urging the Gestapo to file charters against you? How could I possibly gain or benefit from ordering an investigation of you?" He must have noticed the panic I was feeling about being directly connected to a few of his illegal profit making schemes.

"You do not know anything about this, do you?" he inquired.

"I swear to you that I know nothing of this. I authored a neutral report with the promise of positive reform. Amon, if they investigate you they will eventually connect things to me."

He lit a cigarette and exhaled the smoke while waving his hand and shaking his head from side to side. "No, no," he said. "They will not learn about you. I will not tell them about you, Höss, or any other person involved. Of course I can not promise they will not find out by their own means. You took care of most of the paperwork. You know better than I do if there is reason for you to be concerned."

"When are they relieving you of command?"

"I do not know if they are. There has been talk about it. If the charters are filed and if the investigation is opened I will be taken into custody. If we have been careful there might not be anything to worry about."

I felt sick to my stomach and instinctively wondered if this was the reason I had encountered such difficulties reaching my superiors while at Auschwitz. Were they aware of my involvement in Amon's schemes? Were my superiors avoiding me because of the suspicion raised during the assassination attempt on Hitler and because my possible criminal involvement with Göth had cast me into an unfavorable light? Müller and Kaltenbrunner had instituted a purge of Party members thought to have involvement in plots and criminal activity against the Reich. I suddenly believed every person around me knew I was criminally connected to Göth.

Amon tapped his chin a few times while thinking. "Is it possible for you to see the paperwork Gruppe A has filed about me?"

"Only if I can access the documents without drawing suspicion."

"These are perplexing days we are living, are they not?" he asked. He stood and walked to the door. Before exiting he said, "I hope to see you at my next function and not next to me on the gallows."

Goddamned Göth.

I arrived in Berlin on 20 August and entered my office to learn the

Falaise Pocket in France had been encircled by Allied forces. Only six weeks ago I had been there among the men who were now surrounded and fighting for their lives.

RSHA Headquarters was again a scene of frenzied activity. Many departments were boxing up their records and equipment to move their offices to Uelzen, Tangermünde and Stendal. I could not find a familiar face in my department and was informed that Eichmann was attending a meeting in Hannover. I decided to report to Gestapo Chief Müller's office to announce my return and receive new directives.

His office door was open and he was finishing a conversation with several officers. I entered when they left and he looked at me from behind his desk. "What in hell do you want, Schiller?"

"I have just returned from Auschwitz, Sir. Sturmbannführer Eichmann is in Hannover and I am requesting orders, Sir."

He stared at me for a moment and I falsely interpreted his gaze as a degree of suspicion. He rubbed his temples and sighed deeply. "I want you to oversee staffing issues at the Detainment Facilities," he said. "The SS garrisons are being depleted by transfers to Waffen SS regiments on the fronts. We can not trust our conscripts and auxiliary reserves to effectively manage the prisoners. I want all able bodied SS and Wehrmacht soldiers in convalescence to be transferred to the facility garrisons. Get it done, Schiller."

This provided a requirement to visit the Military Personnel Records Department which was on the same floor as Gruppe A. I took my After Action Reports from the liquidations at Auschwitz to the Administrative Law Department and told the clerk I had to file them. He politely offered to file them for me but I told him I had to cross reference information I entered in previous reports. He allowed me unrestricted entry into the Legal Records Department and I felt like a common criminal while hastily locating the documents the Gestapo had filed about Göth. I was pleased and relieved to see that the official investigation was inconclusive and that no recommendations had been approved to file charters against him. However, the inquiry into his activities at Plaszow was still open and ongoing. I went about my days with one eye on my duties and the other over my shoulder.

On 25 August Paris was taken by the Allies and our Intelligence Service reported that the American and French militaries and the citizens of Paris were shooting, hanging and stoning German officers to death in the city. Simultaneous to this, the Finnish provisionary government entered diplomatic discussions with the Soviets. By the end of the month an uprising similar to the one in Paris took place throughout Czechoslovakia and the Russians drove Reich forces out of Bucharest.

By this time I had effectively brought the facility garrisons to maximum quota by installing convalescing Wehrmacht and SS soldiers as Müller had directed. Eichmann had returned to Headquarters days ago and remained deeply immersed in his personal projects and long meetings with Himmler. On or about 1 September he called me into his office and told me that Höss had been given orders to investigate the logistics of destroying the Auschwitz II Birkenau gas chambers, crematories, and most of its key structures. He had also been given orders to dispose of its entire prisoner population.

Eichmann was greatly interested in my suggestions and ideas for the liquidation of the camp and its population as I was familiar with the technical layout of the facility and because I had gained minimal experience for such tasks at Majdanek. I stated that the process should begin immediately to circumvent all possible contingencies regarding the Russian advance. He told me the Soviets had photographed the remains at Majdanek and were circulating the pictures for purposes of anti Reich propaganda. He intently listened to the reasons of why I had been unable to complete my assigned duties at that location and urged me not to allow the same thing to happen at the Auschwitz complex.

Eichmann said he understood but that he had simply been asked to investigate the technicalities of the operation. He had no power of making the decisions of when the liquidation of the facility was to go in effect and he asked me to author reports on the Majdanek process to be sent to Höss for his consideration. Within the week it took for me to compile the reports, the Allies had taken Abbeville, Rouen, and Verdun in France, and Antwerp and Brussels in Belgium. The Finnish provisionary government and the Soviets had also declared a formal cease-fire and our borders were growing smaller and thinner by the day.

Höss came to Berlin the following week and I entered several private meetings with him as well as larger Staff assemblies. On approximately 10 September I attended a meeting in Conference Room E chaired by Hermann Höfle and attended by Höss, Max Burger, Oswald Pohl, and many former Commanders of the eastern Einsatzgruppen Units including Stahlecker, Jöst, Jeckeln, Blobel, Ohlendorf and Rasch. This meeting was not for the weak of heart as we were required to examine and discuss photographs of bodies treated with lye and other chemicals designed to speed the effects of decomposition. Blobel and Rasch gave testimony of their personal experiences in the Ukraine where they had used such chemicals, liquid solutions, and compounds along with Special Equipment to dispose of corpses in mass graves. Blobel advocated for the use of chemicals as it made the bodies unrecognizable as Jews, enemy soldiers, or whoever they might have been. He conceded that while it left bones, there was no plausible means to positively identify the corpse.

Ohlendorf and Stahlecker were greatly concerned with the overwhelming amount of remains and evidence they had deposited in the Ukraine, Bessarabia, the Crimea and Southern Russia. Höfle was insisting that both men had no reasons for concern, but Ohlendorf was committed to the thoughts of a realist. In spite of Höfle's rehearsed administrative answers, Ohlendorf argued that each former Commander of an Einsatzgruppe would be put before a firing squad unless OKW and OKH stabilized the war effort and defeated the enemy on all fronts.

"We have not come to this meeting to discuss the activities of the Einsatzgruppen," said Höfle.

"We never come to these meetings to discuss such activities," countered Ohlendorf. "We have been asked to do what none of our superiors will acknowledge."

"The agenda of this meeting is to discuss methods for the disposal of human remains," stated Höfle.

"Disposal of human remains in your killing factories," said Ohlendorf curtly. "What about the bodies in Bessarabia and the Crimea?"

Höfle looked at him and was obviously lacking the proper words to answer him.

"You do not wish to address that matter, do you?" asked Ohlendorf.

Höss interjected. "This meeting has been called by our superiors in Group A and Group D of the Main Office. We have been asked to devise methods for the disposal of remains in the Detainment Facilities and Termination Stations."

Jöst steepled his fingers. "And you wish for us to tell you how to do it, is that correct?"

Höss nodded firmly. "You have the most experience, gentlemen."

Ohlendorf sat back and looked at Höss and Höfle. "We received no formal acknowledgement for our duties in the field, yet we are expected to help solve the difficulties of Groups A and D?"

"Calcium hydroxide," said Blobel. "Mix quicklime with water and it dissolves the flesh and organs in a matter of hours. It also dissolves cartilage and small bones. Very effective indeed."

Stahlecker slammed his hand on the table as if Blobel had revealed some great secret of industry.

"What is the matter with you?" asked Blobel. "Every minute we waste in this discussion is another minute those Soviet bastards are treading closer to my former area of operations. By God, they have already taken Kiev and Minsk." He looked at the ceiling and quoted from a letter written by the composer Ludwig van Beethoven. "Oh God! Contemplate the beautiful nature and tranquilize their spirits in the presence of the unavoidable." He closed his eyes and his head began to move in time to the symphony playing in his mind.

Ohlendorf dryly stated, "This is a matter for Groups A and D. I suggest they address their own matters."

Höss clenched his fists after having enough of the obstinate refusal from the Einsatzgruppen Commanders. "You are subordinate officers bound by duty to the Reichsführer-SS! You will devote your knowledge and experience to the agenda of this meeting or you will answer directly to Himmler!"

Jeckeln, Rasch and Jöst smiled and laughed smugly. "I will welcome that opportunity," said Jöst. "Permit me to stand before the Reichsführer-SS so that I may tell him the truth. Either he will hang me or my fellow patriots will hang me. If they elect not to do this I am certain the Allies will put a rope around my neck."

"That is a defeatist statement!" shouted Pohl. Jöst had spoken without forethought at a time when the SS and Gestapo were purging its ranks due to the assassination attempt on Hitler.

"Calcium hydroxide," repeated Blobel.

"Away with you all!" stated Höss with firm resolve. "Höfle, Schiller, and Herr Burger, please remain. Obergruppenführer Pohl, will you join us?"

The Einsatzgruppen Commanders rudely exited Conference Room E. After some time Höfle asked, "Shall I draft an arrest warrant for Brigadeführer Jöst?" It seemed quite unnatural for a Captain to inquire about the arrest of a General, but we heard the defeatist remark in the presence of Pohl.

"Those men have been subjected to enormous amounts of stress," I said. "I was in the field with Ohlendorf. I have witnessed it too."

Höss gripped the bridge of his nose between thumb and forefinger and exhaled deeply as if my statement put me in sympathy with Jöst's defeatism.

Pohl stared at me for a moment before setting his gaze on Höfle. "No. I do not see the requirement for a warrant."

We remained in Conference Room E for the better part of the day to discuss technical plans for the destruction of Auschwitz, its prisoner population, and its remains.

Eichmann assigned me various duties at RSHA Headquarters over the next several weeks. At that time I was primarily responsible for gathering updated information about the damage caused to our rail lines by Allied bombings. I referred these reports to the Ministry of Transportation where they were distributed to the RAD and Todt Labor service for repairs. Eichmann insisted that I maintain a steady quota of Jewish freight transports out of Holland, Belgium and northern France, and OKW and OKH constantly argued that my department was clogging the rails.

On 13 September the American army punched through our defenses at the Siegfried Line and entered the Fatherland. On 18 September I received a very informal letter from the Department of Military Records informing me that my brother Lukas had been killed at Saint Quentin, France on 16 September. The war had now taken the whole of my immediate family from me.

It was also on 18 September that I was summoned to the Office of the Reichsführer-SS and I experienced panic at believing the matter was related to the investigation of Amon Göth. To my astonishment Himmler was extremely cordial and invited me to sit down.

"I was saddened to learn of the death of your wife and daughter," he said.

"My Mother and sister were killed that day too, Reichsführer. I lost one of my brothers to the fighting in the Ukraine and just received word that my only remaining brother fell at Saint Quentin."

"Your father must be very proud to have sacrificed so much for the Fatherland," he said.

"He is dead too, Reichsführer. He passed from pneumonia in 1942."

Himmler removed his eyeglasses and looked at me with a very humble and sad expression. "You dear man," he said. "You have sacrificed and lost so much. I knew of your wife and daughter and that is why I called you here today."

I believed the nature of the meeting had something to do with pensions or death benefits when Himmler handed me a folder. I opened it to see it was the personnel records of a female civilian secretary for the SS Recruitment Office.

"That is Petra Schauf," said Himmler. "Der Führer has issued an order that all SS officers are to father children. I am personally endorsing your marriage to Frau Schauf."

I must have looked at him very oddly. I certainly did not know the woman and with respect to Klaudia's memory I did not feel capable of entering into a marriage with a woman I did not know.

"This all must seem very medieval to you," said Himmler. "My endorsement may indeed seem unusual, but der Führer has spoken and I wish to demonstrate the loyalty and devotion of my officers." He put his eyeglasses on again and asked, "You will not disappoint der Führer will you?"

At a time when Field Marshal Rommel had been implicated in the assassination attempt on Hitler and when elite officers were being dragged before the German High Court to answer charters of suspicion, treason, and dereliction of duty; and when I wished to not draw attention to myself because of my dealings with Göth, I agreed to a marital union with a woman I did not even know. She appeared beautiful in her personnel photograph but I knew nothing of her or her family except that they had pure German blood coursing through their veins.

"Splendid," said Himmler. "I will arrange for you to meet at Pohl's banquet on 22 September."

I returned to my office with a stoic sense of duty. I realized the absolute desperation of being completely alone with no immediate family. For this reason, gaining a wife did not seem a tedious ordeal at all. I was excited by the idea that I would have someone to talk to, confide in, and share time with. The idea of love had officially been replaced by duty so there existed a very real sense of safety about not concerning myself with the thought that Petra would find me undesirable. I was indifferent to the matter as it had been arranged and decided upon by elite powers that controlled the lady and me.

Fritz Stammler appeared in my office and we shook hands. It had been a very long time since we had seen each other. We exchanged greetings and he inquired how I had been. I did not tell him about my brother Lukas. I told him the Reichsführer-SS had ordered me to marry a civilian secretary I had never met.

"What is her name?" he inquired.

Thinking he might know her or the Schauf family, I told him.

"Petra?" he asked. "Be thankful it is a woman. I heard that an Obersturmführer at the Ministry of Economics was ordered to marry a man!" He smiled and winked before exiting my office. I laughed for the very first time in months before choking back tears of ultimate sadness.

On the way to Pohl's banquet I learned that the Allied paratrooper assault on Holland had ended in victory for Reich forces. Once again there was a mood of hope that we could control the military situation in the west.

Petra was radiant, talkative, charming and politely witty. She carried herself with an elegant grace and drew the interest of many Reich officers present at the function. She came from a family of bakers who had elevated their social status by establishing shops throughout Germany. She had been well informed of my personal past and offered condolences for my many losses. Petra was not evasive about the arranged terms of our marriage and forwardly stated that she believed we would come to love each other and raise a family for the Reich. I was not used to women who spoke so openly about such things and I realized that she regarded marriage to an SS officer as a beneficial step in further advancing the status of her family. That did not matter to me as the entire meeting had been a duty assignment. There was no reason to question motives, consequences and benefits.

After some time at the table I realized Petra and I were in the presence of two other couples who were meeting for the first time. We enjoyed a sumptuous meal of several courses and after a dessert was served, Pohl tapped a spoon against his wine goblet to gain our attention. He announced the matrimonial intentions of the two other couples and Petra and I, and we stood to applause and congratulations. We all were assigned the date of 7 October to be wed.

I returned to RSHA Headquarters the following Monday and tried to make sense of the damage reports to the rail lines. Boxes and equipment were still being carted out of the building on a regular basis. Estonia fell to the Soviets on the following day and one week later the SS had put an end to the uprising in the Warsaw ghetto.

Stammler entered my office with a very grim expression and set a folder on my desk. "Is he not a friend of yours?" he asked while pointing to it.

I opened the file to learn the Gestapo had arrested Amon Göth on charters of corruption, misappropriation of Reich finances, cruelty, deceit of official ledgers, extortion, and bribery.

"He is no friend of mine," I said.

"For your sake Schiller, I hope not."

I saw Petra during the evenings of that week and met her parents and sisters. They were a very inviting family who understood the arrangements that had been ordered for their daughter and me. Herr Schauf only asked that I protect his daughter. He never mentioned love.

It was agreed that after our marriage Petra would live with me at my RSHA appointed home in Berlin. In the event the city became too dangerous due to Allied air raids, she would live with her parents at the Schauf home in Wernigerode. When the war was over we would take residence at my home in Füssen.

On 7 October Fraulein Petra Schauf became Frauline Schiller. All three nuptial couples that attended Pohl's banquet were married at Saint Mary's Church. My comrades from the SS were the only people who supported me with attendance. There were uncles, aunts and cousins I could have invited, but it was too perilous to ask someone to travel on the autobahn or rails under Allied air raids.

The reception was enjoyable at first but I began feeling sympathy for myself when I saw the other two couples and Petra surrounded by immediate family. It was awkward for me to stand there and smile as I still felt much like an outsider.

Höss approached to shake my hand and congratulate me. There was something very different about his demeanor and for the few moments that we talked, he glanced from side to side as if worried about who might see us conversing. It was as if it was acceptable for him to talk with me briefly to offer obligatory congratulations, but anything more than that might somehow reveal to others that we had a mutual association with Amon Göth.

Eichmann, Stammler, Novak, Dannecker, Müller, Saltzer, Gössler, von Preis, and Tischler had taken time to attend the weddings. Later, Reich Propaganda Minister Josef Göbbels arrived to offer congratulations to one of the other couples. He extended the courtesy of shaking the hand of the other groom and mine with words about the importance of the preservation of the Reich. As the day progressed, Generaloberst Alfred Jodl and the Reichsführer-SS arrived.

From polite conversation with other guests, I learned that one of the other SS officers who married that day had lost his first wife to typhus just months prior. The bride from the other couple had lost her first husband on the Eastern Front.

A Staff Mercedes arrived and a man came from the car and began searching through the guests. My heart was pounding as I believed it could be the Gestapo coming to collect me for an interrogation about my matters with Göth. The man found Höss and privately whispered something to him. Höss looked very annoyed but put a friendly hand on the messenger's shoulder.

I watched as the messenger left and Höss made his way to where Eichmann was talking with Müller. He interrupted the conversation and the men began to collect their personal items as if leaving. I excused myself from a conversation and pushed my way through the crowd to Höss. "What is happening?" I inquired.

He leaned very close and kept a casual smile on his face so as not to alert fellow guests to the problem. "We have an uprising taking place at Auschwitz," he said.

"I will get my coat and hat," I said.

"No," replied Höss. "Remain here with your bride. Join us later at Headquarters if you wish."

When I saw Himmler and Müller preparing to leave I decided such a matter was critical to Reich efforts. I told Petra that I was required to tend to duty and left the reception and entered RSHA Headquarters behind the others. They were surprised to see me and Himmler raised his eyebrows.

"Why are you not with your wife?" asked the Reichsführer-SS.

"I am aware of my obligations to her, Sir. I am also aware of my obligations to the Reich."

Himmler pointed to me and looked at Müller while saying, "He is truly a man who understands loyalty."

Höss was reading several reports and placing telephone calls to various men at Auschwitz. He addressed us with the information he had obtained.

"The Jewish *Sonderkommando* at Auschwitz II Birkenau has engaged our garrison with guns and grenades."

"How did they obtain them?" interrupted Müller.

"The reports state that the weapons and grenades have been crudely manufactured by the inmates," answered Höss. "A few minutes after noon the Jews working in Crematory IV started this rebellion. It now includes the *Sonderkommandos* working in Crematory II and III. Liebehenschel said that Crematory IV is in flames and that a large group of inmates has breached the security wire and are fleeing in the direction of Raisko. I have another report from Liebehenschel that one SS soldier has been shot to death in this rebellion."

Himmler calmly asked, "What is being done to capture the escaped inmates?"

Höss paged through several reports before replying, "Liebehenschel has ordered the deployment of SS, Order Police, Gestapo, and Wehrmacht troops to form perimeters, block roads and secure bridges."

"I want that facility razed," said Müller.

"Oh, not yet," said Himmler. "There is much work that yet needs to be done there. Soon perhaps, but not yet. We must adhere to the terms of the Final Solution."

"The prisoners must not be permitted to destroy the crematories," I said. "The Special Treatment can continue at an efficient level without the use of Crematory IV but the others must be spared."

"I agree," said Himmler. He looked at Höss. "Convey my

personal orders to Liebehenschel that I will hold him accountable if the other crematories are destroyed."

Late in the afternoon we received reports that two more SS soldiers had been killed. We also learned that the prisoners abandoned the crematories and fled to a foliage thicket inside the camp where they were desperately holding out. Liebehenschel stated that most of the escaped prisoners had been caught or killed, and that those holding out in the wooded area were running low on ammunition.

Himmler nodded at the situation being brought under control. "Höss," he said, "I want a complete account of how this happened. I want the names of those who planned and organized it. I want the names of all those who knew about it. And reprisals. We must carry out reprisal executions. I will not tolerate this."

The Reichsführer-SS kindly smiled at me. "Do you not have a wife waiting for you, Schiller?" I did not know how to interpret his question and was not sure if he was dismissing me.

"Off with you," said Himmler with a smile. "Your obligations here have been fulfilled. Go."

CHAPTER TWENTY-TWO
THE DYING FIRES

I returned to my duties at RSHA Headquarters on 10 October; the same day the Soviet Army attacked our lines at Riga in the Ukraine.

The situation in the west had become critical. Our oil reserves were extremely low and the Allies were successfully bombing our synthetic gasoline plants throughout Germany. Hitler was devising a plan to dispatch several SS Panzer Divisions into Hungary to capture the oil fields but could not launch the assault until the tanks had been reoutfitted. Der Führer demanded Mechanized Infantry and Grenadiers to hold out against a numerically superior enemy in the east until the panzers were returned to service.

OKW and OKH had lost much of their influence in the planning of the war. It was common to see Hitler's Staff Officers sitting on the benches in the halls smoking cigarettes, wringing their hands and shaking their heads. The Staff Officers were usually sweating, trembling, pulling at their collars, and rubbing their foreheads in complete exasperation. Someone had stated that der Führer's War Room had become Hitler's toy shop. It was rumored that he stood there and moved tank, infantry, and artillery icons from one point on the map to another without any thought of strategy. His mechanical human soldiers on the front lines were bound to follow these orders and marched from one hell into another. Our troops were ordered to abandon key locations to reinforce other units against numerically inferior opponents. We would win those small battles while losing bridges and cities to the Russians and Allies at other places. Hitler was quite satisfied with these minor victories but our enemies realized the absurdity of this method and began committing decoy units for the purpose. Our Line Generals realized the foolishness of these tactics and some were bold enough to defy der Führer's personal directives to make a stand against the enemy at critical locations. Though some of these valiant Generals were successful, they found themselves relieved of command or sent before a Military Court for disobeying Hitler's orders.

Our Ministry of Propaganda was printing and broadcasting information that we were winning the war but the German people finally faced the truth of impending defeat. There were now too many Mothers, Fathers, sisters, brothers and cousins in the markets and parks who shared the same personal story. They had lost their sons, Fathers and male cousins and the number of deaths was now so great that it could no longer be hidden, excused or molded into a positive projection for victory. Our newspapers were filled with articles about the potential activation of the *Volkssturm.* Hitler was preparing to send elderly men and children into combat. Perhaps some of the old men had gained fighting experience in the Great War and Republic Campaigns, but overall, the people he was preparing to activate as soldiers had no practical skills for war. I had traded shots with the enemy in several engagements and I yet felt inexperienced as a combat soldier. What had my Germany come to that der Führer would ask adolescents and the elderly to take up arms to fight?

On 15 October a State announcement came over our radios that Field Marshal Erwin Rommel succumbed to the wounds he received during the British airplane attack on his open motorcar. Every man in our department looked at the floor or through a window when we heard this. We had all been too close to the Gestapo Offices and heard the rumors from within that Rommel had been implicated in the assassination plot against Hitler. When Heydrich was wounded we received daily progress reports of his failing condition. We received no such reports about Field Marshal Rommel. This was correctly interpreted that he was making a full recovery. There was no logic to the reports as Rommel had been released from the hospital to convalesce at his home. The Field Marshal was given the best physicians and surgeons in all of Germany and it was impossible to believe the doctors would be negligent in their work or release Rommel from their care if he was in physical danger. We immediately believed that der Führer had either ordered the *coup de gras* or permitted Rommel the honor of taking his own life.

Field Marshal Erwin Rommel was a true patriot in the sense that he was devoted to duty, loyal, and believed in the preservation of Germany. He openly disagreed with Hitler and his orders, and openly defied der Führer in North Africa by protecting his troops by allowing them to retreat against Hitler's directives to stand and fight to the last man. Hitler forgave Rommel for this and the two shared a delicate relationship. However, der Führer had descended into a pit of suspicion for his Staff Officers. Since the assassination attempt, he removed any subordinate who so much as combed his hair in a manner Hitler thought to be dubious.

A State funeral was planned for the Field Marshal and Hitler had the audacity to attend it and make a speech about how loyal and devoted Rommel was to the Reich. We listened to this speech on the radio and kept our thoughts to ourselves.

At that time I believed, as all soldiers do, the war could be won. I was not prepared to abandon the philosophies and beliefs of German superiority and our inherent right to guide the Fatherland into a glorious future. In my private thoughts I disagreed with Hitler and many of his policies, but this was a natural and healthy series of mental arguments that every soldier and citizen has with their leaders. I was an administrative Legal Affairs Officer forced to deal with numbers and mathematics on a daily basis. In October 1944 I could not manage to find a plausible solution to the equation. The Soviets were smashing toward Germany from the east and our Lithuanian, Estonian, Baltic and Ukrainian conscripts became turncoats to support the Russian advance. The Allies had turned the French, Italians and Belgians against us and were incorporating them; which were troops we formerly trained, as fighting units against us. We were simply losing the ability to provide suitable numbers of troops to adequately stalemate and repel the countless assaults being launched against us on all fronts. Old men and children were not the solution.

Our factories and plants were being bombed faster than we could repair them. The irony was that we had excess aircraft to combat the Allied bombing raids, but a critical shortage of pilots. Our synthetic gasoline plants were being destroyed, we had limited liters of crude oil and there was very little we could do to obtain more of these decisive resources. We were watching our enemies push closer to our interior borders while Göbbels spewed out asinine propaganda that we were taking steps toward ultimate victory each day. Perhaps some of the people believed this, but I often pondered what our poor soldiers thought on the front lines.

The Allies had encircled Aachen and our SS and Wehrmacht troops were given orders to hold the lines. Surrender was not an option for them. The Allies had come to the very German city where we had launched a portion of our 1940 campaign against France and the Low Countries. It was more irony in that we had been surrounded in the west at the precise location where we had set out to conquer the west. It was humiliating and it almost seemed to be some form of mystical retribution. On 21 October our forces at Aachen defied Hitler and his orders by surrendering in great numbers to the Allies. The Line Generals chose life over tethering themselves to the leash of Hitler's foolishness that would have pulled them into death and hell.

On 23 October Eichmann called a meeting for our entire department and announced that the Office for Jewish Emigrations, Referat IVb4, was being restructured into an elite Administrative unit of 4 or 5 officers. He said that the remainder of us would be transferred to RSHA field duties and assigned new officers to report to.

He also stated that he and his superiors had decided upon the final use of the gas chambers at Auschwitz and that the facility would be converted to a transit camp until the date on which its destruction and dismantling would be determined. He then distributed packets to each of us that contained our new orders and assignments.

I was to report to SS Headquarters West at District VI Düsseldorf approximately 120 kilometers northwest of Aachen. I had been assigned as an RSHA Legal Affairs Officer to the Waffen SS Police Brigade to collect, process, and interrogate Allied Prisoners of War. My orders also included the apprehension of all resistance fighters and local partisans assisting Allied forces. I was to directly report enemy military information to OKW and OKH, partisan information to Kaltenbrunner, and information about Jewish resistance to Eichmann. On 6 November I relinquished my office at RSHA Headquarters Berlin and boarded the train to SS District VI Düsseldorf.

The Allies were aware that the city contained a concentration of their prisoners and had suspended bombing raids in the area. I inspected several of the prisoner compounds which were nothing more than barbed wire enclosures surrounded by guard towers with MG42s mounted on the rails.

Anger and hatred overtook me when I saw the British, American, Canadian, and French prisoners reclining on the frozen ground. They watched me walk along the fence and I interpreted their facial expressions to be apprehension toward their fate. I despised each one of them for bombing our cities, shooting our brothers and Fathers, and for opposing the Reich. What right did they have to come to the European continent for the purpose of meddling in superior German affairs?

The SS Untersturmführer in command of overseeing the barbed wire enclosures told me that the prisoners were taken from these compounds to an interrogation room. After questioning, they were each moved to a cell in the municipal prison before being transported to a *Stalag* in Germany. Most of the Allied soldiers at Düsseldorf were taken to Prisoner of War camps at Köln, Siegen, Meschede, Bielefeld and Paderborn.

I was angered that the prisoners were permitted to smoke and speak with one another inside the enclosures. I gave the order to enforce silence and to have all cigarettes and candy confiscated from them. They were prisoners of the Reich, not guests. After the announcement was made in English and French, the prisoners passed their items through the fence and deposited them in a central pile. The mood had been somewhat tranquil for the prisoners before I arrived and now they were looking at me as if I had come to impose serious restrictions upon them. I had.

I pulled my pistol from its holster in front of the prisoner assembly and released the cartridge. I casually inspected it before thrusting it back inside the grip and cocking the weapon. I held it down at my side and instructed the SS guards to bring an Allied pilot out of the enclosure. The prisoners began to talk excitedly but the Untersturmführer silenced the crowd with several shots fired in the air from his own sidearm.

The American pilot was brought before me and I pulled the metal wings insignia from his coat. I marched him several meters beyond the enclosure until we were out of view from the prisoners and behind a wooden SS administrative building. The American pilot shook his head from side to side and pleaded with me, "Please, Sir. No. Please."

I instructed one of the SS guards to cut the back of the pilot's hand with his bayonet. Once he did this I fired a single shot in the air and smeared the blood of the American on my own hands and face. I ordered the pilot to be taken inside the wooden building through its rear door and I returned to the collection of Allied prisoners with blood on my face and hands. I loosely held the pistol at my side while the silent Allied soldiers stared at me with expressions of terror. I firmly pointed to another pilot inside the enclosure and he was taken out and I repeated the illusion of shooting him behind the building. I did this eight times until replacing the empty cartridge in my Luger in front of the Allies. I abruptly turned and walked away without a word.

I ordered the eight Allied soldiers I took from the enclosure to be dressed in German uniforms and casually marched from the administrative building and away from their comrades. They were given strict orders not to turn their faces toward their fellow soldiers or speak a single word. I effectively transported them to the interrogation facility while maintaining the illusion to the prisoners in the enclosure that I had shot eight of their comrades to death. I had planted the seeds of fear and demonstrated that I held complete authority over them.

Most of the military information gained from the interrogations revealed an eastern and northeastern Allied push from Brussels and France. OKH and OKW had been anticipating this Allied strategy. I was informed that German plans were revised on 1 November for the V, VI and VII Panzer Armies to launch a major offensive through the Ardennes Forest for the purpose of capturing Antwerp, Saint Vith, and Brussels.

OKH and OKW were very pleased with the information as it was considered reliable in accord with confirmed Luftwaffe reconnaissance reports. Much of the information about the status and positions of the American military was provided by British and Canadian officers. The Americans, who did not suspect their Allied comrades of revealing this information, assumed we had gathered accurate intelligence reports on our own. When confronted with what we knew, many of the enlisted American soldiers provided more information in return for winter coats, blankets, shoes, socks and food. The Americans were overindulged by an affinity for material and their soldiers of lower rank were eager to trade information for comforts.

The American officers were novices to the methodology of effective interrogation. Most of them presented a haughty attitude that earned them nothing more than a few sharp blows from a truncheon. When they demonstrated absolute refusal to talk, they were stripped naked, soaked with water, and put in an unheated cell. Most of them talked after 8 or 12 hours of exposure to the cold. Those that did not were transferred to the Gestapo prison where more intense and effective methods of interrogation took place.

On 24 November the French had captured Strasbourg and more of our troops were forced to fall back to defensive lines on our border. Four or five days later I was given new orders to report to Generalleutnant der Waffen SS Hermann Priess, Commander of the I SS Panzer Corps at Headquarters West near Ludwigshafen.

Priess was involved in a strategy meeting with Sepp Dietrich, Joachim Peiper, Infantry General Otto Hitzfeld, General Model and General Manteuffel. The guards ushered me into this room and Priess abruptly stopped the meeting and called me to the front where he introduced me to the men. Each superior officer stood and shook my hand with a firm and confident greeting.

"Haupsturmführer Schiller will serve as our RSHA expert on counterintelligence, partisans, and prisoner interrogations," said Priess. He looked at me with admiration and said, "We were fortunate to learn you were in SS District VI."

I had no idea what he was talking about. Counterintelligence was the formal duty of the Abwehr and I was by no means an expert on partisan affairs. I was confident with my interrogation techniques but had no idea what Generalleutnant Priess expected of me.

Priess continued the meeting and pointed to various maps on easels and pinned to the walls. He had conceived the attack plan for the VI Panzer Army which the I Panzer Corps would follow from Monschau to Kerwinkel. He discussed the difficulties of the terrain at the major launching points and stressed the importance of not permitting tanks and armored vehicles to become bogged down on the way to Hohes Venn where the terrain would become more suitable for the push. Priess would utilize his I SS Panzer Division in coordination with the

XII SS Panzer Corps and would be supported by the 3rd Fallschirmjäger Division and the 12th and 277th Grenadier Divisions.

Sepp Dietrich was adamant about permitting the tank divisions to lead the offensive, but Model argued that the artillery should open the assault followed by infantry penetration at Udenbreth. Once completed, Model wished to move the infantry to capture and secure several key roads leading south from Verviers to open a direct corridor for our tanks to move on Liège. This argument was perpetuated with various strategic scenarios being discussed but in the end Model won the debate.

Hitzfeld spoke of the importance of night movement and fighting, and insisted that in order for the offensive to be successful, the Allies must have no indication of it. The weather was projected to favor this tactic and if the forecast was accurate, all artillery, infantry and armor would be moved into position under the cover of heavy snowfalls.

Priess was very enthusiastic about striking in a sector controlled by the American 99th Infantry Division as our intelligence reports proved it was under the command of an American Major General who had arrived in Europe just days before our meeting. Reports stated that he had been sent to gain combat experience in an area where our attack was considered very improbable. Priess was determined to educate the American officer in the methods of warfare. More intelligence documents reported that the United States 99th Division was mainly comprised of replacements who had never experienced combat and that they were thinly deployed over a 30.5 kilometer defensive line. The Waffen SS troops we were committing to this offensive had 6 years of hardened battle experience that began in Poland in 1939 and continued through the hellish Southern and Eastern Fronts.

We held several meetings over the following two weeks wherein this information was stressed and repeated to the point where each man had memorized it. I was given specific orders as to what was expected of me. I was to secure, count, and record the names, ranks and service numbers of all Allied prisoners captured by the I and XII Panzer Armies and their immediate support battalions. I was to personally interrogate all captured enemy officers while my subordinates questioned the captured Allied enlisted soldiers. I was to arrange transports for the Prisoners of War to the German town of Trier through a series of roads and vehicles assigned for this purpose.

I was to execute all partisans assisting the Allied forces and I was to liquidate all Jews located in the areas of operations.

The weather forecasts had been accurate. On 13 December our armor, artillery and infantry divisions began moving west along the narrow roads through the Ardennes Forest to take our positions for the assault. I had never seen such a large collection of veteran Waffen SS soldiers. The men looked hardened and determined and every person moved with precision and purpose. Seeing the soldiers and tanks on the roads, I felt certain that the war could be won.

CHAPTER TWENTY-THREE
THE ARDENNES OFFENSIVE
16 DECEMBER 1944

I rode in the back of an open halftrack with several officers from the SS Police, Order Police, and Gestapo. I had been issued the StG44 assault rifle which was a relatively new weapon with powerful capabilities. It could be used as a rifle with solid accuracy up to 300 meters, or converted to a lethal submachine gun by pushing a small lever near the trigger. My pouches were filled with extra 30 round cartridges and my belt was stuffed with grenades. Priess had made it very clear that I would be a member of the assault forces before my Police duties were required. I felt minor anxiety about going into battle because I knew we were facing an inexperienced opponent in the American 99th Division. The Waffen SS veterans surrounding me provided confidence and security.

The snow on the roads hindered our advance but after midnight on 16 December we had reached our staging point for the offensive. The artillery was unloaded and guided down into ravines and towed up to positions on high ground. Pionier Squads went forward to conduct reconnaissance and at approximately 0300 hours we gathered for our final orders.

The Pioniers reported Allied barbed wire barriers and potential minefields on the outer perimeters of their positions. They gave the coordinates to several artillery crews who were instructed to blow holes through the wire defenses. We would be left to our own fortunes and skills to forge through the mines. The American 99th Division was on the other side of the obstacles and we were to punch holes through their defenses and secure the roads leading south from Verviers.

At 0530 hours, 200 of our *Nebelwerfer 42s* simultaneously fired rockets from each of their six 160mm tubes as our 88s and 102s joined the barrage against the American 99th Division. We fired rockets and artillery shells into the enemy positions for more than an hour before cooling and replacing some of the barrels. Another hellish barrage was fired when the maintenance was completed and the volleys continued steadily until 0700 hours. A heavy mist arose in the forest and it combined with the smoke and sulfur from our artillery. The infantry was given orders to attack the American position and we moved out through the dense brush and snow.

Soon we came upon massive shattered pine and fir trees that smoldered and glowed red hot from our shells, and broken trunks jutting upward that burned like torches. Soldiers began cutting the first of the barbed wire barriers in several places and stomped it down into the snow. We came to the edge of a clearing and looked over an area that was filled with burning craters. Was the American 99th Division on the other side of it? There had been no shooting and no opposition to our approach. A unit of Waffen SS fired panzerfausts and machine guns across the open expanse. Gunfire was returned.

We ran across the clearing at full sprint while firing our weapons into the opposite tree line. Our soldiers were stepping on mines that sent churned earth skyward and blood and innards across the snow. I was running as fast as I could when an explosion sounded and I was knocked off my feet by a severed leg. I rolled over in the snow, pointed my StG44 at the trees and pulled the trigger. Waffen SS soldiers were running past me in great numbers and someone pulled me to my feet.

We breached the opposite side of the clearing and entered a complex of foxholes, trenches and log covered dugouts. Muzzles flashed from within and German grenades were slid into them. Many Americans broke out of their holes and began to flee in a disorganized panic while others stood just meters away and fired at my comrades. It was a hellish exchange of close range fire and those not able to reload in a prompt manner were forced to use rifle stocks, bayonets, trench knives, helmets, and fists as weapons.

The Waffen SS soldiers formed a semi circular wall and moved across the American area with machine guns and rifles providing a steady thunder. The Allied soldiers threw their hands up in surrender and many of them were gunned down in the carnage. After approximately 20 minutes the shooting faded to sporadic bursts before ending. We heard steady gunfire in the sectors to our north and south but our first engagement was over.

Approximately 35 American soldiers stood in a group with their hands over their heads. The immediate area was littered with more American dead than German, and the Waffen SS moved among the downed Allied soldiers to shoot those that were still alive. As an Officer of the SS Police I should have intervened and prevented the executions, but at that moment there was no possible means to do that. The Waffen SS soldiers were removed from human compassion and still thriving in the vortex of battle. Their bloodstained faces and gunpowder burned hands were eager to destroy the American army that had come to Europe just six months ago. We were a desperate army competing in perhaps our final opportunity to drive the Americans off the continent and secure victory for the Reich. Under such circumstances you can attempt to enforce the law but it is completely futile.

We searched the bunkers and dugouts where approximately 20 more Allied soldiers were found cowering. Of them, perhaps 10 were shot in the holes. Priess had moved a few Tiger tanks up to the captured American outpost and the Order Police secured the prisoners. Among them was an Allied Captain and Lieutenant, but Priess did not allow me to interrogate them. The prisoners were taken to the rear and we were given orders to capture and hold a crossroads south of Verviers.

The enemy had scattered and formed pockets of resistance that ambushed and harassed us on our journey through the forest to the crossroads. We came to a small slope that crested downward to the road. We were north of the crossing and we worked our way south with approximately 100 Waffen SS soldiers walking on each side of the logging lane. I was in the drainage ditch on the east side of the road when the signal was passed back to halt. I crept toward the front of the line and saw 4 American halftracks guarding the crossroads and a series of well fortified bunkers and machine gun nests on all sides. The snow was falling and tiny pillars of smoke were rising from cooking fires in several of the holes. Through my field glasses I studied the machine guns mounted on the halftracks and secretly watched the other crews behind their cover.

Signals were passed back and forth between our soldiers on both sides of the road. My unit was to scale the embankment and flank the American position from behind. Our remaining unit would launch an attack from the north and hopefully draw the American halftracks into committing. We would then take them out from the south with panzerfausts and concentrate grenades on the machine gun nests and bunkers.

Each of us crawled up the slope and assembled in the snowy thicket. We made a wide arc around the crossroad defenses and sprinted across the east-to-west road well out of sight from the Americans. We eventually worked our way west until we came to the north-to-south road. We divided our soldiers to place 50 in the drainage ditches on each side and we made our way to a southern position below the American defenses. Our Pionier Squad used the radio to transmit the message that we were in place.

There was a long and silent pause before the sickening sound of one our MG42s split the air. German grenades popped in the intersection and the American halftracks turned their turrets northward and began spitting out lead. We had drawn the inexperienced Americans into committing all their efforts to the north and my unit was able to stealthily approach to within 18 meters of the enemy position. It was lethal range for our panzerfausts which converted the American armored halftracks into flaming wrecks. We sighted the machine gun nests from behind and began eliminating the crews.

Americans leapt from their bunkers in an attempt to find new cover and realized they were fighting a battle on two fronts. My unit shifted to the west to avoid the crossfire from our troops to the north. As we came near the east-to-west road we fell back in the woods at the approach of three American M4 Sherman tanks. To our astonishment, each tank had a man exposed and standing upright gripping the turret machine gun. The tanks were due to pass our location and we dug ourselves into the top of the embankment and prepared to shoot the three gunners.

While several Waffen SS soldiers shot the American tank machine gunners, others dropped primed grenades down the embankment that slid underneath the chassis. The first two tanks had their treads blown off and this created an impassable roadblock for the third tank.

We were feeling good about disabling the drive systems on two tanks until we realized we had done nothing to knock them out of service. The turrets began searching for us and two panzerfaust rounds were fired through the tanks in the front and the rear. The blasts ignited the ammunition within them and a rain of smoking metal poured down around us. The middle tank swung its turret and fired a round that removed several trees, part of the embankment, and five Waffen SS soldiers from the earth. Two panzerfaust rounds were put through the remaining tank as American halftracks and more M4 Shermans crested the bend and headed toward us from the west.

We ran onto the road in front of the ruined armor roadblock and made our way to the crossroads. The Americans had reinforced from the south and we were forced to cross the road and link with our other unit north of the battle. They had sustained heavy casualties but Priess had dispatched several King Tiger tanks and a Company of Grenadiers as reinforcements.

American bullets kept our faces smashed flat into the snow. Now and then a voice yelled, *"Wo sind die panzers? Wo sind die panzers?"*

None of us knew where our tanks were and all we could do was keep our heads down until they arrived. I saw a group of perhaps 10 American soldiers sprint across the road to the west. I believed they were trying to probe and flank us and before I could call out what I witnessed, several alert Waffen SS soldiers ran off into the trees to meet this enemy patrol. We heard the echo of gunfire in the woods as the American halftracks and M4 Shermans bulled into the crossroads from the west. We watched them jerk forward and backward to form an offensive position, and as the turrets engaged, a dull and hollow thud sounded from behind us before the Sherman to our extreme right burst into flames with a heavy explosion. The King Tigers were rolling down the road behind us as our Grenadiers were setting up mortars on either side of the road. At once the crossroads was under intense German fire and our King Tigers rumbled into the intersection to engage the Shermans and halftracks at point blank range. The shells from the Shermans struck our King Tigers and only managed to produce dents and scorch marks on our armor. The Americans fled from the crossroads leaving behind their heavy machine guns, mortars, supplies, and ruined armor.

The King Tigers immediately began pushing the American wrecks off the road to clear the way. We occupied the remaining American bunkers and treated our casualties. Once all German wounds had been tended to, our combat doctors went about treating the Americans. There was no senseless slaughter after the battle. Several of our halftracks arrived to reinforce the crossroads and ambulances came to take away the wounded from both sides.

Within hours, SS Field Police arrived and began nailing wooden directional signs into the frozen ground. The first of many armored columns began arriving from the north and east and the SS Field Police directed them through the intersection to their destinations. On the following morning we were relieved by a Wehrmacht battalion and ordered to advance to the west.

During our march I saw the men in front of me cautiously climbing part way up the embankment to avoid a motorcycle with sidecar that was sliding from side to side from lack of traction. I began to make way for the lunatic driver but he put the motorcycle in neutral and removed his goggles. "Is your name Schiller, Sir?"

I trudged toward him and he informed me that Generalleutnant Priess had several of his units holding an American Lieutenant Colonel prisoner in a nearby farmhouse and that he ordered the motorcycle driver to take me to the location to interrogate the enemy officer. The driver and I studied a map on the road in the falling snow and I reluctantly climbed into the sidecar.

"You better find something to hold onto, Sir. It is very icy and this is only my third or fourth time driving one of these things."

That explained a lot. We would travel several meters before the rear drive wheel would lose or gain traction and offset the front guiding wheel. Sometimes my weight in the sidecar would send us skidding to one side of the road or the other. I believed I was going to meet my end in a motorcycle accident.

Late in the afternoon we pulled off the main forest road and left the column behind. We slowly descended an icy road on a sweeping hill and approached a farmhouse with a granite retaining wall around it. Inviting smoke poured from the chimney and I looked forward to the warmth and possibly a ladle of hot soup.

The driver stopped the motorcycle next to three parked Kubelwagens and a Blitz Opel. We entered the house to hear static radio transmissions in German. In the great room we saw that several of our officers and three enlisted men had been shot dead. The windows on the opposite side of the room were broken and I noticed the shards of glass were scattered about the room. The shooting had come from outside and it had the markings of a bold and successful Allied rescue mission.

"I believe we should get out of here at once," said the driver.

"Do not be foolish," I said calmly. "If the Allies rescued the prisoner they would have gotten as far away as possible from here."

I examined the bodies and saw that each dead soldier and officer had his weapon holstered or shouldered. The attack from outside had been a complete surprise. I was astounded that our officers had not posted guards around the structure to prevent this. I walked to the window and examined the footprints leading away toward a thick wooded area. I was about to turn around to speak to the driver when I noticed a blood trail and drag marks leading from the outside edge of the window to a woodshed. I waved the driver to come stand next to me and pointed out my discovery.

He engaged the bolt on his K98 rifle and I primed my StG44. We exited the house and walked around the retaining wall to the woodshed. I crouched in front of it with my weapon pointed as the driver pulled open the door. Before us was an older Belgian man clutching his mangled right arm in his left hand. He had several chest wounds and severe burns on his face. I saw the remains of a rifle lying next to him and realized from its condition that it had misfired and exploded in his hands.

"A partisan!" exclaimed the driver.

"Do you have a medical satchel on the motorcycle?" I inquired.

The driver was confused. "He is a partisan!"

"Rottenführer!" I shouted, "Is there a medical satchel on the motorcycle?"

"*Ja wohl.*"

"Fetch it."

"But he is a partisan!"

"Goddamnit Rottenführer! I know what in hell he is! Now fetch the damned medical satchel!"

When the Rottenführer had gone, the wounded Belgian spoke to me in imperfect German. "I did not shoot any of your soldiers, Sir.

Yes, I tried, but my rifle exploded the first time I pulled the trigger. Forgive me, please."

For some reason I had already forgiven him. I do not know why. There was no honor in shooting that old man in the woodshed.

The Rottenführer arrived with the medical satchel and said, "I shall use the radio in the house to report that we have taken a partisan prisoner!"

"You will remain here and assist me in providing medical treatment to this man," I said. We applied moisture salve to his burned face and arm and I did my best to bandage his wounds.

"Can you walk?" I asked him.

"Perhaps," he said. "If you can help me to my feet."

The Rottenführer and I helped him stand and I pointed to the trees. "What is your name?" I asked.

He dabbed at his burned face and replied, "I am Florian Maroutaeff."

"My name is Schiller. Rolf Schiller. Remember that."

"Rolf Schiller," he repeated.

"Tell him your name," I ordered the Rottenführer.

"Jens Pfister."

The old Belgian nodded. "Rolf Schiller and Jens Pfister. I will remember that."

"Go," I told him.

As he straggled toward the tree line, Rottenführer Pfister looked at me with a confused expression. He said, "You have just saved the life of the enemy."

"No, Pfister," I replied. "I may have saved our lives."

In the event our offensive bogged down and we found ourselves retreating and on the defensive, it would be nearly impossible to escape from the Belgian Pocket and the Ardennes Forest. Perhaps the old Belgian would live long enough to reach his partisan comrades and speak our names as men of compassion and honor. Perhaps, I hoped, it would be enough to save our lives if we found ourselves captured by the Belgian resistance. The name Florian Maroutaeff may have been enough to spare us from Belgian partisan guns.

We kicked snow over the blood trail and Pfister and I agreed to keep this matter between ourselves. I used the radio inside the manor house to report to Priess that the American officer had been rescued and our officers and soldiers had been killed. He dispatched a truck carrying Transportation Personnel to retrieve the vehicles parked outside and ordered me to rejoin the I SS Panzer Army on the western road.

We caught up with the unit at another crossroads that had been taken from American hands. Priess was reviewing maps and intelligence reports at a makeshift Command Post as I approached. We stood there in a heavy snowfall until he glanced over at me. "Numbers?"

"Five officers dead and three enlisted soldiers killed," I replied.

"No sign of the American?"

"No, Sir. It appeared to be the work of partisans. I pulled Maroutaeff's damaged rifle from the sidecar. "I found this and footprints outside the windows of the room in which our comrades were killed."

"Son of God," said Priess while looking at the weapon. "My grandfather used to hunt with one of these." He tapped the map in front of him. "We have launched a successful offensive along a 137 kilometer front. The Americans have been taken by surprise and are falling back in sheer panic. Operation Stösser did not have good results. The damned winds blew our *fallschirmjägers* many kilometers outside the intended drop zones. We do not have enough paratroopers in the area to hold the Baraque Michel crossroads. I need to get XII Panzer Army there to cut off the advance of Allied reinforcements and supplies." He put his hands out and collected snowflakes on his black leather gloves. "How am I supposed to fight a war in this shit?"

The pompous coddled ass. Where was he during the Stalingrad campaign? And why was he lamenting to me? "What are my orders, Sir?"

"I want you to lead Kampfgruppe VIII west of Wirtzfeld to learn if the railroad bridge is intact and guarded by the enemy. If it is guarded, do not engage. Report and hold your position until I bring I SS Panzer to you for support."

"If it is unguarded, Sir?"

"Cross it, establish defenses, report, and hold."

"Yes, Sir."

I gathered Kampfgruppe VIII by the field kitchen wagons and was grateful to learn it was part of a Mechanized Unit. Halftracks and Blitz Opels moved out and took my 180 man combat team into the setting darkness. We reached the railroad bridge before dawn and studied it through our field glasses on high ground. "I see nothing over there."

"I do not see anything either," replied a Waffen SS Untersturmführer. "Shall I send a patrol?"

"Let us not be hasty," I answered. Something did not seem right about the opposite side of the bridge. I could not place my suspicion but I would not commit a patrol. I transmitted to Priess that the bridge appeared suspicious in that it was completely void of activity and there was no movement in the small farming village on the near side.

"Send a patrol," ordered Priess.

I selected five men and relayed the directives for them to cross the railroad bridge. One of the young men looked at me and his comrades and asked, "Why us, Sir?"

I did not regard that as questioning the orders, but I thought of it more as a rhetorical response. The men did not argue and they immediately left our position and made their way to the bottom of the high ground. They stalked through the farming village and paused to survey the opposite side of the railroad bridge. One of the men turned and made a chopping motion with his arm to signal that all seemed clear.

We watched them step onto the railroad bridge to begin crossing the river below. They had effectively become dead men if enemy fire was to open on them. The girders on both sides of the bridge were high and the passage was wide but provided no cover. At the midpoint they crouched and stared at the opposite end.

I could feel my heart pounding inside my chest like a hammer. The patrol slowly made their way across the bridge until they successfully reached the other side. Again the man turned and signaled that it was clear. We all breathed a sigh of relief and I transmitted our discovery to Priess.

"Cross, entrench, and hold until I SS Panzer arrives."

"Yes, Sir!"

The bridge accommodated our halftracks and we dug in on the other side as ordered. I established defensive lines of fire and we waited several hours before I SS Panzer arrived. Priess had gathered intelligence reports that stated the town of Butgenbach to the west was occupied by Allied forces and OKH and OKW demanded we capture it. The 277th Grenadiers replaced us as the defense element for the bridge and we advanced alongside I SS Panzer toward the Belgian town.

Resistance was very light at Butgenbach and we had captured the town with minimal efforts. In spite of our paratroopers landing in the wrong locations, Colonel von Heydt had ordered them to form small units to harass the Allies with quick strikes wherever opportunity could be found. Because of the number of these attacks, the Allies assumed a greater number of our paratroopers were in their zones and adopted useless countermeasures because of this theory. Within two days we had split the American lines and cut them off from reinforcements and resupply. The enemy was in full retreat as my Kampfgruppe pushed toward a crossroads between the towns of Malmédy and Ligneuville.

We reached the intersection at approximately 0830 hours on 19 December. I noticed a group of SS soldiers standing in the back of a Blitz Opel and pointing to a field that bordered the crossroads. Several officers were dismounting their vehicles and walking toward the plot of earth and I examined the source of all this attention. Unusual objects were protruding upward through the snow in the field and on closer inspection I realized them to be arms and legs. The falling snow had placed a thin coating on the bodies but we could clearly see they were Americans. There was no indication that they had fallen in combat as most of the corpses were tightly grouped. An inspection of the perimeter revealed more bodies away from the main collection that had bullet wounds in their backs. They had obviously been shot while running in the opposite direction of where the shooting had come from. There were no weapons or grenades found on the bodies which indicated they had been stripped of these items and herded together as prisoners.

"This was Peiper's area of operations yesterday, was it not?" asked a Waffen SS Lieutenant Colonel.

His Staff Officers consulted their documents and charts before confirming it. There was a very uneasy silence among all while the Lieutenant Colonel pondered the present situation.

"Do not touch a thing. Get the column moving! We are to

reinforce Monteuffel and Dietrich at Saint Vith!'"

The Staff Officers chastised the enlisted soldiers that were taking photographs of the slaughtered corpses in the field. As the column pulled out in great haste it felt like we were fleeing from the scene of a shameful crime. We were. We abandoned the site of Peiper's Malmédy massacre.

On the evening of 19 December we linked with Dietrich's outer perimeter forces on the eastern edge of Saint Vith. The General's troops had captured prisoners from the American 7th and 9th Armored Divisions and from the 28th and 106th Infantry Divisions. Dietrich had just received confirmation from OKH and OKW that the American Commander of the Saint Vith forces was a veteran officer called General Clarke.

Our High Command was angry with Dietrich's lack of progress as the original plans called for the capture of Saint Vith on 17 December. Dietrich and Manteuffel had promised victory according to schedule, but the full enemy retreat had resulted in the massive concentration of American soldiers in many of the small towns and cities throughout the forest gap.

Our success for the Ardennes campaign hinged on the capture of many strategic crossroads to cut off the American flow of troops and supplies and to tactically provide lanes for ours. Saint Vith was no different as the town itself was the junction of six strategically important roads. The two northern roads from Saint Vith led to Ligneuville and Ambléve. Its western road connected to Schönhern and the River Our; its eastern road to Rodt and Poteau. One of its southern roads led to Winterspelt and its other lane connected with a critical crossroads between Beho and Reuland. The American forces were greatly hindering our advance.

My Kampfgruppe was permitted a few hours of sleep before being assembled for directives. Dietrich ordered my unit to enter Saint Vith from the northeast to reinforce SS soldiers engaged in fighting near the center of the town.

We passed several Wehrmacht and SS bunker checkpoints before penetrating the city. The town was picturesque despite the noticeable damage that had been done to many of its houses and buildings. The sloped roofs and crossbeam work on the shutters and flowerboxes was somehow elegant against the falling snow and the glow of fires that burned out of control. The gaslight lined cobblestone streets arose and dipped off through quaint little alleys and side streets. Occasional bursts of gunfire softly echoed in the distance.

As we stalked through the streets a voice shouted, *"Halt! Was ist das Zugang Wort?"*

"I looked at my juniors to see if any of them knew of an access word. They shrugged their shoulders.

"SS Kampfgruppe attached to I SS Panzer!" I shouted.

"Was ist das Zugang Wort?"

"I do not know the goddamned access word!"

"Bleiben Sie wo Sie sind! Bewegen Sie nicht!"

We stood firm while SS soldiers came from the shadows with weapons pointed at us. A young and nervous Scharführer looked at us with great suspicion.

" Geben Sie mir Ihre Papiere!"

This all seemed very unusual but I realized the young soldier was dutifully following orders. I handed him my papers and he studied them under the light of his battery powered torch.

He handed my documents to me and asked, "Why do you not know the access word?"

"I was not told that one was required."

He explained that our *Abwehr* had launched a successful operation by infiltrating enemy lines with German soldiers who were dressed in American uniforms and fluent in the English language. The Americans had countered this action with a similar plan and with considerably fewer operatives.

I was furious. "And how many units of 180 disguised Americans have you captured?"

He seemed ashamed but could not mask the fear caused by the circumstances around him.

"What is the situation here?" I inquired.

"American tanks, infantry and artillery in the western and southern sectors of the town, Sir."

"Why are the enemy guns not engaging? Are they low on ammunition reserves? Have they been neutralized?"

The Scharführer rubbed the frost from his wristwatch and looked at it before saying something I could not believe. "The American guns usually open on us between 0730 and 0800 hours, Sir. They prefer to do the bulk of their fighting during daylight hours."

"Much like bankers, Sir," said a Corporal.

Shaking my head and pondering how this enemy came this far against us, I led my unit to the center of Saint Vith and reinforced the SS troops there. At approximately 0700 hours on the morning of 20 December the SS soldiers began taking cover in reinforced areas. True to the Scharführer's claim, the American guns began a barrage a few minutes past 0730 hours.

Most of the shelling was concentrated on our position, and Line Officers were using their radios to request permission to fall back. Our Generals on the outer perimeters of the town ordered us to hold and engage.

"Engage what?!" shouted a Waffen SS Lieutenant into his transmitter. "The Americans are saturating us with artillery fire!"

Moments later our Generals reconsidered and issued orders that we were to move forward and eliminate the artillery guns. I SS Panzer and XII SS Panzer were committing King Tiger Tanks to the effort but we were not to wait for their support.

I do not know what kind of artillery shells the Americans used against us at Saint Vith but they were the loudest explosions I ever heard. Each one detonated with a blinding and disorienting flash and the percussion blasts were so intense that the shockwaves created a powerful vacuum draft under the rims of our helmets. This force literally sucked the heads off the shoulders of our men who had made the mistake of fastening their helmet straps underneath their chins. My own helmet had fallen off while I ran forward to a reinforced position. I was followed by approximately 20 men from my Kampfgruppe and my only desire was to escape the kill box. We ran due east through the streets and traded fire with the American patrols that exposed themselves to harass us. Allied gunfire chattered at us from rooftops, balconies, windows, bunkers, piles of rubble, and doorways. We forced the doors of a Catholic Church open and me and 9 survivors from the Kampfgruppe rested for a moment on the pews. I became aware of someone standing behind me and nervously turned to point my weapon at a marble statue of Saint Josef holding the infant Jesus.

I was overcome with memories of my Father and this bridged to thoughts of my Mother, sister and brothers. I reminisced the few memories I had of Klaudia and my daughter Hannalore and I found myself screaming out loud like a primitive man. I knew the men of my Kampfgruppe were looking at me oddly and wondering why I was performing such an outburst but I had no other choice. I could scream until there was no more breath in my lungs or collapse into a blithering fit of tears in front of my men.

My composure was regained when one of my soldiers called for me while staring out through a broken stained glass window.

"Sir! The Americans are moving up with light infantry!"

I looked out through the hole and saw perhaps 15 or 16 American riflemen advancing toward the church from several blocks to the east.

"Between the pews!" I ordered. "Machine guns on the doors. Each man with a rifle is to engage the bolt and set it on a pew in front of you. Prime grenades and wait for my orders. Remain low and out of sight."

Moments later the crunching of American boots upon the snow covered cobblestones grew louder and faded as they passed.

"More approaching from the south and east, Sir!"

Once again I peered out through the hole in the window and saw enemy infantry moving through the streets. The units approaching us were flanking the doors and conducting visual inspections of each building they came across. I knew that fighting them was unavoidable. Suddenly I became intrigued by a device I had not seen before. It resembled a panzerfaust but had flared ends on each side of the tube. It was the American bazooka.

We took our positions between the thick oak pews and held our breaths as the door to the church opened. The Americans stood there and shouted to each other without any semblance of combat discipline. They began to close the doors to leave when one of my soldiers panicked and threw a primed grenade. It slid between the enemy soldiers and bounced down the stone stairs before exploding. The screams of the wounded Americans was wrenching and a hail of bullets was sprayed into the church. We returned fire and this was followed by a pause in which I cautiously looked out the open door from behind a pew. The falling snow seemed peaceful until a dark green metal ball was thrown from the street into the church. It bounced off the back of the rear pew and detonated harmlessly on the other side of our cover. Two enemy machine guns were thrust inward from around the sides of the door and each emptied a full cartridge. Without aiming, the Americans succeeded in blowing apart the altar and tabernacle.

"Is there another exit?" I asked.

A voice laced with sarcasm answered me from the opposite side of the aisle. "I am pleased you have thought of that now, Sir!"

Something heavy struck the stained glass window above me to the left but the panes did not shatter. I realized it was another American grenade when I heard it explode in the street. "God is protecting us," I thought.

The smoke from a shoulder fired artillery round left a trail between the pews until it detonated on the wall above the altar. Plaster, wood and smoke were blown back upon us and my ears were ringing from the report of the bazooka shell.

"There is your exit," shouted another SS soldier. There was a hole large enough to pass through behind the altar. I gave orders to exit the pews against the walls and retreat to the front of the church. More American machine gun fire sliced down the center aisle from the main door.

Two Waffen SS soldiers courageously risked their lives to move into position behind the altar and provide covering fire while the men began to move through the hole in the wall. I crawled behind the altar and discharged half a cartridge from my StG while shouting at the two brave soldiers to exit the church. When they had passed through the hole, I fired the remainder of rounds in my cartridge and joined them. Suddenly I was reminded of Stalingrad and the complete confusion and disorientation that accompanies urban combat.

We began heading toward our position at the center of the town until we observed heavy American positions ahead of us in the distance. The enemy artillery fire was coming into the town from due west. The 10 of us began working our way north realizing that was the direction we had come to Saint Vith from, and expecting our units to be holding the lines there.

Late in the afternoon we had reached the northern edge of the town having engaged in two minor and undecided gunfights along the way. In a field to the northeast were an American halftrack, machine gun bunker, and mortar crew. Due north and northwest was an open expanse of approximately 115 meters bordered by the dense overgrowth of the Ardennes Forest. I had no radio to use to report the position of the Americans in the field and the sounds of combat inside Saint Vith were growing louder, more intense and closer. I had not reached a complete mood of panic as I had been cut off from my units before at Stalingrad. I was aware that thoughtful planning and obtainable objectives were the keys to a successful extraction from the area and reunion with our troops.

"If we can get across the field and into the forest," I said, "We will be able to swing west to the road. I am certain we will link with our checkpoint units there."

My soldiers looked at the American position approximately 73 meters to the northeast. "How can we avoid them?"

I again drew upon my experience from Stalingrad. "We will wait here and move out under the cover of darkness."

My men agreed that it was a firm and intelligent plan. We waited for darkness at which we realized it had become a foolish and suicidal plan. The snow stopped falling and a bright winter moon lit up the landscape like a searchlight. This encouraged the Americans to continue their attack and within hours we could hear them shouting just blocks away from our position. There was minimal cloud cover that would hide the moon long enough for us to move across the open field in increments. When the moon came from behind the clouds we would have to go prone in the snow to avoid detection. This was our only means of escaping the tightening Allied vice at Saint Vith.

We moved cautiously and laid flat and facedown in the snow whenever the moon shone through the clouds. It was a freezing and painstaking method of extraction but we made steady progress on a northwestern route. We had traversed half the field in this manner before sprinting several meters under darkened cover until one of my men struck a tripwire that launched an illumination flare. We were caught standing up in the open field and the halftrack and machine gun nest opened up on us in the distance. The range and poor visibility greatly hindered their accuracy and realizing this, I led a full charge toward the tree line. A mortar shell exploded behind us as the halftrack pulled forward to give chase. It became a race between men and a steel armored machine with rattling guns. At a distance of 45 meters away the halftrack began rotating its turret to send bullets across our intended path. Most of us dropped to the snow and began crawling but I heard the unmistakable screams of wounded comrades. We traversed the final 18 meters to the tree line on our hands and knees and I did not pause when I grabbed the helmet of an injured comrade to replace the one I had lost in the center of Saint Vith.

We quickly grouped inside the forest and I did not have time to perform a count of the men. The halftrack raked the trees with bullets before there was nothing but the sound of its idling motor. We heard the hatches opening and American voices shouting. We stayed close together as we sprinted into the darkness under the forest canopy and ran for our lives. Eventually we fell through the ice of a small stream and laid on the forest floor to catch our breaths. I looked for a suitable defensive position but could not make out details in the limited visibility. American torches were casting beams through the forest and we heard their loud and disorderly shouting. We picked ourselves up and ran aimlessly through the Ardennes Forest until the cold and exhaustion consumed us. We sat with our backs against trees and I counted seven enlisted soldiers with me. The torch beams and voices had faded and I rationalized that the Americans did not want to stray too far from the safety of their vehicle. I felt reasonably certain they had ended the search for us in the dark forest, primarily because they believed we would succumb to the elements.

"Who has the map and compass?" I asked.

"Breuer has it," said a voice in the darkness. No one moved to bring it to me and we realized Breuer was no longer among us. I could only make out the silhouettes of my men.

"Weapons and ammunition check," I ordered. The men called out with what they had. Two MP42s, five K98s, more than a dozen grenades and my StG44.

I did not know how far we ran until realizing the sounds of combat at Saint Vith were far off in the distance. "Two guards on one hour shifts," I stated. "We will rest for five hours and make our way northwest to the road."

"How, Sir?" asked a voice with a hopeless tone.

"We will use the sounds of battle for orientation. If the sounds stop we will follow our footprints back to Saint Vith to learn the outcome. If we have taken the town we will link with our forces there. If not, we will continue to the road."

Five hours later the sounds of combat were yet raging in the distance. I was certain that I kept the noise to our south while I led the patrol through the forest but recognized there was no physical means to discern where it was actually coming from. The terrain and valleys of the forest provided deceitful reverberations and while I believed I was leading my men to the west, I was in fact taking them east.

21 December 1944
Somewhere in the Ardennes Forest

By noon we had not reached the road we hoped to find and my men knew that we were lost. The water in our canteens had frozen so we ate snow to hydrate ourselves and conserved the very last few crusts of our bread. We crossed several small clearings and streams but each one brought endless trees without the least sign of civilization.

I was proud of the determination and resolve of the soldiers accompanying me. They knew we were on an aimless journey but none of them expressed fear. Instead they encouraged each other with jovial remarks.

"Sir, are we still in Belgium?"

"Perhaps we won the war by now."

"I believe we are just a kilometer or two from my grandmother's house."

"Hansel! Gretl! Where are you?"

This humor ended when we heard the sounds of motors in the distance. "Where is the sound coming from?" asked Unterscharführer Hägen.

Rottenführer Klaussen pointed off to his left. "That way!"

We followed the sounds with haste and caution because we could not discern if the vehicles belonged to us or the enemy. After a short journey our hearts fell as we crouched behind the foliage. American M4 Shermans, jeeps and halftracks were rolling through the forest with alert infantry. I did not know our direction and could not reason if the Americans were falling back from or going to reinforce at Saint Vith. I did not even know for certain if Saint Vith was part of their objective. If I took my squad in the direction of where the Americans were coming from I may have led them into an American field base. If I followed at a distance, and if the enemy was indeed retreating, I may have still led my men to an American encampment.

I led my unit back in the direction we had come from and followed our footprints to where we started our investigation of the vehicles. Each step was laborious through the average of 50 centimeters of snow on the flatlands and even more trying when we had to pass through drifts that piled up to a meter. We were all exhausted and hungry and the jovial remarks had not been made since seeing the enemy vehicles. Near the end of the day we came to a stone farmhouse situated in what seemed to be the center of desolation. A small frozen well, storehouse, coach house, shed and stable were behind it and the fields across from it were fenced.

From our vantage it seemed to be unoccupied but seeing no fresh footprints leading to the main door and outer buildings meant very little. The men were eager to secure the house but for all I knew it was being used as an American outpost. I gave my men tactical orders to flank and investigate the outer buildings and if clear, assemble in the stable. My soldiers would have agreed with any idea at that time as they had set their thoughts on the warmth and comfort of the stone farmhouse.

The outer buildings and coach house were empty and I noticed no hay, oats or dung on the floor of the stable. This indicated to me that the family who owned the house may have fled the dangers of the area long ago and used the horses and coach as a means of transportation.

We crept to the first floor windows of the house but were apprehensive about scraping off the frost, ice and snow to see inside. We listened for movement inside the house but heard nothing at all.

At the rear door I stated, "Tactical entry."

"Son of Mary, Sir," said Scharführer Eberhardt. "There is no one here. Allow us to go inside and get warm!"

"Tactical entry," I repeated.

We took strategic positions and squeezed the door handle. It was locked by a hook latch on the inside. My heart pounded as this seemed sure evidence the house was occupied.

Eberhardt saw the expression on my face. "Perhaps they locked it and exited from the front door. Let us go there and see if that door is latched."

We made our way to the front and took the same tactical positions. I turned the knob on that door and pushed but it did not open. A keyhole that operated a sliding bolt was above the handle. While peering through the door, Scharführer Eberhardt startled me by knocking on it.

"Is there anyone home?" he shouted with a smile. "No?" he asked. He kicked the door off its frame and the men made great haste to go inside where they began searching for food and drink without clearing the house. I stood outside shaking my head and thanking God for protecting the foolish SS.

Eberhardt found two bottles of wine and was pushing the cork through the neck with a fountain pen. "Damned officers," he said with a warm smile. "How is that you men live so long?"

I ordered moderate repairs made to the front door and allowed no one to eat or drink until the lock was functional. The men asked for permission to start a fire in the hearth but I denied the request as I did not wish for roving Allied patrols to see the smoke from the chimney.

Hägen sat in a fabric chair and said, "Please, Sir. Let us start a fire. The only lunatics out here are us."

Sturmmann Reifsneider came out of the kitchen with a grin. "There are potatoes, onions, turnips and carrots in the vegetable box! It is the pity we can not have the fire to melt snow so that I may cook us a delicious soup!"

"Scharführer Eberhardt," I said.

"Yes Sir?"

"Take another man and fetch some kindling."

That night a heavy snowstorm blanketed the area but I did not allow this to soothe me into a false sense of safety. Though there were no sounds of battle or movement around us, the enemy was out there somewhere. I could have been content to remain in the warmth of that Belgian farmhouse eating Reifsneider's soup and waiting for the war to end. It was the first moment of relative peace I had felt for quite some time.

We searched the house for useable items and found blankets and coats that we spread out on the great room floor before the hearth. Hägen had found several ledgers belonging to the owners of the house that seemed to record the sales of produce and woodcrafts. None of us were fluent in the Belgian language but most of the words resembled German. The words *"Markt van Rechtgebied"* were written at the top of each sales column and this told me that we had traveled approximately five kilometers northeast of Saint Vith to the Recht Field region.

From our northward journey toward Recht I realized the American vehicles we encountered were heading west. "The enemy was retreating!" I shouted while waking a few of my men.

"Good," moaned Eberhardt. "Let them retreat and let me sleep."

"Sturmmann Kessler and Rottenführer Reimers. I want each of you outside. One in front of the house and one behind it. Two hour guard shifts. Go."

"And you, Sir?" mumbled Eberhardt, "When will you stand guard tonight?"

I halted Reimers before he reached the door. In my opinion, Eberhardt's humor had transformed to insubordination. "Scharführer, perhaps you can contemplate the correct times to keep your mouth closed while you are out there replacing Rottenführer Reimers on the first guard shift."

He immediately stood, pulled on his winter coat and picked up his MP42. "Yes, Sir," he said while realizing he brought this on himself. As he passed me on the way to the door he sincerely added, "I am sorry, Sir."

After some time in silence Sturmmann Reifsneider inquired, "Sir, what will we do tomorrow? Will we go back to Saint Vith?"

"We will see what the day brings us."

I was with seven good and very loyal men. Sturmmann Reifsneider had grown up on a farm in Kempten just 40 kilometers northwest of my home village of Füssen. He was well formed from years of difficult labor and had a very gentle personality.

Sturmmann Hans Kessler was from somewhere in the north near Mölln. He continually shuffled a deck of cards in the house that night and fanned them out on the floor before scooping them up to do it again. He was very quiet and seemed quite studious.

Rottenführer Klaussen hailed from Munich which is the main city north of Füssen. His Father was a wooden toy crafter with his own business and before the war, Klaussen had been sent for an apprenticeship at the Master Woodworkers Guild in Starnberg. He talked of eventually taking over his Father's business and of the many mechanical spring and clockwork toys he would invent some day.

Rottenführer Reimers had found his identity in the SS. He never mentioned where he was from or spoke a word about his family. He was moody and serious but had the makings of a career soldier with the potential to become an officer.

Unterscharführer Rudolf Hägen was a very likeable fellow with a mild and kind sense of humor. That night he spoke of his desire to return to the family home in Dresden where he would attend the University with hopes of earning a diploma to teach history. He was remarkable with facts about past events and in the house that night he asked each of us our birth dates and quoted several major events that happened on each throughout history.

Unterscharführer Eugen Lichtermann shared a common bond with me in that he lost both his elder brothers to the war. He said very little to any of us and busied himself writing letters all night.

Scharführer Viktor Eberhardt came from Bad Hersfeld in central Germany and was married with three children. He probably had more combat experience than any of us in that house as he had served steadily on the frontlines in Poland, Belgium, France, the Ukraine, Finland, Russia and Italy. I understood and could somewhat sympathize with the suspicion he had for me as it was usually foot soldiers like him who had more practical knowledge and experience than the officers who were rotated into combat units from rear assignments. Officers sent to gain experience; or administrative officers such as me, had an uncanny habit of believing we were qualified to direct and execute successful combat operations. Most often our inexperience and arrogance resulted in the deaths of men like Eberhardt or his companions; men who had survived without our meddling and suggestions and men who would probably have done well without our ideas. In spite of this, I would not allow his sarcasm to undermine the confidence the other men had in me. From the manner in which Eberhardt apologized to me, I believe he understood this.

The men inquired about my home village and family but I told them nothing. It was not appropriate for an officer to reveal personal information to subordinates as it placed you on somewhat of an equal and familiar level with them. Without complete assurance of where we were or which army was nearest us, the structure of command had to remain firm. I listened to the men talking with each other until they fell into a well deserved sleep.

22 December 1944
Recht, Belgium

We reluctantly struck out from the house at dawn and tried to maintain a steady southeastern course toward Saint Vith. I believed something had to be there whether it was friendly or enemy. I felt confident that we would link with our own forces after witnessing the American retreat on the previous day.

At approximately 1000 hours we crossed an open field and heard the distant sound of outgoing artillery. We looked at each other to see if any person among us could identify who the guns belonged to from the sounds.

"It is not heavy enough to be 88s or 102s," said Eberhardt. "Sounds like a PaK 36 or 38."

Our hearts lifted at the thought our PaK anti tank gun crews were in the area. I attempted to ascertain the location of the firing by listening.

"Yes," said Reimers. "Those are PaK rounds going out but why in hell is no one shooting back at them?"

"Those are our guns?" asked Klaussen. "Let us go to them at once!"

"Probably harassment fire," said Eberhardt in response to Reimers.

We changed our course to a northeastern route and entered the thick forest again. The artillery guns grew louder as we picked our way through the snow and trees into an area filled with massive boulders. Beyond the shale and granite deposit was the base of an approximate 9 meter elevation from atop which the guns were firing. Between outgoing rounds we could hear American voices shouting from the summit.

We pulled ourselves down low behind the boulders and Eberhardt looked at me, at the elevation, and then me again.

I nodded to indicate we would have to attempt to capture the enemy outpost and neutralize the guns. The artillery pieces were firing at our comrades somewhere and each moment we hesitated was costing German lives. I recounted my experience on the road outside of Volodarske in the Ukraine when I had been ordered to capture the Russian mortar position on an elevation. With the success in mind of the tactics used there, I gave similar orders for my seven men to flank the hill, climb it, and use grenades before going to our weapons. I cautioned them about the potential crossfire and every man nodded that he understood his duties.

We heard metal strike metal before a rifle shot echoed. Reifsneider's eyes rolled back and he collapsed on the ground with a bullet hole through the top of his helmet.

"Take the hill now!" shouted Eberhardt. A few more bullets deflected off the boulders in front of us and I realized the Americans had spotters on top of the elevation. Rushing the hill seemed a mistake.

"Take it!" yelled Eberhardt. "The angle of our climb will force the Americans to expose themselves to shoot at us!"

I gave the order and while watching my men spread out to surround the hill I saw Unterscharführer Hägen jerk violently from several bullet wounds.

Eberhardt was correct. As I began the steep ascent in the snow I saw that I was looking upward at approximately a 45 degree angle. The top of the hill was void of cover and the moment I saw the muzzle of an American rifle appear; I fired a short burst from my StG44 and drove it back.

An American grenade arced over the summit and sunk into the snow about ten meters to my left. Most of the blast was absorbed but I was struck with ice and earth. More grenades came from the pinnacle and landed in front of and behind me, and to both sides. My body was soaked from the moisture of the snow and the freezing had numbed my body. If it had not been for the blood around me, I would not have known that I was hit with shrapnel.

As the grenades were being thrown in the same area, I began working my way up the hill to my right. Approximately 3 meters from the top I pulled two stick grenades, primed them both and heaved them onto the summit. The distinct sounds of more German grenades sounded from the top and I pulled myself to the edge and saw four American light artillery guns and perhaps 25 enemy soldiers. I fired a burst from my weapon at several Americans taking cover inside a canvas tent and noticed one of their comrades opposite from the position who was pulling a grenade from his tunic. Before I could readjust my aim he was taken down by MP42 fire.

The Americans had no thoughts of surrendering and I assumed they knew we were an opponent of inferior numbers. In spite of this, we continued to heave grenades onto the summit and raised ourselves up to fire quick bursts.

Reimers crawled over the hill opposite my position and crouched while spraying the American soldiers with MP42 bullets. I was forced to lower my head to avoid the crossfire and when I looked again I saw Lichtermann also on the pinnacle. He threw a grenade into the canvas tent and after it exploded I pulled myself onto the top. Following a fifteen minute battle, we had taken the artillery and observation post from the Americans.

Immediately we noticed that there were only three of us on the summit. We examined the Americans to make sure they were dead and that they no longer posed a threat. Then we walked to the edges of the summit and began looking for our comrades.

"Shit!" stammered Reimers. "Klaussen is dead! I think that is him!" I walked to his side and stared down the hill at a body that had been torn open and mangled by a grenade. It indeed was Rottenführer Klaussen. I found Eberhardt's corpse on the north side of the elevation before we discovered Sturmmann Kessler bandaging himself on the west slope.

"Sir," said Rottenführer Reimers. "You have been hit."

I pulled the torn fabric of my trousers aside near my left thigh. I had been struck there by a sniper's bullet, a splinter of wood during an air raid, and now American grenade shrapnel. "Do not concern yourself," I replied. "It missed the femoral artery."

Reimers and Lichtermann assisted Kessler to the top of the elevation. The young man was in pain but his wounds were not fatal. I inspected the dead Americans and found the highest rank among them to have been a 2nd Lieutenant. I took his field glasses and compass to survey the area around us. Each artillery gun was a 30mm cannon still pointed southeast toward Saint Vith. The guns resembled our anti aircraft weapons as each was mounted on a circular base that could pivot 360 degrees. I looked at the summit and walked around the perimeter but was unable to conceive how the weapons had been carted up the elevation to be set in place. Examining the guns closely,

I saw that they were hauled to this location in pieces and then assembled.

I sat down on one of the artillery base chairs and pondered my next series of orders. I instructed Kessler and Lichtermann to keep a watchful eye on the low ground as I was sure our forces being shelled from this location would send a patrol to find the position. For once I was grateful that it was snowing heavily because this voided the possibility of being bombed by our Luftwaffe. It was also logical that the Americans in the area would wonder why their artillery crews had ceased firing.

Using the field glasses to search for more enemy positions or friendly patrols, I focused upon something I did not expect to find. It looked like a road spanning east to west at approximately 0.8 kilometers to the north. It nearly blended in with the terrain as its northern shoulder was a rolling steep slope that extended along it for as far as I could see. The road was level and its southern shoulder was a steep descent into a small valley that crested upward at our current position. Wanting to make certain it was indeed a road, I handed the field glasses to Unterscharführer Lichtermann. "Look out there," I said. "Tell me what you see."

He stared for several minutes in silence. "Trees, Sir?"

"Yes, and a frozen hell full of them. Look closer, Lichtermann."

There was another long pause before he asked, "Is that a road, Sir?"

I was filled with renewed confidence at locating a road that headed west.

Reimers and Kessler were covering the dead American soldiers with snow. It was the most respectful burial we could provide for them with a frozen ground. We removed our helmets while Kessler quoted a simple benediction for the Americans, Reifsnieder, Klaussen, Hägen and Eberhardt.

I decided we would wait until darkness and if a comrade Pionier Squad had not arrived to investigate the American artillery post, we would blow the guns and set off through the valley toward the road. Reimers maintained watch while Lichtermann fetched the American food rations from inside the remains of the canvas tent. He threw the packages on the snow between Kessler and me.

"Salt wafers, biscuits, peanut spread and sardines," said

Lichtermann with disgust. "It is no mystery why the Americans fight so hard. They are trying to capture us for some wholesome food!"

"How can an army survive on this rubbish?" asked Kessler.

I mistakenly replied, "They can not."

"Movement!" shouted Reimers.

We pressed ourselves into the snow near his position and I studied the forest through my field glasses. I saw gray overcoats, K98 rifles and German helmets. "Our comrades have arrived!"

I called out, "First SS Panzer Army, Kampfgruppe Saint Vith!"

There was silence for a very long time before a voice below called out, "Where?"

"On the elevation! We have captured and secured the American guns!"

"Show yourself!" called the voice.

That was a tense request. It was possible that the men were Americans dressed in our uniforms. "Stand up," I said to Reimers.

"With respect to your rank Sir, go to hell! You stand up!"

I stood and six SS Pioniers came through the boulders and began ascending the elevation. At the top an Unterscharführer identified the unit. "II Waffen SS 6th Pionier Squad." He looked at the mound of snow covering the bodies and at the artillery guns. "Four of you took this position, Sir?"

"There were eight of us," I said. "Where does that road lead to?" I asked while pointing northward.

"That is one of the logging roads between Burtonville and Heuem."

I did not know the location of these places. "Can the road be followed to Saint Vith?"

"Yes, Sir. That is where we came from. Intelligence reports are warning of an American counterattack in this area. The enemy will be on that road in a matter of hours."

"How wide is that road, Unterscharführer?"

"How wide is it?" he asked. "Wide enough to accommodate logging vehicles, I suppose. I do not know."

Reimers moved forward. "The average logging lane in Belgium is approximately 4.2 meters wide, Sir. I heard the officers discussing it. Most are wide enough for tanks to travel on."

That was precisely what I wished to know. It seemed logical for the Americans to have established the artillery and observation outpost to spot and defend their advance during the counterattack. There was also a good chance that the Americans would use the Burtonville to Heuem road to transport heavy equipment, troops and armor to the front at Saint Vith. "When is this counterattack expected?"

"Within twenty-four hours," replied the Pionier Unterscharführer.

There was no question of my intentions. I would hold the captured outpost for twenty-four hours. If the Americans used the Burtonville to Heuem road, I would turn their own artillery guns against them.

The 30mm howitzers were easy to operate and I ordered them pointed toward the road. Sighting them properly would be a matter of experimenting with a few rounds, but I would not punch holes in the forest for practice. I did not want to give the enemy the slightest reason to believe we had captured their position.

We waited all night and past dawn until we saw the first of 26 American trucks traveling east on the road. I told my gunners that I wanted the lead and rear vehicles attacked first to provide an effective roadblock. The artillery guns pivoted to the east and west until both spotters reported the targets were in their sights.

I lowered the field glasses and quietly said, *"Geben Sie ihnen Hölle."* And hell was exactly what we gave them.

The lead American vehicle exploded under the first shell but it took three or four before the rear truck was hit. I had successfully stranded the American convoy on the Burtonville to Heuem road as the incline and gulch on both sides made it impossible to move their vehicles.

"Schlagen Sie den zweiten Träger!"

My gunners struck the second lead vehicle and congested the road. All four artillery guns opened up from our position and methodically destroyed the motionless American trucks. Some went up in flames with a thunderous explosion when their freight of ammunition erupted. Some enemy soldiers leapt from other struck vehicles and ran about in flames like human candles. I ordered the destruction of the American convoy and each wagon and artillery piece being towed. We left nothing on that road to be salvaged. The disoriented enemy soldiers fled up the slope and down into the gulch. My gunners and I created a 130 meter line of smoking and flaming American wreckage.

"Put grenades in the muzzles of the guns and prepare to fall back to Saint Vith!" We had not been able to account for the American soldiers that fled into the gulch and I did not wish to wait for them to ascend at our position. My soldiers blew the barrels of the artillery guns and we descended the elevation and followed the Pionier Squad toward Saint Vith.

Late in the day we made contact at a minor forest crossroads with mixed units heading west from Salle. I was told that our forces had effectively surrounded Bastogne to the southeast and the town was a day or two away from German occupation.

My work against the Americans on the Burtonville to Heuem road quickly spread among the Panzer and Artillery Officers and I was being praised for completing a major objective against overwhelming odds. Elements of XII SS Panzer were heading north to link with I SS Panzer which had made such effective progress that it had outrun its resupply and refueling columns. Rommel had been known for this during the 1940 invasion of the Low Countries but this seemed alarming now. Our synthetic gasoline factories were operating well below quota and a critical objective for our Ardennes strategy was to capture American fuel and supply depots.

I boarded a XII SS Panzer halftrack and joined them on the journey to Kaiserbaracke where I SS Panzer was reported to have halted to await our arrival. The crossroads at Kaiserbaracke was filled with burning and smoking American armor and vehicles. A mixture of dead German and United States infantry littered the area with smashed machine gun nests and bunkers. A single abandoned Jagdpanzer IV was knocked out on the side of the road with its hatches open but that was the only sign of I SS Panzer.

The Tank Commander at the head of our column was standing in his hatch and shouting into his throat microphone. He shuffled several maps in his hands and looked around the immediate area with wild gestures. With nightfall approaching word was passed through our column that Priess had advanced I SS Panzer Army northwest beyond Pont and was now waiting for us at Lodomez.

We came upon I SS Panzer in the evening and our commanders argued with Priess to wait for the resupply and refueling trucks. Priess would hear none of this as he believed our consolidated forces were powerful enough to push through the forest east of Stavelot and take the American petrol dump south of Francorchamps. This would enable I SS Panzer and XII SS Panzer to push on to Cheneux to the west and allow Peiper the fuel he needed to capture the bridges at Trois Ponts to the southwest.

The only concern I had about the arguments was that the voices shouting on the radios were keeping me awake. The inside of the covered halftrack was warm enough for a comfortable sleep and there was nothing for me to say that would make any difference in the plans of the Armor Commanders. I realized that my original assignment of interrogating Allied Officers was the least of concerns among my immediate superiors. I was regarded as a Line Officer and my decision to strike the American column on the Burtonville to Heuem road had very positive effects on all German forces in the area. The 277th Grenadiers managed to occupy, secure and control the Burtonville to Heuem road because of my efforts and it had since become a critical right of way to combat fields in the west. My actions had also increased the respect for me held by fellow officers, superiors and the enlisted men as well. Reimers, Lichtermann and Kessler enjoyed telling the story to the other eight SS soldiers in the back of our halftrack. I believed they had earned the right to boast as they effectively operated the enemy artillery guns without any formal training or practice.

The debate was settled within hours and near midnight we moved out to the northeast to skirt Stavelot through the forest. An hour or so later our vehicles came under heavy fire at a three-way intersection east of Stavelot. American M4 Shermans and British Matilda and Crusader IV tanks slammed us with well coordinated mortar and artillery support. Our tanks and vehicles began falling back in such confusion that we were backing into each other, stalling, and hitting trees.

The Commander of XII SS Panzer was urging Priess to take advantage of the break in the weather and call for Luftwaffe bombing support. Priess refused because he feared a massive night bombing campaign could result in the destruction of the American fuel dump. We fell back to form positions approximately one kilometer east of the road where we were ordered out of the halftracks to entrench. The panzers moved half a kilometer behind the infantry positions and the artillery guns were arranged a half kilometer behind the tanks.

We established a defensive line from north to south and I was given command of my position and two nests to my immediate north and two to my immediate south. The bunkers were approximately 22 meters apart and each was armed with a PaK gun, MG42 or panzerfaust. Ten soldiers held each of these posts and the positions were nothing more than snow walls, bags packed with earth and snow, tree branches, and if we were fortunate, a few heavy logs that had been dragged into place. Priess was certain that the Allies would launch an assault against us since they believed we were on the run.

Our positions were located on the edge of a tree line with an 18 meters wide clearing in front of us. Reimers, Lichtermann and Kessler were with me along with two SS soldiers manning an MG42, their spotter, three Waffen SS riflemen and an SS Pionier radio operator. We had disguised and reinforced our bunker throughout the night but the expected attack did not come.

24 December 1944
East of Stavelot

At dawn we heard the sounds of heavy shooting to the north of our position. Word was passed over the radios that the Americans were probing our lines. Our artillery guns in the rear began firing at the northern coordinates and after several minutes there was silence. Moments later we were listening to casualty reports being called in. The American probes had been repelled, but more were expected up and down our lines.

My MG42 crew and spotter were very alert. The gunner leaned his cheek on rags placed against the stock and kept one open eye on the opposite tree line. His assistant gunner kept shifting the belt of ammunition to keep frost and ice from gathering between the rounds as the spotter stared forward through field glasses.

"Unwanted guests to the north," said the spotter. An American patrol was crouching in the snow across the open field. I used the radio to call the positions on my north flank.

"Enemy movement in our sector. Who has that line of fire?"

The north bunker closest to me responded. "We see them. They are in our zone."

The spotter was calm as he said, "I have more to the south and directly across from us."

I alerted my positions and reported the movement to our tanks and artillery gunners at the rear.

Priess announced, "All line units are to hold and engage. We need to draw out the enemy armor. I want them to think we are holding our positions with infantry and light artillery."

I looked at Unterscharführer Lichtermann and shrugged. The previous burst of heavy artillery certainly alerted the Americans to our strength, but Priess seemed to disregard this.

The guns in our bunkers opened up when the Americans came within approximately 13 meters. The MG42 gunner at my position did not give his fellow soldiers a chance to aim. He used his weapon proficiently and sawed the American patrol in front of us in half with bullets. Hell was released up and down the line and the American patrols sprinted into the safety of the western trees across the clearing.

An eerie mood fell over the forest as the voices of the wounded Americans called out for help. Moments later unarmed enemy medical personnel emerged from the opposite tree line with their hands in the air. I promptly used my radio and identified myself as an SS Hauptsturmführer and issued specific orders to be passed to all German line positions that they were not to fire upon the American medical personnel. I was greatly pleased that all SS and Wehrmacht units heeded my directives. The enemy doctors moved about the open field to treat and evacuate their wounded. They came back to drag their dead away.

Before noon the air filled with numerous thudding noises from across the clearing. At once we were under the most intense artillery bombardment I experienced throughout the war. The trees around us were splitting in half from the same blinding and disorienting shells fired against us at Saint Vith. The eleven of us pulled ourselves tightly against the cover of our bunker as this ruthless attack stormed down around us. It was one thunderous blast after another with trees falling and flying over our heads. Snow, stone and earth rocketed skyward on all sides as large flaming pieces of shrapnel sizzled through the air. The ground shook beneath us from this cold blooded and bestial assault and somewhere close by a soldier was shouting, *"Mütter! Gekommen holen mich!"*

I ordered my men to unfasten the chinstraps on their helmets as the appalling drumming of the salvo began to deaden our hearing. I closed my eyes and pressed the front rim of my helmet into the snow and laid there in a fetal position until the bombardment was over. With a ringing in my ears I could barely make out the same soldier repeating his panicked cry. "Mother! Come fetch me!"

My radio came alive with nothing but fatality and casualty reports. Heavy clouds of smoke overtook our bunker from the forest and through it we could see flames, charred tree trunks and deep black craters. The forest burned around us as I counted the men around me. We had all survived the barrage.

Seconds passed before the same grotesque thudding noises were heard again. More American shells ripped apart the forest around us as Rottenführer Reimers laid prone with a hand on his helmet to keep it on. "May God damn you bastards!" he screamed.

Our artillery opened but the crews fired blindly and had no effect on the intensity of the barrage we were under. My hearing was so badly damaged that I could feel the vibrations and only discern faint explosions and rumblings. There was nowhere to run to and nothing to shoot at. We were helplessly pinned against the cover of our bunker when a heavy two meters long log tumbled through the air and crushed two of my Waffen SS riflemen to death.

"You swines!" shouted Reimers. "You sons of whores!"

"Where are our Goddamned Panzers?" shouted Kessler. "Why are they not engaging the American guns?"

"They probably retreated to Berlin and left us out here to manage this shit on our own!" replied the MG42 gunner.

Panic had consumed all of us and it was unbearable to wait for our moment to die. I was certain it was going to happen. The Americans had so far fired behind our line positions but logically it was a matter of time before their spotters corrected and directly shelled us. When the second barrage broke, I was assured they were adjusting their aim on us for the next one.

I was staring at the arms and legs extending from beneath the broken log when the MG42 opened up. Guns fired up and down the line and I turned to see a full American infantry assault advancing toward our softened positions. I fired my StG44 in a sweeping motion but realized I would have to concentrate my aim in order to prevent an American crossing in my sector. The men in our bunkers did well to converge their weapons on their designated fields of fire and this allowed a well executed concentration of bullets toward any enemy who breached the midway point of the clearing.

American bazookas and light artillery shot at our bunkers from the opposite tree line and our spotters coordinated our rear artillery to neutralize the enemy positions. This did not prevent the bunker due south of me from going up in flames from an enemy bazooka round. One badly bleeding and burned survivor crawled to my position.

The Americans fell back and we reinforced our damaged bunkers with men and shattered trees. The enemy launched another well coordinated infantry assault against us at 1300 hours and one more at 1430 hours. Both ended as stalemates with extremely high numbers of casualties and fatalities for both armies.

At approximately 1600 hours the Americans hit us with the most powerful artillery barrage of the day that lasted for 30 minutes or more. Before the smoke cleared another enemy infantry assault had commenced across the clearing. We held off the attack for ten or fifteen minutes until M4 Shermans and Crusader IVs broke the perimeter. Priess wasted no time bringing his King Tigers and Stug IVs to the line and at once a full battle of men and machines was raging for control over the 18 meters wide clearing. Our King Tigers blew the M4 Shermans to pieces while our Stug IVs achieved great success against the Crusader tanks. Both armies lost armor on the field but the Allied attack had been weakened into retreat. Priess gave the order for all SS infantry to move forward to exploit the disorganization of the enemy and to beat them back across the north-to-south road that led to the fuel dump.

Anything was more logical than remaining behind our bunker to await another artillery barrage and with the Americans and British retreating before us, our morale soared and we assaulted with a barbaric roar of voices.

In those moments I believed the tides of war had changed. We ran alongside our tanks and halftracks with our weapons firing and a resounding battle cry. We crossed the clearing and entered the opposite thicket with our tanks cutting paths through the trees. We cut through the Americans like a hot knife through butter and we felt impervious to death and harm.

Our infantry chased the Americans west across the north-to-south road where we saw their light and medium artillery guns between farmhouses, sheds and wells in the field. The enemy crews fled as our Panzers and Stugs rolled over the field guns and smashed them flat in the snow. Our assault was halted when we reached the secondary American defensive lines which opened up on us with heavy machine guns. I took cover with Reimers, Lichtermann, and two Waffen SS soldiers behind a large pile of chopped cordwood. M4 Shermans and Crusader IVs engaged from the north and our Panzers and Stugs turned to face them.

While watching the tank battle develop I noticed Kessler's body lying flat and sprawled in the snow approximately five meters away from our cover. The Allied tanks fell back to the north in the direction of the fuel dump and as our Panzers and Stugs engaged the retreating enemy, American P-51 airplanes dropped from the sky to deliver lethal bombs on our tanks. King Tigers and Stugs had their turrets and hulls blown apart during the first sortie and as the planes departed, our Panzer Commanders seemed to be in a moment of confusion as none of the tanks were moving. A second squadron of P-51 airplanes descended from the sky and Priess gave the order for his tanks to retreat east into the safety of the trees. We felt abandoned as we watched our King Tigers and Stugs drive across the road and disappear into the forest.

We were trying to catch our breaths and I made visual contact with our units who hid behind roundhouses, wells, sheds, houses and stone retaining walls. The enemy had sighted the area perfectly with its heavy machine guns and moving in any direction would expose us to the deadly hail of lead.

"Why is our artillery not firing?" asked Reimers.

"We are too close to the American lines," I responded.

"What if the enemy tanks return? What will we do?" inquired one of the Waffen SS soldiers.

Mortar rounds dropped 20 meters in front of us and the enemy crews began walking the shells back toward our cover. I saw the remains of a stone retaining wall approximately 14 meters to our right and gave the order to move to it. We sprinted as the American machine guns chattered at us.

Reimers had taken a bullet in his chest and one through the elbow joint in his left arm. Both were bleeding badly but the one to his elbow caused so much damage that his forearm, wrist, and hand were hanging from tendons and flesh. Priess issued orders for the infantry to fall back east across the road. Those troops not directly exposed to enemy fire pulled out as ordered but my unit and several others were effectively pinned down by Allied guns. I knew that Reimers would die without medical treatment.

Christmas Eve 1944
Pinned down in a Belgian village

A light snow started falling a few minutes past 1800 hours. The mortar and artillery fire had ceased and silence blanketed the small village. Reimers drifted in and out of consciousness and in spite of the tourniquet we applied around his bicep, he was still losing blood. One of the Waffen SS soldiers, Sturmmann Erik Schreiner, peered around the shattered retaining wall and nearly had his head blown off from a burst of heavy machine gun fire. It was as if the Americans were saying: "We know you are there and we are not going to permit you to leave."

The other Waffen SS rifleman, Sturmmann Horst Puttkammer, sat low with his back against the wall. I pondered how he had been accepted into the Waffen SS as he appeared with a child's face and spoke with the saddened tones of an adolescent. "Happy Christmas," he mumbled.

Again I looked at the other stranded SS units and noticed some of them had injured comrades as well. I was kneeling over Reimers with one hand cradling his head and applying pressure to his chest wound with my other hand.

An American voice across the lines shouted out, "Hell's Kitchen!"

We did not understand these words or the phrases being mixed in, but the tone and inflection sounded like certain threats. This was shouted at us for an hour or more.

"What does that mean?" asked Lichtermann. "Hell's Kitchen?"

Puttkammer pulled a military phrase book from his rucksack and promptly researched the translation. "Hell's Kitchen," he said. "It is the devil's cooking room."

"What in hell does that mean?" asked Lichtermann again.

None of us knew and we began to devise our own meanings. Schreiner said, "Perhaps they intend to cook us alive with artillery."

"Perhaps they intend to slice us up like meat and vegetables," added Puttkammer.

Reimers laughed and coughed out blood. "You fools," he said. "Hell's Kitchen is a place in New York. It is notorious for gangsters. I believe those men are telling us where they hail from." He coughed out more blood and lost consciousness.

"What is happening?" asked Lichtermann.

I had no answer for him. I did not know why our artillery was not firing at points beyond our lines. I did not know why Priess had not overrun the enemy machine gun positions with his tanks and I could not say why our infantry had not launched a support assault.

Lichtermann was not asking about these things. I noticed my men were staring off through the snow to the north. I looked up to see an American jeep slowly driving southward just meters in front of our lines. A white flag of truce had been mounted in the rear next to its heavy machine gun.

"What is happening?" I asked. Lichtermann looked at me oddly for repeating his question. "Stow your weapons," I said.

The jeep stopped on the opposite side of the retaining wall less than two meters in front of us. The driver was a tired and dirty man who looked scarcely old enough to know what to do with the half of a cigar he was chewing on. He wore his helmet at a tilt and if I knew his language, I would have chastised him to wear it properly. The passenger was another child with his boots propped on the control console of the jeep and a story magazine with colorful cartoons resting on his knees. He turned the page and winked an eye at me while popping a bubble with his chewing gum.

The Americans in the back of the jeep appeared much older. The soldier on the far side stood at the ready to seize the triggers on the heavy mounted machine gun and the expression on his face indicated he would not hesitate do this if provoked. The remaining American had a red cross on his helmet and a matching armband. Each of them had the words "Hell's Kitchen" scrawled on their coats. The American doctor pointed at Reimers and in imperfect German asked, "Does he need assistance?"

I did not know their intentions and therefore I did not answer immediately.

"Do you wish me to examine him?" asked the American medic.

I did not have time to mentally debate the advantages and

disadvantages. I believed we were about to become Prisoners of War but I was willing to endure that ordeal if it meant Reimers would receive professional medical treatment. "Yes," I responded.

He exited the jeep and walked around the remains of the retaining wall with his medical bag.

"*Hey Kraut,*" said the driver. *"Haben du eine Flamme?"*

Lichtermann put his left hand out to his side and with his MP42 hanging at his waist, reached into his tunic and pulled out a packet of matches. He walked forward and lit the cigar stub for the American.

This was the American Army? Defacing their uniforms by writing on them? Not wearing their helmets properly and reading cartoons? Winking at their enemies and popping chewing gum bubbles? Who were these men? What were these men? Were they soldiers at all? Were they sent out here to confuse and confound us? If so, they succeeded.

The American doctor injected Reimers with morphine and other medicines to prevent infection. He walked to his jeep and retrieved boxes of bandages, food, and medicines. He packed off the wound on Reimers' chest and retied the tourniquet. He stepped back and looked at me.

"That is all I can do for him," he said with a thick Bavarian accent in his German. "You need to get him back to your doctors if he is to live." He spoke to his comrades in English and the three of them protested what I believed to be his request to permit us to fall back across the road. The Americans in the jeep became silent and acted as if they were pouting. Finally the driver waved his hand and mumbled something.

"Get him across the road and into the trees," said the American doctor. He smiled and said, "Happy Christmas you Kraut bastards. If you wish to give us a gift in return, we will gladly accept your surrender!"

I looked at him somberly and saw he was smiling. I offered him a clipped bow and a click of the heels that somehow seemed to embarrass him. My display of courtesy was almost my undoing as my actions revealed I was an officer. My overcoat had covered my collar tabs and suddenly the American in the back of the jeep became irate and was shouting.

The enemy doctor took a few paces to the rear as the American in the back of the jeep stared at me while pointing to his eyes and his collar. *"Show me! Show me!"* he screamed with all his breath. I knew he wished to see my tabs. He had not placed his hands on the triggers but continued to point to his eyes and collar indicating that he demanded to know my rank.

I reached up and pulled the collar of my greatcoat aside to reveal my Hauptsturmführer insignia. At once he seized the triggers and swung the heavy machine gun and pointed it at me while shouting, "Move away! Move away!"

The doctor translated that his comrade was ordering my enlisted men to move away from me so they were not killed when I was machine gunned.

The driver, passenger, and doctor pleaded with their comrade and pointed to the white flag of truce in the rear of the vehicle. The gunner shouted words I did not need translated. He screamed, *"Malmédy, you bastard! Malmédy!"*

I stood at attention and stared into the dark hole of the machine gun muzzle. I waited for the flash; the sound; whatever was to come from it. A voice was screaming inside my head to raise my StG44 or flee, but I would not leave Reimers lying there in the snow as no man had abandoned me in the snow at Stalingrad.

The Americans shouted at the gunner and despite the freezing temperatures I was perspiring and pondering how long I could remain at attention until the tension took my knees out from me. The American doctor walked toward the back of the jeep and gently pushed the barrel of the machine gun skyward. The gunner took off his helmet and violently slammed it against the breech of the weapon while shouting curses at me in English. The doctor pointed behind us and told us to get moving. We assisted Reimers and turned our backs on the Americans. I was surprised that we crossed the road and made it safely into the trees where SS soldiers assisted us in safety. I truly expected that angry American to gun us all down from behind. I realized then and never forgot that American soldiers may have been coarse and undisciplined, but by God they possessed a remarkable and respectable sense of honor.

I was further impressed by the American restraint and behavior when the SS came forward to carry Reimers to the field hospital. A Waffen SS Untersturmführer said he witnessed my standoff with the enemy and stated he was astonished they had not gunned me down. Having discovered the executed Prisoners of War at Malmédy, the Allies issued reprisal orders that all SS Officers were to be shot on sight.

"What is being done to support or extract our men in the farming village?" I inquired. The Untersturmführer directed me to Priess' field command headquarters.

It was little more than a ditch in the forest surrounded by King Tigers, Stugs and several Panther and Leopard tanks. I reported to Priess and he informed me that he was devising a diversionary attack on the farm village and concentrating his primary efforts on capturing the fuel dump to the north. I urged him to extract or at least support our men who had been cut off on the other side of the road. He assured me they would be protected.

At approximately 2000 hours I entered the makeshift field hospital and found Lichtermann standing by an empty fuel barrel that had been filled with hot coal. He was warming his hands when I asked, "What is the physical condition of Reimers?"

"The doctors can not tell me, Sir. They will not know until after they examine the wounds and perform surgery."

We stood outside the tents and asked each doctor that came out for a breath of cold night air. No one had news for us.

"Christmas Eve," said Lichtermann. There was only a moment of silence before one of the wounded soldiers inside the tent screamed out in agony.

Perhaps an hour passed when a surgeon exited the tent and asked if we were the men requesting information about the condition of Rottenführer Reimers. He told us that the surgeons had been forced to amputate his arm but this had not prevented sepsis from flowing through his veins. The bullet to his chest had destroyed one of his lungs and there was nothing they could do to save him. The surgeon said Reimers probably had a few hours and that he was in and out of consciousness. At least a high dosage of morphine had taken away his pain.

Reimers was on a stretcher and a bandage soaked with blood covered the stump of his arm. There were no tubes or bags of fluid being dripped into his body. There were none remaining in inventory to give. He laid there waiting to drown when his one good lung filled with blood.

Lichtermann read a few verses from Scripture while I silently begged God to cure Reimers. At 2400 hours his eyes fluttered open briefly as the first verse of Silent Night was sung by our troops outside. Reimers stayed with us until Christmas angels took his soul to God at 0330 hours.

Christmas Day 1944
South of the Allied fuel dump

A doctor awoke me and I noticed that Reimers' body had been taken away while I slept.

"Hauptsturmführer Schiller?"

"Yes?"

"You are wanted at the Command Headquarters, Sir."

It was after 0700 hours on Christmas Day when I made my way to the ditch. Most of the men stood by with packages of baked goods from home and the war seemed to have been suspended for the day. Priess told me that our cut off troops had spent the night on the other side of the road but he was planning to bring them back. He then said words that astonished me. "Der Führer has ordered you to Berlin."

"Der Führer?" I asked incredulously.

"Yes," replied Priess. "You had numerous recommendations for the Knight's Cross from SS and Wehrmacht Officers who were impressed with your actions at the Burtonville to Heuem road. Der Führer personally awards this medal and he has asked for you."

"By God! Berlin!" I thought. Any place an improvement over the frozen hellish wasteland of Belgium. I was immediately taken to a Kubelwagen and provided with an armored car escort. I was driven from Stavelot to Lodomez and then on to Pont. Passing the checkpoints, we arrived at Montenau Airfield before noon. From there I was flown to Germany where we landed at Sinzig near the A3 autobahn. The town of Rheinbach just 15 kilometers to the west was under Allied artillery bombardment. A Staff Mercedes sped northwest and I was awakened in the car when we reached the Eisenach Rail Station. I found a working telephone and informed Petra that I would be pulling into the Berlin Station at midnight. Blackout conditions were imposed over the station and I climbed aboard the dark train before it pulled out toward Erfurt and Leipzig before making its final run to Berlin.

I found her at the station and we embraced as if we had been married for ten years instead of two months. She looked at me strangely as I yet had the StG44 shouldered and several days' worth of soil and ash smeared on my flesh and uniform. I placed a telephone call to RSHA Headquarters and was connected to the offices at Tangermünde where I was told to report to der Führer Headquarters on 27 December.

Petra had been residing at the family home at Wernigerode as Berlin was being bombed by the Allies during day and night hours. It was but a few more hours by train until we arrived at the Salzgitter Station where her Father was waiting for us with his motorcar. He drove us to the family manor where I relaxed in a hot soothing bath while my uniform was laundered.

I awoke in a soft bed wearing silk pajamas on 26 December. Children laughed while they played outside in the snow and I looked out the window at the rooftops and buildings of Wernigerode. It had been a very long time since I saw a town that was intact and untouched by the war. I had not seen children laughing and playing since the Russian youths kicked their ball before us on the rail lines at Stalingrad. For those few moments there was no war and no one dying on frozen battlefields. It was a precious suspension of time and current events.

That morning I became the last member of this new family to learn Petra was pregnant with our child. She had written letters but the posts had never reached me. It was all very strange to me as I still felt that I barely knew this woman I called my wife.

The family then asked me questions about being awarded the Knight's Cross and I told them of my actions on the Burtonville to Heuem road. They found the tale to be one of great heroics and did not apprceciate the sacrifices made to accomplish the objective. They repeated propaganda about how we were winning the war and speaking of how exciting and glorious it must be for me to serve on the front lines. I said very little. There were no words that I could speak that would help them understand the horror and pain I had endured.

I arrived in Berlin on the following day and could not believe the countless city blocks that had been turned to rubble by Allied bombers. I entered the Headquarters of der Führer at 1000 hours where my StG44 was taken from me and locked in the armory. I was patted down and searched before this was repeated again at two more security checkpoints. I was escorted up a flight of stairs and into a large conference room where I joined a dozen or so members of the Luftwaffe, Kriegsmarine and Wehrmacht. I was the only SS officer present.

We enjoyed fresh coffee and pastries until a Staff General entered with a delegation of Junior Officers. He lined us up shoulder to shoulder in a row and ordered us to stand at attention.

"Der Führer will present each of you with the Knight's Cross," he said. "You are not to speak to him unless he first speaks to you. If der Führer asks you a question, you are to look him in the eyes and respond with a direct and concise answer."

He left the room and we stood there in silence and at attention waiting for der Führer to enter.

We must have waited an hour or more before General Alfred Jodl entered the room with an elderly man behind him. It took a few moments before I realized the old gentleman with gray hair, slumped posture, wrinkled skin and sunken eyes was Adolf Hitler. He wore a light brown suit with a white shirt and dark necktie and he held Jodl's arm as he shuffled forward. His left hand disappeared into the pocket of his tunic and the elbow and wrist were trembling.

Hitler, Jodl and another Staff General approached the Kriegsmarine men at my far left. The Staff General opened the medal case and Hitler removed the award and handed it to Jodl. Jodl then placed it around the man's neck while Hitler mumbled the words for the formal presentation. He spoke to no one and went from man to man presenting the awards.

At last they came to me and I looked at Adolf Hitler standing before me. He was a tiny man of frail stature without a remote resemblance to his portraits and images. The Staff General opened the case and stated my name. Hitler took the medal in his right hand and gave it to Jodl. As Jodl placed it around my neck, Hitler said, "SS Hauptsturmführer Rolf Schiller. In my name and in recognition for your service to the Reich and its people, I award you the Cross of the Knight."

I stood back with the award around my neck and saw Hitler staring at my collar tabs. "You have come from the west?" he asked.

"Ja Mein Führer!"

"And what news do you bring about the campaign in the west?"

Firmly I stated, "The enemy has made considerable progress, Mein Führer!"

His head turned to Jodl and he looked at him with a puzzled expression. "Have they?" he asked. He looked at me and inquired, "Have they really?" Hitler patted me twice on my left shoulder with his right hand before turning away. Jodl and the Staff General glared at me as if I should have provided a more favorable answer about German efforts. I tried to the best of my ability to give a neutral and diplomatic reply that informed Hitler we needed supplies, ammunition, reinforcements and firm battle plans.

When Hitler and his escorts left the room, another Staff General called out a few names and one of them was mine. He ordered us to report to the Quartermaster for promotions and new rank insignia. I was advanced to the rank of Sturmbannführer on the recommendations of Obergruppenführer Hermann Priess and Oberführer Sepp Dietrich. I was then given two hours before I was expected to be at the Potsdam Airfield where I was to be flown to Sinzig and then returned to the front lines in the Ardennes.

28 December 1944
Medendorf Belgium

On the day after Christmas Priess had launched his operation to capture the American fuel dump between Stavelot and Francorchamps. He had made progress toward his objective but the Allies blew up the dump when Priess came within sight of it. The Allied counterattack was successfully driving our forces back to our borders and I waited their arrival at Medendorf to the northwest of Saint Vith.

Very few tanks arrived with the infantry of I SS Panzer and XII SS Panzer. I was pleased to see Lichtermann in the crowd and noticed he had also been approved for promotion to Scharführer.

He took me aside and informed me of the truth of the situation. He said that the tanks of I SS Panzer and XII SS Panzer were running out of fuel and that Priess and Dietrich had received orders to blow up any stranded vehicle rather then let it fall into enemy hands to be converted, refueled and used against us. Lichtermann also told me that Priess had never crossed the road at the farming village to rescue our soldiers that had been cut off. He said that Priess referred to those men as an "unfortunate but necessary sacrifice."

We stood there for several minutes watching our armies regroup before Schreiner and Puttkammer joined us. "So tell us," said Lichtermann. "What is he like? You are the envy of I SS Panzer and XII SS Panzer!"

I knew he was referring to my experience of meeting Hitler. Puttkammer and Schreiner were also eager to know. I told them that der Führer was well informed, fit and capable of our situation, and that his Staff Generals and OKH and OKW were doing everything possible to secure a complete victory. I was ashamed of myself for lying to them but I believed they would be inclined to surrender or make a suicidal run into a wall of machine gun fire if they knew Hitler was feeble and decrepit. Morale was very important and now that we were retreating and destroying our own vehicles, it was more imperative than ever.

Priess and Dietrich called several meetings while the tanks were being repaired and outfitted. We were heading back to the Stavelot area with the objective of capturing another Allied fuel dump somewhere near Baugnez. It had been spotted by our Luftwaffe pilots but its exact location had not been charted. Priess ended one of the meetings by telling us there had been a noticeable shift in the methods of warfare being employed. No one was certain if this was a direct cause of Peiper's decisions at Malmédy, but the Allies had adopted the policy of shooting all SS they captured. Whereas days ago they contained this policy as exclusive treatment for SS Officers, it was said that it now applied to enlisted men as well.

Priess also said that very reliable reports had been passed through channels detailing the execution of Wehrmacht soldiers and Luftwaffe pilots. There was a legitimate and neutral understanding between all armies in the Ardennes pocket that no military was capable of processing Prisoners of War. The Commanders of each army acknowledged that we were deep in a forest gap with roads and lines that were constantly shifting. It was therefore mostly impossible for the Allies and the Reich to escort prisoners to safe holding facilities.

The orders were clear whether or not they were formal. To prevent captured Allied soldiers from being returned to military circulation, they were to be shot. Officers and soldiers of the Reich were not excluded. The Allies had orders to shoot us if we were captured.

This is not to say that all prisoners were executed from 28 December to the end of the Ardennes Campaign. Certain circumstances existed wherein prisoners could in fact be transported to holding facilities. However, to do this, there had to be available transportation, a ready number of guards to serve as escorts, an allotment of fuel for the purpose, and excess rations. These instances were rare as all armies were short of these critical supplies.

The capture of the fuel dump at Baugnez was acknowledged as the final noble efforts on behalf of I SS Panzer and XII SS Panzer. We were to secure our objective or die in the process. Hitler had once again denied all requests for combat units to retreat or fall back for regrouping and reoutfitting. None of our troops had come close to Antwerp which was our overall objective for the Ardennes Campaign. We needed to secure the Belgian port city to cut off Allied supplies and establish a base of operations in the west from which we could dictate offensives against Holland, France, England, and the interior of Belgium.

Late in the evening I was ordered to consolidate two Waffen SS squads into one and I took command of 24 soldiers including Lichtermann, Schreiner and Puttkammer. We had a fair amount of ammunition, full canteens and enough food. Our vehicles were filled with petrol from the last drops of our forward reserves. The column rumbled out of Medendorf on its advance to Baugnez.

CHAPTER TWENTY-FOUR
CONSIGNED TO HELL
29 DECEMBER 1944 7 JANUARY 1945

T rees were burning and fresh shell craters marked the road north of Ambléve. We saw numerous dead draught horses lying alongside our shattered supply wagons. I rode in the back of an open Blitz Opel and was alerted by Lichtermann to look toward the front of our column. Soldiers were removing their helmets and gathering against the right rails of the trucks. They were standing and squeezing between their comrades to see something in the distance. When we approached I also removed my helmet and looked at the spectacle. Four of our ambulances were motionless on the shoulder of the road and each had its rear doors open. Every man inside of them had been shot to death on his stretcher. The enemy bullets had punched holes through the inside compartments and blown out the glass windscreens. The drivers, doctors and crews were slumped over on the ground in front of the lead ambulance. They had been made to kneel before they were executed. Farther down the road were the bodies of several British soldiers lying next to their weapons. At least they had the simple honor of dying in combat.

We were successfully ambushed on the road south of Hédomont. Our lead Panther tank was unscathed in the attack but the King Tiger behind it lost its treads before several heavy rounds turned it into an inferno. Rounds exploded behind us in the popular tactic of destroying the lead and rear vehicles to create a roadblock. I had brought this misfortune upon the Americans and sighted each vehicle in the column. I gave the orders for my squad to abandon the Blitz Opels and take cover in the thick forest to the south. We climbed up a small embankment and put approximately 23 meters of distance between ourselves and the road. The remainder of the SS infantry had abandoned their vehicles and was taking cover around us.

A Waffen SS Obersturmführer was on his knees in the snow and pulling maps from tubes and cases. His radio operator was crouched next to him and went prone when shells landed close by.

"The shelling is coming north from Hédomont," I shouted.

"How can you be certain?" he called back in panic.

I recalled the maps I had studied at the outset of the offensive. "Hédomont is located on a 495 meters elevation! They are sighting us from the high ground!"

He looked as if he was about to shout something back to me when he and the radio operator were engulfed in an explosion that brought a geyser of earth and snow. We pulled back another 15 or 20 meters and lost sight of the activity on the road. The SS infantry was gathering and every soldier was talking at once. The radio operators were trying to quiet us as they had enough trouble hearing the transmissions over the explosions.

We made our way to the west until we were well in front of the column and worked our way back toward the road. We were outside the kill box and able to get close enough to see that our King Tigers, Leopards and Panthers had swung their turrets northward and were giving back as great as they were getting. The Stug IVs were helpless as they did not have moveable turrets. Some valiant SS soldiers managed to unhitch several field guns and manually position them on the roads to fire north at Hédemont.

Most of our trucks and several of our tanks were in flames but as it was impossible to travel forward or in reverse, Priess and Dietrich remained in their tanks and shot it out with enemy artillery crews half a kilometer away.

Several SS soldiers ran to the front of the column carrying large tripods and six MG42s. They promptly erected the weapons and stood behind them with the guns pointed skyward over the road. The barrage from Hédemont slowly ended and it became a race to clear the wreckage from the road before Allied planes appeared to strafe and bomb our crippled column.

Our prime movers and tanks were banging the wrecks off the road but the thick trees on either side made this very difficult. Our engineers set demolitions in the woods and blew gaps wide enough to shove the wreckage through. While clearing the road we heard the drone of propellers and those of us not able to defend against this took cover in the forest.

American P-47s and P-51s flew in from the east and our MG42s and light anti aircraft guns surprised them enough to change their flight patterns. The enemy planes only fired short bursts from their machine guns before pulling up and flying off toward Hédomont. They came back from the west and our MG42s at the front of our column managed to strike one of the aircraft. We deduced the pilot was killed outright as the plane instantly dipped its nose and slammed into the trees to the north. The other pilots managed to release a few bombs that struck wide south of the column but exploded where our infantry was taking cover in the forest.

Shouts for doctors came from the flaming areas and mixed with the ungodly screams of our wounded. More anti aircraft guns were being set into place along the road while I kept my squad alert and in position. The planes approached again from the south and it became a hellish sequence of guessing where they would shoot or drop their bombs. From the approach of the planes I was forced to move my squad to different locations to avoid the attacks. It was much like a very cruel adult game of seek and find.

Our vehicle commanders courageously worked under this air assault and when the road was almost unobstructed, another artillery barrage rained down upon us from Hédomont. The airplanes appeared again and dropped several bombs squarely on our lead Panther. The tank exploded in a massive fireball and became a 44 ton immoveable roadblock.

The radios crackled with Priess' voice. "SS Squads III to XV. Designated units are to proceed north to Hédomont and neutralize the enemy artillery."

Damn it. I was in command of Squad IV. I was shaking my head from side to side because I certainly did not want to do this. 13 Squads containing 312 SS soldiers sprinted north across the road and into the dense forest. The snow was up to our knees and each step required great physical stamina. The Line Officers began communicating on the radios and we decided to meet in the center to discuss a tactical plan.

I was the senior ranking officer and two Untersturmführers, one Obersturmführer and a Hauptsturmführer were very eager to put the plans into my hands. The 495 meters elevation was a very gradual ascent so there would be no direct climbing to reach Hédomont. We studied the maps while our soldiers caught their breaths and tank and artillery shells flew back and forth above our heads.

"What do you suggest, Major?" asked the Captain.

This was not similar to the Russian mortar position in the Ukraine or the American artillery outpost on the Burtonville to Heuem road. I was facing the experience of knocking out enemy artillery guns in an occupied town.

"The barrage has not been very heavy," said the Senior Lieutenant. "I would estimate 15 field guns. Perhaps 20."

I nodded as if I thought the same thing. Truthfully, I had no idea. "I suggest we surround the town and enter simultaneously."

"Begging your pardon, Major," said one of the Junior Lieutenants, "But are we not to expect fortified enemy bunkers and machine gun positions as defense? What is the radius of this town? Do you not think this is a dangerous idea? There are just more than 300 of us, Sir. Are we to spread ourselves thin?"

The Captain was looking at me suspiciously and I deferred the planning to his expertise. It was humiliating to concede to his experience as I was the officer of senior rank, but I would not allow my novice combat tactics to add up in fatalities.

Waffen SS Hauptsturmführer Knecht suggested a full frontal assault on the town from its northern border. He reasoned the artillery guns were pointed south at the road and if we approached by stealth, the enemy would not have adequate time to pivot the guns to the rear to counter our assault. We skirted the town and worked our way around it until we were in position. It was late in the afternoon and though we could see the village, we could only hear the field guns inside it.

Hédomont
The commencement of dishonor

We charged the town across an open frozen field and were only challenged by light rifle fire. The Belgian citizens were slamming and locking their doors and pulling down their shades as if we would not know they were there. It did not take long before the enemy spotters relayed the news of our penetration and we heard the rumbling motors of Allied tanks. My Squad moved out under an archway and followed a narrow curving cobblestone alley through a row of houses. We came around a corner into a small plaza and were surprised to see nine British soldiers sitting on the edge of a fountain pulling on their boots and drinking from their canteens.

They immediately threw their weapons to the ground and raised their hands while shouting as my Squad of 24 men screamed back at them. I was certain the noise would attract more Allied soldiers to the area and before I could gain control of the situation, several of my men emptied cartridges from their MP42s into the defenseless British soldiers. I looked for a direction to lead my men out of the plaza as rifles and machine guns burst through the windows around us and opened fire. We returned bullets and ran into an opposite alley as enemy voices grew louder.

We paused at an intersection blocked by a Crusader IV tank. We surveyed the area around us and it seemed the tank was the sole guardian of the crossing. Schreiner broke from our perimeter, sprinted across the street and climbed onto the back of the British tank. He primed a grenade and pulled at its main hatch but it was locked from inside. He continued to pull as if his strength would force it open while my men and I screamed at him to get rid of the grenade. It exploded in his hand and sent his limbs scattering.

There was no panzerfaust in my Squad and grenades would only dent the outside of a Crusader IV. My men began firing down the alley behind us as the British had followed our exit from the plaza. During the gun battle the crew of the Crusader IV became aware of our presence and spun its turret. Its coaxial machine gun sprayed us from behind as the British soldiers fired at us from our front. German blood was spraying the walls and windows of the buildings around us and I led the Squad into the intersection as the Crusader IV discharged a round from its cannon. The British tank gunner succeeded in killing his own comrades who had been in front of us. We ran within centimeters of the tank and briefly assembled the 17 surviving members of the squad in a quiet alley. German voices and gunfire were approaching from another street and we successfully linked with Squads IX and XIII.

There were perhaps 60 of us at combined strength and Squad IX used its panzerfaust at close range against the Crusader IV. The weapon did nothing but perhaps ring the ears of the crew inside the tank.

"Son of God," mumbled the Untersturmführer of Squad XIII. We fell back as the tank spun its turret but it did not fire as there was no clear shot for its gunner.

"He can not see us," said the Junior Lieutenant. Personally, I believed he could have put a round through the buildings and killed half our men. My subordinate explained why this did not happen.

"The British have strict orders not to fire unless they have us sighted. It is some foolish rule about not destroying private homes and property. Such things are only for the minds of the British, do you not agree, Sir?"

The British would not risk the destruction of private homes and property and the Americans were reading cartoon books. How were they having such success against us in this Goddamned war?

A voice came over each radio. "The field guns have been abandoned and Squads V and VII are preparing to detonate them." We heard the explosions and assembled at points close to the operation. 17 British artillery guns had been converted to scrap metal.

We took cover and traded shots with the British while the Hauptsturmführer used a radio to contact the column. He reported the guns destroyed and moderate enemy contact in the town. Priess abandoned us the same as he had forsaken our troops at Stavelot. He announced that he was continuing his advance on Baugnez and we were to link with him there.

Darkness was falling and we fortified a Belgian home as our night post. Now and then a Crusader IV or Matilda tank rolled by but the British were not eager to search for us. There was great restraint shown by both armies that night and we attributed this to the probability that we were both operating with a limited number of troops. No one was clear about the size and strength of the other, though it was obvious that we did not have tanks or vehicles in the town.

I sat in the kitchen with Hauptsturmführer Knecht and Obersturmführer Kellermann where we attempted to devise a successful plan for extraction. Now and then bursts of gunfire and grenades sounded from outside.

"They can easily reinforce during the night," said Kellermann. "We have no surrounding support troops to prevent this."

"I counted four Matildas and three Crusader IVs," said Knecht. "And, that is only what I saw. I do not know how many more tanks they have here." He thought for a moment while staring at the table. "Any withdrawal into the wooded areas around here is going to be a confrontation with those tanks."

"And the British are probably setting medium and heavy machine guns at the outskirts of the perimeters," said Kellermann.

"Of course they are," agreed Knecht. "What else would they do to contain us?"

"The important matter," said Kellermann, "is that the armored column was freed to advance on Baugnez. How did Priess put it?" He thought for a moment and stated, "We are unfortunate but necessary sacrifices."

Each of us looked at the table and pondered these words. "Hostages," I said. Kellermann and Knecht slowly raised their heads and looked at me curiously.

"Hostages," I repeated. "There are Belgian civilians in this town. I propose we capture women and children and use their lives to negotiate a safe withdrawal from Hédomont."

"Are you mad, Sturmbannführer?" asked Kellermann.

"No," responded Knecht. "The Major is not mad. That seems a sound idea. If the British will not fire upon Belgian homes and businesses, they certainly will not allow the civilian population to die."

"That is the most dishonorable plan I have heard," declared Kellermann.

"What does honor have to do with it?" asked Knecht. "If it means the difference between pushing the British and Americans into the sea or surrendering to them, I agree with the Major. I have not fought for five years to have it end this way."

"If it is the direct order of the Major then so shall I participate loyally," stated Kellermann.

"It is my direct order."

We assembled our Squads and I personally issued the orders. Most of the men were apprehensive about this plan but none of them wished to enter British captivity. They struck out into the darkness like common kidnappers and throughout the night they returned with Belgian hostages.

At dawn I counted 4 civilian men, 7 women and 9 children, and we marched them out of the house at gunpoint. Knecht, Kellermann and I glanced at the surrounding buildings while waiting for enemy sniper fire to eliminate us. We assembled the Belgians in a group and surrounded them while the remaining 200 or so SS soldiers joined us. Five British soldiers appeared at the end of the street with their hands in the air. They studied the situation and walked out of sight.

"It appears we are about to negotiate," said Knecht.

He was correct. Moments later a British Matilda tank crept down the road with its cannon facing in the opposite direction and a white flag of truce extending from the drivers' hatch. It stopped 10 meters from us and for a reason I can not explain, we were awestruck as its main turret hatch opened.

A gray haired British Commander emerged wearing a bright red beret. He exited and climbed off the tank where four more unarmed British soldiers joined him in front of the vehicle. They walked toward us as Knecht, Kellermann and I went to meet them.

In perfect and precise German the British Tank Commander inquired, "Who is the senior officer here?"

I stepped forward and stared at this man who was old enough to be my father. His weathered face and several scars indicated years of competent military service. We exchanged ranks and I learned he was a Colonel.

"Are you offering terms?" he asked.

I realized the potential for greater gains beyond our simple extraction from the area. "I will accept the surrender of all British forces in Hédomont."

Arrogantly the Colonel said, "I refuse." He intentionally went silent to force me to respond.

"You will have the deaths of twenty Belgian civilians on your hands if you do not comply."

"No," he stated gruffly. "You will have twenty civilian deaths on your hands, boy." His age and experience intimidated me and I tried to remain as firm and direct as possible. Before I could speak he continued. "Your column advanced to the west. You have no vehicles in this area. If I order my soldiers to lay down their weapons, what assurance do I have you will not shoot us?"

There was no sound answer to his question. I did not have any intentions of shooting the British prisoners but there existed the problem of what to do with them if they indeed surrendered.

He cocked his head and said, "My snipers have reported to me that your soldiers refused quarter to my troops who indicated surrender to you." He studied my face and said, "I will see you hanged for that, Major."

I reached into my experience with partisans and enemies of the Reich. Nodding at the Colonel, I turned to Knecht and stated, "Prepare to shoot the Belgians."

This disturbed him into considering alternate terms. I looked at him and used my own arrogant tone while stating, "I would certainly not shoot you, Colonel. I will much more enjoy the thoughts of the retribution your own army brings against you for allowing these civilians to die when you could have prevented it."

"If you shoot those civilians, Major, every one of us will die here today," he said.

"Perhaps," I replied. "But you have the ability to prevent that."

He raised his left hand and cautiously opened his holster. The Colonel slowly removed his sidearm and presented it to me by the handle. "I surrender the King's 9th Armored Infantry to you, Major."

I thought of every horrible memory to prevent a novice smile from forming on my lips. Knecht ordered the Colonel to drive all tanks and British vehicles into the center of Hédomont and for all enemy soldiers to deposit their weapons, ammunition and grenades in front of the hospital building. All British soldiers and officers were then to assemble in a fenced in field on the western side of the town.

When this was completed I allowed the British to begin marching off to the west. I contacted I SS Panzer by radio and informed them of the captured British vehicles. He ordered the fuel tanks to be siphoned while we waited for elements of the 277th Grenadiers to arrive at Hédomont to relieve us.

Once the British had gone, the SS began looting the houses and abusing the civilian population. Several citizens were shot and beaten to death for no other reason than my men had found bottles of spirits and were releasing bestial frustration. I saw such conduct on the Eastern Front and from becoming insensitive to it there; I permitted it to happen at Hédomont.

When the 277th Grenadiers arrived they immediately joined the chaotic surge of abuse. We departed from the town late on 31 December and left behind dozens of dead Belgian civilians and torched houses. The Junior Officers did not complain to me about the abhorrent behavior of the men, nor did they issue orders to prevent it. However, when we returned to the main road heading toward Baugnez, they began questioning the matter of accountability for such actions.

On the morning of 2 January 1945 we met elements from XII SS Panzer coming in the opposite direction from Baugnez. We were informed that the Allies had again blown their fuel dump as Priess got close to capturing it. Most of our tanks and trucks had run out of fuel and had been blown up on Priess' orders. XII SS Panzer was eager to secure the fuel we had siphoned from the British vehicles at Hédomont and wasted no time connecting hoses from the trucks of the 277th to their tanks. I SS Panzer arrived in the midst of this and Priess was irate that the fuel was not being dispensed to his tanks. He waved his pistol around and cursed at every soldier and officer near him. Our orders were to fall back to Honsfeld and hold the rail lines east of the town. It was one of the last lines left intact that was capable of delivering supplies for our efforts.

The Allied counteroffensive gained strength each day. With seemingly limitless supplies of fuel, ammunition, vehicles and men, they pushed us east from Charneux, Francorchamps, Stavelot, Recht and Crombach. The Allied front was too wide for us to contain or counter and this became closer to impossible as we intentionally destroyed more of our stranded tanks each day. It was a pitiful irony that we possessed superior tanks and vehicles capable of halting the enemy advance but could not use them because the fuel tanks were dry.

We entered Honsfeld on 4 January and used the day to establish lines of fire and fortify our positions. We secured the rail line to the east and Priess dispatched an emergency request to Berlin for fuel. In the meantime we pointed our stranded tanks to the north, west, and south of the town, and reinforced their positions with debris and stones. The turrets could spin, but our tanks had been reduced to nothing more than stationary heavy assault guns.

On the morning of 5 January we received Luftwaffe reconnaissance reports stating the British were moving toward Honsfeld from their positions northeast at Waimes. The Americans were moving on us from the southeast at Ambléve. It was suspected that these two Allied forces would converge and hit Honsfeld to break our hold on the town. Our orders were precise. We were to take no prisoners.

Late in the day a supply train delivered 758 liters of gasoline, ammunition, food, bandages and medicine. It also delivered several crates of feldpost and within my mail was the December 1944 letter from Petra announcing her pregnancy. The mail raised morale for most of us as we waited for seemingly endless hours in our bunkers.

On 6 January we learned the outcome of Operation Bodenplatte. Our Luftwaffe launched raids on Allied airfields throughout Belgium in an attempt to destroy enemy air superiority. It had resulted in disaster for us and we had lost over 250 planes while destroying just over 100 Allied aircraft. With the shortage of fuel and pilots, our Luftwaffe had effectively been removed from the war.

That evening British and American artillery guns fired at Honsfeld. Allied patrols tried to breach our perimeters but with fuel in our tanks we were able to prevent enemy penetration. Throughout the night shells would fall on our positions without any adherence to the British policy of not destroying Belgian homes and businesses. Allied patrols continued to engage us at close range but at 0430 hours it had become a stalemate.

At approximately 0830 hours on 7 January 1945 we received orders from der Führer. In recognition of the Allied advance and the critical shortages of fuel and supplies, most Wehrmacht and all SS Divisions were directed to pull out of the Ardennes and return to Germany to be reoutfitted, resupplied, repaired and made available for the final defense of the Fatherland.

We all shared the feeling that we failed at accomplishing our objectives. We had firm opportunities to drive the Allies west into the sea but we had not been able to do it. Limited fuel and supplies were disgusting excuses that we refused to consider. We were the elite Waffen SS and we had been decisively beaten by American gangsters from the likes of Hell's Kitchen, and pompous arrogant Englishmen. While returning to Germany in the back of trucks we knew that the war was now coming not only to us, but to our families as well. We could not fail again. It was now a time to protect every person, thing and idea that was dear to us. There was not a dry eye among us.

The trucks took us through Holland and we crossed the German border west of Duisburg before halting at Essen on the morning of 9 January 1945. On the following day SS Supply began a series of deliveries to outfit and repair our tanks. Over the following weeks we collected reports about Allied combat troops smashing through our country and bombing our industrial cities. German refugees from the small towns and villages sought shelter at Essen and we were ordered to send them to central and western Germany. On 2 February 1945 our Panzer Divisions were cleared to reenter service.

CHAPTER TWENTY-FIVE
THE GERMAN APOCALYPSE
THE RUHR VALLEY, FEBRUARY 1945

Our Division was appended to Army Group B under the command of Field Marshal Walther Model. Hitler had finally approved the activation of the Volksstürm and we watched companies of these citizen soldiers marching by for drills and prompt instruction. The units were nothing more than elderly men wearing old helmets from the Great War and others wore the spiked pickelhaube. They tried to dress as soldiers but some of them wore postal and fire brigade uniforms with hopes it would make them appear militaristic. Others wore patched gray wool coats, leather motorcycle helmets and fishing boots. These old gentlemen looked so pathetic and ridiculous that it brought me to the edge of weeping.

Boys from the *Hitlerjugend* had come to Essen and these children between the ages of 14 and 17 looked greatly confused and frightened. They were given basic supplies and some of them were barely taller than the rifles they received.

On 8 February Model released elements of Army Group B to drive southwest and assist with the fighting at Düren. I remained with Headquarters Group B and interrogated Allied prisoners regarding troop movements, supply lines, headquarters locations, and numbers of troops, field guns and armor.

During the afternoon of 12 February American troops launched an attack against Rörmond to the west and Model dispatched the last SS elements he was willing to part with to assist in the battle.

The Volksstürm had been sent into battle alongside the Wehrmacht and SS, and each day we listened to radio broadcasts from Göbbels telling us that we were shifting the tides of victory and that der Führer was preparing our ultimate victory celebration.

None of the officers spoke much about this. We were resigned to defending the Fatherland and were aware the hour was approaching. Each day I desperately tried to reach RSHA Headquarters Berlin by telephone but the communication lines were constantly being cut and destroyed by Allied bombers.

On or about 14 February I managed to contact Fritz Stammler at our offices in Uelzen. He was very surprised to hear my voice and stated it was imperative that we speak. He said the telephone was not a secure means and urged me to meet him at Minden on the following day. I explained my present situation and my duty attachment to Army Group B and he promised a messenger would deliver the necessary authorization.

We were just learning about the bombing at Dresden. It was estimated at that time that 30,000 or more civilians had perished from the cowardly Allied dropping of incendiary devices. Those who had relatives in the city were insane with worry and there was nothing any officer could do to keep these men away from the telephones. The bombing of this city went on for two days with no Luftwaffe to oppose it.

True to Stammler's promise, the messenger arrived with my orders and Field Marshal Model cleared me to depart. The train pulled into the Minden Station where Fritz was waiting for me in a Mercedes. He did not engage the motor of the vehicle and we sat there away from other ears that may hear.

"The Soviets took Auschwitz," he said. "They know all about it. They know what happened there and what we did."

"What does Eichmann say about this?"

"No one has seen Eichmann since January. It is said he visits the offices at Stendal and Tangermünde, but none of us at IVb4 have seen him. We have used the past three weeks to burn documents."

"What about Höss?" I asked.

"The last report on him stated that he was seeing to matters at Dachau. Rolf, our department is destroying every scrap of paper and reference to the Jewish solution."

"Have you seen anything with my name on it? Or my reference numbers?"

"I destroyed everything with my name, yours, Novak's and Dannecker's, but some of the documents from our department in Berlin were transported to the offices at Uelzen, Tangermünde and Stendal."

"We operated within the guidelines of the law," I assured him.

"The Soviets shot the SS garrison at Auschwitz. They know about the Russian Prisoners of War killed there."

"There was no signed code of conducts agreed upon between the Reich and the Soviet Union."

Fritz stared out the window of the car. "It is rumored that some of our superior officers have simply disappeared."

"What does that mean exactly?"

"It means," said Fritz with a tone of anger, "that they may be getting out while they can. I know what is being said in our Ministry of Propaganda but I also know the truth. Churchill and Stalin are demanding the blood of every member of the SS."

"Is there a way I can get off the line at Essen and be transferred back to RSHA Headquarters?"

"Why would you want to do that, Rolf? Have you not listened to a single thing I have just told you? No one wants to be at Headquarters at this moment!"

There were a few minutes of silence as a heavy rain began to drum on the roof of the car. "Have you heard from Petra?" he asked.

"Months old feldposts, that is all."

"Her family left Wernigerode in January because of the bombings. They are safe in Göppingen."

"Göoppingen is in the south," I said. "How safe can they be?"

Fritz looked at me and nodded as if I finally understood. "How safe are any of us, Rolf?"

I returned to Army Group B Headquarters at Essen and monitored the reports of our troops holding back the Allies in the west. The radio broadcasts were still rich with Göbbels preaching about victory, loyalty to der Führer and rhetoric I had grown weary of. Each day I went about my assignment of interrogating prisoners before sending them to the holding facilities at Willingen and Siegen. It was all very peculiar as I walked about the Headquarters area of Army Group B as if performing some job for the civil service. I had survived Stalingrad and the Ardennes Campaign and now I was going about my duties with set and regular hours.

During the first days of March we could hear Allied shelling to the south and west. More civilian refugees flooded Essen and we did our best to relocate them in Central Germany. A battle was raging far off to the east in our very last effort to capture the oil fields in Hungary.

On 7 March we received news that the Allies had established a bridgehead at Remagen and orders were given to relocate Army Group B Headquarters to Bochum. The next five days were a chaotic outbreak of activity to move all equipment, vehicles and personnel to the new location.

Late in the day on 12 March we received word that our town of Emmerich was under heavy Allied artillery bombardment. In spite of this, our forces drove the Americans out of Honnef and Hönningen and pushed them back to their bridgehead at Remagen. Rumors were abounding that the citizens of small German towns were hanging white bed linens from their windows to surrender to the Americans! How can this be? We have been fighting, bleeding and dying for our Germany! Do not give our towns to the enemy!

On the following day radio broadcasts supported the rumors. It was announced that any town suspected of intentions to welcome the enemy will be razed and its citizens shot as traitors. This was encouraging news. We did not fight all these years to face our own people as an enemy.

So much hinged on the Remagen bridgehead and our forces were suffering heavy casualties but inflicting them as well. Intelligence reports stated that the Americans considered abandoning the objective but the British urged them to hold it to prevent giving us time to regroup with a counterattack. Field Marshal Model continued to commit troops to the fight and then spent the next several hours cursing that it weakened his forces in the Ruhr. Göbbels finally stumbled over his own rhetoric by announcing with one breath that der Führer expects complete victory and in a second breath he announced preparations for the defense of Berlin. For the next few weeks the area around the Ruhr continued to decrease. The Americans, British and Canadians broke out from the bridgehead and advanced virtually unopposed on our headquarters. Göbbels continued to preach about victory and success that he said would result from an abundance of fuel and supplies. However, I saw the citizens that straggled into

Bochum suffering from starvation and disease. As the area around the Ruhr collapsed I saw the injured Wehrmacht, SS, and Luftwaffe, old men, boys and civilians brought into our headquarters zone for treatment. None of this had the appearance of victory.

On 29 March Field Marshal Walther Model called a meeting of all officers. He told us the truth of our present situation. The Allies, he said, were moving to encircle the Ruhr Valley. Hitler had forbidden retreat and it was here during the next few days that the outcome of the war would be decided for each and every one of us.

1 April 1944

The Ruhr was effectively surrounded by the Allies and Field Marshal Model countered this by placing his tanks and field guns facing outward in a large circle. Late in the afternoon the Americans engaged with M4 Shermans and infantry from the north and west.

I had been placed in command of a *Schlacht Gruppe* of 40 SS troops heavily armed with machine guns, PaKs and panzerfausts. We were ordered to concentrate our fire on all enemy units that attempted to cross a small canal bridge to the southwest of Bochum. I was grateful to have Lichtermann and Puttkammer with me.

For the first two days the fighting did not take place in our sector but on 3 April a column of American infantry moved toward the bridge. Our MG42s repelled them but we were answered by enemy howitzers and bazookas. We were firmly entrenched behind an earthen wall in a series of trenches. This provided adequate cover and allowed us to sight the canal bridge in spite of the American artillery rounds.

The enemy attempted several more crossings that day but retreated each time when confronted by the three MG42s aimed at the position.

The problem with the canal was that it was man made and only had a gradual earthen bank on its south side. The bank on the north was a constructed wall that dropped 3 and a half meters straight down to the water. If the enemy was to attempt a raft crossing, we would not know about it until they climbed over the canal wall.

We laid against the soil throughout the night as the sounds of combat to the north and west were fierce. Searchlights swept the battlefield and now and then the enemy launched illumination flares to probe our positions. Near dawn there was a series of explosions to the east.

Later that morning two M4 Shermans pulled up on the southeast bank of the canal and fired at our position from a distance of 36 and a half meters. The tank shells blew the earth apart around us and we were forced to move our MG42s farther down the line and reestablish an offensive position. I reported this situation to Field Marshal Model's Command Post and he instantly delivered two Panther tanks behind our trench line. Tank shells flew over our heads in both directions and the Panthers each took a harmless hit until the M4 Shermans were destroyed. One of the Panthers fell back to reinforce our soldiers at the north and the other stayed in place for support. We felt impervious with that marvelous behemoth over our shoulders.

We repelled a few more Allied attempts to cross the canal bridge but just before evening, a combined attack of American and British soldiers poured toward the canal. I ordered the MG42s to remain concentrated on the bridge while panzerfausts and our PaK gun fired at the troops on the other side. The Panther released a few shells but the enemy was determined to cross. What they did not know was that I was determined to keep them back.

When it was over, one of the barrels had melted on an MG42 and the opposite side of the canal was in flames. Through my field glasses I saw many dead enemy soldiers on the bridge but not one had fallen on our side of it.

That night a Staff General requested radio reports of our status. I told him none of the men in my *Schlacht Gruppe* had sustained injuries and that I felt certain we could hold the canal bridge provided the Panther tank remained with us as support.

He informed me that the Panther was being redeployed to the north where it was direly needed. The General told me that he would send engineers to the bridge to wire it with demolitions. The detonators would be given to me and it was to be my personal decision to blow the bridge in the event we could no longer hold or defend it. If I blew the bridge, we were to fall back to a row of ruined houses on the outskirts of Bochum.

Late that night the engineers arrived and mined the bridge. They extended the cord back to our trench line, connected it to a plunger and showed me how to remove the safety feature to push the handle. They gave us words of encouragement and as they departed, the Panther turned over its motor and backed up. It engaged its treads and turned to the north and disappeared in the night. Lichtermann and I gave each other a nervous smile.

On 8 April we experienced difficulty in our efforts to defend the bridge. The Allies attempted to cross the expanse while simultaneously launching a raft assault. I ordered two MG42s to concentrate on the massive number of enemy infantry that tried to overwhelm us on the bridge and directed the other MG42 and all soldiers to focus their fire on the top of the canal wall.

The enemy managed to get across on the bridge but our PaK and panzerfausts drove them back. We continued shooting as they retreated across the bridge.

Several of my men had been hit during the exchange of bullets and one had been killed. The remainder of the night was very uneventful in our sector.

9 April 1944

The Ruhr pocket was collapsing on all sides but not one attack was launched against the canal bridge that morning. Before noon several M4 Shermans and Matilda tanks approached on the opposite side. I immediately called the Command Post to request tank support but was told all armored vehicles were engaged in the north and west. I was told to blow the bridge if necessary.

We were curious as the Sherman tanks headed straight for the canal bridge and I removed the safety catch on the plunger. As the treads of the enemy vehicle touched the bridge I pushed the plunger but nothing happened. I pushed it two or three more times.

"Goddamnit!" yelled Lichtermann. "They must have seen the wires when they crossed on the rafts! That is why they did not attack us last night! They were disconnecting the demolitions!"

"Son of God!" I shouted. I ordered the PaK to take one final shot at the lead Sherman and directed our panzerfausts to fire. The lead Sherman burst into flames and we used this diversion to fall back to the row of burned out buildings. Several of my men were cut down by Allied bullets and I looked back to see a Matilda pushing the wrecked Sherman off the bridge and into the canal.

American and British soldiers stormed into the trench lines we had occupied up until that morning. The Shermans and Matildas fired arbitrarily into the buildings we were using for cover. I called the Command Post and reported the Allied crossing.

"Fall back to the final defense lines."

We cautiously made our way through the streets of Bochum to a large area that had been leveled into a debris field during a previous air raid. The Volkssturm, Wehrmacht and Luftwaffe soldiers would hold out as long as possible on the perimeters while the SS armed and entrenched around Field Marshal Model's Command Post.

During the next five days Model sent elite Waffen SS patrols out to assist our beleaguered forces but they never returned. The buildings farthest away were no longer being targeted by Allied artillery. Those just blocks away from us were now showering the Command Post with debris. On 16 April, to avoid annihilation, our troops on the outer perimeters surrendered against orders. Field Marshal Model was not angered by this. At the end of the day he called a meeting of all officers in the final defense perimeter.

Perhaps 12 of us sat on pieces of rubble or whatever we could find as Model stood before us. Shells banged down around us just blocks away and the sounds of enemy tank engines and gunfire forced him to raise his voice.

"We are close to the final hour," he said. "Each officer must make his own decision. I have made mine. I order that no one here is to ever be thought of as a coward or not having honor for the decision he makes. That is all."

Field Marshal Model entered his Command Post as we sat there looking at each other. "Certainly he does not mean surrender," stated a Staff General.

"What other option remains?" asked a Colonel.

"That is a defeatist statement!" shouted the Staff General.

"We are defeated!" countered the Colonel.

Some of the officers walked away to ponder the gravity of the situation that had befallen us. I walked to a pile of debris and stood there thinking.

What had become of my Germany? How is it that we elevated ourselves to the ultimate glory and now stood here in mud and debris like lost and frightened children? My Father had been the victim of surrender and I once vowed I would never bow to that humiliation. But was I to continue fighting Hitler's war when it had cost me my brothers, sister, cousins, comrades, Mother, Father, wife and daughter? Would my surrender bring retribution upon Petra and her family? Hitler had issued orders to execute the families of all officers who surrendered. Would this be considered my personal decision against Hitler or would Model be responsible? Was I to sacrifice Lichtermann, Puttkammer and the remainder of my *Schlacht Gruppe*?

It did not seem real. Standing in the center of Bochum covered in filth, it did not seem possible that I once dined with Himmler, Eichmann and members of the elite circles of the Reich. Where were they now? Why had they not protected me from Stalingrad, the Ardennes and the hell falling on my head at the Ruhr?

It was not about me or the consequences I might face for surrendering. I had only to look at the men in my *Schlacht Gruppe* to make the decision. They had fought hard and endured hell for many years and most of them had families they could return to. Even if my family and I were executed for my treasonist act of surrender, my men would be spared from retribution. I was in command of them and as I started my career at Porajów, so was I now responsible for the safety and security of Reich forces. They were my men and I was accountable for them.

No collective decision had been made by the end of 17 April and the argument was so tense that officers were threatening to shoot each other. On the following morning, Field Marshal Model came to all of us and announced that he personally informed Berlin that he alone had surrendered Army Group B to Allied Forces. He stated there would be no consequences for any of the Junior Officers as he told General Jodl that we had protested his decision to surrender. He looked at all of us and nodded before placing his visor hat on his head and entering his command bunker. We stood there talking amongst ourselves until a gunshot sounded inside the bunker. Model's personal adjutant entered hastily and exited moments later. He held his own hat in his hand. Looking at us somberly he said, "The Field Marshal is dead." Model had taken his own life.

We entered into a debate about which Allied army we would surrender to. The Canadians, British and Americans all had a reputation of mistreating and shooting SS prisoners since the Malmédy incident. The shelling was getting closer and the dangers of shrapnel and debris deflection were serious concerns. It was decided that each officer would report to his men and surrender to the Allied army of his choice.

I walked slowly to my *Schlacht Gruppe* and made the brief announcement that we were going to surrender. Some of the men became very emotional and started to weep while others seemed relieved that the war was over for them. I consulted with Lichtermann and we decided we would surrender to the Army of the United States of America.

We shredded linens and bandages and fastened the white cloths to boards and poles. I ordered the men of my *Schlacht Gruppe* to keep their weapons shouldered and I walked behind the white flags held by Puttkammer and Lichtermann. We exited the town and began walking across an open muddy field when Americans appeared from behind their cover and stalked forward with their weapons pointed at us. The firing in our sector subsided as the Americans surrounded us. Two of them approached and one spoke to me in German.

"Are you surrendering?" he asked.

I believed the white flags and shouldered weapons made our intentions rather obvious but I realized it was not a moment for arrogant sarcasm.

"I wish to present the American army with *SS Schlacht Gruppe South*."

The young man spoke to his superior in English. Words were exchanged and translated before he addressed me.

"My Lieutenant accepts your surrender."

"Tell your Lieutenant," I said, "That I wish to present the American army with my unit. I will only extend this formality to an officer of equal or greater rank."

The young man translated and the American Lieutenant let forth with a haughty and displeased chortle. He spoke to one of his men who ran off far behind their lines. Moments later an Allied jeep drove into the area and I saw the Oak Leaves of a United States Major. We spoke through the translator.

"Sturmbannführer Rolf Schiller, Waffen SS, Army Group B."

"Major Walt Douglas, 99th U.S. infantry." He shook my hand as if we had once been schoolmates.

He was waiting but I could not bring myself to say the words. However, there was no reversing my decision at that point. My men were exposed and under the guns of the American army. I inhaled deeply to maintain composure and made eye contact with him. When I saw sorrow and pity on his face for me having to do this, I began to stammer. He stepped toward me and whispered words in English that I somehow understood. Softly he said, "Easy, son."

With tears in my eyes and a broken voice I stated, "Sturmbannführer Rolf Schiller, Waffen SS. I surrender and present you with *SS Schlacht Gruppe South*." I opened my holster and gently removed my Luger and presented its handle to Major Douglas. He took it in his left hand, stepped back and presented me with a salute. I bit hard on my lower lip to hold back the tears and returned the courtesy.

On 18 April 1945, I officially became a Prisoner of War to the United States 99th Infantry in the Ruhr Valley.

We were disarmed and marched over the canal bridge we had previously defended and I could not deny the thought we were going to be shot. We walked for many kilometers through American held territory while enemy soldiers jeered and pelted us with rubbish and stones. All dignity had vanished when Major Walt Douglas turned us over to his subordinates.

CHAPTER TWENTY-SIX
IN ALLIED CAPTIVITY

I did not know the Allies rescinded their policy of shooting Prisoners of War at the end of the Ardennes Campaign. We came to an American command and supply area where I saw a damaged road sign indicating we were near Duisburg. Strips of barbed wire had been wrapped around fence posts and they resembled the same kind of enclosures we used for Allied prisoners. The paddocks at Duisburg were filled with Wehrmacht, Luftwaffe, SS, and members of the Volkssturm. Our helmets were taken as we were ushered inside one, and the gate was chained behind us.

A young boy from the *Hitlerjugend* was pulling at my sleeve. "Please, Sir," he said, "Come away from the fence. You do not want to remain there."

I relied on the experience of the boy and squeezed through the dense crowd of prisoners. I stood next to an elderly Wehrmacht Colonel and looked at our wounded soldiers reclining on the ground.

The Wehrmacht Officer looked at me and bowed his head in greeting. "Major."

I bowed my head and acknowledged him. "Colonel."

As the hours passed I learned why the boy told me it was not prudent to stand near the edge of the wire. American soldiers often walked by carrying buckets of urine and excrement from their latrines. The contents of the receptacles were flung at German soldiers while the Americans laughed and shouted horrible curses at us in our language. Twice a British fire police vehicle appeared at which the high powered water hoses were turned on us with the velocity of cannons. Our soldiers did not offer the meekest protest to this treatment. Each of us felt that a complaint would bring worse conduct from our Allied captors.

Before evening, an open American truck pulled up alongside the wire and a soldier stood in the back scanning us through field glasses. A tinny voice was blaring through a speaker in German. "All SS Officers to the edge of the wire! All SS Officers to the edge of the wire!"

I did not know the meaning of this. Perhaps we were to be taken for interrogation, transported, put in a separate holding facility, or for all I knew, shot. I stood between two Waffen SS Untersturmführers as a covered American truck arrived. Several enemy soldiers rushed to its back and lowered the gate. My heart thumped and I became short of breath when I saw the Americans helping former Jewish prisoners out of the vehicle. The Jews were frail and still dressed in the gray and blue striped facility uniforms. There were 14 of them and the Americans led them to the enclosure where the Jews began studying our faces.

I was perspiring heavily as the Jews began walking along my section of the fence. They went very slowly and all of them studied each of us for several long moments. There was a commotion off to my right when two Jewish prisoners pointed to an SS officer.

"Mein Leben ist jetzt ein Haufen Scheiße!" shouted one of the Jews, *"Jetzt sind Sie im Arsch der Welt! Du machst mich krank! Ich wünsche Ihnen Tod!"*

If permitted the opportunity, I am certain those malnourished and weakened Jews would have torn our limbs from our bodies. The SS officer was escorted out of the enclosure as the Jew continued screaming the same curses over and over. It was as if he knew no other words or held firm conviction with what he shouted:

"My life is a pile of shit! Now you are in the ass of the world! You make me ill! I wish you death!"

As they approached I clenched my fists to hide my trembling fingers but opened my hands at realizing this could be regarded as a sign of aggression. Was I to give them a kindly look? Was I to stare at them emotionless? What might anger them? With all my formal Police and legal training I had no idea how to act now that the warden had become the prisoner.

When they came close I noticed their rancid odor and saw the patches sewn on their breasts. Each wore a yellow Star of David above the letters: KZ NdH. I immediately recognized the letters as the Reich administrative designation for the Nordhausen Detainment Facility. I had been there several times but suddenly I could remember the purpose for no other visit except the gas van experiments with Doctor Rausch.

The first Jew came before me and glanced at my rank insignia before staring at my face while licking his lips and repeatedly squinting. He acted like a hound preparing to sink his fangs into a side of meat. He moved to the next officer and I mentally counted backward from 14 until the last one inspected me and moved along. I had not been identified as someone associated with the Nordhausen facility.

After the examination we were told to remain in place as more Jews were being transported to the area. The SS Untersturmführer identified by the Jews had been taken outside the wire and was held under armed guard. Perhaps he had once been a member of the Nordhausen garrison, but all of his rank and insignia properly identified him as a Waffen SS Artillery Officer. I do not know if he was the victim of mistaken identity or singled out for perverted Jewish justice, but he protested most convincingly.

"Who are these people?" he shouted. "What are these people?" It was the second question that he asked so sincerely. All Germans knew we had been deporting Jews to Detainment Facilities and Termination Stations, but those not directly involved with the process would have had no idea what the prisoners looked like or how they were dressed. There was such honesty in the Untersturmführer's voice when he inquired, *"What are these people?"* that I have always believed him innocent.

While waiting for the other Jews to arrive I was doused with a bucket of urine, struck with apple cores, jeered at, and hosed by the British fire police vehicle. We remained in that enclosure for two days undergoing visual inspections by Jewish prisoners and at the hands and mercy of our captors.

I was escorted from the paddock and taken into a large canvas tent where an American Captain was seated next to an enlisted man with a typewriter. The Captain spoke to me in German. "Sit down, Major."

The simple act of following his instructions to sit seemed like submission to enemy orders. But what purpose yet existed for me to defy him? By God, what if our position in the Ruhr was reinforced and we were turning the tides of war as I stood before him? Had I been hasty with my decision? I had wished to protect my men, but what had I led them to? They were being abused by their American captors and subjected to single sided inspections by Jews with a penchant for retribution.

"Sit down, Major." His voice was not stern and I had been standing upright in the enclosure for hours. I sat as he opened a thin file containing two or three pages.

"Schiller?" is it? "Sturmbannführer Rolf Schiller? Am I pronouncing that correctly?"

I nodded.

"Waffen SS *Schlacht Gruppe South*," he said. "What is a *Schlacht Gruppe*?"

"A unit of 40 to 55 heavily armed combat soldiers. These groups are strategically employed as defensive forces to hold tactical areas."

He nodded with a satisfied smile and motioned to his subordinate who began typing. "Army Group B," he said. "That is under the command of the Wehrmacht, is it not?"

"It was under the command of Field Marshal Walther Model," I replied.

"Was?" he asked. "Has he been relieved of command?"

"The Field Marshal took his own life."

He immediately picked up his telephone, placed a call and began speaking to someone in English. I believe he was relaying the information I had given him about the Field Marshal.

"Which Waffen SS Division and Regiment were you assigned to?" he inquired.

"Waffen SS Regiment Deutschland, VII Panzer Division Kempf under the command of SS-Brigadeführer Paul Hausser."

He picked up several maps and read over several documents. "That was mainly an Eastern Front regiment. How did you get assigned to Army Group B?"

I did not have a sound answer and I hoped to avoid questions about the Ardennes Campaign. I was also pleased that the Captain believed me to be a career member of the Waffen SS and that he had not connected me to RSHA duties.

That quickly my anxiety level was elevated when he inquired, "What Division were you assigned to in the Ardennes?"

I remained silent and the Captain rested his chin on his folded knuckles. "If your name is not Peiper, Höltz or Fleischer, you do not have reason for concern. What Division were you assigned to in the Ardennes, Major? Every German combat soldier in this area was recalled from the forest."

"I SS Panzer Army."

"That is Priess' Division, is it not?" he inquired.

I nodded.

"I SS Panzer operated mostly with XII SS Panzer, is this not true?"

The Americans knew much more than I thought they did. Until I received news of the official capitulation of the Fatherland, I would not assist the Allies in destroying us. I became quiet and evasive. He asked me several more questions but I refused to answer them.

"Very well, Major Schiller. You are going to be placed on a truck and driven to Antwerp. You will then be escorted across the Channel where you will be held as a Prisoner of War in England."

On 29 April I arrived at the English port of Dover. We were immediately put aboard buses and driven to Bridgend Island Farm, Camp IX. The buses passed road signs reading: Coity, Swansea and Coychurch and I foolishly made mental notes of these names as if they would help me orient myself in the event of my escape. I noticed a large circular chimney in the distance as our buses entered a lane with thick metal fencing on each side of the road. We fell in line with other transport vehicles and waited there for a very long time before we were driven through the gates.

We were marched inside an empty building and stopped in front of several long tables upon which were placed pressboard boxes with a wax pencil inside. We were ordered to strip and place our uniforms and undergarments in the boxes and to write our names and ranks on the lid and sides. Each of us was then subjected to a humiliating cavity and mouth search before being doused with a white delousing powder. We were then given ill fitting shirts and trousers. On the back of each shirt and on its left breast were the letters: P.O.W.

One of the British guards spoke to us in German. Sarcastically he said, "King George welcomes you to England!"

I was taken for an interview before being given a barracks assignment. The British had the information I gave to the American Captain at Duisburg but they were not satisfied that they did not have a more accurate account of my military service and assignments. I insisted that my entire career had been in the Waffen SS and repeated the details of SS Regiment Deutschland, VII Panzer Division Kempf, and my assignment to I SS Panzer Army. I told the British that I had been a Combat Line Officer but they did not believe me. They stated that the piping on my uniform indicated I was a member of the SS Police and they attempted to implicate me in Peiper's actions at Malmédy and some unfortunate occurrence at Ouradour-sur-Glane in France. They asked one final question that took everything within me in order to maintain my composure. "Major, do you know anything about the killing of Belgian civilians at Hédomont?"

"Certainly not!" I lied.

"And you were attached to I SS Panzer Army between 20 December 1944 and 5 January 1945?"

"Yes," I replied and then acted as if I was firmly thinking. "I was engaged in a battle for an Allied fuel depot during those days."

"Who ordered the assault on Hédomont, Major?"

"It could have only been Priess or Dietrich," I replied.

"General Sepp Dietrich?"

"That is correct."

My interrogators paused for a moment before one asked, "You are stating that you had absolutely nothing to do with the assault on Hédomont, Major?"

"That is correct. I recall we were shelled from that vicinity and attacked by planes. We blew gaps in the trees to move our wreckage off the road and advanced on Baugnez. Infantry Squads were deployed in the direction of Hédomont, but I do not know who commanded them or who issued the orders for the assault."

"But you believe it was General Sepp Dietrich?"

"That is only a guess."

They ended the interrogation and I was taken to a barracks with Kriegsmarine, Wehrmacht, Luftwaffe and a few enlisted SS men. Some of my fellow prisoners told me they had been at Bridgend Island Farm Camp IX since 1940.

On 3 May 1945, all German prisoners were assembled in the center of the camp and a British Officer unceremoniously announced that der Führer, Adolf Hitler, was dead. Our guards handed us Belgian, French, Dutch and Italian newspapers that contained articles stating der Führer had taken his own life and Germany was now under the leadership of Grand Admiral Karl Dönitz.

Of course we believed this to be lies and trickery set in place to confound us. Hitler would not lead us through the gates of a cataclysmic hell and abandon us by taking his own life! Certainly der Führer was killed during the defense of the Reich! This is what we believed. It was impossible for us to accept that our years of obedience, loyalty, devotion, suffering, bleeding, sweating and countless deaths were punctuated by the cowardly suicide of der Führer. We believed the British were trying to break our spirits and destroy our morale.

On 6 May we were permitted to listen to a radio broadcast made by Grand Admiral Dönitz. He stated to us and the world that he had authorized General Alfred Jodl to conclude an armistice with the Western Allies. He said nothing about Hitler and immediately rumors spread among the men that der Führer was alive. We wished to believe anything other than that the complete surrender of Germany was imminent.

We were assembled once more on 8 May to listen to another broadcast by Dönitz. He stated that all land, sea and air units of the Reich had unconditionally surrendered to the Western Allies on 7 May. It was now official. Many of us wept and consoled our comrades while others were greatly relieved. I believed we would all be released and permitted to go home. That night the bells at Coychurch rang just after 2300 hours. I did not look forward to the humiliation I would face for having offended my country as part of its second surrender.

Within a few days I was called before a group of British Officers and was instructed to fill out a lengthy questionnaire. They informed me this was part of the Denazification Process that was required before I could be returned to Germany. The form seemed quite innocent with its questions about residence address, height, weight, eye color, hair color, family, education level, trade skills and medical conditions. However, I had seen and used similar forms during my experiences with Jewish Emigrations and was aware that the answers given on such a form could be effectively used to compile a criminal profile. It was a double edged sword for me because lying on the form could delay the verification of my information and force me to remain in England for a longer period of time. Conversely, the truth could help the Allies track my enlistment and service. At that time I had heard no formal mention that the Allies wished to hold any Reich Officer for deeds committed during the war, so I provided accurate answers to the questions.

During the following six weeks all former SS officers at Bridgend Island Farm Camp IX were ushered into the facility cinema house from 0900 hours until 1500 hours where British Officers and psychiatrists lectured us about the evils of National Socialism and condemned its philosophies, objectives and existence. We had paper manuals that contained group responses. We collectively muttered nonsense about desiring a new political constitution; having offended the world, and promising to live productive lives and not to invade Europe again. It was foolish rhetoric designed as part of the Allied Denazification Process required for sending us home. It was not effective and none of us believed or supported the responses we were forced to give, but we would have said anything at that time to be released from Bridgend Island Farm Camp IX.

On 3 July 1945 the last details of my paperwork were completed and I was placed aboard a bus with four other former SS officers. We were driven to Dover and directed toward a supply truck to retrieve the pressboard boxes containing our uniforms, medals and personal items. We underwent a series of questions and had our paperwork and documents verified by members of the Royal Navy before we were marched across a gangplank and onto a medium British vessel. The sailors were quite friendly and offered us cigarettes and coffee.

The vessel docked at the German port of Emden on 5 July. Allied soldiers were walking about, laughing, and flirting with German women. There were many of us in the port wearing our P.O.W uniforms and holding our little pressboard boxes. An American Naval Officer called us forward and checked our papers. He instructed us to report to a warehouse at the end of the pier and we entered to find large piles of clothing. We were permitted to trade our prison uniforms for civilian clothes and I was fortunate enough to find a matching suit and shoes. This probably would not have been important to me if I did not believe the P.O.W uniform was a proclamation of shame. I wished to blend in with my fellow countrymen and not be recognized as the failed soldier I thought myself to be.

There were extremely long lines for free soup and telephones but having no money, I needed to reach Petra with the hope someone could come to fetch me. I waited for hours and when I told the exchange operator the number I wished dialed, I was informed the line had been cut. With no money, how was I to reach Göppingen?

I asked several people but was terrified to approach the Allied Military Police who looked like they had all the answers. I was informed that several buses and trains were open to free passage, but these were on a minimal basis and each had a massive congregation of people waiting for them. I was frightened to simply begin walking for fear that an Allied patrol would accost me and take me away for whatever reason. I tried to read the information placards and memorize details about free food, curfews and transportation but it was too much to organize. I joined the lines outside the rail station for free passage and two days later on 7 July I boarded a train to Paderborn.

The Allied Military Police was checking identity papers as we stepped from the train. One Policeman showed my card to his comrade and they pulled me aside at which they made a telephone call. The Policeman on the telephone spoke my name and former rank into the mouthpiece. "Rolf Schiller. Waffen SS Sturmbannführer. Füssen." The wait was unbearable but he disconnected from the call and returned my documents. They walked away and left me standing there wondering if there was more to do. When I saw them checking other documents and no longer paying attention to me, I blended with the crowd.

I walked south along the autobahn toward Kassel and was saddened by the extensive destruction all around me. Allied tanks, trucks and jeeps rolled up and down the roadway with civilian German motorcars in between them. An elderly gentleman pulled over and inquired if I needed a ride. The Americans shouted and cursed as they drove by and I wasted no time climbing into the back of his motorcar.

The bridged intersection of the autobahn and the roads to Willingen and Kassel were blocked by an Allied Military Police checkpoint. Approximately 20 soldiers were directing traffic and reviewing identity documents. I handed mine through the rear window and the Policeman stared at me for a long time before walking away and showing my papers to three of his comrades. They approached with drawn weapons and the old man driving the car was covering his head in great panic. The Americans shouted, *"Aus! Aus!"* and I obeyed by stepping from the car. They waved the driver through the intersection and pushed and shoved me off the road and down a small embankment where they raised their weapons at me. They taunted me and all I understood of their words was a repeated references to *"The SS!"*

At once I was struck in the abdomen with a rifle stock and I fell to the ground where I was repeatedly kicked and beaten. After some time I no longer felt the pain.

I regained consciousness with my face and hands encrusted with my dried blood. I crawled to where they had thrown my identity documents and gathered up the papers and my pressboard box. Staggering back up to the bridge, I saw that the guards had changed shifts. Some of them looked at me but none offered to help or inquired about what happened. They did not even ask to see my papers again as I limped south past the checkpoint.

As night was falling an American truck pulled over in front of me and I braced myself for another beating or to be arrested. German voices called out to me and two former Wehrmacht soldiers and a British Officer assisted me into the vehicle. The truck took me all the way to Fulda where I was fortunate to gain a seat on a free passage bus that drove me to the ruins of Würzburg. I waited countless hours for the train that took me to the Aalen rail station and from there I walked and rode part of the way in a farm wagon to Göppingen. On 10 July 1945 I knocked on the door of Petra's family home.

They reacted as if a ghostly visage stood before them. Every person shed tears and was horrified by my beaten and disheveled appearance. They drew a hot bath and I reclined in the tub feeling safe enough to fall asleep.

I opened my eyes to see Petra holding our son. I cried bitterly at the sight of the precious little infant. I was ashamed of myself for having disappointed that beautiful little boy by failing to preserve the Germany I had intended for him. I was elated that the war was over and he would not have to endure the hell I walked through. My emotions were mixed and I could not stem my tears. I wailed and wept like a very infant myself; so loud that Petra carefully closed the window while cradling our son in her other arm. She nodded an understanding that only a wife could give and left me there alone to confront my emotions. Shame, dishonor, relief, guilt, remorse, loss, destruction and death flashed before my eyes. I slammed my hands in the bath water and beat the tiled walls with my fists while wailing at the top of my breath. I do not know how long I did this before going silent. Petra entered the room again, sat on the side of the tub and we embraced for a very long time.

None of her family members spoke a word about my outburst when I joined them at the dining table. A sumptuous feast had been laid before me and we ate in silence at first because no one knew what to say. At last Petra's Mother broke the uneasy quietness.

"Have you given thought to a trade?" she asked.

Politely, but without much concern I replied, "Perhaps I will seek work in a law office." I was given support for this statement but we all knew it was an empty remark. There were very few jobs available as most businesses had been destroyed by Allied air raids. I could not take my eyes from my precious son in his little elevated wooden chair.

"Rolf," said Petra's Father, "Men have come to this house asking about you."

Everyone looked away for a moment and then began busily eating in silence again.

"What men?" I inquired.

"American and British Officers of the Police. They wish to speak with you about things that happened during the war."

"What things?" I asked innocently so as not to cause alarm or imply that I had involvement with the Detainment Facilities and Termination Stations.

"They would not tell us," he said. "They left a telephone number and wish for you to call them or report to the Allied Field Office in town."

"I will contact them in the morning."

There was a moment of silence as we continued eating. He stated, "We know about the camps, Rolf. Every person knows about them."

"Father!" Petra's voice was rich with a tone that implied he should not have mentioned this at the dining table.

"Did you have involvement with those places? It seems the Allies are very interested in locating Höss, Eichmann, and Müller. Were these men not in your department? Did I not see them at the wedding?"

"Yes," I replied. "I organized deportations to the Detainment Facilities and personally supervised executions at the Termination Stations." I refused to hold the truth from them. If they wished to disown and disassociate themselves with me and deprive me of my wife and son, I provided them with the opportunity.

They were not surprised. They had obviously known what I did during the war but never had the opportunity to mention it to me before that moment.

"There is a printer in town," said Petra's Father. "He is a good man. He can help you. We have told the Allied Police that you served in the Waffen SS. Nothing more. I will give you money for the printer."

I declined the offer. If I was discovered to be in possession of false identity documents it would implicate the Schauf family and the man who printed them. I would bring them no harm or misfortune. If questioned by the Allies, I would maintain that I was a Waffen SS Combat Officer until otherwise was proven.

The Allies were not interested in my actions during the war. I was made to register with the provisional authorities and now and then the Occupational Police would stop at the house or call me to the Field Office to look at photographs of former SS officers. Men such as Hans Frank, Walter Funk, Alfred Jodl, Kaltenbrunner and Dönitz had been arrested by the Allies and there was a rumor that these Party Officials and a roster of others, were to be tried as War Criminals.

Names such as Höss, Burger, Stangl, Wirth, Glücks and Eichmann had not even been mentioned and therefore I started to feel secure that my department, fellow officers and superiors were outside the circle of Victors' Justice. Joachim Peiper's photograph was the first I was shown and the Allies were very interested in learning his whereabouts as they intended to hold him accountable for the Malmédy incident. I was shown photographs of many SS officers and was asked questions about men such as Rudolf Lange, Klaus Barbie, Heinz Jöst, Walter Schellenberg, Jakob Grimminger, Werner Best, Friedrich Jeckeln and Otto Ohlendorf.

I grew suspicious of why the Allied Police was asking me about RSHA officers, Commanders of the Einsatzgruppen, and Administrative SS members if they indeed believed me to be a member of the Waffen SS. They never implied they thought differently, and this too seemed dubious to me. I developed a very balanced method in which I answered questions truthfully but reserved a lot of personal information.

By September I had forged a neutral relationship with the Allied Policemen as I was visiting them and looking at photographs at least twice a week. Job opportunities came through their office as employers were searching for candidates who had been cleared by the Occupational Police. It was not prudent to hire men with personal histories marred by dishonorable deeds committed during the war. The Allies informed me about an available job at Bergdorf's Department store and wrote a letter of recommendation for me. I had not earned a coin since the end of the war and I applied for this job in the nearby city of Heiderscheim. I was given fair work unloading crates of handbags, shoes and perfumes imported from Switzerland. I never suspected that the Allies knew exactly who I was and what my duties were during the war. They arranged this job for me to keep me rooted to the area as they gathered the required evidence to arrest me.

CHAPTER TWENTY·SEVEN
ARRESTED FOR WAR CRIMES

On Tuesday, 11 December 1945, the Allied Occupational Police knocked on the door of the Schauf family home. Petra's Mother invited them inside and they approached us as we sat at the dinner table. Such visits were not uncommon at odd hours as the Allies never took respite from their duties. The Schauf family believed I would be shown photographs and asked questions about other men. However, I knew why they had come. I saw the expressions on their faces and recognized their mood to be the same one I experienced on Brzozowa Street in Porajów when I entered the apartment of a Polish lady and her children to arrest them for throwing an incendiary device at German forces. I wiped my mouth with a cloth napkin and stood up. The Captain of the Allied Occupational Police force of Göppingen said, "Rolf Schiller, the Government of the United States of America, the Constitutional Monarchy of Great Britain, the Provisionary Government of France and the Politburo of the Soviet Communist Party place you under arrest for War Crimes, Crimes against Humanity, the Murder of the King of England's soldiers, Waging a War of Aggression and General Breaches of the Peace."

Petra was ordered to fetch my identity documents and the pressboard box I brought home from Bridgend Island Farm Camp IX. I was to wear the uniform of the Reich during the formal reading of the accusations against me.

While being placed in the back of a Citroen car I denied the allegations against me. I knew it was wise to say nothing but I also recognized the importance of immediately stating an objection.

The Americans never placed me in shackles and they treated me with dignity at the Göppingen Field Office. The Allied Police Captain, who I had come to know well over the previous five months, was direct and surprisingly fair. He sat down across from me at his desk and opened several large files.

"Major Rolf Otto Schiller," he said. He proceeded to relate my date of birth, religion, and the names of my parents, sister, and brothers. Then he named my SS sponsor, noted my enlistment date in 1937 and stated my assignment to Theodor Eicke's Unit upon my graduation from the SS Training Depot at Dachau. He knew I had been posted at Sachsenhausen, waged war in Poland, and was assigned as the SS Chief of Police and Security at Porajów. He revealed the source of all this information when he said, "A former comrade of yours has called you the Blackbird of Porajów." The Captain knew about the executions of Polish civilians and when I inquired who called me the Blackbird, he would not reply. In my opinion there was only one former SS officer who would have divulged this information in exchange for personal leniency. The Captain informed me that the crux of their case against me had been highly circumstantial and based primarily on hearsay.

I was taken from Göppingen to the city of Stuttgart and placed in a windowless cell in the municipal jail. I can not say how long I was confined there until I was visited by an elder German in a gray suit. He said he was a Criminal Defense barrister and that he had been contacted by the Occupational Police to represent me throughout the preliminary hearings, interviews and trial.

I did not understand what was happening or why I had been arrested. The sole statement of the American Captain at Göppingen that equaled legal merit, if any at all, was the potential liability for killing the King's soldiers. I rationalized this charter was in reference to the actions of my unit at Hédomont in 1944, but certainly my soldiers did not commit the exclusive wartime act of shooting surrendering prisoners. More to my wonder was how that one particular incident could have been singled out against a wartime full of events.

War Crimes? This charter befuddled me as I did not even know what a traditional war crime was. There had certainly been no formal legal precedent governing criminal offenses excluding the Geneva

Convention of which all armies who signed this code violated its terms and conditions. To my knowledge, so called war crimes were those stated under the Roman Justinian Code and not formally recognized in Europe for over seven centuries.

Crimes against Humanity? This charter held potential merit but only because I recalled Eichmann's and Stammler's concerns about the discoveries of Einsatzgruppen activities and the camps. Technically, the Reich had classified Jews and untermenschen under veterinary laws and this formal categorization exempted them from filing civil and criminal claims for damages. The Nürnberg Laws lucidly stated the provisions, precedents and legal codes under which Jews and untermenschen were to be processed. I felt certain that the Allies were not yet familiar with Reich laws and deduced they would be satisfied to strike this charter once they read and understood them.

Waging a War of Aggression? What war in history has not been aggressive? This was another charter that confused me until the elder barrister explained that the Allied governments held the Reich's Campaign against Europe to be a criminal conspiracy for illegal domination and subjugation of the foreign populace.

General Breaches of the Peace was a clever classification into which the Allies could include additional charters whenever they trumped them up. I told the barrister to instruct the Allies to read and familiarize themselves with Reich law so that I may be released at once. The barrister said the Allies were only interested in Reich law as far as declaring it criminal. He stated I would be tried, found guilty and more than likely hanged. He urged me to strike a deal with the Allies in exchange for leniency and told me that to do so I would have to reveal information about criminal activity committed by my superior officers.

That strategy seemed greatly flawed. Admitting knowledge of criminal activity on behalf of my superior officers equaled complicity in executing the orders I was given. I was an Administrative Liaison which authorized me to conceive and give orders that under this plan, would also be considered criminal. I believed that none of us had committed any legitimate criminal act and therefore refused part in this proposal.

Again I must state that I do not know how long I remained in the cell after the barrister departed. A single bulb burned constantly and except for several bowls of soup, I had no contact with other people. The deprivation of senses eliminated all possibilities for deducing the time of day.

Eventually I was placed in shackles and taken from the cell to the prefecture at Stuttgart where the elder German barrister was waiting for me. He explained I would appear before a Council of Allied Prosecutors who would read a formal list of charters against me and that I was to respond with a plea to each individual accusation. Afterward, the Council would examine alleged evidence and make a ruling on whether I was to stand formal trial. I was led into a small room where I was given the pressboard box I received at Bridgend Island Farm Camp IX. The Allied Police instructed me to dress in my former uniform and once I did this, they removed the SS and Party insignias from my clothing. I was permitted to wear my medals, awards and epaulettes and they did not pull the metal insignia from my visor hat.

I was taken into the courtroom where an American, French, British and Russian government was each represented by a General. Court recorders sat at desks and tables and armed bailiffs guarded each exit. The barrister and I took seats before this commission and a woman serving as an interpreter sat with us. The British officer spoke and she interpreted.

"It is the purpose of this Council to determine if you, Rolf Otto Schiller, are to withstand trial for War Crimes, Crimes against Humanity, The Unlawful killing of the King of England's soldiers, Waging a War of Aggression, and General Breaches of the Peace. Do you understand the intentions of this Council?"

The barrister answered for me and stated that I understood. However, I interjected that I only understood the interpretation of the woman serving as a translator and entered that the words she used to repeat the statement were subjective and possibly did not reflect the true or general intentions of the Allied Council. This caused immediate confusion and brought about a conversation between the British prosecutor and the female interpreter. I took the barrister's fountain pen and paper and made notes of this incident.

The Allied Council stated its preparation to accuse me of War Crimes but before the first charter was read, I requested the official written definition of War Crimes as perceived by the Council to be criminal, and further requested the precedents upon which the charter had been founded. In addition, I demanded a written version of the procedure by which the charter was ratified by the governments of the prosecuting Council as well as written versions of objections to the charter made by its approving members and the amending clauses authored in response to said arguments. The Council acknowledged my legal right to understand the charters against me and admitted the documents I requested were not readily available in the German language for my review. I moved for a formal adjournment until all documentation was provided. I stated I would wait. The Council discussed the matter and granted my motion. I released the civilian barrister from my defense as I had gained advantageous control over the legal proceedings before they formally commenced.

I found no logic in employing a civilian barrister for legal representation. I would have graciously accepted a former Reich barrister such as Werner Best or Johanne Startl, but these men were themselves defendants elsewhere. In my opinion it was dangerous to trust a civilian barrister to arbitrate military law. No civilian without ties to the National Socialist Party would wish to bring suspicion upon himself for defending a man who had connections to it.

Eventually I was provided a copy of the London Charter and read the Allied conception of the circumstances that constituted war crimes. Section II, Article 6, Subheading B gave the definition as: *Violations of the laws or customs of war. Such violations shall include, but not be limited to, murder, ill-treatment or deportation to slave labor or for any other purpose of civilian population of or in occupied territory, murder or ill-treatment of prisoners of war or persons on the seas, killing of hostages, plunder of public or private property, wanton destruction of cities, towns or villages, or devastation not justified by military necessity.*

This was pursuant to Section I, Article I of the London Charter and agreed upon by the governments of France, Great Britain, the United States of America, Northern Ireland and the Soviet Union on 8 August 1945. Legally, this categorized the London Charter as an ex post facto document. Had these terms, provisions, articles and sections been recognized by the Allied governments prior to the Reich's 1939 commencement of war, perhaps the London Charter would have held minimal influence as the basis for an indictment. However, the

London Charter existed as a document created by the Allied governments 3 months after the Reich had surrendered. Furthermore, the Allied governments legally accepted the unconditional surrender of the Reich under the prevailing laws of warfare and military codes of conduct enforced and recognized as of 8 May 1945. It is disgraceful and absolutely illegal for any international government, agency, organization, operative, representative or official to arrest and accuse a member of a former foreign military under the precedent of laws established subsequent to the legal acceptance of the formal capitulation.

Crimes against Humanity was listed under Section II, Article 6, Subheading C as: *murder, extermination, enslavement, deportation, and other inhumane acts committed against any civilian population, before or during the war; or persecutions on political, racial or religious grounds in execution of or in connection with any crime within the jurisdiction of the Tribunal, whether or not in violation of the domestic law of the country where perpetrated. Leaders, organizers, instigators and accomplices participating in the formulation or execution of a common plan or conspiracy to commit any of the foregoing crimes are responsible for all acts performed by any persons in execution of such plan.*

The statement: *any crime within the jurisdiction of the Tribunal,* appeared quite dubious to me as the authority of the court was clearly defined in writing as having the ability to: *have the power to try and punish persons who, acting in the interests of the European Axis countries, whether as individuals or as members of organizations, committed Crimes against Peace, War Crimes, and Crimes against Humanity.* The London Charter openly stated in this provision that: *These acts, or any of them, are crimes coming within the jurisdiction of the Tribunal for which there shall be individual responsibility.*

This was ambiguous in that the so called jurisdiction had no defined legal boundaries but was rather set in place as a broad and open set of conditions capable of being interpreted, enforced, and applied according to the whims and fancy of the Allied Prosecuting Commissions. Under the terms of the London Charter, the Allied governments themselves were to be held as War Criminals under the stated provision of: *murder or ill-treatment of prisoners of war or persons on the seas, killing of hostages, plunder of public or private property, wanton destruction of cities, towns or villages, or devastation not justified by military necessity.*

Was the world to deny the murder and ill-treatment of German prisoners of war committed by the Allied governments accusing me? Was the world to deny that the Russians killed thousands of German hostages and civilians? Was the world to deny that all Allied governments plundered and looted German homes, businesses, museums and archives? Was the world to deny the wanton destruction of cities, towns and villages under Allied bombers? Dresden, Hamburg, Berlin, Bremen, Frankfurt, Wolfsburg, Liepzig, Dessau, Potsdam? Hiroshima and Nagasaki? Was the world to deny this was devastation not justified by military necessity? Yes. The world was willing to deny Allied complicity in the very charters being leveled against Reich Officers. Victors' Justice was weaving a rope for me.

I was told that the preliminary proceedings were not an official trial, but rather evidentiary hearings to determine if a case existed against me. I was therefore cognizant to restrain myself from answering the ridiculous accusations against me as I recognized the Allied Council was shouldered with establishing a burden of proof. In spite of being assured the evidentiary hearings were not an official trial, it often took the form of one. The Allied Council had very few documents to use as evidence against me and they did not understand these items. The Reich was accomplished in authoring communications with euphemistic design. Therefore, the documents entered against me could have been interpreted in a number of ways. I argued that the Allied Council was bound to produce similar documents related to similar matters for the purpose of establishing a coherency to their meanings.

The Allied Council went about the evidentiary hearings with a novice level of functioning. I gained the distinct belief that they wished to not only remand me for trial, but wished for my conviction as well. With these goals either ordered or expected from higher sources, the Council was very guarded and careful with its approach to indistinct legal matters. They often called private meetings in which they talked amongst themselves about the objections I entered and many times they reversed their decisions in my favor. Though novice, it appeared they were willing to concede to me on certain arguments rather than allow questionable or unresolved matters to resurface later and damage their case.

The Allied Council claimed to have eyewitnesses capable of placing me at Sachsenhausen, Auschwitz, Nordhausen, Esterwegen, Sobibor, Koveri, Theresienstadt, Amersfoort and Radogosz. This greatly interested me as an opportunity to discredit witnesses as in my entire career I never set foot inside Koveri in Finland, Theresienstadt and Radogosz in Poland, nor Amersfoort in Holland. It was also a curiosity that no witnesses had placed me at Belzec, Plaszow, Drancy, Chelmno and Majdanek.

According to the Council, there were more eyewitnesses and written depositions that linked me to the deportation transports and the actions committed at the gas chambers of Auschwitz II Birkenau. I was not furnished with a list of witnesses or copies of the alleged written depositions. I had to treat this matter as a novice ploy on behalf of the Allied Council to break me into admitting things they had no evidence of.

The hearings had merit when the Council discussed my involvement with Department IVb4 and the Office for Jewish Emigrations. They had ascertained that I knew and worked with Eichmann, Stammler, Dannecker, Novak and Höfle, and placed me under the authority of Heydrich, Globocnik and Himmler. In spite of this, they could not directly identify my formal duties and responsibilities within the department. They inquired if I was aware of the Detainment Facilities, which they had taken to calling "Death Camps". I objected to this term and stated for the record that it was prejudicial. The Council agreed to strike the term and henceforth referred to the locations as Concentration Camps.

I admitted knowledge of the Concentration Camps as the Allies had discovered them and Department IVb4 was directly associated with the locations. There was no plausible means with which to deny their existence. I realized that the many field duty assignments I received during the war had created multiple holes in the Council's attempt to establish that I served as a permanent member of Bureau IVb4. At that time the Council did not understand or acknowledge that I was on field assignments more frequently than I was in Berlin. They knew I served in the department, but could not complete an accurate assessment or chronological chain of events of my duties in the office. This permitted me leave to introduce the theory that I had been transferred to the Waffen SS in 1939, as evidenced by my assignment to SS Regiment Deutschland, VII Panzer Division Kempf under the command of SS-Brigadeführer Paul Hausser. I acknowledged my subsequent assignments to XXV Panzer Regiment, VII Armored Division under the command of General Erwin Rommel in 1940, and my 1941 assignment to EK5 in the Ukraine, VI Army Kampfgruppe XI at Stalingrad from1942 to 1943, and I SS Panzer and XII SS Panzer in the Ardennes as well as *SS Schlacht Gruppe South* in the Ruhr Valley from 1944 to 1945.

My career as a Combat Line Officer had been much better documented and the records were available for review. Fortunately, it seemed that Stammler had completed an excellent service of destroying many of the papers that detailed my duties and responsibilities with Department IVb4. The Council pressed the matter that I served as a Police Officer of the SS and desperately attempted to invent connections between my field combat duties and the responsibilities of the Gestapo, SD and Security Police.

On Friday, 11 January 1946, the Allied Council had abandoned their efforts to associate me with the Detainment Facilities but advanced the motions that I was responsible for the illegal killing of British soldiers at Hédomont and connected to the organization of the deportation transports.

The information regarding the shootings at Hédomont, to wit: the nine British soldiers shot while surrendering, was contained in sworn affidavits presented by 4 former enlisted members of I SS Panzer Army Squad IV. I received copies of the signed and dated affidavits and would be required to answer the accusations.

The information regarding my involvement in the deportation transports to Termination Stations in Poland was gathered from documents captured by the Soviet Army at SS Headquarters Warsaw, and at Auschwitz and Majdanek.

In spite of the two formal charters against me, the Council's case was primarily comprised of circumstantial evidence and hearsay. I was held accountable for the Hédomont shootings through a matter of general complicity. I had been the acting officer of Squad IV and was therefore responsible for the actions of my men. None of the signed affidavits stated that I had given the order to open fire on the surrendering British soldiers and none of the documents identified the shooters. However, the enlisted men had agreed to reveal me as their former Commander in exchange for leniency. I did not regard this as a dishonorable act on behalf of my former soldiers. I was indeed responsible for the actions of Squad IV and would duly face my accountability.

Proving my culpability for the shootings at Hédomont was much more difficult than expected. The signed affidavits exclusively mentioned that I was the acting officer of Squad IV. This information was combined with the statements I made while in British captivity at Bridgend Island Farm Camp IX. I had openly lied about my involvement in the invasion of Hédomont and this understandably damaged the credibility of any subsequent statements I made about the matter. I entered a defense cited in common Military Conduct that a Prisoner of War is to make every viable attempt to confuse and confound his captors. This was a weak strategy but it established my argument and placed the burden of proof upon the Allied Council.

Analytically I was forced to admit knowledge of the incident based on the four affidavits. I maintained that there had been an exchange of gunfire in the plaza at Hédomont but that I did not see visual signs of enemy surrender nor hear audible shouts for quarter. I stated that to my knowledge, we engaged the enemy in a legitimate battle.

The four former SS soldiers who signed the affidavits were led into the courtroom and presented as witnesses for the prosecution. I did not recognize any of them in their civilian clothes. None of them was capable of looking me in the eyes but I felt no disdain for them. They were common soldiers and throughout the war remained obedient and loyal to men the likes of me. They were not men who made decisions; they were men who followed orders.

Each of them repeated my name when asked by the Allied Council who was in command of I SS Panzer Army Squad IV at Hédomont. However, none of them said anything more incriminating than that. When queried about the British surrender, each man stated he did not see enemy actions or hear enemy words that indicated capitulation under hostile combat. Each gave an account of the encounter with the enemy and stated that gunfire was evenly traded. The British Prosecutor raised his voice and shouted at the young men but they refused to alter their statements. There was no need for me to question the men as their steadfast resolve and silence damaged the case of the

Allied Council.

I was told that five British soldiers were to be called as witnesses and that these men had observed the alleged illegal killings from various vantage points around the plaza. I implored the Tribunal to call each witness separately and the motion was granted.

The first man took the podium and gave statements of his name, rank and service record. He identified himself as an artillery spotter and was requested to give his account of the matter. He told a fabulous tale of how the nine British soldiers threw down their weapons and placed their hands behind their heads; a very embellished tale in opposition to the actual circumstances.

I covered my left collar tab with my hand as I stood to question him. He had looked directly at me prior to this and I proceeded to question him about his vantage point, the number of SS soldiers he observed, the actions committed by both sides, the approximate distance in meters from his location to the site of the alleged illegal killings, and what means; field glasses or bare eyes, with which he made his observations. His answers were prompt and full of lively details but irrelevant to my line of interrogation. In closing, I summoned every Gestapo ability I had perfected during the war and asked him with a cold stare and steady tone if he distinctly saw me present during the commission of the combat. He replied he recognized me from the plaza at Hédomont. With my tab still covered I inquired how many metal pips he observed on my collar at Hédomont and stated for the record that I wished his answer to establish whether or not I was the officer of senior rank present in the plaza. The British soldier replied that he counted four metal pips on my collar at Hédomont. I stated to the soldier that I was being subjected to this trial while wearing the uniform of a Sturmbannführer with four metal pips on my left collar, but during my service at Hédomont, I was at the rank of Hauptsturmführer and at the time in question wore three diagonal metal pips and a distinct silver bullion stripe on my tab. The soldier changed his answer and entered a statement on the formal record in which he admitted to making a mistake in his identification of my tabs and he altered his testimony to indicate that at Hédomont he had observed me wearing the insignia of a Hauptsturmführer. I quoted my service records to indicate that at the time in question I had indeed been wearing the collar rank and insignia of an SS Sturmbannführer. I moved to discredit his testimony and won the motion.

This strategy worked in my favor during the interviews of the subsequent four British soldiers and of the five, only two had correctly remarked they had observed the rank of Sturmbannführer on my collar at Hédomont. This was not damaging as the accounts of those two soldiers greatly conflicted with inconsistent details. I was able to advance my argument that no solid evidence had been entered to determine the actual events that took place in the plaza. The British soldiers offering this testimony were members of the King's 9th Armored Infantry, and I stated for the record that this was the very unit I had given full quarter to, and granted free passage out of Hédomont to. I inquired if it had been my objective to execute Allied Prisoners of War, what logic existed in that I allowed unarmed British soldiers to evacuate a location captured by the Waffen SS?

The Allied Council conceded this point to me too easily and though dismissing it as a Capital War Crime, used it as a bridge to establish that I used Belgian hostages to negotiate the surrender of the King's 9th Armored Infantry. I had unwittingly performed precisely to their expectations by admitting that I accepted the surrender of the King's 9th Armored Infantry. Whereas they could not establish suitable evidence to remand me to trial for the shootings of nine British soldiers, they amended the charter against me to Crimes against Humanity and stated that I had: *Terrorized the local population for purposes of completing a military objective.*

The Colonel of the King's 9th was escorted into the courtroom and I recognized him as the man who had surrendered to me. The Colonel limped and his right arm had been amputated at the elbow. Portions of his hair had been burned away and thick scars covered the right side of his face. I was informed that 8 of the hostages were also waiting to be called as witnesses against me.

Once he took the podium he stated his name and the required formalities, and then identified me as the Waffen SS Major he surrendered to at Hédomont. He gave a very accurate account of the number of Belgian hostages and remembered the group consisted of 4 men, 7 women and 9 children. I assumed the Colonel was not called as a witness against me for the shootings of the nine British soldiers because he had not physically witnessed the event.

The Allied Council asked him about the disposition of the hostages and the manner with which my soldiers treated them. The Colonel replied the people were afraid for their lives and that they were weeping and pleading. He also stated that my units surrounded the civilians, held them at gunpoint and shouted threats at them. I was annoyed that the Allied Council permitted the Colonel to express his own opinions about the treatment of a civilian populace during the waging of war. I argued that British and German laws conflicted in regard to his statements, but my motion was denied and my remarks were not entered as part of the formal record.

I approached the Colonel slowly and stared at him for several moments before inquiring about the cause of his visible injuries.

Curtly he replied, "This happened when one of your Goddamned Elephants put a shell through my Matilda."

"I noticed that a portion of your right arm is missing."

The Allied Council moved to redirect my line of questioning but I motioned that it was necessary to draw attention to any prejudice the Colonel may have harbored toward Reich soldiers for the wounds he sustained. The Colonel agreed to answer my questions in order to establish he held no bias. The Allied Council allowed me to proceed.

"What were the circumstances under which you received your injuries?"

The British Colonel related an account of his tank bogging down in the mud east of Limburg and stated that he became a stationary target for a Panzerjäger Tank Destroyer. This heavy tank was commonly referred to as *The Elephant* as it was perhaps the largest self-propelled tracked vehicle used during the war. He said the German tank was attached to Kampfgruppe Ritter and that he did not consider this incident and the one at Hédomont to be related.

I inquired about his amputation and he explained his arm had been severed by shrapnel inside the tank.

I asked about any other wounds he sustained and the Colonel replied he received multiple fragment wounds and massive head injuries.

"Were you rendered unconscious?" I asked.

He admitted that he was.

"Do you suffer from a loss of memory about this attack? Are there instances previous or prior to the shell strike that you can not remember?"

The Colonel glanced at the Allied Council to put a halt to my line of inquiry. He promptly realized the direction I had taken.

"Do not look at them, Colonel. Look at me and answer the question."

He implored the Allied Council to withdraw my question but they reminded him that he opened the floodgate by agreeing to answer queries regarding any potential bias.

I repeated the question and the Colonel answered that he remembered his driver shouting he saw the Elephant preparing to fire upon the Matilda. He admitted that he did not remember the moment of shell impact and that his cognizance returned when he regained consciousness after he was pulled from the wreck by fellow soldiers.

I asked a series of questions I learned from watching SS physicians evaluate Jewish prisoners as they arrived at the Detainment Facilities. "Do you suffer from headaches, dizziness, spells of fainting, distorted vision, hearing impairment, memory loss, confusion, numbness or delusions?"

A member of the Allied Council banged a gavel. "That is enough, Major!"

I entered a motion on the formal record to call a qualified physician to testify in my defense that all of the symptoms I mentioned were often consistent with serious head trauma that resulted in sudden unconsciousness.

The Allied Council was not comprised of medical experts and debated my motion. They called the American physician in charge of Prisoner of War welfare and at the podium he stated he had been a former combat surgeon. He agreed that serious head trauma resulting in sudden unconsciousness could produce any one of or a combination of the symptoms I quoted. The British Colonel argued that he suffered none of them, but without signed affidavits from physicians to support this, and with his own admission of memory loss while unconscious, I moved to strike his testimony regarding the events at Hédomont and to remove him as a tenable witness against me. The Allied Council had no other choice but to grant this motion based on having no formal medical evaluations to support the Colonel's current level of mental functioning.

The 8 Belgians were brought before me and each answered a series of questions asked by the Allied Council. 6 of them stated firm recollections that I was present during the events and all 8 identified me as the officer that negotiated the British surrender. However, when I questioned each of them, none could describe the details of Reich collar tabs worn by German officers that day at Hédomont. Some admitted that greatcoats obscured tabs from view and others gave general descriptions of metal pips and the patterns they were arranged in. Not one of the 8 Belgian witnesses could positively state that I was the officer of senior rank present that day. It was the contention of the Allied Council that the British Colonel would have surrendered to the Reich Officer of senior rank, but court process required the submission of factual evidence to prove this.

I was enjoying a confident level of satisfaction at discrediting the witnesses brought against me and forcing the Allied Council to meet the burden of proof required by the laws of their proceedings. At last the Council made its final presentation and offered documentation to prove my direct involvement with the deportations of Jews, Gypsys, Poles, Austrians, Germans, Russians, Hungarians, Italians, Belgians, the Dutch and the French to the Concentration Camps.

The Allied Council had photographed the documents and displayed them during a presentation of slides. Most of them contained my signature under the words: *"Ermächtigung, Frachtmaßeinheiten zu transportieren"*. This clearly demonstrated my personal authorization to transport freight units, but the freight was not specified by anything other than a number of individual pieces. The Allied Council maintained the numbers represented people but I argued it could have indicated anything at all such as liters of milk, containers of shoe polish, crates of ammunition or boxes of nails. The Council had gained an understanding of the coded numbers and letters on the documents and directly associated them with various deportation and transit stations employed by Bureau IVb4. I was told there were thousands of depositions and affidavits on file that had been composed by previous Concentration Camp prisoners. Many of them directly identified the deportation and transit stations listed on the documents being used against me as locations used to transport human cargo. In spite of this, the Allied Council was required to prove that human beings were indeed the source of the items numerically charted on the documents they referred to.

This led to difficult questions that began to chisel away at my defense of having been transferred to the Waffen SS. The dates on the documents conflicted with my statements that I was not assigned to RSHA Headquarters, Department IVb4, Office for Jewish Emigrations.

I endured several days of such questioning and I maintained that while a member of the Waffen SS, I had limited Police duties connected to the Ministry of Transportation and that these responsibilities were only for the priority shipment of necessary war supplies to various locations.

On 6 February 1946 I was permitted a short visit from my family members before being transferred to Nürnberg to go before the Principal Allied Prosecuting Commission to learn if enough evidence existed to remand me to a formal trial.

I arrived at the ruins of Nürnberg late in the night with my hands and feet shackled in chains. People had gathered outside the prefecture to shout curses and throw stones and compacted ice and snow at those of us coming for formal hearings. The two French guards escorting me fell back from this bombardment and pushed me to the ground. I laid there with a hail of stones, ice and snow striking me while people shouted, *"Sie Lumpenhund!"* and *"Sie Mörder!"*

The people throwing stones, ice, and snow and cursing me as a bastard and murderer were fellow Germans. They were elders, children, and men and women of my age. What had I done to deserve this from them? Everything I did during the war was for their protection and benefit. How could they have treated me like that?

The French guards waved off the crowd and ordered me to my feet with hellish grins and one pushed my hat back onto my head. I was led inside the prefecture and was seated on a chair in my soaked uniform. The French guards transferred all my documents and paperwork to a Soviet soldier and before leaving, one of the Frenchmen struck me so sharply across the face that it knocked off my hat and caused my nose to bleed.

The Soviet soldier did not look at me as he sat behind a desk and reviewed my paperwork. He spun the dial of a telephone and said something in his native language. Moments later two large Soviet soldiers appeared and the man behind the desk showed them my paperwork. "SS," he said. The two guards motioned for me to stand up and they took me through a corridor and halted while opening a cell containing another SS officer. Pushing me inside one of them shouted, *"Ziehen Sie sich aus!"*

I removed my wet and filthy uniform and undergarments as ordered. The Soviets took my clothing before slamming and locking the cell door. My fellow officer handed me a small blanket and said, "They will launder and return your uniform."

Looking at him I saw the SS runes and Party insignia had been removed from his uniform as well. He wore his medals, cuff band, and the rank of an Untersturmführer. "How long have you been here?" I inquired.

"I came last night," he replied. "I see the local people introduced themselves to you too."

"Why did they do that?" I asked. "Why do they hold hatred for us? They are our fellow people."

"Not any more," he answered. "They must publicly denounce us for their sake and the welfare of their relatives who served the Reich."

"Why are you here?" I queried. He looked away as if his answer would provide me with information I could use to gain leniency.

"Why are you here?" he asked.

I did not respond either. His junior rank afforded him the potential to gain leniency for whatever he was accused of if he was to provide information about a superior officer such as me.

He laughed wryly. "Does this not defy belief? They are calling the lot of us criminals, Major."

"What happens here?" I inquired.

The Untersturmführer shrugged and replied, "They told me I have been brought here to learn if I am to stand trial."

"That is what they told me at Stuttgart."

"Stuttgart?" he asked. "I am from Esslingen just south of the city." There was silence for several moments. "Where are you from, Sir?"

"Füssen."

"Do you think we will ever see our families and homes again, Sir?"

"Of course," I replied. "The Allies can not convict us with ex post facto precedents. We have committed no crimes. We have done no wrong."

"Perhaps you have done no wrong, Sir. I am not certain I can make a similar claim. And if the Allies do not have at me, I am sure someone will."

"What have you done?" I asked. I did not expect him to answer me but the question came from his resigned hopelessness.

"Things," he replied softly. "I have done things."

My uniform was returned many hours later and I dressed in a great hurry. Immediately my nose, lungs and throat burned, my eyes stung and watered, and my skin was irritated. The Untersturmführer patted at my sleeve and looked at his fingers.

"What is this?" he asked. "Is this lye?"

The Soviets had coated my clothing with a liberal amount of lye to cause me great discomfort.

On Monday, 11 February we were taken from the cell and marched into a large room occupied by 30 or 40 fellow SS officers and enlisted men. We were each given a placard with a number and told to take a seat under the watchful eyes of armed guards. We were told that when our number was called we were to walk to the front of the room and stand before the table behind which the Principal Allied Prosecuting Commission sat. They would make the pronouncements of our fates.

I held Number 16 and we all waited nervously for the Chief Bailiff to begin calling the numbers. After an unbearable length of time the process began.

The first man wore the rank of an Unterscharführer and the room was very still and quiet as we all waited to hear the poor fellow's outcome.

An interpreter repeated the words of the Chief Prosecutor as he stated the man's name and rank. This was followed by, "On the charter of Crimes against Humanity, this Commission does not find evidence or reason to remand you to trial. You are hereby released."

Each of us wanted to applaud and cheer as this was a very encouraging experience. The following seven enlisted SS men were also released and I felt very confident as my former cell partner, the Untersturmführer holding placard Number 9, went before the panel.

"On the charters of War Crimes, Crimes against Humanity, Crimes against Peace and General Breaches of the Peace, this Commission finds evidence and reason to remand you to trial as a War Criminal of the former Third Reich. You are hereby ordered into custody."

I watched the guards take him away and all things around me temporarily ceased to exist. I could not believe the Allies were actually intending to proceed with trials.

My number was called and I walked before the panel expecting to be remanded to trial but hoping and praying for release. The Allied prosecutors silently read over my documents before one spoke. I could not believe the words of the interpreter.

"Rolf Otto Schiller, SS Major. On the charters of War Crimes, Crimes against Humanity, Crimes against Peace and General Breaches of the Peace, this Commission does not find evidence or reason to remand you to trial."

A surge of relief flooded through my body and I was pleased that the ordeal was over. In truth it had just begun. The following words catapulted me into a hellish nightmare.

"You are hereby ordered to be extradited to Poland where you will be remanded to an evidentiary hearing before the Polish Peoples' Tribunal and the Occupying Soviet Army. Members of the British, French and American governments will observe and assist. You are hereby ordered into custody for said extradition."

I was immediately shackled again and led from the prefecture by Soviet guards. They violently pushed me into the back of a truck where three armed Russian soldiers pointed their weapons at me. A young soldier with a fat face smiled to reveal several of his teeth were missing. He put his bayonet to the bridge of my nose and in German asked, *"Was taten Sie im Polen Arschloch?"*

It did not seem wise to say a word. He continued to ask me, "What did you do in Poland, asshole?" As the truck pulled out of the courtyard he said, "Perhaps this truck will not arrive in Poland. Perhaps we will stop along the way and hang you ourselves. Or perhaps we will cut you into pieces."

As the truck bounced on the broken cobblestone roads the soldier placed the butt of his rifle on the floor of the truck and angled his bayonet just millimeters under my chin. I was forced to keep my head raised for fear that one harsh bounce would impale my head on the end of his rifle. He pulled the weapon away when the truck was searched at checkpoints, but once under way again; he placed the bayonet back under my chin. I could not rest or sleep. When he grew weary of holding his rifle, one of his comrades replaced the threat.

CHAPTER TWENTY-EIGHT
THE POLISH PEOPLES' TRIBUNAL
POLAND 1946

The truck came to a halt on 14 February and with my hands and feet shackled, I was thrown from the back to the street. The Russian guards kicked me as I laid there until I heard a voice shouting, " *Zaden! Zaden! Zatrzymywac!* " I had learned enough Polish to understand that someone was yelling, "No! No! Stop!"

An elder Polish man with gray hair came between me and the Russians and said something to them with a harsh tone. He stooped and helped me to my feet and looked at me as if I was a nuisance. When I looked around my heart sunk into the depths of my belly. I was standing outside my former office in Porajów. He ushered me inside and I was surprised to see Polish and Soviet flags in the building. The same furniture and fixtures remained but it somehow seemed not real. I was seated across from my old desk and the gray haired man ordered the Russian guards to unlock the shackles from my hands. He told two of the Soviets to leave the room and the one with the fat face remained.

The man introduced himself in German and told me his name was Ryszard Dziatkowicz and that he was the presiding interim Mayor of Porajów. Without so much as a glance at my paperwork he said, "So you are the one the townspeople call the Blackbird."

"Am I to receive a fair trial here?" I asked.

"Do you expect one?"

"Yes, I do."

Without taking his eyes from my paperwork he replied, "So did many former residents of this town while you were their overseer."

"I declare bias on the basis of the prejudicial disposition of this town," I said. "I demand my evidentiary hearing to be moved to another location."

Ryszard squinted at me and removed his wire eyeglasses. "Where do you think you are? Before the Allies in Nürnberg? The only rights you have in Poland, Major, are the rights I see fit to give you."

The fat faced Russian guard giggled like a little boy and began nodding his head with a broad smile.

"This is ludicrous," I declared. "The people of this town will see me hanged without fair legal process."

"Perhaps," said Ryszard with his eyes upon my documents. He seemed casual when he mumbled, "We have seen many cases of that happen here in our recent past. What is one more?"

"The trial is to be a formality?" I asked. "Something of which you can record in your journals to state it was done? Why not spare the time and shoot me now?"

"No, Blackbird." Ryszard was arrogant with his tone. "The families of those you called smugglers and illegal printers are most eager to confront you."

"That was not my decision," I said.

"No?" he asked sarcastically. "You were not the SS Chief of Police and Security here?" He set the documents on his desk and removed his glasses again. "Who should I hold accountable for that and an endless count of other crimes against the Polish people in this town? Göth? Is that who you wish to blame? Polish authorities have Göth in custody, Major. We spoke to him about his involvement here at Porajów. He holds you responsible for what happened in your district of operations. And bluntly, Major, so do I and the people of this town."

I began to understand why I won my arguments against the Allied Council at Nürnberg with such ease. The evidentiary hearings had been nothing more than a formality to extradite me to Poland. I considered the Poles to be a collection of simple human beings with inferior intellect and this became a dangerous awareness. The Polish Peoples' Tribunal was not obligated to conduct itself with any amount of internationally accepted courtroom procedure. I could not expect any degree of justice from the Occupying Soviet Army presidors and I did not believe the American, British and French assistants and observers would petition the court for fair or due process.

Dziatkowicz set a thick file on the desk and instructed me to open it. There were multiple documents fastened together in triplicate that read in German, Polish and Russian. These were the charters being brought against me by the Polish Peoples' Tribunal.

It was all there before me. The charters began with the 30 October 1939 shooting of a Pole by an SS Schütze under my command. I had forgotten about the report of the Pole who refused to surrender a knife. The Schütze had since been killed in combat but the Poles and Russians maintained the Schütze had acted under the so called illegal Occupational Code of Law I had authored and established for the town of Porajów.

I learned that the members of the former Polish Council I had appointed, including Mayor Bartlomiej Nieuzyla, and his two primary administrators, Municipal Chief Henryk Cholewa, and the former Police Chief Piotr Wietrzychowski, and all eight remaining members of this cabinet, had been transported to Auschwitz and were gassed during July 1944.

I was being held accountable for the summary, reprisal and arbitrary executions of 161 former citizens of Porajów; each of whom was listed by age, gender and name. The Polish also intended to hold me liable for the gassing executions of 116,000 Poles, Jews, Gypsys, Hungarians and Austrians on Polish soil at Majdanek, Sobibor, Belzec and Auschwitz. I was also chartered with the illegal killings of 11,000 Jews, partisans and Poles in the Radom, Lublin and Porajów ghettos.

The Russians had chartered me with the illegal gassing executions of 19,000 Soviet Prisoners of War and an additional 4,000 killings of Ukrainian, Baltic, Slavic and Russian peoples and partisans including the 156 Jews, and 12 citizens of Vilovik at Andrivka. In summation, I was to be placed on trial for the illegal killings of 150,329 people.

I heard and read the numbers and accusations and I scoffed at Dziatkowicz. My reaction was not intended to be a display of disrespect, but no man is capable of comprehending that he alone has caused irrevocable damage of that magnitude. There is no plausible argument that I alone was responsible for 150,329 deaths. However, it is reasonable to assume that I had taken part in each of those deaths and probably many more in some capacity, whether diminished or proactive. I was aware that through clerical, administrative, personal, collective, direct and indirect means, I had sometimes been a component in this machine and other times the fuel and driving force of it.

The 161 executions at Porajów and the shootings of the 156 Jews and 12 citizens from Vilovik at Andrivka were my personal decisions and were carried out on my orders. I alone accepted full responsibility for the deaths of those 329 people but I refused to personally shoulder the blame for the 150,000 others I was accused of killing.

I told Dziatkowicz that I believed a sound argument could be made against me for the 329 killings as documents and witnesses existed. Conversely, I maintained that each of my actions had been within the boundaries of legal codes that were recognized and enforced at the time. The 150,000 additional killings were the decisions of multiple superior and fellow officers and carried out through a systematic chain of delegation. To put one man on trial for the killings required all those implicated to be tried.

Dziatkowicz was not moved. He stated that I had been brought to Porajów to hear my official remand to trial. There would be no hearings in the town. I was to be taken before the Polish Peoples' Tribunal and stand trial at Kraków .

17 February 1946
Kraków , Poland

Kraków seemed to be the heart of looming disaster. It was the central location with veins stretching out to Plaszow, Auschwitz, Bielsko, Tarnów, and Katowice. It was about this time that I contemplated the reality before me. I was going to be hanged. I was going to be escorted to a gallows like a common criminal and a bag and noose would be placed over my head. A priest would mutter words designed to be a soothing benediction and the bottom would drop out beneath me. If fortune was to be mine, perhaps my neck would break and I would be spared the agony of twisting and choking to death. What would all of that feel like, I pondered. How would I react when they came to fetch me from the cell for that final walk?

I was taken from my cell at Kraków and escorted to an office where a Soviet officer was reading my paperwork. "You have the right to representation," he said. "You may choose a barrister or advisor from any of the prosecuting governments."

What sort of representation would be offered by a barrister or advisor of the prosecuting governments? I did not want a barrister but I did wish to talk to someone capable of explaining the proceedings to me and who could tell me what to expect. I detested the Soviets and felt that a Pole would be biased. I could only expect misleading advice from the French and I did not know the disposition the British held toward me as the Hédomont incident was part of my permanent file. I requested an American advisor.

An American Colonel and his assistant were brought to the office and the Soviet officer left us. His German was flawless and he introduced himself and his Lieutenant Secretary. He reviewed the accusations against me and asked, "What do you wish to tell me about these charters?"

"Ludicrous," I replied.

"It is a lengthy and damning list, Major. The Polish and Russians are preparing over 300 witnesses to be called against you. Their testimony and the documents and photographs will be enough to hang you."

It disturbed me that he did not have the slightest inclination that I might be innocent of the accusations. Whether or not innocence was a factor, as an officer of the court and a representative of the American legal system, he was obligated to regard me as innocent until proven guilty by a preponderance of evidence. His statement inadvertently advised me that it would be necessary to fight my way out of a death sentence from the start.

"You were with Department IVb4?" he asked.

I remained silent. I had become suspicious of his so called advice.

"Frankly Major, you do not mean much to the Tribunal. Perhaps we can reach a formal agreement?"

A good and successful lawyer never sets foot in the courtroom. I was open to his attempt at negotiations. "What kind of formal agreement?"

He sat back and looked me in the eyes. "Where is Adolf Eichmann, Major?

I could not prevent the smile that formed on my lips and the

American Colonel was disturbed by it. I did not mean to smile but I could not control the urge. It meant that one of us or maybe more had avoided capture. It was satisfying that a superior officer, friend and confidant had escaped the Allied net. It was a small victory for the defeated and humiliated soldiers and officers of the Reich.

"I do not know where Eichmann is," I responded.

"Is that so?" inquired the Colonel. "We had him in the Prisoner of War camp at Ober-Dachstetten and he simply disappeared."

"Perhaps you should have increased security, Sir."

He stared at me for some time as if evaluating me. "What about SS Doctor Josef Mengele? Where might he be, Major?"

"By God," I replied. "You allowed two of us to escape?"

"Do not get sharp with me, Major. Do you know the potential whereabouts of Heinrich Müller or Martin Bormann?"

"No, I most certainly do not."

"What about Fritz Stangl and Amon Göth?"

"I know that Göth was taken into custody by the Gestapo in 1944."

"Yes," replied the Colonel. "Our VII Army captured him at Bad Tolz in February 1945. He was turned over to the Poles here in Kraków on 29 August 1945."

"And he is no longer here? In Kraków?" I asked.

The Colonel did not reply.

"I know he was from Austria," I said. "Vienna, I believe. He spoke of a wife there, Colonel."

Monday, 22 April 1946

During the 64 days I spent confined in Poland I had lost 11.5 kilograms of body weight on a diet of weak tea, broth and a soup that contained a hint of meat and potato. The Polish Peoples' Tribunal used this time to perfect its case and I was fairly furnished with copies of the documents and paperwork they intended to use against me, their witness lists, and a list of the formal charters being argued against me. I was also given a typewriter, paper, and pencils to prepare my defense and was given great assistance in constructing my own witness list. The Russians, now the occupying force in Poland, were also preparing to enter their case against me with the Polish Peoples' Tribunal.

At that time I yet believed that no criminal actions had been committed on behalf of the Reich, its officers and soldiers. We had waged a legal war and operated under legitimate legal codes and National Socialist State Laws. I could find no merit in the Tribunal's argument that the Reich had since been declared an illegal regime and therefore all actions committed under its former banners were illegal. This was the direct result of adherence to an ex post facto document, to wit: the London Charter which served as the basis for the arguments of all Allied governments and the territories formerly occupied by Germany.

The decision to represent myself at trial was not one I arrived at with ease. It was one I arrived at as a matter of having no other logical alternative. My experience before the Allied Evidentiary Hearing Committee at Nürnberg had been an interesting but complicated event that raised many personal questions. Had I performed expertly as a trial lawyer and had I indeed successfully discredited the witnesses there? Or, did the Allied Commission allow me to acknowledge those charters for the sake of establishing the amount of so called complicity necessary to remand me for extradition to Poland?

The trials being conducted in Nürnberg during my incarceration in Poland provided me with the reality that the Allies, Poles, Ukrainians, Soviets, and others were indeed prepared to proceed with legal arguments against us. At times it seemed the Poles and Allies were gaining nothing but moral satisfaction from keeping us confined and terrorizing us with threats of going to the gallows. In truth, and I knew this; it was legally impossible to execute a Reich officer for actions committed during the war. I again stress that I believed each event, no matter how abominable it might have seemed, was enacted under the prevailing laws and codes of my government.

I duly contend that the London Charter should be, and needs to be enforced for the protection of future generations and to govern the laws of warfare, occupation, and civilian subjugation. However, it should have been gracefully made law without staining its pages with the blood of Reich Officers.

At 0800 hours on Monday, 22 April 1946 I stood before the Polish Peoples' Tribunal and its assisting Allied representatives to hear the formal pronouncement of the charters against me. As I stood there watching my prosecutors look at each other with uncertainty as to how the tribunal was to proceed, one could clearly discern history was being born. There had been so much excitement and commotion about the commencement of the War Crimes Trials and suddenly the moment was upon not only me, but the prosecutors, bailiffs, witnesses and the world. No one knew the exact formal procedure to open the sessions and that fleeting moment terrified me. It was as if I was standing before the great medieval Spanish Inquisitor Torquemada to be pronounced guilty of heresy, or appearing before the Magistrates John Hathorne and Jonathan Corwin at the Salem, Massachusetts witch trials. How I knew what those so called heretics and witches must have felt; their innocence not being considered by the frenzied mob wishing to kill them for a self-righteous requirement to destroy evil.

The trials had been paved by years worth of expertly orchestrated Allied propaganda. The governments convinced their soldiers and people that National Socialism was an abhorrent evil and that its members of the SS were abominable inhuman monsters. This belief served to balance and justify the illegal actions committed against us on the fields of war and afterward during our arrests and trials. Ironically, this was no different than the method with which the Reich convinced its people and soldiers that Jews, Poles and other races were inhuman. How frightfully satirical it was that the Allies were permitted to violate the terms of the London Charter in order to successfully use the document against us.

In spite of the countless contradictions, ironies and absurdities, I was forced to acknowledge the road before me. It was necessary for me to recognize myself as a War Criminal in order to successfully arbitrate the matters being presented against me. Whether or not I agreed with being considered a War Criminal mattered only to me. The fact was, the Allies, Poles and world thought of me as one. It therefore became necessary to approach my litigation from the partial standpoint of one. I knew that blind arrogance and outward disdain for my prosecutors would construct a network of tension and mutual disagreement that would eventually become as real as concrete walls and barbed wire fencing. I therefore decided that I would not dispute the charters against me, but I would attempt to discredit the evidence. I believed this was the only possibility for a mistrial or sentence other than death. An acquittal? Not possible. The Allies and Poles would not allow that for an SS Officer.

At last the Polish Peoples' Tribunal came to order and the following charters were pronounced against me:

1. On 17 April 1939 while posted at Sachsenhausen, I ordered the Directive 19 executions of 23 Polish civilians whom, having immigrated to Germany as legal workers, were subjected to confinement at the Sachsenhausen Detainment Facility.
2. On 1 September 1939 I actively participated in waging a War of Aggression against Poland.
3. Between September 1939 and March 1940 I ordered the Directive 19 executions of 161 citizens of the Polish town of Porajów while serving as the SS Chief of Police and Security of the Occupied Zone.
4. During March 1941 I ordered the Directive 19 executions of 622 Polish Jews at the Lodz ghetto.
5. During May 1941, I ordered the Directive 19 executions of 1,211 Jews in the quarry pits near the Lublin ghetto.
6. On 22 June 1941 I actively participated in waging a War of Aggression against the Soviet Union staged from Occupied Zones in Poland.
7. On or about 26 June 1941 I incited a pogrom at Lokachi, Ukraine in which Ukrainian Nationalists, operating under my orders, murdered 31 Ukrainian Jews.
8. On or about 30 June 1941 at Lutsk, under Standing Orders from RSHA Headquarters, I implemented the Directive 19 shooting executions of 2,625 Ukrainian Jews.
9. During July 1941, 3,591 Ukrainian Jews died from suffocation on my orders to place them into transport freight wagons at Sokal.
10. During July 1941, I personally executed by shooting, 16 Russian Prisoners of War at the Rovno Prefecture in the Ukraine.
11. On or about 12 August 1941, I participated in the liquidation of the population of the Ukrainian village of Redivka at which 206 Ukrainians were executed by shooting.
12. On or about 23 December 1941 I ordered, planned and carried out the experimental Zyklon B gassing executions of 89 infirmed inmates at the Auschwitz Detainment Facility.

13. On 26 February 1942, while conducting searches and seizures at the Lublin ghetto, 78 Polish and Jewish ghetto residents were shot to death on my orders.

14. On 5 April 1942 I ordered the Directive 19 shooting executions of 156 Ukrainian Jews at the village of Andrivka and personally carried out the shooting executions of 12 citizens from the village of Vilovik.

15. On 29 April 1942 I ordered, planned and carried out the Zyklon B gassing executions of 2,100 prisoners at the Auschwitz Detainment Facility.

16. On 4 May 1942 I ordered, planned and carried out the Zyklon B gassing executions of 7,500 prisoners at the Auschwitz Detainment Facility.

17. On or about 26 April 1943 I ordered, planned and carried out the carbon monoxide gassings of 642 Polish Jews at the Belzec Detainment Facility.

18. Between 15 and 25 August 1943 I participated in the liquidation of the Bialystok ghetto during which 1,241 ghetto residents were slain and approximately 11,000 deported to the Termination Stations for Special Processing.

19. On or about 29 June 1944 I carried out the destruction of criminal evidence at the Majdanek Termination Station.

20. On 1 July 1944 I ordered the shooting deaths of 302 Radom Jews assisting with the destruction of criminal evidence at the Majdanek Termination Station.

21. On 19 July 1944 I ordered, planned and carried out the shooting executions of 412 Polish Jews assisting with the destruction of criminal evidence at the Majdanek Termination Station.

22. On 2 August 1944 I supervised the Zyklon B gassing executions of 2,897 members of the Gypsy Family Camp at the Auschwitz II Birkenau Termination Station.

23. Between 14 and 18 August 1944 I ordered, planned and carried out the Zyklon B gassing executions of 70,000 Polish Jews arriving at the Auschwitz II Birkenau Termination Station from the Lodz ghetto.

24. Between December 1941 and May 1944 I ordered, planned and carried out the illegal deportation of Polish citizens,

participated in the construction and implementation of gas chambers and crematoriums to be used for criminal killings, organized the logistical expansion of illegal Detainment Facilities and authored contracts for industries that profited from the slave labor of Polish Jews.

25. Articles resulting from the previous charter resulted in the deaths of 22,414 Polish Jews.

26. Russian Charter 1 enforced by Soviet Occupation of Poland: Between 22 June 1941 and December 1943 I ordered, planned and carried out the Directive 19 gassing and shooting executions of 19,000 Soviet Prisoners of War.

27. Russian Charter 2 enforced by Soviet Occupation of Poland: Between 22 June 1941 and December 1943 I ordered, planned and carried out the Directive 19 executions of 4000 Ukrainian, Baltic, Latvian, Estonian, Slavic and Russian peoples.

22 of the 27 charters accused me of the deaths of 150,329 people. Charters 25, 26 and 27, contained grossly dubious suppositions in the reported numbers but the remaining charters were fairly accurate in reference to the actions I had committed as a member of Department IVb4 Office for Jewish Emigrations during the war.

Furthermore, the Allied Commission assisting and supervising the trial conducted by the Polish Peoples' Tribunal informed me that following the proceedings against me in Poland, I would face subsequent charters for illegal actions I committed against the French population of Paris and the Dutch population at Eindhoven and Westerbork. I would also face a final review of charters for the incident involving the shooting of British Prisoners of War at Hédomont. I was informed that while the Allied Evidentiary Commission at Nürnberg had not found sufficient evidence to try me on this charter, the accusations were forwarded to a Higher Investigative Allied Committee.

After the formal pronouncement of the charters against me I was led back to my cell. On Monday, 3 June 1946, the Polish Peoples' Tribunal formally opened its case against me and I stood trial for War Crimes in Kraków.

EPILOGUE

SS Sturmbannführer Rolf Otto Schiller endured 8 months before the Polish Peoples' Tribunal at Kraków. His expert knowledge of Reich Law and his argument that the London Charter was an ex post facto document greatly confounded the prosecution.

SS Sturmbannführer Schiller proficiently discredited 140 of the 236 witnesses that testified against him including former Polish and Soviet military officers who claimed to have observed Schiller's orders and actions in the camps. He competently overcame many prosecuting arguments and focused his defense on the manner with which select pieces of evidence were used against him.

Schiller argued that many of the documents presented as evidence by the Polish Peoples' Tribunal contained various interpretations within the legal structure of the former Reich. The creation and sustaining of reasonable doubt was upheld for most of his arguments.

Near the end of his trial, Schiller was permitted to call his own witnesses. Among those who testified in his defense were Catholic priests, former kapos, prior members of ghetto Judenrats, former SS and Wehrmacht soldiers, SS Hauptsturmführer Fritz Stammler, and the former Belgian partisan, Florian Maroutaeff. When the official proceedings against him closed on 10 February 1947, the Polish Peoples' Tribunal convened for 24 days to deliberate its decision.

On Thursday 6 March 1947, the Polish Peoples' Tribunal proclaimed its final verdict. SS Sturmbannführer Rolf Otto Schiller was convicted on 2,711 of the 150,329 capital murders he was accused of under the statutes and provisions of the London Charter. Sentencing was deferred until the Allied Prosecuting Commission at Nürnberg completed its trial against him for the illegal shootings of British Prisoners of War at Hédomont and incidents occurring at Paris,

Eindhoven and Westerbork.

Schiller was transferred into Allied custody where he remained confined as a convicted War Criminal until his subsequent trial began at Prenzlau, Germany on Tuesday, 14 October 1947. Almost three months later on Monday 12 January 1948, Schiller was found guilty of the shooting executions of 9 British Prisoners of War at Hédomont. He was acquitted due to lack of evidence of alleged crimes against the French and Dutch populations. The Secondary Allied Commission deferred sentencing to the Polish Peoples' Tribunal. Schiller was again transported to Kraków and on Monday, 19 January 1948, sentenced to 30 years confinement at Grudziadz Prison in Poland.

Officer Ranks

Waffen SS	Wehrmacht	Western
Reichsführer-SS	-	-
-	Generalfeldmarschall	General of the Army
SS-Oberstgruppenführr	Generaloberst	General
SS-Obergruppenführer	General der Infanterie, der Artillerie etc.	Lieutenant General
SS-Gruppenführer	Generalleutnant	Major General
SS-Brigadeführer	Generalmajor	Brigadier General
SS-Oberführer	-	Colonel
SS-Standartenführer	Oberst	-
SS-Obersturmbannführer	Oberstleutnant	Lieutenant Colonel
SS-Sturmbannführer	Major	Major
SS-Hauptsturmführer	Hauptmann	Captain
SS-Obersturmführer	Oberleutnant	1st Lieutenant
SS-Untersturmführer	Leutnant	2d Lieutenant

Noncommissioned Ranks

Waffen SS	Wehrmacht	Western
SS-Sturmscharführer	Stabsfeldwebel	Sergeant Major
SS-Standarten-Oberjunker	Oberfähnrich	-
SS-Hauptscharführer	Oberfeldwebel	Master Sergeant
SS-Oberscharführer	Feldwebel	Technical Sergeant
SS-Standartenjunker	Fähnrich	-
SS-Scharführer	Unterfeldwebel	Staff Sergeant
SS-Unterscharführer	Unteroffizier	Sergeant

Enlisted Ranks

Waffen SS	Wehrmacht	Western
SS-Rottenführer	Obergefreiter	Corporal
SS-Sturmmann	Gefreiter	-
SS-Oberschütze	Oberschütze	Private 1st Class
SS-Schütze	Schütze	Private

Glossary of Terms

Abwehr - German Military Intelligence Agency

Anschluss - The diplomatic agreement to annex Austria to the Third Reich

Appellplatz - Roll Call Area

Arbeit Lager - Work Camp

Buchenwald - One of the Concentration Camps in Germany

Commissar Order - The official directive issued during the Russian Campaign permitting German forces to shoot Russian Political Officers, spies, partisans and saboteurs

Coup de gras - A fatal shot delivered to the back of the head

Detainment Facility - Reich administrative term for "Concentration Camp"

Directive 19 - Official Third Reich administrative term for a death sentence

Einsatzgruppen/EGC/EK5 - Mobile Killing Squads assigned to liquidate Jews, partisans, spies and saboteurs on the front lines. There were four primary Einsatzgruppen Units: A, B, C and D. EGC represents Einsatzgruppen C. EK5 represents an Einsatz Kommando (small detachment) of a main Einsatzgruppe

Fallschirmjäger - Paratrooper

Gestapo - Abbreviation of Geheime Staats Polizei, the German secret state police

Hitlerjugend - Hitler Youth Corps

Kampfgruppe - German battle group consisting of up to 180 soldiers

Kapo - Inmate of a Concentration Camp or ghetto assigned as an internal policeman

Kriegsmarine - German Navy

KRIPO - German Criminal Police

KZ - Third Reich abbreviation for *Konzentrationslager* or "Concentration Camp"

Lebensraum - Third Reich philosophy of providing living space for German citizens

Luftschutze - Civil Air Police

Luftwaffe - German Air force

MG42 - German tripod mounted machine gun

MP38/40/42 - German handheld machine pistol

Nebelwerfer 42 - A German towed grenade launcher with six individual 160mm tubes

NKVD - The Russian *Narodnyi Komissariat Vnutrennikh Del* or, People's Commissariat of Internal Affairs

OKH - The Oberkommando des Heeres (OKH) was Germany's Army High Command from 1936 to 1945

OKW - The Oberkommando der Wehrmacht (OKW) commanded the OKH. However, the de facto situation after 1941 was that the OKW directly commanded operations on the Western front while the OKH commanded the Russian front

Order Police - Military police assigned to keep order among the subjugated populations and ghetto residents

PaK Gun - German towed anti tank gun

Panzerfaust - German shoulder fired anti tank weapon

RAD - Reich Arbeit Dienst - Reich controlled laborers

Referat (Office) IVb4 - RSHA Office for Jewish Emigrations

Reines Deutschland - Third Reich term for "Pure Germany"

RSHA - Abbreviation of Reichssicherheitshauptamt, the combined offices of the SD, Gestapo and KRIPO. This office was responsible for controlling enemies of the Reich within Germany and in its Occupied Zones including Jews and Gypsys

Sachsenhausen - One of the Concentration Camps inside Germany

SD - Abbreviation of Sicherheitsdienst, the Third Reich internal and external security service controlled by SS General Reinhard Heydrich

Sonderkommando - Specialty work units comprised of Concentration Camp inmates

SS - Abbreviation of Schützstaffel, or literally, "Defense Echelon. This was the elite body of the Reich and was comprised of the Totenkopfverbände and Waffen SS

Stalag - German Prisoner of War camp

StG44 - Late model German assault rifle that could also be toggled as a machine gun

T4 Euthanasia Program - Reich liquidation program to exterminate the elderly, terminally ill and insane

Termination Station - Reich administrative term for any Concentration Camp fitted with gas chambers and designated as a mass killing center

Todt Labor Service - Reich controlled labor service for the construction of buildings

Totenkopfverbände - SS Death's Head formations assigned as guards and administrators of the Concentration Camps

Untermenschen - Reich designation for "inferior peoples" such as Jews, Gypsys and non-Aryan

Volksstürm - German Peoples Militia

Wehrmacht - German general army

Zyklon B - Hydrogen Cyanide/Prussic acid crystals used as a gassing agent to exterminate people. There was a Zyklon A used strictly as a delousing agent

88mm - German anti aircraft and field artillery gun

102mm - German artillery gun

Printed in the United States
110335LV00003B/466/A